HOW TO USE PAGES IN YOUR HANDBOOK

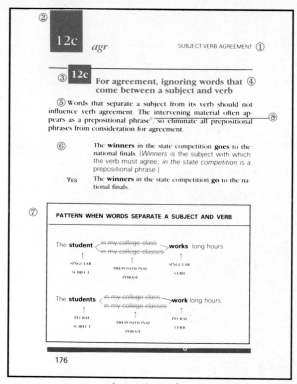

(composite page)

LOCATION ELEMENTS

①**Shortened Chapter Title** at the top of left pages (shortened subsection title at the top of right pages) helps you check where you are in the book.

②**Tab** gives a number-letter combination that tells the chapter number and the subsection letter **abbreviation**, or symbol, next to tab stands for the material covered chapter or subsection.

③**Section code**, like the tab, gives a number-letter combination that tells the chapter number and the subsection letter.

CONTENT ELEMENTS

④**Rule or guiding principle,** printed in red, gives the _____ nmary of the ma__

_____ailed

_____l.

_____ed

_____es.

_____ights a grammar

____st, set of guidelines, or

__ **degree mark** after a word signals that the word is defined in the "Glossary of Terms" toward the back of the book.

ABOUT
THE AUTHOR

Lynn Quitman Troyka, earned her Ph.D at New York University, and has taught since 1967 at the City University of New York (CUNY), including Queensborough Community College, the Center for Advanced Studies in Education at the Graduate School, and in the graduate program in Language and Literacy at City College. She is now Senior Research Associate in the Instructional Resource Center of the CUNY Office of Academic Affairs.

Editor of the *Journal of Basic Writing* 1985–88, Dr. Troyka has published essays in leading scholarly journals and books.

She is author of *Structured Reading,* Third Edition, Prentice Hall, 1989; and co-author (with Richard Lloyd-Jones, John Gerber, et al.) of *A Checklist and Guide for Reviewing Departments of English,* Associated Departments of English of the Modern Language Association, 1985; and of *Steps in Composition,* Fifth Edition (with Jerrold Nudelman), Prentice Hall, 1990.

Dr. Troyka has been a consultant to and/or guest lecturer at dozens of colleges, universities, and government agencies. She is past chair of the Conference on College Composition (1981), of the College Section of the National Council of Teachers of English (1985–1987), and of the Writing Division of the Modern Language Association (1987).

"All this information," says Dr. Troyka, "tells what I've done, not who I am. I am a teacher. It is my life's work, and I love it."

Simon & Schuster

CONCISE
HANDBOOK

Lynn Quitman Troyka

Prentice Hall
Englewood Cliffs, NJ 07632

Library of Congress Cataloging-in-Publication Data

Troyka, Lynn Quitman
    Simon & Schuster concise handbook / Lynn Quitman Troyka.
        p.   cm.
    Includes index.
    ISBN 0-13-174269-8
     1. English language—Rhetoric—Handbooks, Manuals, etc.
  2. English language—Grammar—1950—Handbooks, manuals, etc.
  I. Title. II. Title: Concise Simon and Schuster handbook.
  PE1408.T694   1992
  808'.042—dc20   90-27023
                                                          CIP

for David,
who makes it all an adventure

Development Editor: Kate Morgan
Production Editor: Mark Tobey
Interior Design: Lorraine Mullaney
Prepress Buyer: Herb Klein
Manufacturing Buyer: Patrice Fraccio
Associate Art Director: Janet Schmid
Page Layout: Lorraine Mullaney
Cover Design: Rose Paccione

 © 1992 by Lynn Quitman Troyka

All rights reserved. No part of this book may be
reproduced, in any form or by any means, without
permission in writing from the publisher.

Printed in the United States of America
10 9 8 7 6 5 4 3 2 1

ISBN   0-13-174269-8
           0-13-174277-9 (INSTRUCTOR's EDITION)

Prentice Hall International (UK) Limited, *London*
Prentice-Hall of Australia Pty. Limited, *Sydney*
Prentice-Hall Canada Inc., *Toronto*
Prentice-Hall Hispanoamericana, S.A., *Mexico*
Prentice-Hall of India Private Limited, *New Delhi*
Prentice-Hall of Japan, Inc., *Tokyo*
Simon & Schuster Asia Pte. Ltd., *Singapore*
Editora Prentice-Hall do Brasil, Ltda., *Rio de Janeiro*

Contents

Preface

Preface

The *Simon & Schuster Concise Handbook* reflects my belief that students are empowered by knowledge. I wrote my first handbook, the *Simon & Schuster Handbook for Writers* (1990), because I believe that access to information about writing processes and written products greatly increases students' chances to fulfill their academic, business, and personal potentials. In an effort to reach out to all students, I have adaped my longer handbook into this briefer, paperback *Simon & Schuster Concise Handbook*. My goals remain the same: to offer uncomplicated explanations, a supportive tone, and an accessible format.

The *Simon & Schuster Concise Handbook*—as does the longer book—draws on respected traditional and contemporary rhetorical theory, composition research, language studies, learning theory, and modern practices in the teaching of writing to serve both as a classroom text and as a reference source for students to use in college and beyond. Here are the *Handbook's* major features:

- It starts with six chapters about whole essays, thereby giving students a context for studying writing.
- It explains the entire writing process, emphasizing that the steps of the process are rarely linear and that the process varies with the writer, the topic, and each writing situation.
- It traces the evolution of three drafts of a student's essay, located in a separate chapter with gray-tinted edges so that students can find the pages easily when the book is closed.
- It offers a separate chapter on reading and thinking critically.
- It covers all aspects of grammar, style, language, and punctuation and mechanics, with explanations and examples designed to facilitate verbal as well as visual learning.
- It provides a separate chapter on avoiding plagiarism and effectively using paraphrase, summary, and quotation.
- It discusses research in four comprehensive chapters from two perspectives: the research process *and* the writing process. A separate chapter on documenting sources—a "mini-handbook" on MLA style and APA style—has red-tinted edges for quick location of citation examples.

In writing the *Simon & Schuster Concise Handbook* I sought to be inclusive of all people. Sexist language and role stereotyping are avoided; *man* is not used generically for the human race; male and female writers are represented equally in examples. Also, I use various pedagogic innovations to help students make connections among the diverse elements in this *Handbook*. They include

■ Charts in tinted boxes present guidelines, checklists, grammar patterns, and summaries.

■ "Focus on Revising" sections give students opportunities to observe and to participate in case studies that apply concepts of revision to matters of grammar, language, and style.

■ Clusters of examples have related content to allow students to focus on the instruciton and not be distracted by a new topic with each example.

■ Exercises in connected discourse replicate the processes of revising and editing as closely as possible.

■ Content from across the curriculum is used for all case studies, examples, and exercises to expose students to academic contexts for writing.

■ An ❖ ALERT ❖ system helps students remember smaller matters in larger contexts. For example, a brief Punctuation Alert in an explanation of coordination puts into context one particular function of the comma, cross referenced to the section where commas are fully discussed.

■ A degree symbol (°) after a word signals that the term is defined in the Glossary of Terms. This feature allows students to concentrate on the material at hand, with the assurance that they can easily locate definitions they need.

■ Response Symbols (on the fold-out back cover) include not only Correction Symbols, but also complimentary symbols to facilitate instructors' and peers' praise of student writing.

Acknowledgments

Composing this book affirmed once again my conviction that writing is a social act for writer as well as reader. Being able to turn to a community of colleagues, friends, and family for advice and perspective sustained me. Responsibility, of course, for any short-comings on these pages is mine.

Of special importance was Emily R. Gordon, Hofstra University and Queensborough Community College, CUNY, who offered invaluable friendship as well as outstanding talent as senior author of the *Simon & Schuster Concise Workbook* and author of the testing package. I also heartily thank Duncan Carter, Portland State University; Ann B. Dobie, The University of Southwestern Louisiana; Michael Goodman, Fairleigh Dickinson University; Rebecca Innocent, Southern Methodist University; Linda Julian, Furman University; Pat Morgan, Louisiana State University; and Judith Stanford, Merrimack College.

I am indebted for the reviews—"conversations on paper"—of many wise, caring faculty: Norman Bosley, Ocean County College; John L. Hare, Montgomery College; Margo K. Jang, Northern Kentucky University; Susan J. Miller, Santa Fe Community College; Jon F. Patton, University of Toledo; Edward J. Reilly, St. Joseph's College; Peter Burton Ross, University of the District of Columbia; Jack Summers, Central Piedmont Community College; and Vivian A. Thomlinson, Cameron University.

From Prentice Hall, the higher education group of Simon & Schuster, I am warmly grateful to Kate Morgan, Senior Editor and Development Editor for English; Tracy Augustine, Senior Editor for English; Phil Miller, Humanities Editor-in-Chief; Mark Tobey, Production Editor; Gina Sluss, Senior Marketing Manager for English; and Heidi Moore and Deborah Roff, Editorial Assistants.

Closer to home, family and friends were indispensable: Kristen and Dan Black; Rita and Hy Cohen; Edith Klausner, my sister; Jo Ann Lavery; Jerrold Nudelman; Belle and Sidney Quitman, my parents; Betty Renshaw; Magdalena Rogalskaja; Shirley and Don Stearns; Marilyn Sternglass; Muriel Wolfe; and Gideon Zwas. Above all, I am grateful to my husband, David Troyka, for his discerning reader's eye, for his unflagging belief in my work, and for the joy of each new day with him.

Lynn Quitman Troyka
New York, New York

One

WRITING AN ESSAY

 When you write an essay, you engage in a process. The parts of that process vary with the writer and the demands of the subject. Part One explains all aspects of the act of writing, and of thinking and reading in relation to writing, so that you can evolve your personal style of composing and thereby become an effective writer.

1

1 Thinking about Purposes and Audiences

Why write? In this age of telephones and tape recorders, television and film, computers and communication satellites, why should you bother with writing? The answer has overlapping parts, starting with the inner life of a writer and moving outward.

Writing is a way of thinking and learning. Writing gives you unique opportunities to explore ideas and acquire information. By writing, you come to know subjects well and make them your own. Even thirty years later, many people can recall details about the topics and content of essays they wrote in college, but far fewer people can recall specifics of a classroom lecture or a textbook chapter. Writing helps you learn and gain authority over knowledge. As you communicate your learning, you play the role of a teacher, someone who knows the material sufficiently well to organize and present it clearly and effectively.

Writing is a way of discovering. The act of writing allows you to make unexpected connections among ideas and language. As you write, thoughts emerge and interconnect in ways unavailable until the physical act of writing begins. An authority on writing, James Britton, describes discovery in writing as "shaping at the point of utterance." Similarly, a well-known writer, E. M. Forster, talked about discovery during writing by asking, "How can I know what I mean until I've seen what I said?" You can expect many surprises of insight that come only when you write and rewrite, each time trying to get closer to what you want to say.

Writing creates reading. Writing creates a permanent, visible record of your ideas for others to read and ponder. Writing is a powerful means of communication, for reading informs and shapes human thought. In an open society, everyone is free to write and thereby to create reading for other people. For that freedom to be exercised, however, the ability to write cannot be concentrated in a few people. All of us need full access to the power of the written word.

Writing ability is needed by educated people. In college you are expected to write many different types of assignments. Also, most jobs in today's technological society require writing skill for preparing documents ranging from letters and memos to formal reports. Indeed, throughout your life, your writing will reveal your ability to think clearly and to use language effectively.

1a
Understanding the elements of writing

Writing can be explained by its elements: *Writing is a way of communicating a message to a reader for a purpose.* Each word in this definition carries important meaning.

Communicating in writing means sending a message that has a destination. The **message** of writing is its content, which you can present in a variety of ways. Traditionally, forms for writing are divided into *narration, description, exposition,* and *argumentation.* In this handbook, narration and description are two among many strategies for developing ideas, explained in section 5d. Exposition and argumentation are the major **purposes** for academic writing, explained in section 1b. The final element of writing is the **reader,** or audience, explained in section 1c.

1b **Understanding purposes for writing**

Writing is often defined by its **purpose.** Writing purposes have to do with goals, sometimes referred to as *aims of writing* or *writing intentions.* Thinking about purposes for writing means thinking about the motivating forces that move people to write. As a student, you might assume that your only purpose for writing is to fulfill a class assignment. More is involved, however. Fulfilling an assignment is external to the content of the writing. As a writer, you need to think about writing purpose in the context of what you are writing and how you are writing it.

PURPOSES FOR WRITING*

- To express yourself
- To provide information for a reader
- To persuade a reader
- To create a literary work

The purposes of writing *to express yourself* and *to create a literary work* contribute importantly to human thought and culture. This handbook, however, concentrates on the two purposes most prominent and practical in your academic life: *to inform a reader* and *to persuade a reader.*

1 **Writing to inform a reader**

Informative writing seeks to give information and, frequently, to explain it. Such writing is known also as **expository**

*Adapted from the ideas of James L. Kinneavy, a modern rhetorician, discussed in *A Theory of Discourse.* 1971; New York: Norton, 1980.

writing because it expounds on, or sets forth, ideas and facts. It includes reports of observations, ideas, scientific data, facts, and statistics. It can be found in textbooks, encyclopedias, technical and business reports, books of nonfiction, newspapers, and magazines. Consider this passage.

> In 1914 in what is now Addo Park in South Africa, a hunter by the name of Pretorius was asked to exterminate a herd of 140 elephants. He killed all but 20, and those survivors became so cunning at evading him that he was forced to abandon the hunt. The area became a preserve in 1930, and the elephants have been protected ever since. Nevertheless, elephants now four generations removed from those Pretorius hunted remain shy and strangely nocturnal. Young elephants evidently learn from the adults' trumpeting alarm calls to avoid humans.
>
> —CAROL GRANT GOULD, "Out of the Mouths of Beasts"

This passage is successful because it *communicates* (transmits) a *message* (about young elephants learning to avoid humans) to a *reader* (the general reading public who might be interested in the subject) for a *purpose* (to inform). In this passage, the writer's last sentence states the main idea. Each sentence before the last offers information that builds support for the main idea.

2 Writing to persuade a reader

Persuasive writing seeks to convince the reader about a matter of opinion. This writing is sometimes called **argumentative** because it argues a position. When you write to persuade, you deal with the debatable, that which has more than one side to it. It seeks to change the reader's mind, to bring the reader's point of view closer to the writer's. Examples of persuasive writing include editorials, letters to the editor, reviews, sermons, business or research proposals, opinion essays in magazines, and books that argue a point of view. Consider this passage.

We know very little about pain, and what we don't know makes it hurt all the more. Indeed, no form of illiteracy in the United States is so widespread or costly as ignorance about pain—what it is, what causes it, and how to deal with it without panic. Almost everyone can rattle off the names of at least a dozen drugs that can deaden pain from every conceivable cause—all the way from headaches to hemorrhoids. There is far less knowledge about the fact that about ninety percent of pain is self-limiting, that it is not always an indication of poor health, and that, most frequently, it is the result of tension, stress, idleness, boredom, frustration, suppressed rage, insufficient sleep, overeating, poorly balanced diet, smoking, excessive drinking, inadequate exercise, stale air, or any of the other abuses encountered by the human body in modern society.

—NORMAN COUSINS, *Anatomy of an Illness*

This passage is successful because it *communicates* (transmits) a *message* (ignorance about pain) to a *reader* (someone who might not be aware of the multiple causes of pain) for a *purpose* (to persuade a reader that human knowledge about pain is insufficient). The writer's first sentence summarizes the point of view that he argues in the rest of the paragraph. The other sentences support the writer's assertion.

EXERCISE 1-1

For each paragraph, decide if the dominant purpose is *informative* or *persuasive*. Explain how you came to your decision.

A.   For the past few years, our city has been in a downward slump, especially in terms of its recreational facilities and economy. Our parks and buildings have been the target of considerable vandalism. The lake, which has been sorrowfully neglected, could be improved with more trees, better roads, and additional security. Our unemployment is the highest in the state and our economy the worst. Both situations could be improved by attracting new industries to our city. Reclaiming our land by planting orange trees, onions, and melons would help the farm economy. Our city could be one of the best places to live if it would employ its available work force to effect these kinds of improvements.

—GERARDO ANTONIO GARZA, student

B.   During the past generation, the amount of time devoted to historical studies in American public schools has steadily decreased. About twenty-five years ago, most public high-school youths studied one year of world history and one of American history, but today, most study only one year of ours. In contrast, the state schools of many other Western nations require the subject to be studied almost every year. In France, for example, all students, not just the college-bound, follow a carefully sequenced program of history, civics and geography every year from the seventh grade through the twelfth grade.

—DIANE RAVITCH, ''Decline and Fall of Teaching History''

EXERCISE 1-2

Assume that you have to write on each of these topics twice, once to inform your reader and once to persuade your reader. Be prepared to discuss how your two treatments of each topic would differ.

1. diets
2. garbage
3. Emily Dickinson
4. forest fires
5. weight training
6. resumés
7. Canada
8. car insurance

1c **Understanding audiences for writing**

Your writing will often be judged by its ability to reach its intended **audience,** your readers. To be effective, informative and persuasive writing (see 1b) need to imply an awareness that someone is receiving the communication. If you write without considering your readers, you risk communicating only with yourself.

If you know or can reasonably assume even a few characteristics in the checklist below, your chances of reaching your audience improve. The more explicit information that you have about your audience, the better you can think about how to reach it. Often, of course, you can only guess at the details.

CHECKLIST OF BASIC AUDIENCE CHARACTERISTICS

WHO THEY ARE
Age, gender
Ethnic backgrounds, political, philosophies, religious beliefs?
Roles: student, veteran, parent, wage earner, voter, other?
Interests, hobbies?

WHAT THEY KNOW
Level of education?
Amount of general or specialized knowledge about the topic?
Preconceptions brought to the material?

---

1 Understanding the general reading public

The **general reading public** is composed of educated, experienced readers, people who frequently read newspapers, magazines, and books. These readers often have some general information about the subject you are dealing with, but they enjoy learning something new or seeing something from a different perspective. The general reading public expects material to be clear and to be free of advanced technical information.

2   Understanding your instructor as a reader

When you write for a class assignment, your audience will almost certainly be your **instructor.** Your instructor is a member of the general reading public and also someone who recognizes that you are an apprentice. Still, your instructor always expects your writing to reflect that you took time to learn the material thoroughly and to write about it well.

In part, therefore, an instructor is a *judge,* someone to whom you must demonstrate that you are doing your best. Instructors are also very experienced readers who can quickly recognize a minimal effort or a negative attitude. Your instructor is also an *academic,* a member of a group whose professional life centers on intellectual endeavors. You must, therefore, write within the constraints of academic writing. Inexperienced writers sometimes wrongly assume that instructors will fill in mentally what is missing on the page. Instructors expect what they read to include everything that the writer wants to say or imply. Do not leave out material. Even if you write immediately after your instructor has heard you give an oral report on the same subject, write as if your reader is unaware of what you know.

3   Understanding specialists as readers

Specialists are members of the general reading public who have expert knowledge on specific subjects. In writing for specialists, you are expected to know the specialty and also to realize that your readers have advanced expertise.

Specialized readers often share not only knowledge but also assumptions, interests, and beliefs. They may have similar backgrounds and similar views. For example, they may be members of a club interested in folkdancing. When you write for readers who share specialized knowledge, you have to balance the necessity to be thorough with the demand not to go into too much detail about technical terms and special references.

1d Understanding the effect of tone on readers

The **tone** of your writing is established by *what you say* and *how you say it*. You want to achieve a reasonable tone, both in the content of your material and in your choice of words. Your tone should reflect the purpose (see 1b) for your writing and your awareness of the basic characteristics of your audience (see 1c). As you move from writing privately for yourself to writing for an audience, the level of formality in your writing should reflect your goal. Although readers enjoy lively language, they can be jarred by an overly informal tone being injected into a serious discussion. Readers of academic writing expect to be treated respectfully. A medium level of formality is most effective (For more on levels of formality and choosing appropriate words, see 25a).

EXERCISE 1-3

Each of these passages was written for a general reading audience. Read each paragraph and decide (1) if its tone is appropriate for academic writing and (2) if the choice of words implies a specialist as reader.

A.　　　There is for many young girls another less tangible factor in the sequence of events leading to parenthood. It is a sense of fatalism, passivity, even pleasure at the prospect of motherhood—especially among the poor. For young girls trapped in poverty, pregnancy becomes a means of fulfillment. In the largely white community of North Adams, Massachusetts, an old mill town where unemployment has been high, or in the mostly white, down-at-the-heels southern counties of Illinois, underlying reasons for the high rate of unwed teenage pregnancies are no different from those in urban ghettos: lack of opportunity, absence of interesting alternatives to childbearing.

　　　　　　　—CLAUDIA WALLIS, "The Tragic Costs of Teenage Pregnancy"

B.   Without mucus, a slug would quickly be invaded by a host of microbial denizens and die. It would also be immobile, for slugs require mucus underfoot on which to crawl. Secreted from the pedal gland, located just beneath the head, the mucus flows down to the slug's single muscular foot. Like a miniature asphalt machine, the slug first lays its road and then, with wavelike motions of its foot, moves over it. As the mucous "road" dries, it becomes a silvery map of a slug's travels.

> SCOTT McCREDIE, "They're Still Slimy, But Naked Snails
> Are Finding New Friends"

C.   The consumer of electricity usually accepts the fact that power outages frequently occur during wind and thunderstorms. However, when outages occur during calm and dry weather, the consumer becomes upset and blames the power company. In reality, most non-weather-related outages occur either because of circumstances beyond the control of the power company or in order to insure the safety of its workers. Squirrels and other animals with the ability to reach the top of power poles cause outages by unknowingly completing a circuit between a hot wire and a ground wire, an act which can knock out power to many houses. Occasionally, rehabilitating old lines to decrease future outages forces the power company to kill the lines temporarily to insure safety. And, a power company that purchases its power from larger companies often loses power because of trouble on the other company's line

> —BURL CARRAWAY, student

2 Planning and Shaping

2a **Understanding the writing process**

Many people assume that a real writer can pick up a pen (or sit at a typewriter or word processor) and magically write a finished product, word by perfect word. Experienced writers know better. They know that **writing is a process,** a series of activities that start the moment they begin thinking about a subject and end when they complete a final draft. Experienced writers know, also, that good writing is rewriting. Their drafts are filled with additions, deletions, rearrangements, and rewordings.

For example, on the next page you can see how the paragraph you just read was reworked into final form. Notice that two sentences were dropped, two sentences were combined, one sentence was added, and various words were dropped, changed, or added. Such activities are typical of writing.

Writing is an ongoing process of considering alternatives and making choices. The better you understand the writing process, the better you will write and the more you can enjoy writing. For an overview of the steps in the writing process, see the chart on the opposite page.

For the sake of explanation, the parts of the writing process are discussed separately in this chapter. In real life, you will find that the steps overlap, looping back and forth as each piece

~~Chapter One discusses what writing is.~~ ~~This chapter~~
~~explains how writing happens.~~ Many people assume that a real

writer can _^*pick up a pen* ~~put pen to paper~~ (or sit at ~~the keyboard of~~ a

typewriter or word processor) and _^ write *magically—a* finished product _, *word*
by perfect word.

_^Experienced writers ~~all~~ know better.   They know that writing

is a process _, ~~Writing is~~ a series of activities that start

the moment _^ *they begin* thinking about a subject ~~begins~~ and end when they
complete ~~the~~ *a*

_^final draft. ~~is complete.~~ Experienced writers know, also,

that good writing is rewriting. *Their drafts are filled with*
additions, deletions, rearrangements, and rewordings.

Draft and Revision of Opening Paragraph of Chapter 2 by Lynn Troyka

AN OVERVIEW OF THE WRITING PROCESS

Planning calls for you to gather ideas and think about a focus.

Shaping calls for you to consider ways to organize your material.

Drafting calls for you to write your ideas in sentences and paragraphs.

Revising calls for you to evaluate your draft and, based on your decisions, rewrite it by adding, cutting, replacing, moving—and often totally recasting material.

Editing calls for you to check the technical correctness of your grammar, spelling, punctuation, and mechanics.

Proofreading calls for you to read your final copy for typing errors or handwriting legibility.

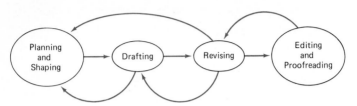

Visualizing the Writing Process

of writing evolves. Understanding writing as a multistage process allows you to work efficiently, concentrating on one activity at a time rather than trying to juggle all facets of a writing project simultaneously.

If you are a writer who likes to visualize a process, see the writing process diagram above). A simple straight line would not be adequate because it would exclude the recursive nature of writing. The arrows on the diagram imply movement. Planning is not over when drafting begins, drafting is not necessarily over simply because the major activity shifts to revision, and editing sometimes inspires writers to see the need for additional revising—and perhaps some new planning.

As you work with the writing process, rest assured that there is no *one* way to write. When you start, allow yourself to move through each stage of the writing process and see what is involved. Then as you gain experience, begin to observe what works best for you. Once you have a general sense of the pattern of *your* writing process, you can adapt the process to suit each new situation you encounter as a writer.

Most writers struggle some of the time with ideas that are difficult to express, sentences that will not take shape, and words that are not precise. Do not be impatient with yourself and do not get discouraged. Writing takes time. The more you write, the easier it will be—although writing never happens magically, even for highly experienced writers.

An aside about words used to talk about writing: Some words are used interchangeably, but often they have specific meanings for specific instructors. Listen closely and ask if you are unsure of what you hear. The words *essay, theme,* and *composition* usually—but not always—refer to writing that runs from about 500 to 1,000 words. This handbook uses *essay.* The words *report* and *project* usually mean writing that draws on outside sources. The word *paper* can mean anything from a few paragraphs to a long and detailed report of a complex research project. This handbook uses **paper** to refer to research writing.

2b Adjusting for each writing situation

Writing begins with thinking about each **writing situation.** The decisions you make depend on the particulars of each writing situation.

ELEMENTS OF EACH WRITING SITUATION

- topic
- purpose
- audience
- special requirements

Underlying all aspects of the writing situation is the **topic.** If you are supposed to choose your own topic or to narrow an assigned topic, keep in mind the constraints of academic writing. If the topic is assigned, you have to write without going off the track. No matter what the topic, *you* are the starting place for your writing. Draw upon yourself as a source. Whatever you have seen, heard, read, and even dreamed contributes to your fund of ideas and knowledge.

Each writing situation depends also on your **purpose** for writing. In college, the major purposes for writing are *to inform* and *to persuade* (see 1b). Some writing assignments include or clearly imply a statement of purpose. Many assignments, however, do not stipulate the writing purpose. In such cases, one of your tasks is to choose either an informative or persuasive purpose for the topic.

The **audience** for your writing (see 1c) also affects each writing situation. Some writing assignments name a specialized audience, which means that your audience has more technical knowledge than does the general reading public. Some assignments stipulate that your writing will be read by other students in the class. In such situations student readers serve as surrogate instructors, so you are expected to write with the same tone and level of information as you would for your instructor alone.

Every writing situation includes **special requirements.** These include the time allotted for the assignment, the expected length of the writing, and other practical constraints. (For advice on writing under pressure, see 3g.) Your assignment is a key resource as you write. Reread it as you work to make sure you have not lost track of what is expected. Throughout this chapter and Chapter 4, you will see the work of a student, Tara Foster, in response to the assignment below.

Tara Foster was given this assignment: Write an essay of 500 to 700 words that discusses an important problem facing adult men and women today. An early draft is due in one week. I will read it as an "essay in progress" and will make comments to help you toward a third, final draft.

In analyzing her writing situation, Foster saw that the assignment specified the special requirements of length and time. She decided that her audience would be her instructor. She tentatively chose an informative purpose, knowing that as she got further into planning she might change her mind.

EXERCISE 2-1

For each assignment listed below, answer these questions: (1) Is its purpose to inform or to persuade? (2) Is the audience the general reading public or specialists? (3) What special requirements of length and time are stated or implied?

1. *Biology:* You have twenty minutes to list and explain three ways that the circulatory system contributes to homeostasis in the human body.

2. *Political Science:* Write a 1,000-word essay about television's impact on elections.

3. *English:* Write a 300-word editorial for the student newspaper praising or criticizing the college's library. Draw on your personal experience. Also, interview at least one member of the library staff for his or her reaction to your point of view.

4. *Art:* Write a one-paragraph summary of the difference between a wide-angle lens and a telephoto lens.

2c Choosing a topic for writing

Experienced writers know that the quality of their writing depends on how they handle a topic. You should therefore think through a topic before you rush in and get too deeply involved to make topic adjustments within the time allotted. Of course, some assignments leave no room for making choices about the topic. Your job with such assignments is to do precisely what is asked and not go off the topic.

1 Selecting a topic on your own

Some instructors ask students to choose their own topic. In such situations, do not assume that all subjects are suitable for writing in college. For example, the old reliable essay about a summer vacation is probably not safe territory if you have nothing extraordinary to report. Your essays need to dive into issues and concepts, and they should demonstrate that you can use specific, concrete details to support what you want to say. The need for specifics should not, however, tempt you to go to extremes by writing very technical information, especially when an audience is unfamiliar with the particular specialized vocabulary.

---

2 Narrowing an assigned topic

The real challenge in dealing with topics comes when you choose or are assigned a subject that is very broad. You have to *narrow the subject.* Narrowing means thinking of subdivisions of the subject. Most very broad subjects can be broken down in hundreds of ways, but you do not need to think of all of them. When one seems possible for an essay, think it through before rushing in. Consider carefully whether the topic as narrowed can be developed well in writing. **One major factor that separates most good writing from bad is the writer's ability to move back and forth between general statements and specific details.**

As you narrow a broad subject to obtain a writing topic, keep in mind the writing situation of each assignment, as explained in 2b. Think about what you can handle well according to the conditions of each assignment.

SUBJECT	*music*
WRITING SITUATION	freshman composition class informative purpose instructor as audience 500 words, one week
POSSIBLE TOPICS	the moods that music can create classical music country-western music

Subject	*cities*
Writing situation	sociology course
	persuasive purpose
	students and then instructor as audience
	500 to 700 words, one week
Possible topics	comforts of city living
	discomforts of city living
	how cities develop

Tara Foster faced the task of narrowing her topic. Foster's assignment asked for a discussion of "an important problem facing adult men and women today." She knew immediately that "an important problem" was too general. As one of today's "adult men and women," she thought of many problems: war, the dangers of nuclear energy, unemployment, divorce. She wanted to try out what she might say on various topics, so she used some of the planning strategies explained in 2d to 2k. She became aware that the topic of adults living alone had good potential as a topic.

EXERCISE 2-2

For three of these general topics, think of three narrowed topics suitable for a 500- to 700-word essay for a writing course. Assume that each essay is due in one week and that the audience is the general reading public, as represented by an instructor. Explain why each of your three narrowed topics is suitable for the writing situation (see 2b). Then think of one general topic that is not on this list but that interests you and repeat the exercise with that topic.

1. computers
2. movies
3. political campaigns
4. literature
5. self-respect

6. vocational education
7. slang
8. cartoon
9. football
10. health

2d Gathering ideas for writing

Techniques for gathering ideas, sometimes called *prewriting strategies* or *invention techniques,* can help you discover how much you know about a topic. You need this information before you decide to write on a topic. Sections 2e to 2k describe various ways to gather ideas for writing.

Students sometimes worry that they have nothing to write about. Often, however, students know far more than they give themselves credit for. The challenge is to uncover what is there but seems not to be.

WAYS TO GATHER IDEAS FOR WRITING

- Keeping an idea book (2e)
- Writing in a journal (2e)
- Freewriting (2f)
- Brainstorming (2g)
- Using journalist's questions (2h)
- Mapping (2i)
- Reading for writing (2j)
- Incubating (2k)

No one technique of generating ideas always works for all writers in all situations. Experiment. If one method does not provide enough useful material, try an alternative. Also, even if one strategy works well for you, try another to see whether additional possibilities turn up.

2e Keeping an idea book and writing in a journal

Your ease with writing will grow as you develop the habits of mind that typify writers. Many writers always carry an **idea book**—a pocketsize notebook to jot down ideas that spring to mind. Good ideas tend to melt away like snowflakes when you rely entirely on your memory.

Keeping a **journal** gives you the chance to have a "conversation on paper" with yourself. Unlike a diary, a journal is not merely for listing what you did that day. When writing in your journal, you can draw on your reading, your observations, your dreams. *You* are your audience for your journal so the content and tone can be as personal and informal as you wish. Writing is a way of discovering, of allowing thoughts to emerge as the physical act of writing moves along.

Keeping a journal can help you in three ways. First, writing every day gives you the habit of productivity. The more you write, the more you get used to the feeling of words pouring out of you onto paper, and the easier it will become for you to write in all situations. Second, writing in a journal can help you think through ideas that need time to develop. Third, a journal serves as an excellent source of ideas when you need to write in response to an assignment.

2f Using freewriting

Freewriting means writing down whatever comes into your mind without stopping to worry about whether ideas are good or spelling is correct. When you freewrite, you do nothing to interrupt the flow. Let your mind make all kinds of associations. Do not censor any thoughts or flashes of insight. Do not go back and review. Do not cross out. Some days your freewriting might seem mindless, but other days it can reveal interesting ideas to you.

If you use a word processor, you can avoid the temptation to stop and criticize your writing by doing "invisible writing." Dim the monitor screen so you cannot see your writing. The computer's memory will still be recording your ideas, but you will not be able to see them until you brighten the screen again. The same effect is possible for writing by hand if you use a worn-out ballpoint pen and a piece of carbon paper between two sheets of paper.

Focused freewriting means starting with a set topic. You may focus your freewriting in any way you like—perhaps with a phrase from your journal or a quotation you like. Use the focus as a starting point and write freely until you meet the time or page limit you have set. Again, do not censor what you say. Keep moving forward.

2g Using brainstorming

Brainstorming means making a list of all the ideas that come to mind associated with a topic. The ideas can be listed as words or phrases. Let your mind range freely, generating quantities of ideas before analyzing them.

Brainstorming is done in two steps. First, you make a list. Then you go back and try to find patterns in the list and ways to group the ideas into categories. Set aside any items that do not fit into groups. The categories that have the most items are likely to be ones you can write about most successfully. If an area interests you but its list is thin, brainstorm on that area alone. If you run out of ideas, ask yourself questions to stimulate your thinking. You might try exploratory questions about the topic, such as: What is it? What is it the same as? How is it different? Why or how does it happen? How is it done? What caused it or results from it? What does it look, smell, sound, feel, or taste like?

plan **2h**

Tara Foster, whose essay drafts appear in Chapter 4, used brainstorming to help her narrow her topic about a problem facing today's adult men and women. She decided to see what she could brainstorm about divorce. She discovered that she had more to say about living alone (see items with asterisks) than any other aspect of the topic.

Brainstorming results of divorce

—living alone*
—being on your own again*
—shopping alone*
—children's reactions
—financial worries
—making new friends
—splitting up the money
—buying a car alone*
—finding a lawyer
—hurt and disappointment
—having to start over
—fears of loneliness*

EXERCISE 2-3

Brainstorm on a subject that you chose for Exercise 2–2.

2h **Using the journalist's questions**

Another means for generating ideas is using the **journalist's questions:** *Who? What? When? Why? Where? How?* Asking these questions forces you to approach a topic from several different perspectives.

To expand her ideas about living alone, Tara Foster used the journalist's questions: *Who* lives alone? *What* does living alone entail? *When* do people have problems living alone? *Why* do people live alone? *Where* do people live alone? How do people cope with living alone?

EXERCISE 2-4

Ask the journalist's questions about one of the subjects in Exercise 2-2.

2i Using mapping

Mapping, also called *clustering* or *webbing,* is much like brainstorming, but it is more visual. To map, start with your subject circled in the middle of a sheet of unlined paper. Next draw a line out from the center and label it with the name of a major division of your subject. Circle it and from that circle move out further to subdivisions. Keep associating to further ideas and to details related to them. When you finish with one major division of your subject, go back to the center and start again with another major division. As you go along, add anything that occurs to you for any section of the map. Continue the process until you run out of ideas. Part of Tara Foster's map is shown below.

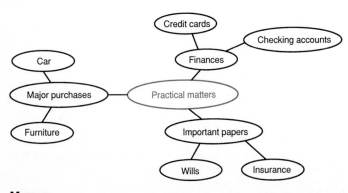

MAPPING

2j Using reading for writing

Reading can inspire you to think about a topic *before* you write. For example, Tara Foster had read "The Rewards of Living a Solitary Life," by May Sarton in her Freshman English class a few weeks before she wrote her essay on living alone. When Tara wanted to improve the introductory paragraph in the second draft of her essay, she thought of Sarton's essay and decided to select a quote from it to open the paragraph.

Reading can also help you plan *after* you receive an assignment. Reading is a way to confirm what you already know and to get new information. Be aware, however, that reading is not always part of an assignment. Unless an assignment specifically calls for the use of outside sources, ask your instructor if you can use them.

On the other hand, some assignments ask students to read a specific work, such as an essay or short story, and write in reaction to it. Other assignments ask for research writing (see Chapter 40). When you read to write, be sure to read critically (see 6c).

2k Using incubation

When you allow your ideas to **incubate,** you give them time to grow and develop. Incubation works especially well when you need to solve a problem in your writing (For example, if material is too thin and needs expansion, if material covers too much and needs pruning, or if connections among your ideas are not clear for your reader.) Time is a key element for successful incubation. You need time to think, to allow your mind to wander, and then to come back and focus on the writing.

One helpful strategy is to turn attention to something entirely different from your writing problem. Concentrate *very hard* on your new focus of attention so that your conscious mind is totally distracted from the writing problem. After a while, relax and guide your mind back to the writing problem you want to solve. Another strategy is to allow your mind to relax and wander, without concentrating on anything special. Open your mind to random thoughts, but do not dwell on any one thought very long. After a while, guide your mind back to the writing problem you are trying to solve. When you come back to the writing problem, you might see solutions that did not occur to you before.

21 Shaping ideas by grouping and ordering

Once you have gathered ideas on a topic as a result of any or all of the planning activities in this chapter (see 2e to 2k), you are ready to group and order your ideas. **Shaping** activities are related to the idea that writing is often called *composing,* the putting together of ideas to create a *composition,* one of the synonyms for *essay.* To shape the ideas that you have gathered, you need to group them

As you shape ideas, keep in mind that the form of an essay is related to the ancient notion of a story's having a beginning, a middle, and an end. An academic essay always has an introduction, a body, and a conclusion. The length of each paragraph is in proportion to the overall length of the essay. Introductory and concluding paragraphs are generally shorter than body paragraphs, and no body paragraph should overpower the others by its length. (Types of paragraphs useful for informative and persuasive writing are discussed and illustrated in Chapter 5.)

1 Grouping ideas

When you group ideas, you make connections and find patterns. As you do this, put each batch of related ideas into its own group. As you create groups, use the concept of **levels of**

generality to help you make decisions. One idea is more general than another if it falls into a larger, less specific category than the other. (For example, "cures for diseases" is more general than "cures for cancer.") Remember that generality is a relative term. An idea may be general in relationship to one set of ideas, but specific in relation to another set.

To group ideas, review the material you accumulated while gathering ideas (see 2e–2k). Then look for general ideas. Next group less general ideas under them. If you find that your notes contain only general ideas, or only very specific details, return again to gathering techniques to supply what you need. One of the standard tools for ordering ideas is making a "subject tree." It shows ideas and details in order from most general at the top to most specific at the bottom. Part of the tree Tara Foster made for her essay on living alone (shown in Chapter 4) is illustrated below. As happens with most writers, Foster did not use every item on the tree when she wrote her essay. The material did, however, give her a good start for drafting.

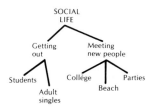

GROUPING IDEAS BY USING A SUBJECT TREE

2 | Ordering ideas

When you order ideas for writing, you decide what you want your readers to encounter first, second, and on until the last. When readers can follow your line of reasoning, they are more likely to understand the message that you want your material to deliver.

WAYS TO ORDER IDEAS WITHIN ACADEMIC ESSAYS

■ **Climactic order:** from least to most important
■ **Chronological order:** according to a time sequence
■ **Spatial order:** according to physical location

Climactic order, also called *emphatic order,* moves from least to most important. Ideas are arranged according to degree of impact on your reader or importance to your subject. The order builds to a climax. (You can see an example of climactic order in Tara Foster's final draft on living alone, shown in Chapter 4.) Climactic order also operates in essays that move from the simplest to most complex idea, or from the most familiar to least familiar idea. For example, you might start an essay about softball by explaining how to grip the bat. You could then talk about achieving a good swing and finish by discussing how to hit a pitched softball. The strategy of climactic order is useful not only for ordering major groups of ideas within a large framework, but also for ordering supporting details within each major group.

Chronological order presents ideas according to a time sequence. Chronological order is frequently used in narrating a series of events and in showing a process where steps are normally given in the order in which they occur. For example, you might use chronological order to discuss the career of Martin Luther King.

Spatial order presents ideas arranged according to their physical locations in relation to one another. This can include top to bottom, near to far, left to right. Spatial order is useful for such topics as describing a stage set or a street scene. Similarly, it would work well for moving from the East Coast to the West Coast when comparing historic preservation programs in New York, Chicago, and San Francisco.

plan **2m**

2m **Shaping writing by drafting a thesis statement**

A **thesis statement** is the central message of an essay. An effective thesis statement prepares your reader for the essence of what you discuss in an essay. As the writer, you want to compose a thesis statement with care so that it accurately reflects the content of your essay. If you find a mismatch between your thesis statement and the rest of your essay, revise to coordinate them better. Here is a list of the basic requirements for a thesis statement.

BASIC REQUIREMENTS FOR A THESIS STATEMENT

1. It states the essay's **subject**—the topic that you are discussing.
2. It reflects the essay's **purpose**—either to give readers information or to persuade readers to agree with you.
3. It includes a **focus**—your assertion that conveys your point of view.
4. It uses **specific language**—vague words are avoided.
5. It *may* give the major subdivisions of the essay's topic.

Often, instructors ask for more than the basic requirements for a thesis statement. For example, you might be required to put your thesis statement at the end of your introductory paragraph. The final draft of the essay on living alone (see Chapter 4) is an example. In addition, many instructors require that the thesis statement be contained in one sentence. Other instructors permit two sentences if the material warrants such length. All requirements, basic and additional, are designed to help you learn to think in structured patterns that communicate clearly with readers.

In most writing situations, all parts of a thesis statement might not accurately reflect what you say in the essay until you have written one or more drafts. To start shaping your essay, however, you need a **preliminary thesis statement.** Often a preliminary thesis statement is too broad ("Rain forests must not be destroyed") or too vague ("Rain forests are important to the human race"). Expect to revise a preliminary thesis statement as you write successive drafts of your essay, but an early version helps you find direction in your writing. When you revise into a **final thesis statement,** make sure that it clearly applies to the content of the essay as it has evolved through its drafts.

Consider the final thesis statement in Tara Foster's essay on living alone (in Chapter 4).

> Chances are high that most adult men and women will have to know how to live alone, briefly or longer, at some time in their lives.

Foster's thesis statement shows that she has fulfilled the basic requirements for a thesis statement in the chart on page 29. The *subject* is living alone, the *purpose* is to give information, and the *focus* is that chances are high that most people will have to know how to live alone at some time in their lives. She uses *specific language* such as "adult men and women," "how to live alone," and "briefly or longer."

Here is another example of a thesis statement written for a 500- to 700-word essay with an **informative purpose.** The ineffective version resembles some types of preliminary thesis statements. The effective version is a final thesis statement written by a student after she had gathered and grouped ideas. The material here on music is built on one of the "possible topics" evolved on page 18. Note that the good version contains the five characteristics listed in the Basic Requirements chart on page 29.

TOPIC	*classical music*

No Classical music combines many different sounds.

YES Classical music can be played by groups of various sizes, ranging from chamber ensembles to full symphony orchestras.

Here is an example of an evolving thesis statement written for a 500- to 700-word essay with a **persuasive purpose.** The ineffective version resembles some types of preliminary thesis statements. The effective version is a final thesis statement written by a student after he had gathered and grouped ideas. The material here on city living is built on one of the "possible topics" evolved on page 19. Note that the good version contains all five characteristics listed in the Basic Requirements chart.

TOPIC *discomforts of city living*

No The discomforts of living in a modern city are many.

YES Rising crime rates, increasingly overcrowded conditions, and growing expenses make living comfortably in a modern city difficult.

EXERCISE 2-5

Identify the topic, purpose, and focus of each thesis statement.

1. Reading poetry can help students improve their analytical skills.
2. Emphasizing foreign languages in U.S. schools would benefit U.S. culture, business, and politics.
3. The earth's surface can be divided into four major landforms: plains, plateaus, hills, and mountains.
4. In the first year of life, babies acquire increasingly sophisticated motor skills as they move from reflexive to nonreflexive activities.
5. Journalists should have an extensive liberal arts education.

EXERCISE 2-6

Each of the following sets of sentences offers several versions of a thesis statement. Within each set, the thesis statements progress from weak to strong. The fourth thesis statement in each set is the best. Based on the Basic Requirements chart on page 00, identify the characteristics of the fourth thesis statement in each set. Then explain why the other choices in each set are weak.

A. 1. Advertising is complex.
    2. Magazine advertisements appeal to readers.
    3. Magazine advertisements must be creative.
    4. To appeal to readers, magazine advertisements must skillfully use language, color, and design.
B. 1. Tennis is excellent exercise.
    2. Playing tennis is fun.
    3. Tennis requires various skills.
    4. Playing tennis for fun and exercise requires agility, stamina, and strategy.
C. 1. *Hamlet* is a play about revenge.
    2. Hamlet must avenge his father's murder.
    3. Some characters in *Hamlet* want revenge.
    4. In *Hamlet,* Hamlet, Fortinbras, and Laertes all seek revenge.

2n Knowing how to outline

Many writers find outlining a useful planning strategy. If you are working from an outline and you make changes in organization as you write, be sure to revise your outline at the end. An outline helps pull together the results of gathering and ordering ideas and preparing a thesis statement. It also provides a visual guide and checklist. Some writers always use outlines;

others prefer not to outline. Writers who outline do so at various points in the writing process: for example, before drafting, to arrange material; or while revising, to check the logic of an early draft's organization. Especially for informative and persuasive writing, outlines can clearly reveal flaws—missing information, undesirable repetitions, digressions from the thesis. Some instructors require outlines because they want students to practice planning the arrangement and organization of a piece of writing.

An **informal outline** does not have to follow all the formal conventions of outlining. An informal outline is particularly useful for planning when the order within main ideas is still evolving or when topics imply their own arrangement, such as spatial arrangement for describing a room. An informal outline can also be considered a *working plan,* a layout of the major parts of the material intended for an essay. It can be the next logical step after a brainstormed list (see 2g), a map (see 2i), or a subject tree (see 2l-1). Here is part of an informal outline that served as a working plan for Tara Foster when she was writing her essay on living alone. This excerpt includes the essay's thesis statement and one of its body paragraphs.

> Thesis statement: Chances are high that most adult men and women will need to know how to live alone, briefly or longer, at some time in their lives.
>
> *Circumstances that force living alone*
>   Grown children leave
>   College, graduate school
>   Jobs in other cities
>   Some marriages don't last forever
>   Divorce
>   Widows

SAMPLE INFORMAL OUTLINE

A **formal outline** follows conventions concerning content and format. The conventions are designed to display material so that relationships among ideas are clear and so that the content is orderly. A formal outline can be a *topic outline* or a *sentence outline.* Each item in a topic outline is a word or phrase; each item in a sentence outline is a complete sentence. Formal outlines never mix the two.

PATTERN FOR FORMAL OUTLINE OF AN ESSAY

Thesis Statement: ....
....
I.   First main idea ....
....
   A.   First subordinate idea ....
....
      1.   First reason or example ....
....
      2.   Second reason or example.......................
....
         a.   First supporting detail.......................
....
         b.   Second supporting detail....................
....
   B.   Second subordinate idea ....
....
II. Second main idea ....
....

When writing a formal outline, you are expected to observe the following conventions.

1. **Numbers, letters, and indentations.** All parts of a formal outline are systematically indented and numbered or lettered. Capital roman numerals (I, II, III) signal major subdivisions of the topic. Indented capital letters (A, B) signal the next level of generality. Further indented arabic numbers (1, 2, 3) show the third level of generality. Indented lowercase letters (a, b) show the fourth level, if there is

one. If an outline entry is longer than one line, the second line is indented as far as the first word of the preceding line.

2. **More than one entry at each level.** At all points on an outline, there is no I without a II, no A without a B, and so on. Unless a category has at least two parts, it cannot be divided. If a category has only one subdivision, you need to either eliminate that subdivision or expand the material to at least two subdivisions.

> **No**
> A. Grown children leaving home
> 1. Moving to other cities
> B. Married people not being together forever

> **Yes**
> A. Grown children moving to other cities
> B. Married people not being together forever

> **Yes**
> A. Grown children moving to other cities
> 1. Going away to school
> 2. Taking jobs
> B. Married people not being together forever

3. **Levels of generality.** All subdivisions are at the same level of generality. A main idea cannot be paired with a supporting detail.

> **No**
> A. Opening a checking account
> B. Comparing the services offered by different banks

> **Yes**
> A. Opening a checking account
> B. Making major purchases

4. **Overlap.** Headings do not overlap. What is covered in 1, for example, must be quite distinct from what is covered in 2.

> **No**
> A. Grown children moving to other cities
> 1. Going away to school
> 2. Continuing an education

> **Yes**
> A. Grown children moving to other cities
> 1. Going away to school
> 2. Taking jobs

5. **Parallelism.** All entries are grammatically parallel. For example, all items start with *-ing* forms of verbs, all items begin with verbs not in the *-ing* form, or all items are adjectives and nouns.

> **No**   A. Understanding the feeling
> B. Avoid depression
>
> **Yes** A. Understanding the feeling
> B. Avoiding depression
>
> **Yes** A. Understand the feeling
> B. Avoid depression

6. **Capitalization and punctuation.** Except for proper nouns°*, only the first word of each entry is capitalized. In a sentence outline, end each sentence with a period. Do not punctuate the ends of entries in a topic outline.

7. **Introductory and concluding paragraphs.** The content of the introductory and concluding paragraphs is not part of a formal outline. The thesis statement comes before (above) the roman numeral I entry.

EXERCISE 2-7

Here is a sentence outline. Revise it into a topic outline. Decide which of the two forms you would prefer as a guide to writing. Explain your decision.

Thesis Statement: Common noise pollution, although it causes many problems in our society, can be reduced.

I. Noise pollution comes from many sources.
  A. Noise pollution occurs in many large cities.
    1. Traffic rumbles and screeches.
    2. Construction work blasts.
    3. Airplanes roar overhead.

*Throughout this book a degree mark (°) indicates a term that is defined in the book's Glossary.

plan **2n**

    B. Noise pollution occurs in the workplace.
      1. Machines in factories boom.
      2. Machines used for outdoor construction thunder.
    C. Noise pollution occurs during leisure-time activities.
      1. Stereo headphones blare directly into eardrums.
      2. Film soundtracks bombard the ears.
      3. Music in discos assaults the ears.

II. Noise pollution causes many problems.
    A. Excessive noise damages hearing.
    B. Excessive noise alters moods.
    C. Constant exposure to noise limits learning ability.

III. Reduction in noise pollution is possible.
    A. Pressure from community groups can support efforts to control excessive noise.
    B. Traffic regulations can help alleviate congestion and noise.
    C. Pressure from workers can force management to reduce noise.
    D. People can wear earplugs to avoid excessive noise.
    E. Reasonable sound levels for headphones, soundtracks, and discos can be required.

3

Drafting and Revising

In the writing process, drafting and revising follow from planning and shaping, discussed in Chapter 2. **Drafting** means getting ideas onto paper in sentences and paragraphs. **Revising** means taking a draft from its preliminary to its final version by evaluating, adding, cutting, moving material, editing, and proofreading.

3a Getting started

If ever you have trouble getting started when the time arrives for drafting, you are not alone. If you run into a writing block, make sure that you are not being influenced by any of these common myths about writing.

MYTH   Writers are born, not made.
TRUTH   Everyone can write.

MYTH   Writers must have mastered grammar and spelling.
TRUTH   Writers often check grammar rules in a handbook (like this one), and their spelling in a dictionary or with a computer program.

MYTH   Writers do not have to revise.
TRUTH   Writers expect to revise. Being a good writer means being a patient reviser.

| **MYTH** | Writing can be done at the last minute. |
| **TRUTH** | Writing and revision take time. |

| **MYTH** | Writers have to be 'in the mood" to write. |
| **TRUTH** | If writers always waited for "the mood" to descend, few would write at all. After all, news reporters have to write to meet deadlines for stories, and professional writers often have to meet deadlines set by their contracts. |

Once you realize the truths behind myths about writing, you are ready to try the time-proven ways experienced writers get started when they are blocked. The key to getting these suggestions to work is not to criticize yourself when you are trying to get underway.

1. **Avoid staring at a blank page.** Relax and move your hand across the page or keyboard. Write words, scribble, or draw while you think about your topic. When you see an idea worth pursuing, use "focused freewriting" (see 2f).

2. **Visualize yourself writing.** Imagine yourself in the place where you usually write, with the materials you need, busy at work. Many professional writers say that they write more easily if they first picture themselves doing it.

3. **Picture an image or scene, or imagine a sound or taste, that relates to your topic.** For example, to report on a concert, recall the sound of your favorite part. Start writing by describing and discussing what you see or hear.

4. **Write your material in a letter to a friend.** Doing this gives you a chance to relax and chat on paper to someone you like and feel comfortable with. You can also try to write your material as if you were someone else. Once you take on a role, you might feel less inhibited about writing.

5. **Start in the middle.** Write from the center of your essay out, instead of from beginning to end. Instead of starting with your introductory paragraph, draft a paragraph that might come later in your essay.

3b   Knowing how to draft

Once you have shaped and planned your ideas, you are ready to **compose.** When you compose, you put together sentences and paragraphs into a unified whole. In a first draft, concentrate on content and its clarity. A first draft is a preliminary draft. It is not meant to be perfect; it is meant to give you something to revise. Try any of these ways of writing a first draft. **Put aside all your notes from planning and shaping.** Write a "discovery draft." Be open to discovering ideas and making connections that spring to mind as you write. You can use your discovery draft either as a first draft or as part of your notes when you write a structured first draft. **Keep your notes from planning and shaping in front of you and use them as you write.** Write a structured first draft. Work through all of your material. Depending on the expected length of your essay, draft either the entire essay or blocks of a few paragraphs at one time. **Use a combination of approaches.** When you know the shape of your material, write according to that structure. When you don't know what to say next, switch to writing a "discovery draft."

The direction of drafting is forward: *keep pressing ahead.* If you are worried about the spelling of a word or a point in grammar, underline the material so that you can come back later and check it—and keep moving ahead. If you cannot think of a word that says precisely what you want, write an easy synonym and circle it so that you will remember to change it later—and move on. If you are worried about your sentence style or the order in which you present the supporting details within a paragraph, write *Style?* or *Order?* in the margin so that you can return to that spot later to revise—and press forward. If you feel that you are running dry, reread what you have written—but only to propel yourself to further writing, not to distract you into rewriting.

As you draft, use the essay's thesis statement as your springboard. A thesis statement° has great organizing power. It expresses the central theme that controls and limits what the essay will cover. As you use your thesis statement, remember that its role is to serve as a connecting thread that unifies the essay. **Unity** is important for communicating clearly to an audience. You achieve unity when all parts of the essay relate to the thesis statement and to each other. Also, an essay is unified when it meets two criteria. First, the thesis statement must clearly tie into all topic sentences (see 5a-1). Second, the support for each topic sentence—the paragraph development—contains examples, reasons, facts, and details directly related to the topic and, in turn, to the thesis statement (see 5a-2).

Your essay also must be **coherent** to communicate clearly to an audience. An essay is coherent when it supplies guideposts that communicate the relations among ideas. You can achieve coherence through the use of transitional expressions, pronouns, repetition, and parallel structures (see 5c).

When you write, try to work in a place where you are comfortable and will not be disturbed. Have enough paper on hand so that you need to use only one side of each sheet. When you revise, you should be able to spread your full draft in front of you so that you can see how the parts relate to one another. Leave large margins and plenty of room between lines so that you have space to enter changes when you revise.

Chapters 2 through 4 of this handbook use the example of a student, Tara Foster, going through the process of writing an essay. For Foster's writing assignment, see page 00. For her planning and shaping strategies, see Chapter 2. Three drafts of her essay appear in Chapter 4.

3c Knowing how to revise

To **revise,** you must evaluate your draft and decide where improvements are needed. Then you make the improvements and evaluate them, alone and in the context of the surrounding material. This process continues until you are satisfied that the essay is in a final draft.

To revise successfully, you need first to expect to revise. Some people think that anyone who revises is not a good writer. The opposite is true. Writing is largely revising. Experienced writers know that the final draft of any writing project shows on paper only a fraction of the decisions made from draft to successive draft. Revision means "to see again," to look with fresh eyes. Good writers are revisers, people who can truly *see* their drafts and rework them into better form.

To revise successfully you need also to distance yourself from each draft. You need to read your writing with objective eyes. A natural reaction of many writers is to want to hold onto their every word, especially if they had trouble getting started with a draft. If you ever have such feelings, resist them and work on distancing yourself from the material. Wait a few hours, if at all possible, before going back to look anew at your work. As you revise, use the steps in the box below.

STEPS FOR REVISING

1. Shift mentally from suspending judgment (during idea gathering and drafting) to making judgments.

2. Read your draft critically to evaluate it. Be guided by the questions on the Revision Checklists on pages 45–46 or by material supplied by your instructor.

3. Decide whether to write an entirely new draft or to revise the one you have. Do not be overly harsh. Many early drafts provide sufficient raw material for the revision process to get underway.

4. Be systematic. Avoid evaluating at random. Pay attention to many different elements of a draft, from overall organization to choice of words.

If time does not help you develop an objective perspective, try reading your draft aloud; hearing the material can give you a fresh new sense of an essay's content and organization. Another useful method is to read the paragraphs in your essay in reverse order; eventually, of course, you must read your essay from beginning to end, but to achieve distance you can temporarily depart from that sequence.

1 Knowing the activities of revision

As you revise, you are working to improve your draft at all levels: whole essay, paragraph, sentence, and word. You need to engage in all the activities in the chart below. As you engage in each activity, keep the whole picture in mind. Check that your separate changes operate well in the context of the whole essay or a particular paragraph.

MAJOR ACTIVITIES DURING REVISION

Add. Insert needed words, sentences, and paragraphs. If your additions require new content, return to planning techniques (see 2d-2k).

Cut. Get rid of whatever goes off the topic or repeats what has already been said.

Replace. As needed, substitute new words, sentences, and paragraphs for what you have cut.

Move material around. Change the sequence of paragraphs if the material is not in logical order (see 2l-2). Move sentences around if arrangements seem illogical.

<table>
<tr><td>

2

</td><td>

Using the organizing power of your thesis statement and essay title

</td></tr>
</table>

When you revise, pay special attention to your essay's thesis statement and title. Both of these features help you stay on the track, and they orient your reader to what to expect.

If your **thesis statement** does not match what you say in your essay, you need to revise either the thesis statement or the essay—and sometimes both. A thesis statement must present the topic of the essay, the writer's particular focus on that topic, and the writer's purpose for writing the essay (see 2m). The first draft of a thesis statement is often merely an estimate of what will be covered in the essay. Early in the revision process, you may want to check the accuracy of your estimate. You can then use the thesis statement's controlling role to bring it and the essay in line with each other.

The **title** of an essay also plays an important organizing role. A *direct* title tells exactly what the essay will be about. A direct title is specific and prepares the reader for the topic of the essay. The title of Tara Foster's essay in Chapter 4 is direct: "Knowing How to Live Alone." An *indirect* title is also acceptable in some situations, according to the writer's taste and the instructor's requirements. An indirect title hints at the essay's topic. This approach can be intriguing to the reader, but the writer has to be sure that the title is not too obscure.

As you write, plan your essay's title carefully. Do not wait until the last minute to tack on a title. As you revise your essay, make sure that your title continues to relate to the content of your evolving essay. Make sure that your title stands alone. The opening of the essay should never refer to the title as if it were part of a preceding sentence.

<table>
<tr><td>

3

</td><td>

Using revision checklists

</td></tr>
</table>

A revision checklist can help you focus your attention as you evaluate your writing. Use a checklist provided by your instructor, or compile your own based on the revison checklists here. These checklists are comprehensive and detailed; do not let them overwhelm you. Feel free to adapt the following detailed checklists to your writing assignments and your personal needs.

REVISION CHECKLIST: THE WHOLE ESSAY AND PARAGRAPHS

The answer to each question should be "yes." If it is not, you need to revise. The reference numbers in parenthesis tell you what chapter or section of this handbook to consult.

1. Is your essay topic suitable and sufficiently narrow? (2c)

2. Does your thesis statement communicate your topic and focus (2m) and your purpose (1b)?

3. Does your essay reflect awareness of your audience? (1c)

4. Is your tone appropriate? (1d)

5. Is your essay logically organized? (2l-2)

7. Have you cut material that goes off the topic?

8. Is your reasoning sound (6c-6e) and do you avoid logical fallacies (6f)?

9. Is your introduction related to the rest of your essay? (5e)

10. Does each body paragraph express its main idea in a topic sentence as needed? (5b-1)? Are the main ideas clearly related to the thesis statement? (2m)

11. Are your body paragraphs sufficiently developed with concrete support for their main idea? (5b-2, 5d)

12. Have you used necessary transitions? (5c-1, 5e)

13. Do your paragraphs maintain coherence? (5c)

14. Does your conclusion provide a sense of completion? (5e)

15. Does your title reflect the content of the essay? (3c-2)

REVISION CHECKLIST: SENTENCES AND WORDS

The answer to each question should be "yes." If it is not, you need to revise. The reference numbers in parentheses tell you what chapter or section of this handbook to consult.

1. Have you eliminated sentence fragments? (15)
2. Have you eliminated comma splices and fused sentences? (16)
3. Have you eliminated confusing shifts? (17)
4. Have you eliminated misplaced and dangling modifiers? (18a, 18b)
5. Have you eliminated mixed and incomplete sentences? (19a, 19b)
6. Are your sentences concise? (20)
7. Do your sentences show clear relationships among ideas? (17)
8. Do you avoid faulty parallelism? (22)
9. Does your writing reflect variety and emphasis? (23)
10. Have you used exact words? (24)
11. Is your usage correct? (Usage Glossary)
12. Do your words reflect an appropriate level of formality? (25a)
13. Do you avoid sexist language (25b), slang and colloquial language (25a-3), slanted language (25a-4), cliches, (25d) and artificial language (25e)?

---

4 Knowing how to use criticism

When criticism is constructive, you can learn a great deal about your writing through the eyes of others. Still, you have much company among writers if your initial reaction to criticism is defensive. Someone else's reactions to your writing can feel like an intrusion at first. Writing is a personal act, even when a writer is trying to communicate with a reader. The more you write, however, the more you will come to welcome constructive criticism.

Another person can give you an objective view of your material. In working with comments, look at each one separately. First, make sure that you understand what the comment says. If you are unsure, ask. Next, be open-minded about the comment. If you resist every comment, you will miss many opportunities to improve. Finally, use the comments to revise according to what you think will improve your draft.

5 Knowing how to be a peer critic

Being a **peer critic** means using structured procedures to react to and make suggestions about another student's writing. Peer critiquing is an interactive communication process. It involves reading and thinking together, asking and explaining, talking and listening. As a student writer, be sure that your instructor wants you to use peer critiquing before you do so. There can be a fine line between giving opinions and doing others' work for them.

When you are a peer critic, you are part of a respected tradition of colleagues helping colleagues. Professional writers often seek to improve their rough drafts by asking other writers for comments. When you give comments as a student writer, know that you are not expected to be an expert. What you do offer can be quite valuable: opinions from the point of view of a writer who understands what his or her peer is going through. Try always to base your comments on an understanding of the writing process and of the features that characterize effective writing. The more concrete and specific your comments, the more helpful.

3d   Knowing how to edit

When you **edit,** you pay attention to correct grammar, spelling, and punctuation, and to correct use of capitals, numbers, italics, and abbreviations. Before you start editing, be sure that you have revised (see 3c) for quality of ideas, content, organization, development, and sentence structure. Your job during editing is to fine-tune the surface features of the draft you have.

Editing takes patience. When you edit, resist any impulses to hurry. Matters of grammar and punctuation take concentration—and frequently the time to check yourself by looking up rules and conventions in this handbook. As you edit, be systematic. Feel free to adapt the following editing checklist to your writing assignments and your personal needs.

EDITING CHECKLIST

The answer to each question on this checklist should be "yes." If it is not, you need to edit. The reference numbers in parentheses tell you what chapter or section of this handbook to consult.

1. Is your grammar correct? (Chapters 7 to 14)

2. Is your spelling correct (Chapter 26)?

3. Are your hyphens correct (Chapter 27)?

4. Have you correctly used commas (Chapter 29)?

5. Have you correctly used other marks of punctuation (Chapter 34)?

6. Have you correctly used capital letters (Chapter 35), italics (Chapter 36), abbreviations (Chapter 37), and numbers (Chapter 38)?

3e Knowing how to proofread

When you **proofread,** you carefully check a final, clean version of your essay before handing it in. Make sure that your essay is correctly formatted (see Appendix B). Proofreading involves a careful, line-by-line reading of your writing. You may want to proofread with a ruler so that you can focus on one line at a time. Starting at the end of a paragraph or an entire essay can help you avoid becoming distracted by the content of your paper. Another effective proofreading technique is to read your final draft aloud, to yourself or to a friend. Doing this can help you hear and see errors that might have slipped past your notice.

In proofreading, look for letters inadvertently left out. If you handwrite your material, be legible. If you type, neatly correct any typing errors. If a page has numerous errors, retype the page. Do not expect your instructor to make allowances for crude typing; if you cannot type well, arrange to have your paper typed properly. No matter how hard you have worked on other parts of the writing process, if your final copy is inaccurate or messy, you will not reach your audience successfully.

For information on properly presenting your final manuscript, see Appendix B.

3f Using a word processor to draft, revise, and edit

Many writers feel more creative when they use a computer. Their ideas seem to flow more freely when each new thought does not mean recopying. Do know, however, that some writers find that recopying by hand helps them think of new ideas. Be careful not to ignore what has always served you well when you wrote by hand.

1 **Using the computer for drafting**

As you are drafting, if you have questions or think you may want to elaborate on something but cannot think how at the moment, insert a symbol that will alert you to "talk to yourself" later. When you finish the draft and begin revising, your symbols will help you focus on areas that need reworking.

Resist the urge to think that neatness means completion. An essay is not complete simply because it has a beginning and an end, with paragraphs in between. Many writers are tempted to consider a rough draft the final version, and they type it up. This urge can be even stronger with computer drafts, because they are already typed.

2 **Using the computer for revising**

Revision—addition to, deletion from, substitution for, and rearrangement of material—is a many-faceted activity (see 3c). A computer makes these activities easy to do. As you read through your draft, word by word, use symbols and notes to yourself in brackets to alert yourself to what you want to revise. Remember, the computer screen does not become illegible from too many notations, as a written or typed draft can. Alternatively, some writers prefer to make changes on hard copy and enter those changes on disk.

If you think of something to add, move the cursor to the place in the draft that might be improved and type in the material. You can add anything from a word to a paragraph. If you are unsure about the best place for an addition, type it at the end of the draft, then move the addition into more than one place. See where it helps most, then delete the extras.

The computer makes rearranging relatively painless. You may create endless versions of your draft until you are satisfied with the order. Try reordering your body paragraphs, splitting or joining some existing paragraphs, and moving your last paragraph to the first position. You may be surprised.

Delete with caution. Move material you think you want to drop to the end of your document. Later you may find you want to return the deletion to your draft. You can always drop it later.

3 Using the computer for editing and proofreading

You can use the screen to help you proofread and edit. Use the block command to highlight a five- or six-line section, and read each section slowly and carefully. This strategy allows you to work in small segments and thus reduce the tendency to read too quickly and thereby fail to detect errors.

You might try making your own "spell-and-style checker" by keeping a file of the mistakes that you have made in the past. You can then call up the file, and search your draft for those items. Each time the search stops, check the item against the appropriate sections in this handbook.

After you have edited and proofread and you are ready to print out your final version, make sure that your pages conform to manuscript format requirements from your instructor, or use Appendix B.

3g Writing under pressure

Writing answers for essay tests is one of the most important writing tasks in college. Essay tests give you the chance to synthesize and apply your knowledge, thereby helping your instructor determine what you have learned.

If you develop strategies for writing essay tests, you will be more comfortable as you take essay tests and your writing will likely become more effective. Remember that your purpose in answering essay exam questions is to show your instructor what you know in a clear, direct, and well-organized way. Most essay tests have a time limit, so test-taking strategies will help you work efficiently.

The more you use the strategies in the chart below, the better you will be able to use them to your advantage. Try to practice them, making up questions that might be on your test and timing yourself as you write the answers. Doing this offers you another benefit: if you study by anticipating possible questions and writing out the answers, you will be very well prepared if one or two of them show up on the test.

STRATEGIES FOR WRITING ESSAY TESTS

1. Do not start writing immediately.
2. If the test has more than one question, read them all at the start. If you know from the beginning what you will have to answer, you will know what to expect and you will have a better sense of how to budget your time by either dividing it equally or allotting more for some questions. If you have a choice, select questions about which you know the most—and the ones whose cue words you can work with best.
3. Reread each question you are going to answer and then underline the cue and key words to determine exactly what the question asks for.
4. Use the writing process as much as possible within the constraints of the time limit. Try always to find time to plan and revise. For a one-hour test of one question, take about 10 minutes to jot down preliminary ideas about content and organization, and save at least 10 minutes to reread your answer and to revise and edit it. For a one-hour test with more than one question, divide your time for planning, drafting, and revising accordingly. If you suddenly become pressed for time—but try to avoid this—consider skipping a question you cannot answer well or a question that counts less on your total score.

4 Case Study: A Student's Writing Process

This chapter presents a case study of a student, Tara Foster, going through the process of writing an academic essay. Foster wrote three drafts of her essay. As you examine the drafts, refer back to Foster's writing assignment, shown on page 00. Also, look over the techniques that she used for planning and shaping her material (see Chapter 2) before she started drafting and revising.

4a Writing and revising a first draft

Foster's assignment was to write on an important problem facing adult men and women today. As a result of her planning and shaping (see Chapter 2), she chose the topic of living alone. Also, she decided that her purpose (see 1b) would be informative. When Foster revised her first draft, she concentrated first on the overall essay and then on paragraphs, sentences, and words. She proceeded systematically through the elements so that she was sure she had covered everything. Nevertheless, as many writers do, sometimes she changed words as she looked at the whole essay, and revised paragraphs as she looked at her sentences. Here is Foster's first draft, along with her notes to herself for revisions she wanted to make.

FIRST DRAFT REVISED BY STUDENT

(I need a title) terrified
~~Lots of~~ People are ~~scared~~ of living alone.
are used to living
They ~~like to live~~ with others. When the statistics

catch up with you, therefore, you are never prepared.

Chances are high that most adult men and women will   (I need a
better
have to know how to live alone, briefly or longer,   introduction.
check
at some time in their lives.   Chapter 4)

Many grown children move away from their
continue their
hometowns to ~~get an~~ education, or take jobs. ~~Also,~~
s
might feel they will
Married people ~~think they'll~~ always be together, but
currently one out of two
~~many~~ marriages end in divorce. [The divorce ~~rate~~ is

frightening. People are not making the right choices,   (Cut.
I'm off
or they are too immature to work out their differences.   the topic
here.)
Fighting over money, parents, or religion although

the underlying reason is lack of compatibility.

Divorce brings the couple and their children a great

deal of pain.]

(I should
change
order of
these
two
sentences)   ~~I read recently in the newspaper where~~ estimates
n   eight   ten
are that in the next twety years, ~~8~~ out of ~~10~~

married women end up widows. ~~This will happen to~~
usually   An
~~most of them~~ late in life. ~~This~~ statistic ~~is~~ even

sadder ~~than divorce. I feel sorry for any happily~~
concerns the death of a spouse.
~~married person whose spouse dies.~~

(I'll
move
this
¶ to
come after
next
¶.)   People living alone need to establish new
they can have an
friendships. When single people feel self-reliant,
time
~~It's easier~~ for ~~them to start~~ getting out and meeting
for instance
new people. Some students are in the habit of always
but   pleasantly surprised
going to classes with a friend, ~~and~~ they can be find   to
a
that they can concentrate better on the course, And

also have a chance to make some new friends.

The idea of going places alone can paralyze some

~~Friends can help people take care of practical~~

people. *Once you make the attempt, however, you find*

~~by keeping them company and going with them.~~

→ *that everyone welcomes a new friendly face.*

One good way to prepare for living alone is to

learn how to take care of practical matters. ~~Many~~

For example, they might not

~~people don't~~ know how to do something as simple as

Similarly,

opening a checking account. ~~M~~aking major purchases

How long can a person

is something people have to handle. ~~Such as a~~ *manage with*

cannot

refrigerator that ~~can't~~ be repaired or a useless car?

after *ping* *ing* *Most*

some Shop~~around~~ and mak~~e~~ price comparisons. ~~All~~ decisions

less complicated *they seem*

are much ~~easier~~ than~~,~~ at first.

Probably the most difficult problem for people living alone

Feelings of lonliness ~~are the hardest to take.~~ *is dealing*

with

~~I think this is what people fear the most.~~ First,

the feeling, they confuse

people have to understand ~~what is going on.~~ ~~B~~eing

with *people living alone*

alone ~~does not mean~~ being lonely. Second, ~~singles~~ have

everyone needs to get involved

to fight depression. Third, ~~they have to keep busy.~~

with activities such as volunteering their services to help others

People living alone have to handle practical,

social, and emotional problems.

I want to move this paragraph up.

Last paragraph is boring. I need a more interesting concluding device. Check Chapter 4.

Revising a second draft

After Foster finished revising her first draft (see 4a), she typed a clean copy and gave it to her instructor. Foster's instructor considers second drafts "essays in progress" and all comments would be geared toward helping students write an effective third, final draft. Here is Foster's second draft with two types of comments from her instructor: questions to stimulate further writing and codes to consult in this handbook.

SECOND DRAFT WITH INSTRUCTOR'S COMMENTS

Knowing How to Live Alone

How does this interesting quotation tie in to your point?
Also, who is Sarton?

"Alone one is never lonely," says May Sarton.

Most people, however, are terrified of living alone.

Can you be more specific? They are used to living with others. When the 15a

statistics catch up with you, therefore, you are

Qualify this statement (see 5c). never prepared. Chances are high that most adult men

and women will have to know how to live alone, briefly

or longer, at some time in their lives. *Can you be more specific?*

Many grown children move away from their

hometowns to continue their educations or take jobs.

What is your main idea in this paragraph? (See 4a-2 about topic sentences.) Married people might feel they will always be

together, but recent news reports say that one out of 11a

two marriages end in divorce. An even sadder sp

statisitic concerns the death of a spouse. Estimates

are that in the next twenty years eight out of ten

married women will end up widows, usually late in

10b Unclear pronoun ref. life. *informal (see 21a-1)*

One good way to prepare for living alone is to

learn how to take care of practical matters. For *Can you help your readers tie this information in to your thesis?* example, they might not know how to do something as

simple as opening a checking account. Similarly,

making major purchases is something people might

have to handle. How long can a person manage with a

18 *parallelism* refrigerator that cannot be repaired or a useless

REVISING A SECOND DRAFT

(13b) *fragment*
car? [After some shopping around and making price

comparisons.] Most decisions are much less

complicated than they seem at first.

How does this idea relate to the previous one?

People living alone need to establish new

24b-1 comma error

friendships. When͡ single people feel self-reliant͡

they can have an easier time getting out and meeting

new people. [For instance, some students are in the

what is the relationship among these ideas? See Chap. 17 about subordination.

habit of always going to classes with a friend, but

they can be pleasantly surprised to find that they

can concentrate better on the course and also have a

chance to make some new friends.] The idea of going

Can you be more specific?

(places) alone can paralyze some people. Once you

(15a)

make the attempt, however, you find that (everyone)

Are there no exceptions?

welcomes a new friendly face.

Probably the most difficult problem for people

(5p)

living alone is dealing with feelings of lonliness.

(14a) comma splice

First, people have to understand the feeling͡ they

number and shift agreement problem

confuse being alone with being lonely. Second,

(people) living alone have to fight depression.

Develop your paragraph as explained in 4a-2.

Third, (everyone) needs to get involved with activities,

such as volunteering (their) services to help others.

How does this question tie in to your thesis?

People need to ask themselves, "If I had͡to

live alone starting tomorrow morning, would I know

how?" This is an important question.

You revised your first draft well, so this second draft shows good progress. Your thesis statement clearly reflects your purpose and focus. Now you are ready to develop your paragraphs more fully. When you revise, think through the questions I ask, and refer to the handbook material I point out. I'm looking forward to reading your final draft. You are writing on a fresh and interesting topic.

4c Revising, editing, and proofreading a final draft

Foster read her instructor's comments carefully as she revised her essay into a final draft. Some of the comments showed Foster that she needed to revise her ideas. She started by working on paragraph-level matters, such as adding more specific examples, giving additional information, and showing relationships between certain points. She then revised her sentences and words by looking up the codes from the handbook that her instructor had written on the paper.

Before typing a clean version of her final draft, Foster edited her writing by referring to the editing checklist in this handbook (see 3d). She then typed a clean copy of her third, final draft and proofread it before handing it in.

Here is the third and final draft of Foster's essay. The labels in the margin are guideposts used *only* in this handbook. Do not use them on your final drafts.

FOSTER'S THIRD AND FINAL DRAFT

Tara Foster

Professor Rittenhouse

English 101, Section G2

31 October 19XX

Knowing How to Live Alone

Introduction:
Identification
of situation

"Alone one is never lonely," quotes May
Sarton in her essay "The Rewards of Living A
Solitary Life." Most people, however, are
terrified of living alone. They are used to

---

living with others--children with parents,
roommates with roommates, friends with friends,
husbands with wives. When the statistics catch up
with them, therefore, they are rarely prepared.

Thesis
statement

Chances are high that most adult men and women
will need to know how to live alone, briefly or
longer, at some time in their lives.

Background:
facts that
relate
to the
thesis

In the United States, circumstances often
force people to live alone. For example, many
high school and college graduates move away from
their hometowns to continue their educations or
take jobs. Most schools assign roommates, but
employers usually expect people to take care of
their own living arrangements. Also, married
people might feel they will always be together, but
recent news reports say that one out of two marriages
ends in divorce. An even sadder statistic concerns
the death of a spouse. Estimates are that in the next
twenty years eight out of ten married women will
become widows, usually late in life. These facts
show that most people have to live by themselves at
least once in their lives whether they want to or not.

Support:
first area

One good way to prepare for living alone is to
learn how to take care of practical matters. For
example, some students and newly single people might
not know how to do something as simple as opening a
checking account. When making arrangements alone,
they might be too tense to find out that they can

compare banks as well as the benefits of various types of accounts. Similarly, making major purchases is something people living alone might have to handle. When divorced or widowed people were married, perhaps the other spouse did the choosing or the couple made the decisions together. But how long can a person manage with a refrigerator that cannot be repaired or a car that will not run? After shopping around and making price comparisons, most people find that these decisions are much less complicated than they seem at first.

Support: second area

The confidence that single people get from learning to deal with practical matters can boost their chances for establishing new friendships. When singles feel self-reliant, they can have an easier time getting out and meeting new people. For instance, some students are in the habit of always going to classes with a friend. When they break this dependency, they can be pleasantly surprised to find that they can concentrate better on the course and also have a chance to make some new friends. Likewise, the idea of going alone to the beach or to parties can paralyze some singles. Once they make the attempt, however, people alone usually find that almost everyone welcomes a new, friendly face.

Support: third area

Probably the most difficult problem for people living alone is dealing with feelings of loneliness. First, they have to understand the feeling. Some people confuse being alone with feeling lonely. They need to remember that unhappily married people can feel very lonely with spouses, and anyone can suffer from loneliness in a room crowded with friends. Second, people living alone have to fight any tendencies to get depressed. Depression can lead to much unhappiness, including compulsive behavior like overeating or spending too much money. Depression can also drive people to fill the feeling of emptiness by getting into relationships or jobs that they do not truly want. Third, people living alone need to get involved in useful and pleasurable activities, such as volunteering their services to help others.

Conclusion: call for awareness

People need to ask themselves, "If I had to live alone starting tomorrow morning, would I know how?" If the answer is "No," they need to become conscious of what living alone calls for. People who face up to life usually do not have to hide from it later on.

Keep in mind that the drafts you have just read represent one student's personal writing process. Your own process will probably differ somewhat from Tara Foster's. Chapters 1, 2, and 3 discuss different possibilities for the process of planning, drafting, and revising.

5 Writing Paragraphs

5a Understanding paragraphs

A **paragraph** is a group of sentences that work in concert to develop a unit of thought. Paragraphing permits a writer to subdivide material into manageable parts and, at the same time, to arrange those parts into a unified whole that effectively communicates its message.

Paragraphing is signaled by indentation. The first line is indented five spaces in a typewritten paper and one inch in a handwritten paper. Some business writing (see Appendix A) uses "block format" to signal paragraphs.

A paragraph's purpose helps determine its structure. In college, the most common purposes for academic writing are to inform and to persuade (see 1b). Some paragraphs serve special roles: they introduce, conclude, or provide transitions (see 5c). Most paragraphs are **topical paragraphs,** also called *developmental paragraphs* or *body paragraphs.* They consist of a statement of a main idea and specific, logical support for that main idea. A topical paragraph is effective when it has the major characteristics listed in the chart on the next page.

MAJOR CHARACTERISTICS OF AN EFFECTIVE PARAGRAPH

1. **Unity:** clear, logical relationship between a main idea and supporting evidence for that main idea (see 5b)
2. **Coherence:** smooth progression from one sentence to the next within a paragraph (see 5c)
3. **Development:** specific, logical support for the main idea of the paragraph (see 5d and 5e)

5b Writing unified paragraphs

A paragraph is **unified** when all its sentences relate to the main idea. Unity is lost if a paragraph goes off the topic by including sentences unrelated to the main idea. Consider this paragraph which is effective because all its sentences relate to the subject of data bases.

1 We have all used physical data bases since our grammar school days. Our class yearbooks, the telephone book, the shoebox full of receipts documenting our deductions for the IRS—these are all data bases in one form or another, for a data base is nothing more than an assemblage of information organized to allow the retrieval of that information in certain ways. A telephone book, for example, assuming that you have the right one for the right city, will enable you to find the telephone number for, say, Alan Smith. Coincidentally it will also give you his address, provided there is only one Alan Smith listed. Where there are several Alan Smiths, you would have to know the address or at least part of it, to find the number of the particular Alan Smith you had in mind. Even without the address, however, you would still save considerable time by the telephone database. The book might list 50,000 names but only 12 Alan Smiths, so at the outset you could eliminate 49,988 telephone calls when trying to contact the elusive Mr. Smith.

—ERIK SANBERG-DIMENT, "Personal Computers"

For the sake of comparison, here is the beginning of the paragraph about data bases, with the second and the last sentences added deliberately to illustrate lack of unity.

No   We have all used physical data bases since our grammar school days. Grammar school was fun, but high school was more challenging. Our class yearbooks, the telephone book, the shoebox full of receipts documenting our deductions for the IRS—these are all data bases in one form or another, for a data base is nothing more than an assemblage of information organized to allow the retrieval of that information in certain ways. The IRS requires that taxpayers have documentation to support all but standard deductions.

1   Knowing how to use a topic sentence

The sentence that contains the main idea of a paragraph is called the **topic sentence.** A topic sentence focuses and controls what can be written in the paragraph. Some paragraphs use two sentences to present a main idea. In such cases, the topic sentence is followed by a **limiting** or **clarifying sentence,** which serves to narrow the paragraph's focus. In paragraph 1 the second sentence is its topic sentence, and the third sentence is its limiting sentence. The rest of the sentences support the main idea.

Topic sentence at the beginning of a paragraph

Most informative and persuasive paragraphs have the topic sentence first so that a reader knows immediately what to expect.

> 2   The cockroach lore that has been daunting us for years is mostly true. Roaches can live for twenty days without food, fourteen days without water; they can flatten their bodies and crawl through a crack thinner than a dime; they can eat huge doses of carcinogens and still die of old age. They can even survive "as much radiation as an oak tree can," says William Bell, the University of Kansas entomologist whose cockroaches appeared in the movie *The Day After.* They'll eat almost anything—regular food, leather, glue, hair, paper, even the starch in book bindings. (The New York Public Library has quite a cockroach problem.) They sense the slightest breeze, and they can react and start running in .05 seconds; they can also remain motionless for days. And if all this isn't creepy enough, they can fly too.
>
> —JANE GOLDMAN, "What's Bugging You"

Sometimes the main idea in the topic sentence falls early in a paragraph and is then restated at the end of the paragraph.

Topic sentence at the end of a paragraph

Some informative and persuasive paragraphs present supporting details before the main idea. The topic sentence, therefore, comes at the end of a paragraph. This approach can be particularly effective for dramatic effect, because it builds detail upon detail before revealing the organizing effect of a main idea.

> 3   A combination of cries from exotic animals and laughter and gasps from children fills the air along with the aroma of popcorn and peanuts. A hungry lion bellows for dinner, his roar breaking through the confusing chatter of other animals. Birds of all kinds chirp endlessly at curious children. Monkeys swing from limb to limb perform-

ing gymnastics for gawking onlookers. A comedy routine by orangutans employing old shoes and garments incites squeals of amusement. Reptiles sleep peacefully behind glass windows, yet they send shivers down the spines of those who remember the quick death many of these reptiles can induce. The sights and sounds and smells of the zoo inform and entertain children of all ages.

—DEBORAH HARRIS, student

Topic sentence implied

Some paragraphs make a unified statement without the use of a topic sentence. Writers must carefully construct such paragraphs so that the main idea is very clear even though it is not explicitly stated. Consider this paragraph which uses many details to communicate the implied main idea that exotic foods and restaurants are appearing all across the country.

4
Already, in the nation's heartland—Des Moines or Omaha—you'll find widespread use of Oriental and Mexican vegetables. Houston has some of the best Vietnamese restaurants in the world. The Los Angeles area has more than two hundred Thai restaurants. Mexican fast food has become a $1.6 billion industry covering the whole country—even Barrow, Alaska, north of the Arctic Circle, has a Mexican restaurant. And springing up throughout the land are Ethiopian, Afghan, Brazilian, and other exotic ethnic eating places. Indeed, it is no longer enough for a restaurant to be just Chinese; it may be Szechuan, Hunan, or Shanghai, but also Suzhou, Hangzhou, or some other ethnic specialty within an ethnic specialty.

—NOEL VIETMEYER,
"Exotic Edibles Are Altering America's Diet and Agriculture"

2 Developing a paragraph

Writing that has effective **paragraph development** delivers its message to its audience successfully. In writing most topical paragraphs, you must be sure to *develop the paragraph*. Development is provided by specific concrete details that support the generalization given in a topic sentence. When you write a topical paragraph, remember that **what separates most good writing from bad is the writer's ability to move back and forth between generalizations and specific details.**

Using details is the key to effective, successful development in topical paragraphs. "RENNS" is a memory device that writers can use to check whether their topical paragraphs are developed with sufficient detail. The chart below shows what each letter in RENNS stands for.

USING "RENNS" TO CHECK FOR SPECIFIC, CONCRETE DETAILS
■ **R**easons
■ **E**xamples
■ **N**ames
■ **N**umbers
■ **S**enses (sight, sound, smell, taste, touch)

Most well-developed paragraphs usually have only a selection of RENNS. Also, RENNS do not have to occur in the order of the letters in RENNS. For example, paragraph 5 has three of the five types of RENNS. Locate as many RENNS as you can before you read the analysis of RENNS that follows the paragraph.

5 Whether bad or good, in tune or not, whistling has its practical side. Clifford Pratt is working with a group of speech therapists to develop whistling techniques to help children overcome speech problems through improved breath control and tongue flexibility. People who have a piercing whistle have a clear advantage when it comes to hailing cabs, calling the dog or the children, or indicating approval during a sporting event. And if you want to leave

the house and can't remember where you put your keys, there's a key chain on the market now with a beep that can be activated by a whistle: You whistle and the key chain tells you where it is.

—CASSANDRA TATE, "Whistlers Blow New Life Into a Forgotten Art"

Paragraph 5 effectively develops the topic sentence by offering concrete, specific illustrations to support the generalization that whistling has its practical side. **Examples** include treatment for children with speech difficulties; convenience for hailing cabs, dogs, and children, and for sounding off at sporting events; and a signaling key chain. **Names** include Clifford Pratt, speech therapists, and children (not the general term *people*), and dogs (not the general term *animals*). **Senses** include the feeling of tongue flexibility, the piercing sound of a whistle, the roar at a sporting event, and the sound of a key chain beeping for its owner.

EXERCISE 5-1

Using your own words, fill in the blanks below. Then choose one sentence as a topic sentence, and write a well-developed paragraph based on it. Use RENNS to give the topic sentence concrete, specific support.

1. The place where I feel most comfortable is _____.
2. Getting a good job depends largely on _____.

5c   Writing coherent paragraphs

A paragraph is **coherent** when its sentences are related to each other, not only in content but also in grammatical structures and choice of words. Decisions about coherence are often made during revising, after you have written a first draft and can begin to see how your sentences might more effectively relate to one another. This section discusses five major ways of achieving coherence in writing.

| 1 | Using transitional expressions for coherence |

Transitional expressions—words and phrases that signal connections among ideas—can help you achieve coherence in your writing (see chart, page 71). Each expression is a signal that can connect one idea to the next.

The most commonly used transitional expressions are shown in the chart on the next page. The types of signals are quite varied in their purpose. For example, transitional expressions that signal *addition* cannot be interchanged with those that signal *result*.

To use transitional expressions effectively, do not overuse them. Also, make sure each fits the meaning you want your material to deliver, and vary the expressions when possible. ❖ COMMA ALERT: Especially when they begin a sentence and have more than one syllable, transitional expressions are usually set off from the rest of the sentence with commas (see 29c–3). ❖

Consider how the transitional expressions (shown in boldface) help to make paragraph 6 coherent.

6 Jaguars, **for example,** were once found in the United States from southern Louisiana to California. Today they are rare north of the Mexican border, with no confirmed sighting since 1971. They are rare, **too,** in Mexico, where biologist Carl Koford estimated their population at fewer than a thousand in a 1972 survey. Some biologists think the number is even smaller today. **Similarly,** jaguars have disappeared from southern Argentina and Paraguay.

—JEFFREY P. COHN, "Kings of the Wild"

TRANSITIONAL EXPRESSIONS

SIGNAL	WORDS
ADDITION	also, in addition, too, moreover, furthermore, equally important, next, then, finally,
EXAMPLE	for example, for instance, thus, as an illustration, namely, specifically,
CONTRAST	however, on the other hand, nevertheless, in contrast, on the contrary, at the same time,
COMPARISON	similarly, likewise, in the same way, in comparison,
CONCESSION	of course, certainly, naturally,
RESULT	therefore, thus, consequently, accordingly,
SUMMARY	as a result, in short, in summary, in conclusion, finally,
TIME SEQUENCE	first, second, third, next, then, finally, afterwards, soon, later, meanwhile, subsequently, eventually, in the future, currently,
PLACE	in the front, in the foreground, in back, in the background, at the side, nearby, in the distance,

---

| **2** | **Using pronouns for coherence** |

Pronouns that clearly refer to nouns or other pronouns can help you build bridges from one sentence to the next. (For advice on maintaining clear pronoun reference, see Chapter 11.) Consider how the pronouns (shown in boldface) help make paragraph 7 coherent.

In the morning, before the sun has broken through, the sandpiper begins to look for food. A tiny thing with gray feathers and a white underbelly, the "peep" looks, front to back, like awl and ball and cotton ball. **He** darts along the wave front, probing the sand for buried flecks of nourishment. Each feeding lasts but seconds and is sneaked in between a departing wave and the one soon to

7   follow. With **his** head poked down into the sand, it seems impossible for the sandpiper to notice the water about to overtake **him.** Yet, at the last possible instant—later than the last possible instant, it sometimes seems—**he** turns, body suddenly erect, and races to higher ground. Rejecting flight, **he** races overland, body perfectly still, feet pounding a noiseless rat-tat-tat-tat-tat into the wet sand. The water is never more than a stride behind **him.**

—RICK HOROWITZ, "The Sandpiper's Politics"

---

3   Using deliberate repetition for coherence

The **deliberate repetition** of key words can help you achieve coherence in a paragraph. A key word is usually one that is related to the main idea in the topic sentence or to a major detail in one of the supporting sentences. This technique must be used sparingly, however, to avoid being monotonous. The shorter a paragraph, the less likely that repeated words will be effective. Consider how the careful reuse of the key words *sounds, words, hear,* and *hearing* (shown in boldface) helps make paragraph 8 coherent.

I was then a listening child, careful to **hear** the very different **sounds** of Spanish and English. Wide-eyed with **hearing,** I'd listen to **sounds** more than to **words.** First, there were English (gringo) **sounds.** So many **words** still were unknown to me that when the butcher or the lady at the drugstore said something, exotic polysyllabic **sounds** would bloom in the midst of their sentences. Often the speech of people in public seemed to me very loud, booming with confidence. The man behind the

8   counter would literally ask, "What can I do for you?" But

by being so firm and clear, the **sound** of his voice said that he was a gringo; he belonged in public society. There were also the high, nasal notes of middle-class American speech—which I rarely am conscious of **hearing** today because I **hear** them so often, but could not stop **hearing** when I was a boy. Crowds at Safeway or at bus stops were noisy with birdlike **sounds** of *los gringos.* I'd move away from them all—all the chipping chatter above me.

—RICHARD RODRIGUEZ, "Aria: A Memoir of a Bilingual Childhood"

4 Using parallel structures for coherence

Parallel structures can help you achieve coherence in a paragraph. **Parallelism** is created when grammatically equivalent forms are used several times. The repeated tempos and sounds of parallel structures reinforce connections among ideas and create a dramatic effect. Be aware, however, that a thin line exists between effective parallelism (see Chapter 22) and lack of conciseness (see Chapter 20). In paragraph 9, the author uses parallel structures (shown in boldface) for key words in his paragraph. Additional parallel structures not shown in boldface are more subtle but highly effective: *sight and sound; under blazing suns, in rainstorms, in pitch-black nights; walking to or walking from.* Read paragraph 9 silently and then aloud to hear as well as to see parallelism working.

9
The world of work into which Jacinto and the other seven-year-olds were apprenticed was within sight and sound of the pueblo. **It was work** under blazing suns, in rainstorms, in pitch-black nights. **It was work** that you were always walking to or walking from, **work without wages** and **work without end. It was work** that gave you a bone-tired feeling at the end of the day, so you learned **to swing a machete, to tighten a cinch, and to walk without lost motion.** Between seven and twelve you learned all this, each lesson driven home when your *jefe* said with a scowl: "Así no, hombre; así." And he showed you how.

—ERNESTO GALARZA, *Barrio Boy*

5 Showing relationships among paragraphs

Paragraphs in an essay do not, of course, stand in isolation. You can use the techniques of coherence discussed in this chapter to link ideas from paragraph to paragraph throughout an essay. Another effective way to show relationships among paragraphs is to start a new paragraph with a reference to the previous paragraph. The essay by Tara Foster (see Chapter 4) uses this technique. In the final draft of "Knowing How to Live Alone" (pages 58–61), Foster wrote a paragraph about learning to make important practical decisions. She started her next paragraph—about making new friends—by briefly referring back to practical matters: *The confidence that single people get from learning to deal with practical matters can boost their chances for establishing new friendships.*

EXERCISE 5-2

Identify the techniques of coherence—words of transition, pronouns, deliberate repetition, and parallel structures—in this paragraph.

> Kathy sat with her legs dangling over the edge of the side of the hood. The band of her earphones held back strands of straight copper hair which had come loose from two thick braids that hung down her back. She swayed with the music that only she could hear. Her shoulders raised, making circles in the warm air. Her arms reached out to her
> 10 side; her opened hands reached for the air; her closed hands brought the air back to her. Her arms reached over her head; her opened hands reached for a cloud; her closed hands brought the cloud back to her. Her head moved from side to side; her eyes opened and closed to the tempo of the tunes. Kathy was motion.
>
> —CLAIRE BURKE, student

5d   Using patterns for developing a paragraph

By knowing a variety of patterns for **paragraph development,** you have more choices when you are seeking ways to help your paragraphs deliver their meanings most effectively. For the purpose of illustration, the patterns shown here are discussed in isolation. In essay writing, however, paragraph patterns often overlap. For example, narrative writing often contains descriptions; explanations of processes often include comparisons and contrasts; and so on. As you write paragraphs of various patterns, you likely will find that many patterns share characteristics. Your goal is to use paragraph patterns in the service of communicating meaning, not for their own sakes.

Narration

Narrative writing tells about what is happening or what has happened. In informative and persuasive writing, narration is usually written in chronological sequence.

11

When I visited the birthplace of my mother twelve years ago, I was embarrassed by the shiny rented car that took me there. Even in 1974, there were no paved roads in Clonmel, a delicate dot of a mountain village in Jamaica. And despite the breathtaking altitude, you could not get yourself into a decent position for "a view": The vegetation was that dense, that lush, and that chaotic. On or close to the site of my mother's childhood home, I found a neat wood cabin, still without windowpanes or screens, a dirt floor, and a barefoot family of seven, quietly bustling about. I was stunned. There was neither electricity nor running water. How did my parents even hear about America, more than half a century ago? In the middle of the "Roaring Twenties," these eager black immigrants came, by boat. Did they have to borrow shoes for the journey?

—June Jordan, "Thank You, America!"

Description

Descriptive writing appeals to a reader's senses—sight, sound, smell, taste, and touch. Descriptive writing permits you to share your sensual impressions of a person, a place, or an object.

12
To a fugitive from the surface world, an underground construction site seems like a cave filled with unidentifiable structures angling off in various directions. Two rust-coated electrical conduits are suspended from the street-level planks that form the cavern's roof. A vertical slab of masonry on one side of the 150-foot-long corridor turns out to be one wall of an abandoned coal chute. A large pipe perpendicular to the rest, which crosses the corridor, is a sewerline connector. The place has a strange bluish light at the end open to the outside, where a large blue curtain has been hung to keep out the weather. A little swirl of dust and gas collects near the roof of the tunnel, and there is an occasional whiff of sewage. Ladders, tools, and plank walkways clutter the narrow workspace. At the point where the corridor ends, a dozen pipes and conduits of varying sizes disappear into a solid 12-foot-high wall of New York dirt.

—DONALD DALE JACKSON,
"It Takes a 'Sixth Sense' to Operate Underneath the Streets of New York"

Process

Process is a term used for writing that describes a sequence of actions by which something is done or made. Usually a process description is developed in chronological order. To be effective, process writing must include all steps. The amount of detail depends on whether you want to instruct the reader about how to do something or you want to offer a general overview of the process.

Stand or tread water, until you see the right wave far out, gathering momentum. Then position yourself—swim farther out or farther in if necessary—so that you

are ready to plunge toward shore in the trough created in front of the cresting wave. Once you are in the trough, swim as hard as you can. Ideally, you will be sucked down into the trough. Suddenly the cresting water above you lifts you, holds you, and shoots you forward. At the mo-
13 ment, arch, point your body with your arms like tensed wings down at your sides, flat and bulletlike. You become a missile projected by the churning, breaking wave. If it works, you are *in;* if you *catch* the wave, you become part of it, the forward part of the cresting wave, like the prow of a boat made somehow of churning foam, and you can ride all the way home to the sand, and come home *into* the sand like a wedge, grinding into the shore like the wave itself.

—RUTH RUDNER, *Forgotten Pleasures*

Example

A paragraph developed by example uses illustrations to provide evidence in support of the main idea. Examples are highly effective for developing topical paragraphs. They supply a reader with concrete, specific information.

In fact, mistranslation accounts for a good share of verbal errors. The slogan "Come Alive with Pepsi" failed understandably in German when it was translated: "Come Alive out of the Grave with Pepsi." Elsewhere it was translated with more precision: "Pepsi Brings Your Ancestors Back from the Grave." In 1965, prior to a reception for
14 Queen Elizabeth II outside Bonn, Germany's President Heinrich Lübke, attempting an English translation of *Gleich geht es los* ("It will soon begin"), told the Queen: "Equal goes it loose." The Queen took the news well, but no better than the President of India, who was greeted at the airport in 1962 by Lübke, who, intending to ask "How are you?" instead said: "Who are you?" To which his guest answered responsibly: "I am the President of India."

—ROGER ROSENBLATT, "Oops! How's That Again?"

Definition

A paragraph of definition develops a topic by explaining the meaning of a word or a concept. A paragraph of definition is an *extended definition*—it is more extensive than a dictionary definition (although the paragraph may include a dictionary definition). An effective paragraph of definition does not use abstractions to explain abstractions.

15
> Surely the Board knows what democracy is. It is the line that forms on the right. It is the don't in Don't Shove. It is the hole in the stuffed shirt through which the sawdust slowly trickles; it is the dent in the high hat. Democracy is the recurrent suspicion that more than half of the people are right more than half of the time. It is the feeling of privacy in the voting booths, the feeling of communion in the libraries, the feeling of vitality everywhere. Democracy is the score at the beginning of the ninth. It is an idea which hasn't been disproved yet, a song the words of which have not gone bad. It's the mustard on the hot dog and the cream in the rationed coffee. Democracy is a request from a War Board, in the middle of the morning in the middle of a war, wanting to know what democracy is.
>
> —E. B. White, "Democracy"

Analysis and classification

Analysis (sometimes called *division*) divides things up. Classification groups things together. A paragraph developed by analysis divides one subject into its component parts. Paragraphs of analysis written in this pattern usually start by identifying the one subject and continue by explaining that subject's distinct parts.

> The trouble with the clans and tribes many of us were born into is not that they consist of meddlesome ogres but that they are too far away. In emergencies we rush across continents, and if need be, oceans to their sides, as they do to ours. Maybe we even make a habit of

16 seeing them, once or twice a year, for the sheer pleasure of it. But blood ties seldom dictate our addresses. Our blood kin are often too remote to ease us from our Tuesdays to our Wednesdays. For this we must rely on our families of friends. If our relatives are not, do not wish to be, or for whatever reasons cannot be our friends, then by some complex alchemy we must try to transform our friends into our relatives. If blood and roots don't do the job, then we must look to water and branches, and sort ourselves into new constellations, new families.

—JANE HOWARD, "A Peck of Salt"

A paragraph developed by classification groups information according to some scheme. The separate groups must be *from the same class*—they must have some underlying characteristics in common. Here is a paragraph that discusses three classes of sports signals.

17 Many different kinds of signals are used by the coaches. There are flash signs, which are just what the name implies: the coach may flash a hand across his face or chest to indicate a bunt or hit-and-run. There are holding signals, which are held in one position for several seconds. These might be the clenched fist, bent elbow, or both hands on knees. Then there are the block signals. These divide the coach's body into different sections, or blocks. Touching a part of his body, rubbing his shirt, or touching his cap, indicates a sign. Different players can be keyed to various parts of the block so the coach is actually giving several signals with the same sign.

—ROCKWELL STENSRUD, "Who's on Third?"

Comparison and contrast

Comparison deals with similarities, while contrast deals with differences. Paragraphs using comparison and contrast can be structured in two ways. A *point-by-point structure* allows you to move back and forth between the two items being compared. A *block structure* allows you to discuss one item completely before discussing the other.

POINT-BY-POINT STRUCTURE

Student body: college *A,* college *B*

Curriculum: college *A,* college *B*

Location: college *A,* college *B*

BLOCK STRUCTURE

College A: student body, curriculum, location

College B: student body, curriculum, location

Paragraph 18 is structured point-by-point for comparison and contrast.

18   My husband and I constantly marvel at the fact that our two sons, born of the same parents and only two years apart in age, are such completely opposite human beings. The most obvious differences became apparent at their births. Our first born, Mark, was big and bold—his intense, already wise eyes, broad shoulders, huge and heavy hands, and powerful, chunky legs gave us the impression that he could have walked out of the delivery room on his own. Our second son, Wayne, was delightfully different. Rather than have the football physique that Mark was born with, Wayne came into the world with a long, slim, wiry body more suited to running, jumping, and contorting. Wayne's eyes, rather than being intense like Mark's, were impish and innocent. When Mark was delivered, he cried only momentarily, then seemed to settle into a state of intense concentration, as if trying to absorb everything he could about the strange, new environment he found himself in. Conversely, Wayne screamed from the moment he first appeared until the nurse took him to the nursery. There was nothing helpless or pathetic about his cry either—he was darn angry!

—ROSEANNE LABONTE, student

Here is a block-form comparison of the impact of building construction a thousand years ago and now. Notice how the word *today* signals the transition between the two parts of paragraph 19.

A thousand years ago in Europe, acres of houses and shops were demolished and their inhabitants forced elsewhere so that great cathedrals could be built. For decades, the building process soaked up all available skilled labor; for decades the townspeople stepped around pits in the streets, clambered over ropes and piles of timber, breathed mortar dust, and slept and worked to the crashing noise of construction. The cathedrals, when finished, stood half-empty six days a week, but most of them at least had beauty. Today, the ugly skyscrapers go up, shops and graceful homes are obliterated, their inhabitants forced away, and year after year New Yorkers step around the pits, stumble through wooden catwalks, breathe the fine mist of dust, absorb the hammering noise night and day, and telephone in vain for carpenter or plumber. And the skyscrapers stand empty two days and seven nights a week. This is progress.

19

—ERIC SEVAREID, *This Is Eric Sevareid*

Analogy

Analogy is one type of comparison. Analogy compares objects or ideas from different classes—things not normally associated. Analogy is particularly effective when you want to explain the unfamiliar in terms of the familiar.

Casual dress, like casual speech, tends to be loose, relaxed, and colorful. It often contains what might be called "slang words": blue jeans, sneakers, baseball caps, aprons, flowered cotton housedresses, and the like. These garments could not be worn on a formal occasion without causing disapproval, but in ordinary circumstances they pass without remark. "Vulgar words" in dress, on the other hand, give emphasis and get immediate attention in almost any circumstances, just as they do in speech. Only the skillful can employ them without some loss of face, and even then they must be used in the right way. A torn, unbuttoned shirt, or wildly uncombed hair can signify strong emotions: passion, grief, rage, despair. They are

20

most effective if people already think of you as being neatly dressed, just as the curses of well-spoken persons count for more than those of the customarily foul-mouthed.

—ALISON LURIE, *The Language of Clothes*

Cause-and-effect analysis

Cause-and-effect analysis involves examining outcomes and reasons for those outcomes. Causes lead to an event or an effect; effects result from causes.

21 Because television is so wonderfully available as child amuser and child defuser, capable of rendering a volatile three-year-old harmless at the flick of a switch, parents grow to depend upon it in the course of their daily lives. And as they continue to utilize television day after day, its importance in their children's lives increases. From a simple source of entertainment provided by parents when they need a break from child care, television gradually changes into a powerful and disruptive presence in family life. But despite their increasing resentment of television's intrusions into their family life, and despite their considerable guilt at not being able to control their children's viewing, parents do not take steps to extricate themselves from television's domination. They can no longer cope without it.

—MARIE WINN, *The Plug-In Drug*

EXERCISE 5-3

Write three of the following paragraphs.

1. A classification of drivers.
2. A personal definition of *political freedom*.
3. A narrative of your first experience as an authority figure.
4. A cause-and-effect analysis of the increase in crime in the United States.
5. An analogy about learning to use a college library.

5e Writing introductory, transitional, and concluding paragraphs

Introductory, transitional, and concluding paragraphs are generally shorter than the topical paragraphs with which they appear.

Introductory paragraphs

An effective introductory paragraph is indispensable to a successful essay. An introductory paragraph prepares the reader for what lies ahead. It must, therefore, relate clearly to the rest of the essay. As you write successive drafts of an essay, expect to revise your introduction to work in concert with your topical paragraphs.

For college writing, many instructors require that an introductory paragraph include a statement of the essay's thesis—the central idea of an essay. These instructors want students to demonstrate from the start that all parts of any essay are related. Professional writers do not necessarily include a thesis statement in their introductory paragraphs; with experience comes skill at maintaining a line of thought without overtly stating a central idea. Student writers, however, often need to demonstrate openly external clues to essay organization.

When instructors require a thesis statement, they often want it to be in the last sentence or two of the introductory paragraph. For example, see the final draft of the essay by Tara Foster (see Chapter 4). Here is an example by a professional writer (thesis statement shown in italics).

22   Most sprinters live in a narrow corridor of space and time. Life rushes at them quickly, and success and failure are measured by frustrating, tiny increments. Florence Griffith Joyner paints her running world in bold, colorful strokes. *For her, there's a lot of romance to running fast.*

CRAIG A. MASBACK, "Siren of Speed"

23   Today, what respectable person would call a candidate for the highest office in the land a carbuncle-faced old drunkard? A pot-bellied, mutton-headed cucumber? A pickpocket, thief, traitor, lecher, drunkard, syphilitic, a gorilla, crook, anarchist, murderer? *Such charges were commonplace in Presidential contents in the nineteenth century.*

—PAUL F. BOLLER, JR., "Electiron Fizzle-Gigery"

An introductory paragraph often includes one or more **introductory devices,** listed in the chart below, that serve to stimulate a reader's interest in the subject of the essay. Usually the introductory device precedes the thesis statement.

SELECTED DEVICES FOR INTRODUCTORY PARAGRAPHS

- Provide relevant background information.
- Tell an interesting brief story or anecdote.
- Give a pertinent statistic or statistics.
- Ask a provocative question or questions.
- Use an appropriate quotation.
- Make a useful analogy.
- Define a term used throughout the essay.
- Identify the situation.

WHAT TO AVOID IN INTRODUCTORY PARAGRAPHS

1. **Do not be too obvious.** Avoid statements such as "In this paper I will discuss the causes of falling oil prices."

2. **Do not apologize.** Avoid self-critical statements such as "I am not sure I am right, but here is my opinion."

3. **Do not use overworn expressions.** Avoid statements such as "Haste makes waste" or "Love is what makes the world go around."

Transitional paragraphs

A transitional paragraph usually consists of one or two sentences that help you move from a few pages on one subtopic to the next large group of paragraphs on a second subtopic. Transitional paragraphs are uncommon in short essays. Here is a two-sentence transitional paragraph written as a bridge between a discussion of people's gestures and people's eating habits. This paragraph is followed by a number of paragraphs each of which discusses a different type of eater.

24   Like gestures, eating habits are personality indicators, and even food preferences and attitudes toward food reveal the inner self. Food plays an important role in the lives of most people beyond its obvious one as a necessity.

—JEAN ROSENBAUM, M.D., *Is Your Volkswagon a Sex Symbol?*

Concluding paragraphs

A concluding paragraph serves to bring your discussion to a logical end. A conclusion that is merely tacked onto an essay does not give the reader a sense of completion. An ending that flows gracefully and sensibly from what has come before it reinforces the writer's ideas and enhances an essay. A concluding paragraph often includes one or more **concluding devices,** listed in the chart below.

SELECTED DEVICES FOR CONCLUDING PARAGRAPHS

- Use the devices for introductory paragraphs (see list on page 84), but avoid using the same device in both the introduction and conclusion.
- Summarize the main points of the essay.
- Call for awareness and/or action.
- Point to the future.

Here is a concluding paragraph that summarizes a persuasive essay about the problem of teenagers getting married for the wrong reasons.

> Teenagers may contemplate marriage for a variety of reasons—most of them misguided. Before they pledge
> **25** their lifelong devotion to their "one and only," however, teenagers should secure the counsel of an impartial party, and they should seriously consider their options.
>
> —ADRIAN GONZALEZ, student

As you draft and revise your conclusion, be sure to avoid these problems.

WHAT TO AVOID IN CONCLUDING PARAGRAPHS

1. **Do not go off the track.** Avoid introducing an entirely new idea or adding a fact that belongs in the body of the essay.

2. **Do not reword your introduction.** Check to see whether the introduction and conclusion are interchangeable; if they are, revise.

3. **Do not announce what you have done.** Avoid statements such as "In this paper, I have explained the drop in oil prices."

4. **Do not make absolute claims.** Always qualify your message. Avoid statements such as "This proves that . . ."

5. **Avoid logical fallacies** (see 6f). Concluding paragraphs are particularly vulnerable to errors in reasoning.

6. **Do not apologize.** Avoid statements such as "Even though I am not an expert, I feel my position is correct."

EXERCISE 5-4

Write an introduction and conclusion for each essay informally outlined below.

A. Humor in current movies

    Thesis: Today's movies illustrate several types of humor.

    Topical paragraph 1: slapstick

    Topical paragraph 2: understatement and overstatement

    Topical paragraph 3: wit

B. Uses of computers

    Thesis: Many new applications for computers are emerging in the worlds of business, finance, and the arts.

    Topical paragraph 1: business

    Topical paragraph 2: finance

    Topical paragraph 3: the arts

C. Starting a new job

    Thesis: Starting a new job demands much concentration.

    Topical paragraph 1: learning or adapting skills

    Topical paragraph 2: fitting inw ith co-workers

    Topical paragraph 3: adjusting to the surroundings

6 Thinking and Reading Critically

Defining critical thinking

Thinking is not something you choose to do, any more than a fish "chooses" to live in water. To be human *is* to think. Although thinking comes naturally to you, awareness of *how* you think does not. Thinking about thinking is the key to thinking critically.

The word **critically** here has a neutral meaning. It does not mean taking a negative view or finding fault, as when someone criticizes another person for doing something wrong. Critical thinking is an attitude as much as an activity. If you face life with curiosity and a desire to dig beneath the surface, you are a critical thinker. If you do not believe everything you read or hear, you are a critical thinker. If you find pleasure in contemplating the puzzle of conflicting ideologies, theories, personalities, and facts, you are a critical thinker.

Some features of critical thinking differ slightly among academic disciplines, but all critical thinking is rooted in the activities of analysis, synthesis, and evaluation. These activities apply when you think about lectures and discussions in your college classes, when you read your textbooks and other assignments for your college courses, and also when you conduct your daily life. They are explained in the following chart.

ACTIVITIES FOR CRITICAL READING AND THINKING

1. **Analysis.** Taking ideas apart to consider their components separately
2. **Synthesis.** Making connections among different ideas or components of ideas to seek relationships and interactions to tie the ideas together
3. **Evaluation.** Assessing the ideas for quality of reasoning (see 6d-6e) and soundness of logic (see 6f)

6b   Understanding the reading process

Reading, like writing, helps you to come to "know"—to compose meaning. In college, you get many reading assignments that assume you have the ability to read critically. Critical reading means reading with a questioning mind that is open to new ideas. A critical reader also recognizes when material is slanted, is incomplete, or is based on incorrect information. Understanding **the reading process** can help you effectively meet the demands of critical reading.

Reading is an active process—a dynamic, meaning-making encounter involving the interaction of the page, eye, and brain. When you read, your mind actively makes connections between what you know already and what is new to you.

Experts who have researched reading processes report that the key activity in reading is *making predictions.* As you read, your mind is always involved in guessing what is coming next. Once it discovers what comes next, it either confirms or revises its prediction and moves on. Predicting during reading happens at split-second speed without the reader's being aware of it. Without predictions, the brain would have to consider infinite possibilities for assimilating every new piece of information; with predictions, expectations can be narrowed to reasonable proportions.

1 Purposes for reading

Purposes for reading vary. Most reading in college is for the purpose of learning new information, appreciating literary works, or reviewing notes on classes or readings. These types of reading involve much *rereading;* one encounter with the material rarely suffices.

Your purpose in reading determines the speed at which you can expect to read. When you are hunting for a particular fact in an almanac, you can skim the material until you come to what you want. When you read about a subject that you know well, you can move somewhat rapidly through most of the material, slowing down when you come to something new. When you are unfamiliar with the subject, you need time to absorb the new material, so you have to slow down.

2 Using a system for reading to learn

Reading to learn involves three universals that hold for all material. These universals have parallels in the writing process, with slightly different labels, as explained in the chart on the next page.

Various structured systems for applying these universals have been suggested by experts in reading. Here is one widely endorsed system, popularly known as SQ3R.*

S = *Survey*. Surveying is part of *skimming*. You survey to get an overview of the material before you start reading closely. As you survey, your mind begins unconsciously to make predictions about the material. To survey a textbook, quickly survey

---

*Originated by Francis P. Robinson in 1946, the system been adapted by many others since. The version here is adapted for college students.

UNIVERSALS IN READING TO LEARN	
SKIM	Like *planning* (see Chapter 2) in the writing process, **skimming** means getting ready to read.
READ	Like *drafting* (see 3a-3b) in the writing process, **reading** means moving through the material, according to your purpose for reading.
REINFORCE	Like *revising* (see 3c) and *editing* (see 3d) in the writing process, **reinforcing** means rereading, clarifying, fine tuning, and getting into final form.

the entire text. Then, survey more slowly each chapter you want to read closely. If the material has headings, subheadings, words in italics or boldface, or visuals, use them as a road map during your surveying. To survey a book that has no headings, (1) read the title; (2) establish a general sense of the length of the material you need to read; (3) read the opening and closing paragraphs—unless you do not want to know the ending—and, if the material is long, glance over some intervening paragraphs.

Q = *Question.* Questioning is part of *skimming.* Asking questions stimulates your mind to prepare for learning. Questioning helps most when each question refers to a small "chunk," such as a paragraph or a group of paragraphs. The goal is to get your thinking started so that your brain will be alerted to focus on key matters as you read.

R = *Read. Reading* is the core activity in SQ3R. The speed at which you read depends on your purpose. Your goal is to comprehend the material. Comprehension can break down for a number of reasons: (1) If the subject is totally unfamiliar, you probably cannot associate it to what you already know. In such a situation, take the time to build up your store of information by reading easier material in other sources on the subject. Of course, return as quickly as possible to the more difficult material you want to read. (2) If your mind wanders, you are allowing valuable energy to be wasted on extraneous material. Be determined to concentrate and resist the appeal of other thoughts. (3) If you cannot comprehend material, you might be rushing. Be sure to allot sufficient time to use SQ3R. College students are pulled in many different directions and have to discipline themselves to balance their schedules for class, studying, and socializing; and nothing prevents learning as much as lack of time.

R = *Recite.* Reciting is part of *reinforcing.* Reciting calls for you to look away from the page and repeat the main points, aloud or to yourself. For best success, recite in "chunks"—subsections of textbook chapters, for example. Being aware ahead of time that you will have to recite can stimulate your concentration during reading. If you cannot recite the main points of the material, reread it and try again.

R = *Review.* Reviewing is part of *reinforcing.* When you finish reading, survey again. This process refreshes your memory about the initial overview you got during surveying. Be honest with yourself about what you cannot recall and need to reread. The next day, and again about a week later, repeat your review—always adding whatever new material you have learned since the previous review. Review again at set intervals during a course. The more reinforcement, the better.

Collaborative learning can help you reinforce your learning. Ask a friend or classmate who knows the material well to discuss it with you, even test you. Conversely, offer to teach the material to someone. You will know quickly whether you have mastered it sufficiently to communicate it.

Writing can also help you reinforce your learning. There is little that promotes authority over knowledge as does writing about it. Try keeping a learning log: draw a line down the center of your notebook page; on one side take notes on the reading material, and on the other side list key words, ask questions, make connections among ideas, and have a "conversation on paper" with the material.

ct **6c**

6c Reading critically

During the reading process, the full meaning of a passage emerges on three levels: the **literal,** the **inferential,** and the **evaluative.** If you are like most readers, you stop reading at the literal level. Unless you move to the next two levels, however, your critical reading and thinking skills will suffer.

STEPS FOR READING CRITICALLY

1. **Read for literal meaning.** You read "on" the lines to see what is stated.
2. **Read to make inferences.** You read "between" the lines to see what is not stated but implied.
3. **Read to evaluate.** You read "beyond" the lines to assess the soundness of the writer's reasoning, the accuracy of the writer's choice of words, and the fairness of the writer's treatment of the reader.

---

1 Reading for literal meaning

Reading for literal meaning, sometimes called *reading "on" the line,* calls for you to understand what is said. It does not include impressions or opinions about the material. Depending on the academic discipline in which you are reading, the literal level has to do with (1) the key facts, the central points in a line or argument, or the central details of plot and character; and (2) the minor details that lend texture to the picture.

When you encounter a complex writing style, take time to "unpack" the sentences. Try to break them down into shorter units or reword them into a simpler style. Do not assume that all writing is clear merely because it is in print. Authors write with a rich variety of styles, not all equally accessible on a first reading.

When you find a concept that you need to think through, take the time needed to come to know the new idea. Although no student has unlimited time for reading and thinking, rushing through material to "cover" it rather than understand it ends up costing more time in the long run.

2 Reading to make inferences

Reading to make inferences, sometimes called *reading "between" the lines,* means understanding what is implied but not stated. The process of inferring is a critical thinking skill that adds invaluable background for the interpretation of any passage.

CHECKLIST FOR MAKING INFERENCES DURING READING

1. What is implied rather than stated?
2. What words need to be read for both their implied meanings, (connotations) and their stated meanings, (denotations) (see 24b-1)?
3. What information does the author expect the reader to have before starting to read the material?
4. What does the author seem to assume are the reader's biases?
5. What information does the author expect the reader to have about the author's background, philosophy, and the like?
6. What does the reader need to be aware of concerning author bias?

---

3   Reading to evaluate

Evaluative reading, sometimes called *reading "beyond" the lines,* is also essential for critical thinking. Once you know an author's literal meaning, and once you have drawn as many inferences as possible from the material, you must evaluate.

Evaluative reading calls for many skills: knowing how to recognize faulty reasoning (see 6d-6e), logical fallacies (see 6f), slanted language (see 25a-4), and artificial language (see 25e). When you read to evaluate, you need to recognize the impact of an author's tone, detect prejudice, and differentiate fact from opinion.

Recognizing appropriate tone

Tone is communicated by all aspects of a piece of writing, from its choice of words to the content of the message. An author's tone should be appropriate to the author's purpose (see 1b) and audience (see 1c).

Most readers are wary of a highly emotional tone whose purpose is to incite the reader.

No   Urban renewal must be stopped! Urban rede-
              velopment is ruining this country. Money-hungry
              capitalists are robbing treasures from law-abiding
              citizens! Corrupt politicians are murderers, caring
              nothing about people being thrown out of their
              homes into the streets.

Usually, inappropriate tone is not quite as obvious as in the example above. Signals of inappropriate tone include—most especially—logical fallacies (see 6f) and remarks or satire that is nasty for no obvious reason.

If the tone sounds reasonable and moderate, readers are likely to pay attention and respect the writer. For more about tone, see 1d.

YES   Urban renewal is revitalizing our cities, but it has caused some serious problems. While investors are trying to replace slums with decent housing, they must also remember that they are displacing people who do not want to leave their familiar neighborhoods. Surely a cooperative effort between government and the private sector can lead to creative solutions.

Detecting prejudice

An author's **prejudice** can be revealed when his or her beliefs are stated as facts or evidence. Also, some authors express negative opinions in positive language, even though the underlying assumptions are negative. For example, *men make good boxers because they like to fight.* Often writers imply their prejudices rather than state them outright. For example, *women are not agressive enough to succeed in business.* Critical readers will question any argument that rests upon a weak foundation of distorted information or unsound reasoning (see 6d-6f).

Differentiating fact from opinion

Facts are statements that can be verified. A person may use experiment, research, and/or observation to verify facts. *Opinions* are statements of personal beliefs that are open to debate. Opinions often contain information that cannot be verified, such as abstract ideas. Writers sometime intentionally blur the difference between fact and opinion. A discerning reader must be able to tell the difference. Sometimes that difference is quite obvious, but often it is not.

One aid in differentiating between fact and opinion is to *think beyond the obvious.* For example, is "Strenuous exercise is good for your health" a fact? Although the statement has the ring of truth, it is not a fact. People with severe arthritis or heart trouble could be harmed by some forms of exercise. Also, what does "strenuous" mean—a dozen pushups, jogging, or aerobics?

A second aid in differentiating between fact and opinion is to *remember that facts sometimes masquerade as opinions, and opinions sometimes try to pass for facts.* To read critically as you evaluate, be ready to concentrate and think through matters that are relative and sometimes ambiguous. For example, in an essay for or against capital punishment, you would likely evaluate the argument differently if you knew that the author is currently on death row, or a victim of a crime committed by someone on death row, or a disinterested party with a philosophy to discuss.

EXERCISE 6-1

Decide if each statement is a fact or an opinion.

1. Jogging promotes good mental health.
2. "Every journey into the past is complicated by delusions, false memories, false namings of real events." (Adrienne Rich, poet, *Of Woman Born*)
3. "History is the branch of knowledge that deals systematically with the past." (*Webster's New World Dictionary,* Third College Edition)
4. The earth's temperature is gradually rising.
5. "You change laws by changing lawmakers." (Sissy Farenthold, political activist, interview reported in *The Bakersfield Californian*)

EXERCISE 6-2

After you read this passage, (1) list all literal information, (2) list all implied information, and (3) list the opinions stated.

It is the first of February, and everyone is talking about starlings. Starlings came to this country on a passenger liner from Europe. One hundred of them were deliberately released in Central Park, and from those hundred descended all of our countless millions of starlings today. According to Edwin Way Teale, "Their coming was the result of one man's fancy. That man was Eugene Schieffelin, a wealthy New York drug manufacturer. His curious hobby was the introduction into America of all the birds mentioned in William Shakespeare." The birds adapted to their new country splendidly.

—ANNIE DILLARD, *Pilgrim at Tinker Creek*

6d Using evidence to think critically

The cornerstone of all reasoning is **evidence.** Evidence may consist of facts, statistical information, examples, or opinions of experts. Keep these guidelines in mind as you gather, evaluate, and use evidence.

1. **Evidence should be sufficient.** In general, the more evidence, the better. A survey that draws upon a hundred respondents is likely to be more reliable than a survey involving only ten.

2. **Evidence should be representative.** Evidence should be presented as objectively and fairly as possible. An assertion or conclusion must be based on evidence that is a truly representative—typical—sample of the group.

3. **Evidence should be relevant.** Evidence should relate directly to the assertion or conclusion made. Determining relevance can demand subtle thinking. If you heard evidence that one hundred students who had watched television for more than two hours a day throughout their high school years earned significantly lower scores on the Scholastic Aptitude Test than one hundred students who had not, you might conclude that students who watch less television perform better on achievement tests. Yet closer examination of the evidence might reveal other, more important differ-

ences between the two groups—differences in geographical region, family background, socioeconomic group, even quality of schools attended.

4. **Evidence should be qualified.** Evidence rarely deserves claims that use words such as *all, always,* or *never.* Conclusions based on evidence are more reasonable qualified with words such as *some, many, probably, possibly,* and *usually.*

5. **Evidence must be accurate.** Without accuracy, evidence is useless. That evidence must be presented carefully without misrepresentation or distortion.

6e Using inductive and deductive reasoning

To think critically, you need to be able to understand reasoning processes. **Induction** and **deduction** are reasoning processes that follow natural thought patterns. People use induction and deduction every day to think through ideas and to make decisions.

1 Recognizing and using inductive reasoning

Induction is the process of arriving at general principles from particular facts or instances, as summarized in the chart below. Suppose that you go to the Registry of Motor Vehicles to renew your driver's license, and you have to stand in line for two hours until you get the document. Then a few months later, when you return to the Registry for new license plates, a clerk gives you the wrong advice, and you have to stand in two different lines for three hours. Another time you go there in response to a letter asking for information, and you discover that you should have brought your car registration form, although the letter failed to mention that fact. You conclude that the Registry is inefficient and seems not to care about the convenience of its patrons. You have arrived at this conclusion by means of induction.

SUMMARY OF INDUCTIVE REASONING

1. **Inductive reasoning moves from the specific to the general.** It begins with the evidence of specific facts, observations, or experiences and moves to a general conclusion.

2. Inductive conclusions are considered *reliable* or *unreliable,* not true or false. An inductive conclusion indicates probability, the degree to which the conclusion is likely to be true. Frustrating though it may be for those who seek certainty, inductive thinking is, of necessity, based only on a sampling of the facts.

3. An inductive conclusion is held to be reliable or unreliable in relation to the quantity and quality of the evidence (see 6d) supporting it.

4. Induction leads to new "truths." Induction can support statements about the unknown on the basis of what is known.

2

Recognizing and using deductive reasoning

Deduction is the process of reasoning from general claims to a specific instance. If several unproductive visits to the Registry of Motor Vehicles have convinced you that the Registry cares little about the convenience of its patrons (as the experiences described in 6e-1 suggest), you will not be happy the next time you must return. Your reasoning would be inductive, and it would progress something like this:

> The Registry wastes people's time.
>
> I have to go to the Registry tomorrow.
>
> Therefore, tomorrow my time will be wasted.

Deductive arguments have three parts: two **premises** and a **conclusion.** This three-part structure is known as a **syllogism.** The first premise of a deductive argument may be a fact or an assumption. The second premise may also be a fact or an assumption.

Whether or not an argument is **valid** has to do with the argument's form or structure. Here the word *valid* is not the general term people use in conversation to mean "acceptable" or "well grounded." In the context of reading and writing logical arguments, the word *valid* has a very specific meaning. A deductive argument is *valid* when the conclusion logically follows from the premises. The following argument is valid.

VALID

PREMISE 1	When it snows, the streets get wet. [fact]
PREMISE 2	It is snowing. [fact]
CONCLUSION	Therefore, the streets are wet.

The following argument is invalid.

INVALID

PREMISE 1	When it snows, the streets get wet. [fact]
PREMISE 2	The streets are wet. [fact]
CONCLUSION	Therefore, it is snowing.

The invalid argument has acceptable premises because the premises are facts. The argument's conclusion, however, is wrong. It ignores other reasons for why the streets may be wet. The street could be wet from rain, from street-cleaning trucks that spray water, or from people using hoses to cool off the pavement or to wash their cars. Because the conclusion does not follow logically from the premises, the argument is invalid.

Here is another example of a valid argument. Only if the writer can give evidence to support the first premise can the argument be considered *true*.

VALID

PREMISE 1   When the unemployment rate rises, an economic recession occurs. [assumption: the
writer must present evidence in support of
this statement]

PREMISE 2   The unemployment rate has risen. [fact]

CONCLUSION   An economic recession will occur.

In any deductive argument, beware of premises that are implied but not stated—called **unstated assumptions.** The response to such an argument is to question the assumptions, not the conclusion. Often the assumptions are wrong. Whenever you find an unstated assumption, supply it and then check to make sure it is true.

The following argument is valid. Its conclusion follows logically from its premises. Is the argument, however, true? No. Because the argument contains an assumption in its first premise, the argument can be true only if the premise is proved true. Such proof is not possible. Therefore, although the argument is valid, it is not true.

VALID

PREMISE 1   If you buy a Supermacho 357 sports car, you
will achieve instant popularity. [assumption]

PREMISE 2   Kim just bought a Supermacho 357 sports car.
[fact]

CONCLUSION   Kim will achieve instant popularity.

SUMMARY OF DEDUCTIVE REASONING

1. **Deductive reasoning moves from the general to the specific.** The three-part structure that makes up a deductive argument includes two premises and a conclusion drawn from them.

2. A deductive argument is valid if the conclusion logically follows from the premises.

3. A deductive conclusion may be judged true or false. If both premises are true, the conclusion is true. If the argument contains an assumption, the writer must prove the truth of the assumption to establish the truth of the argument.

4. Deductive reasoning applies what the writer already knows. Though it does not yield anything new, it builds stronger arguments than does inductive reasoning because it offers the certainty of a conclusion's being true or false.

EXERCISE 6-3

Ignoring for the moment whether the premises seem to you to be true, determine if each conclusion is valid. Explain your answer.

1. The Pulitzer Prize is awarded to outstanding literary works.
   The Great Gatsby never won a Pulitzer Prize.
   The Great Gatsby is not an outstanding literary work.

2. All military veterans are entitled to education benefits.
   Elaine is a military veteran.
   Elaine is entitled to education benefits.

3. Midwestern universities have great college basketball teams.
   Georgetown has a great college basketball team.
   Georgetown is a midwestern university.

6f Recognizing and avoiding logical fallacies

Flaws in reasoning that lead to illogical statements are called **logical fallacies.** Logical fallacies tend to occur most often when ideas are being argued, although they can be found in all types of writing. Most logical fallacies masquerade as reasonable statements, but they are in fact attempts to manipulate readers by reaching their emotions instead of their intellects, their hearts rather than their heads. Most logical fallacies are known by labels. Each indicates a way that thinking has gone wrong during the reasoning process.

A **hasty generalization** occurs when someone generalizes from inadequate evidence. Supporting the following statement with only two examples creates a hasty generalization: *My hometown is the best place in the state to live.* **Stereotyping** is a type of hasty generalization that occurs when someone makes prejudiced, sweeping claims about all of the members of a particular religious, ethnic, racial, or political group: *Everyone from country X is dishonest."* **Sexism** occurs when someone discriminates against people on the basis of sex. (See 13d and 25b for advice on how to avoid sexism in your writing.)

A **false analogy** is a comparison in which the differences outweigh the similarities, or the similarities are irrelevant to the claim that the analogy is intended to support. Homespun analogies often seem to have an air of wisdom about them, but just as often they fall apart when examined closely: *Old Joe Smith would never make a good President of the United States because an old dog cannot learn new tricks.* Learning how to be a good President of the United States is hardly comparable to a dog's learning new tricks.

A **circular argument,** sometimes called a *circular definition,* is an assertion merely restated in slightly different terms: *Boxing is a dangerous sport because it is unsafe.* Here, "unsafe" conveys the same idea as "dangerous" rather than adding something new. This **"begs the question"** because the conclusion is the same as the premise.

Non sequitur in Latin translates as "does not follow," meaning a conclusion does not follow from the premises: *Jane Jones is a forceful speaker, so she will make a good mayor.* It does not follow that someone's ability to be a forceful speaker means that person would be a good mayor.

Post hoc, ergo propter hoc—which means "after this, therefore because of this"—results when someone assumes that sequence alone proves something. This cause-and-effect fallacy is very common: *Because a new weather satellite was launched last week, it has not stopped raining.*

Self-contradiction occurs when two premises are used that cannot simultaneously be true: *Only when nuclear weapons have finally destroyed us will we be convinced of the need to control them.* This statement is self-contradictory in that no one will be around to be convinced after everyone has been destroyed.

A **red herring,** sometimes referred to as *ignoring the question,* sidetracks an issue by bringing up a totally unrelated issue: *Why worry about pandas becoming extinct when we should be concerned about the plight of the homeless?* Someone who introduces an irrelevant issue hopes to distract the audience, as a red herring might distract bloodhounds from a scent.

An **appeal to the person,** also known as *ad hominem,* attacks the appearance, personal habits, or character of the person involved instead of dealing with the merits of the issue: *We could take her plea for money for the homeless seriously if she were not so nasty to the children who live next door to her.*

The **bandwagon approach,** also known as *going along with the crowd,* implies that something is right because everyone is doing it. Truth, however, cannot be determined by majority vote: *Smoking is not bad for people because millions of people smoke.*

Using **false or irrelevant authority,** sometimes called *ad verecundiam,* means citing the opinion of an "expert" who has no claim to expertise about the subject. This fallacy attempts to transfer prestige from one area to another. Many television commercials rely on this fallacy—a famous tennis player praising a brand of motor oil or a popular movie star lauding a brand of cheese.

Card-stacking, also known as *special pleading,* ignores evidence on the other side of a question. From all the available facts, the person arguing selects only those facts that will build the best (or worst) possible case. Many television commercials use this strategy. When three slim, happy consumers praise a new diet plan, they do not mention (1) the plan does not work for everyone and (2) other plans work better for some people. The makers of the commercial selected evidence that helps their cause, ignoring any evidence that does not.

The either–or fallacy, also known as *false dilemma,* offers only two alternatives when more exist. Such fallacies often touch on emotional issues and can therefore seem accurate at first. When people reflect, however, they come to realize that more alternatives are available. Here is a typical example of an either-or fallacy: *Either go to college or forget about getting a job.* This statement implies that a college education is a prerequisite for all jobs, which is not true.

Taking something out of context separates an idea or fact from the material surrounding it, thus distorting it for special purposes. Suppose a film critic writes about a movie: "The plot was predictable and boring, but the music was sparkling." Then, an advertisement for the movie says, *Critic calls this movie "sparkling."* The critic's words have been taken out of context—and distorted.

Appeal to ignorance assumes that an argument is valid simply because there is no evidence on the other side of the issue. Something is not true merely because it cannot be shown to be false. Conversely, something is not false simply because it cannot be shown to be true. Appeals to ignorance can be very persuasive because they prey on people's superstitions or lack of knowledge. Here is a typical example of such flawed reasoning: *Since no one has proven that mental depression does not cause cancer, we can assume that it does.* The absence of opposing evidence proves nothing.

EXERCISE 6-4

Identify and explain the fallacy in each item. If the item is correct, circle its number.

EXAMPLE Seat belts are the only hope for reducing the death rate from automobile accidents. [This is an *either-or fallacy* because it assumes that nothing but seat belts can reduce the number of fatalities from car accidents.]

1. Joanna Hayes should write a book about the Central Intelligence Agency (CIA). She has starred in three films that show the inner workings of the CIA.

2. It is ridiculous to have spent thousands of dollars to rescue those two whales from being trapped in the Arctic ice. Why, look at all of the people trapped in jobs that they don't like.

3. Every time my roommate has a math test, she becomes extremely nervous. Clearly, she is not good at math.

4. Plagiarism is deceitful because it is dishonest.

5. The local political coalition to protect the environment would get my support and that of many other people if its leaders did not drive cars that get poor gasoline mileage.

6. UFO's must exist because no reputable studies have proven conclusively that they do not.

7. Water fluoridation affects the brain. Citywide, students' test scores began to drop five months after fluoridation began.

8. Learning to manage a corporation is exactly like learning to ride a bicycle: once you learn the skills, you never forget how, and you never fall.

9. Medicare is free; the government pays for it from taxes.

10. Reading good literature is the one way to appreciate culture.

Two

UNDERSTANDING GRAMMAR

 When you understand grammar, you have one tool to help you think about and discuss the ways that your sentences deliver their meaning to your readers. Part Two describes the elements of language and explains the standard rules for using those elements. As you use Chapters 7 through 14, remember that grammar is only a tool. Other parts of this handbook offer you additional perspectives on writing.

7 Parts of Speech

When you know the **parts of speech,** you have a basic vocabulary for identifying words and understanding how language works. Sections 7a through 7h explain the **noun, pronoun, verb, adjective, adverb, preposition, conjunction,** and **interjection.** As you use this material, be aware that no part of speech exists in a vacuum. To correctly identify a word's part of speech, see how the word functions in the sentence you are analyzing. Often, the same word functions differently in different sentences.

We ate **fish.** [*Fish* is a noun. It names a thing.]

We **fish** on weekends. [*Fish* is a verb. It names an action.]

7b Recognizing pronouns

A **noun** names a person, place, thing, or idea. For types of nouns, see the chart on opposite page.

Articles often appear with nouns. These little words—*a, an, the*—are also called **limiting adjectives, noun markers,** or **noun determiners.** *A* and *an* "limit" a noun less than *the* does: *a plan, **the** plan.* When you choose between *a* and *an,* remember that *a* is the right word to use when the word fol-

TYPES OF NOUNS		
PROPER	Names specific people, places, or things (first letter is always capitalized)	**John Lennon** **Paris** **Buick**
COMMON	Names general groups, places, people, or things	**singer** **city**
CONCRETE	Names things experienced through the senses: sight, hearing, taste, smell, and touch	**landscape** **pizza** **thunder**
ABSTRACT	Names things *not* knowable through the senses	**freedom** **shyness**
COLLECTIVE	Names groups	**family** **team**
MASS	Names "uncountable" things	**water**

lowing it starts with a consonant sound: ***a*** *carrot;* ***an*** is the right word to use when the word following it starts with a vowel or a vowel sound: ***an*** *egg,* ***an*** *honor.*

7b Recognizing pronouns

A **pronoun** takes the place of a noun. The word (or words) a pronoun replaces is called an **antecedent.**

> **David** is an accountant. [noun]
>
> **He** is an accountant. [pronoun]
>
> David gave **his** report to the finance committee. [The pronoun *his* replaces the antecedent *David.*]

111

PRONOUNS

PERSONAL
I, you, they, we, her, its, ours,
and others

I saw **her** take **your** book
to **them.**

RELATIVE
who, which, that, what,
whoever, and others

Whoever took the book
that I lost must return it.

INTERROGATIVE
who, whose, what, which, and
others

Who called?

DEMONSTRATIVE
this, these, that, those

Is **this** a mistake?

REFLEXIVE; INTENSIVE
myself, yourself, themselves,
and others

They claim to support
themselves.

RECIPROCAL
each other, one another

We respect **each other.**

INDEFINITE
all, anyone, each, and others

Everyone is welcome.

Pronouns are often involved in issues of correct grammar. For detailed information about pronoun case, see Chapter 10; about pronoun reference, see Chapter 11; and about pronoun-antecedent agreement, see Chapter 13.

EXERCISE 7-1

Underline and label all <u>nouns</u> (N) and <u>pronouns</u> (P). Circle all (articles.)

1. Queen Elizabeth II served as a driver and mechanic in World War II.

2. As a princess, she joined the Auxiliary Territorial Service in 1944.
3. She was treated like all the others, though.
4. When she started, she did not know how to dirve.
5. The princess quickly learned to strip and repair many kinds of engines.

7c   Recognizing verbs and verbals

Main verbs express action, occurrence, or state of being. For a detailed discussion of verbs, see Chapter 9.

> I **dance.** [action]
>
> The audience **became** silent. [occurrence]
>
> Your dancing **was** excellent. [state of being]

Main verbs can act as linking verbs. **Linking verbs** indicate a state of being or a condition. They link a subject°* with a subject complement—a word (or words) that renames or describes the subject.

<u>The Salary</u>   **<u>was</u>**   <u>low.</u>

SUBJECT   LINKING VERB   COMPLEMENT = DESCRIBES SUBJECT

Auxiliary verbs, also called **helping verbs,** are forms of *be, do, have, can, may, might, will,* and others. Auxiliary verbs combine with main verbs to make **verb phrases.**

I   **am**   **looking**   for a new job.

AUXILIARY VERB   MAIN VERB

VERB PHRASE

Verbals are formed from verbs, but do not function as verbs.

*A degree mark indicates a term that is defined in this book's Glossary

---

VERBALS

INFINITIVE: *to* + simple form° of verb	**To eat** now is inconvenient.
PAST PARTICIPLE: *-ed* form of regular verb° or equivalent in irregular verb°	**Boiled, filtered** water is usually safe to drink.
PRESENT PARTICIPLE: *-ing* form of verb	**Running** water may not be safe.
GERUND: *-ing* form of verb	**Eating** while driving is dangerous.

EXERCISE 7-2

Underline all <u>verbs</u> and circle all (verbals.)

1. Albert Einstein was offered the presidency of Israel.
2. Israel's first president had died in office.
3. An Israeli newspaper suggested Einstein for the presidency.
4. Many people wanted him for that demanding position.
5. Disinterested in politics, he refused the nomination.

7d Recognizing adjectives

Adjectives modify—describe or limit—nouns°, pronouns°, and word groups that function as nouns. For a detailed discussion about using adjectives correctly, see Chapter 14.

> I saw a **green** tree. [*Green* modifies the noun *tree.*]
>
> It was **leafy.** [*Leafy* modifies the pronoun *it.*]
>
> The flowering trees were **beautiful.** [*Beautiful* modifies the noun phrase *the flowering trees.*]

LIMITING ADJECTIVES

DEMONSTRATIVE
this, these, that, those   **Those** students rent **that** house.

INDEFINITE
any, each, some, and   **Few** students live off campus.
others

INTERROGATIVE
what, which, whose   **What** is your address?

NUMERICAL
one, first, tenth, and
others   The **third** floor is empty.

POSSESSIVE
my, your, their, and others   **My** room is larger than **yours**.

RELATIVE
that, which, whose,   They own a cat **that** makes me
whatever   sneeze.

Descriptive adjectives can show levels of intensity: *green, greener, greenest.* **Proper adjectives** are formed from proper nouns: *American, Victorian.* Articles (*a, an, the*) are one type of **limiting adjectives** (see 7a). Other types of limiting adjectives, listed in the chart above, can also function as pronouns. To identify each word's part of speech, see how it functions in a sentence.

7e   Recognizing adverbs

An **adverb** modifies—that is, describes or limits—verbs°, adjectives°, other adverbs, and entire sentences. For a detailed discussion about using adverbs correctly, see Chapter 14.

Chefs plan meals **carefully.** [*Carefully* modifies the verb *plan.*]

Vegetables provide **very** important vitamins. [*Very* modifies the adjective *important.*]

Those potato chips are **too** highly salted. [*Too* modifies the adverb *highly.*]

Fortunately, people are learning that salt can be harmful. [*Fortunately* modifies the entire sentence.]

Many adverbs are easy to recognize because they are formed by adding *-ly* to adjectives: *sadly, normally.* Be aware, however, that some adjectives end in *-ly: brotherly, lovely.* Also, many adverbs do not end in *-ly: very, much, always, not,* and *well* are a few.

COMMON CONJUNCTIVE ADVERBS AND THE RELATIONSHIPS THEY EXPRESS	
RELATIONSHIP	**WORDS**
ADDITION	*also, furthermore, moreover, besides,*
CONTRAST	*however, still, nevertheless, instead, otherwise,*
COMPARISON	*similarly, likewise,*
RESULT OR SUMMARY	*therefore, consequently, accordingly, then,*
TIME	*next, meanwhile, finally, subsequently,*
EMPHASIS	*indeed, certainly,*

Conjunctive adverbs modify by creating logical connections in meaning. Conjunctive adverbs can appear in the first position of a sentence, in the middle of a sentence, or in the last position of a sentence.

> **Therefore,** we consider Isaac Newton a great scientist.
>
> We consider Isaac Newton, **therefore,** a great scientist.
>
> We consider Isaac Newton a great scientist, **therefore.**

7f Recognizing prepositions

Prepositions function with other words, in **prepositional phrases.** Prepositional phrases often set out relationships in time or space: *in April, under the umbrella.*

> **In the fall,** we heard a concert **by our favorite tenor.**
> **After the concert,** he flew **to Paris.**

COMMON PREPOSITIONS

about	by	of
above	concerning	off
across	down	on
after	during	out
against	except	over
along	for	past
among	from	through
around	in	till
at	in addition to	toward
before	in front of	under
behind	inside	until
below	instead of	up
beneath	into	upon
beside	like	with
between	near	within
beyond	next	without

Some words that function as prepositions also function as other parts of speech. To check whether a word is a preposition, see how it functions in its sentence.

> The mountain climbers have not radioed in **since** yesterday. [preposition]
>
> **Since** they left base camp yesterday, the mountain climbers have not radioed in. [subordinating conjunction: see 7g]
>
> At first I was not worried, but I have **since** changed my mind. [adverb: see 7e]

7g Recognizing conjunctions

Coordinating conjunctions join two or more grammatically equivalent structures.

COORDINATING CONJUNCTIONS

and	nor	so
but	or	yet
for		

Correlative conjunctions also join grammatically equivalent structures. They function in pairs.

CORRELATIVE CONJUNCTIONS

both . . . and	not only . . . but (also)
either . . . or	whether . . . or
neither . . . nor	

> **Both** English **and** Spanish are spoken in many homes in the United States.

Subordinating conjunctions introduce structures that are grammatically less important than those in an independent clause within the same sentence.

> Many people were happy **after** they heard the news.
>
> **Because** it snowed, school was cancelled.

COMMON SUBORDINATING CONJUNCTIONS AND THE RELATIONSHIP THEY EXPRESS	
RELATIONSHIP	**WORDS**
TIME	*after, before, once, since, until, when, whenever, while*
REASON OR CAUSE	*as, because*
RESULT OR EFFECT	*in order that, so, so that, that*
CONDITION	*if, even if, provided that, unless*
CONTRAST	*although, even though, though*
LOCATION	*where, wherever*
CHOICE	*rather than, than, whether*

7h Recognizing interjections

An **interjection** conveys surprise or another strong emotion. Alone, an interjection is usually punctuated with an exclamation point: ***Hooray!*** As part of a sentence, an interjection is usually set off with a comma: ***Oh,*** *they are late.* In academic writing, use interjections sparingly, if at all.

EXERCISE 7-3

Identify the part of speech of each word in italics. Choose from noun, pronoun, verb, adjective, adverb, preposition, coordinating conjunction, and subordinating conjunction.

One[1] of the most devastating *natural*[2] *disasters*[3] *of*[4] recorded history *began*[5] on April 5, 1815, *when*[6] Mount Tambora, located *in*[7] present-day Indonesia, erupted. The *volcano*[8] blew off the top 4,000 feet of the mountain, creating a seven-mile-wide crater. Twelve thousand people *were killed*[9] *immediately,*[10] *and*[11] 80,000 died *later*[12] of starvation because the ash *from*[13] the volcano *destroyed*[14] farmland. The *blast,*[15] eighty times stronger than that of Mount St. Helens, was heard over 900 miles away. The cloud of *volcanic*[16] ash *circled*[17] the globe, reaching North America the following summer. The cloud *was*[18] *so*[19] thick that even the sun's rays could not penetrate *it.*[20] *Freezing*[21] temperatures and snow continued through the *entire*[22] summer, resulting in crop failures and death.

8 Structures of the Sentence

8a Defining a sentence

When you know how sentences are formed, you have one tool for understanding the art of writing. The sentence has several definitions each of which views it from a different perspective. On its most mechanical level, a sentence starts with a capital letter and finishes with a period, question mark, or exclamation point. A sentence can be defined according to its purpose. Most sentences are **declarative**; they make a statement: *Sky diving is dangerous.* Some sentences are **interrogative**; they ask a question: *Is sky diving dangerous?* Some sentences are **imperative**; they give a command: *Be careful.* Some sentences are **exclamatory**: *How I love sky diving!* Grammatically, a sentence contains an independent clause, a group of words that can stand alone as an independent unit: *Sky diving is dangerous.* Sometimes a sentence is described as a "complete thought," but the concept of "complete" is too subjective to be reliable.

An infinite variety of sentences can be composed, but all sentences share a common structural foundation. Sections 8b through 8g present the basic structures of sentences.

8b Recognizing subjects and predicates

A sentence consists of two basic parts: a subject and a predicate. A **simple subject** is the word or group of words that acts, is described, or is acted upon.

> The **telephone** rang. [Simple subject, *telephone,* acts.]
>
> The **telephone** is red. [Simple subject, *telephone,* is described.]
>
> The **telephone** was being connected. [Simple subject, *telephone,* is acted upon.]

A **complete subject** is the simple subject and its modifiers°: *The **red telephone** rang.* A compound subject consists of two or more nouns or pronouns and their modifiers: *The **telephone and doorbell** rang.*

The **predicate** is the part of the sentence that contains the verb. The predicate tells what the subject is doing, or is experiencing, or what is being done to the subject.

> The telephone **rang.** [*Rang* tells what the subject, *telephone,* did.]
>
> The telephone **is** red. [*Is* tells what the subject, *telephone,* experiences.]
>
> The telephone **was being connected.** [*Was being connected* tells what was being done to the subject, *telephone.*]

A **simple predicate** contains only the verb: *The lawyer **listened**.* A **complete predicate** contains the verb and its modifiers: *The lawyer **listened carefully**. A* **compound predicate** contains two or more verbs: *The lawyer **listened and waited**.*

SENTENCE PATTERNS: GROUP I

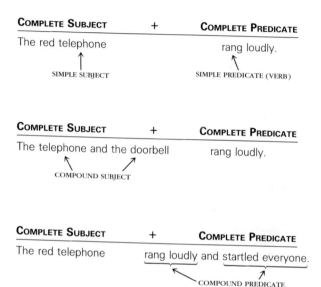

COMPLETE SUBJECT	+	**COMPLETE PREDICATE**
The red telephone		rang loudly.

SIMPLE SUBJECT   SIMPLE PREDICATE (VERB)

COMPLETE SUBJECT	+	**COMPLETE PREDICATE**
The telephone and the doorbell		rang loudly.

COMPOUND SUBJECT

COMPLETE SUBJECT	+	**COMPLETE PREDICATE**
The red telephone		rang loudly and startled everyone.

COMPOUND PREDICATE

8c   Recognizing direct and indirect objects

Direct and indirect objects occur in the predicate° of a sentence. A **direct object** receives the action—it completes the meaning—of a transitive verb.° To find a direct object, make up a *whom?* or *what?* question about the verb. An **indirect object** answers a *to whom? for whom? to what?* or *for what?* question about the verb.

SENTENCE PATTERNS: GROUP II

COMPLETE SUBJECT	+	COMPLETE PREDICATE
The caller		offered money.

                ↑   ↑
           VERB DIRECT OBJECT

COMPLETE SUBJECT	+	COMPLETE PREDICATE
The caller		offered the lawyer money.

     ↑   ↑   ↑
   VERB INDIRECT DIRECT
        OBJECT   OBJECT

8d Recognizing complements, modifiers, and appositives

A **complement** renames or describes a subject° or an object°. A **subject complement** follows a linking verb°. An **object complement** immediately follows a direct object° and either describes or renames it.

SENTENCE PATTERNS GROUP III

COMPLETE SUBJECT	+	PREDICATE
The caller		was a student.

     ↑   ↑
  LINKING SUBJECT
   VERB COMPLEMENT

COMPLETE SUBJECT	+	COMPLETE PREDICATE
The student		called himself a victim.

   ↑   ↑   ↑
  VERB DIRECT OBJECT
      OBJECT COMPLEMENT

Modifiers are adjectives° and adverbs°. They can appear in the subject or the predicate of a sentence.

SENTENCE PATTERNS: GROUP IV

COMPLETE SUBJECT	+	COMPLETE PREDICATE
The red telephone		rang loudly.

↑
ADJECTIVE

COMPLETE SUBJECT	+	COMPLETE PREDICATE
The telephone		rang very loudly.

↖ ↗
ADVERBS

An **appositive** is a word or group of words that renames the noun° or noun group preceding it. Most appositives are non-restrictive, which means they are not essential for identifying the noun being renamed. ❖ PUNCTUATION ALERT: Use a comma or commas to separate a nonrestrictive appositive° from what it renames (see 29f). ❖

SENTENCE PATTERNS: GROUP V

COMPLETE SUBJECT	+	COMPLETE PREDICATE
The victim, Joe Jones,		asked to speak to his lawyer.

↑
APPOSITIVE

COMPLETE SUBJECT	+	COMPLETE PREDICATE
The victim		asked to speak to his lawyer, Ms. Smythe.

↑
APPOSITIVE

8e Recognizing phrases

A **phrase** is a group of related words that contains only a subject° or only a predicate°. A phrase cannot stand alone as a sentence. Phrases function as parts of speech. A **verb phrase** functions as a verb° in a sentence (see 9e).

A **prepositional phrase** functions as an adjective° or an adverb in a sentence° (see 7f).

> The taking **of a population census** dates back **to the seventeenth century.**

A **verbal phrase** is a word group that contains a verbal—an infinitive°, a present participle°, or a past participle° (see 8e). Verbal phrases function as various parts of speech except verbs.

> In 1624, Virginia began **to count its citizens** in a census. [infinitive phrase]

> **Going from door to door,** census takers interview millions of people. [participial phrase using present participle]

> **Amazed by some people's answers,** the census takers always listen carefully. [participial phrase using past participle]

EXERCISE 8-1

Combine each set of sentences into a single sentence, converting one sentence in each set into a phrase. Underline that phrase. You can omit, add, or change words. Most sets can be combined in several equally correct ways, but be sure to check that your combined sentence makes sense.

EXAMPLE   The word *chauvinism* comes from the name of Nicholas Chauvin, a retired French soldier. Chauvin was obsessed with Napoleon's greatness.

The word *chauvinism* comes from the name of Nicholas Chauvin, a retired French soldier obsessed with Napoleon's greatness.

1. Chauvin was wounded in battle at least seventeen times. When he retired he received a medal, a ceremonial sword, and a pension of about $40.

2. Chauvin turned away from bitterness. He became a champion of Napoleon and France.

3. Word of his hero worship spread beyond his village. Chauvin was used as a character in a comedy.

4. Many other words started out as someone's name. These include *sandwich* and *bloomer*.

5. Other words enter the language in other ways. Some words were originally slang.

8f **Recognizing clauses**

A *clause* is a group of words that contains a subject and a predicate°. Clauses are divided into two categories: **independent clauses** (also known as **main clauses**) and **dependent clauses** (including *subordinate clauses* and *relative clauses*).

An **independent clause** can stand alone as a sentence because it is an independent grammatical unit (see 7a).

A **dependent clause** contains a subject° and a predicate° and cannot stand alone as a sentence. A dependent clause must be joined to an independent clause°. Some dependent clauses are subordinate clauses. They start with **subordinating conjunctions.** Each subordinating conjunction expresses a relationship between the meaning in the dependent clause and the meaning in the independent clause (see 7g).

Most clauses that start with subordinating conjunctions function as adverbs°. **Adverb clauses** usually answer some question about the independent clause: *how? why? when?* or *under what conditions?* ❖ PUNCTUATION ALERT: When an adverb clause comes before its independent clause, the clauses are usually separated by a comma (see 29c-1). ❖

If the bond issue passes, the city will install sewers. [The adverb clause modifies the verb *install;* it explains "under what conditions."]

They are drawing up plans as quickly **as they can.** [The adverb clause modifies the adverb *quickly;* it explains "how."]

Adjective clauses start with relative pronouns (such as *who, that, which,* or *when, where,* or *why*). An adjective clause is also called a *relative clause.* The word starting an adjective clause refers to something in the independent clause.

The car **that Jack bought** is practical. [The adjective clause describes the noun *car; that* refers to *car.*]

The day **when I can buy my own car** is getting closer. [The adjective clause modifies the noun *day; when* refers to *day.*]

SENTENCE PATTERNS: GROUP VI

| DEPENDENT (ADVERB) CLAUSE | | | + | INDEPENDENT CLAUSE | |

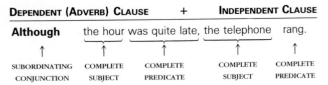

| **Although** | the hour | was quite late, | the telephone | rang. |
| SUBORDINATING CONJUNCTION | COMPLETE SUBJECT | COMPLETE PREDICATE | COMPLETE SUBJECT | COMPLETE PREDICATE |

| FIRST PART OF INDEPENDENT CLAUSE | + | DEPENDENT (ADJECTIVE) CLAUSE | + | SECOND PART OF INDEPENDENT CLAUSE |

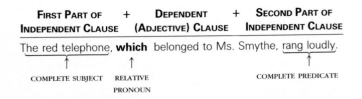

The red telephone, **which** belonged to Ms. Smythe, rang loudly.

| COMPLETE SUBJECT | RELATIVE PRONOUN | | COMPLETE PREDICATE |

Sometimes, *that* can be omitted from a sentence. For purposes of grammatical analysis the omitted *that* is considered to be implied and therefore present.

The car [that] **I buy** will have to get good mileage.

Noun clauses replace a noun° with a clause. They do not serve as modifiers.

Promises are not always dependable. [noun]

What politicians promise is not always dependable. [noun clause]

EXERCISE 8-2

Underline the *dependent clauses.* Write (ADJ) at the end of adjective clauses and (ADV) at the end of adverb clauses.

1. The bacteria that led to typhoid fever and cholera were spread when water was contaminated by solid human waste.
2. Sewers were built so that water supplies could be protected.
3. Waste water pipes from the sewers were connected to storm drainage systems, which took the waste to distant rivers.
4. The people who constructed these sytems believed this practice to be safe because a river can purify itself.
5. They were wrong because the rivers cannot renew themselves as quickly as we can pollute them.

8g Recognizing sentence types

Sentences can be **simple, compound, complex,** and **compound-complex.** A **simple sentence** is composed of a single independent clause° with no dependent clauses°.

Charlie Chaplin was born in London on April 16, 1889.

A **compound sentence** is composed of two or more independent clauses°. These clauses should be connected by a coordinating conjunction *(and, but, for, or, nor, yet,* or *so)* or *a semico-lon.* ❖ PUNCTUATION ALERT: Use a comma before a coor-dinating conjunction connecting two independent clauses. ❖

> His father died early, **and** his mother often had to spend time in mental hospitals.
>
> Chaplin lived in orphanages or boarding schools; sometimes he left them to perform in theaters.

A **complex sentence** is composed of one independent clause° and one or more dependent clauses° (see 8f and 21c). ❖ PUNCTUATION ALERT: When a dependent clause comes before its independent clause, the clauses are usually separated by a comma. ❖

> **When times were bad,** Chaplin lived in the streets. [dependent clause starting *when;* independent clause starting *Chaplin*]

A **compound-complex sentence** is composed of a compound sentence and a complex sentence. It contains two or more independent clauses° and one or more dependent clauses°.

> Chaplin's comedies were immediately successful, **and** his salaries were huge **because the public loved to see his tramp character, who was famous for his tiny mustache, baggy trousers, big shoes, and trick derby.** [independent clause starting *Chaplin's;* independent clause starting *his salaries;* dependent clause starting *because;* dependent clause starting *who*]

EXERCISE 8-3

Identify each sentence as simple, compound, complex, or compound-complex.

EXAMPLE   The teachings of Voltaire, Montesquieu, and Rosseau contributed to the French Revolution. (simple)

1. Each helped to convince middle-class French intellectuals that the monarchy was corrupt and that they could create a better government.
2. Voltaire considered many social institutions insensitive; his favorite target was the Catholic Church.
3. Voltaire saw the Church as narrow-minded and unsympathetic to the people, so he sought its elimination from politics.
4. The Baron de Montesquieu was a political theorist who traveled all over Europe studying various governments.
5. Montesquieu popularized the English system of checks and balances among the branches of government, and this ideal was adopted as a model by the writers of the American constitution.
6. He also argued that people should select their form of government, an idea of appeal to the French as well as the Americans.
7. Jean Jacques Rousseau saw humanity as pure and good.
8. Rousseau, who was born in Switzerland but lived in Franch, believed that children are born in a natural and unspoiled state but that civilization corrupts people.
9. Because of private ownership of property, people become selfish, and they must be taught to act for the common good.
10. Rousseau's ideas have had a strong impact on modern socialist and communist thought.

9 Verbs

Understanding verbs

Verbs convey information about what is happening, what has happened, and what will happen. In English, a verb tells of an action, an occurrence, or a state of being.

> Many people **overeat** on Thanksgiving. [action]
>
> Mother's Day **falls** on the second Sunday in May. [occurrence]
>
> Memorial Day **is** one of this country's most solemn holidays. [state of being]

Verbs convey additional information by various changes in their forms.

INFORMATION VERBS CONVEY	
PERSON	who or what acts or experiences an action—the **first person** (the one speaking), the **second person** (the one being spoken to), or the **third person** (the person or thing being spoken about)
	(continued on next page)

	INFORMATION VERBS CONVEY *(continued)*
NUMBER	how many subjects act or experience an action—**one** (singular) or **more than one** (plural)
TENSE	when an action occurs—in the **past, present,** or **future** (see 9g–9k).
MOOD	what attitude is expressed toward the action—**indicative, imperative,** or **subjunctive** (see 9l–9m).
VOICE	whether the subject acts or is acted upon—the **active voice** or the **passive voice** (see 9n–9o).

VERB FORMS

9b ### Recognizing the forms of main verbs

A **main verb** names an action (*people* **overeat**), an occurrence (*Mother's Day* **fell**), or a state of being (*Memorial Day* **is** *tomorrow*). Every main verb has three principal parts: a **simple form,** a form for **past tense,** and a form for **past participle.**

The **simple form** shows an action, an occurrence, or a state of being that is taking place in the present. The simple form is also the basis for the future tense (see 9g).

The **past tense** indicates an action, an occurrence, or a state of being completed in the past. If the past tense of a verb is **regular,** it is formed by adding *-ed* or *-d* to the simple form. If the past tense is **irregular,** the forms change in various ways (**go, went, gone**). For a list of irregular verbs, see 9d.

The **past participle** in regular verbs uses the same form as the past tense. In irregular verbs, these forms usually differ. Alone, a past participle can never function as a verb. To function as a verb, a past participle must combine with an auxiliary verb in a **verb phrase** (see 9e). Used alone, past participles function as adjectives: *crumbled* cookies, *stolen* pies.

Verbs also have a **present participle.** It is formed by adding *ing* to the simple form: *eating, falling, learning.* Alone, a present participle can never function as a verb. To function as a verb, the present participle must combine with an auxiliary verb in a verb phrase (see 9e). Used alone, present participles function as adjectives° (a *diving* board) or nouns° (*Swimming* is good exercise).

The **infinitive** is another verb form that functions as a noun° or an adjective° but not as a verb. Infinitives use the simple form and usually, but not always, are preceded by *to.*

> **To own** a bakery is my dream. [*to own* = infinitive functioning as noun subject°]
>
> The owner expects you **to bake** cookies. [*to bake* = infinitive as noun object°]
>
> We heard you **leave.** [*leave* = infinitive, without *to,* as noun object°]

A participle or an infinite not functioning as a verb is called a *verbal.*

9c   Using the -*s* form of verbs

The -*s* form of a verb occurs in the third-person singular in the present tense. The -*s* ending is added to a verb's simple form: *smell, smells.*

> The **bread** smells delicious.

The verbs *be* and *have* are irregular verbs. For the third-person singular, present tense, *be* uses **is** and *have* uses **has.**

> The strawberry shortcake **is** popular.
>
> The coffee cake **has** nuts on top.

If you tend to drop the -*s* or -*es* ending when you speak, do not forget to use it when you write. Proofread carefully for the correct use of the *-s* form. (For an explanation of the *-s* form in subject-verb agreement, see 12b).

EXERCISE 9-1

Rewrite each sentence, changing the subject to the word given in parentheses. Change the form of the verb to match this new subject. Keep all sentences in the present tense.

EXAMPLE   In many cultures, shamans heal the sick. (a shaman)
          In many cultures, *a shaman heals* the sick.

1. They also protect the community from danger. (he)
2. They cure patients by calling on supernatural powers. (he)
3. Some shamans are extremely rich. (The shaman)
4. Some shamans have great political power. (The shaman)
5. Shamanism still exists in societies of the far north, such as those in Siberia, Alaska, and Canada. (Shamans)

9d Using regular and irregular verbs

A **regular verb** forms its past tense and past participle by adding *-ed* or *-d* to the simple form. Most verbs in English are regular. Some English verbs are **irregular.** They form the past tense and past participle in various ways. A list of common irregular verbs appears on pages 136-138.

SIMPLE FORM	PAST TENSE	PAST PARTICIPLE
enter	entered	entered
smile	smiled	smiled
swim	swam	swum
drive	drove	driven

Speakers sometimes skip over the *-ed* sound in the past tense, hitting the sound lightly or not at all. If you are unused to hearing or pronouncing this sound, you may forget to add it when you write. Be sure to proofread your writing for *-ed* endings.

No	The birthday cake was **suppose** to be ready.
Yes	The birthday cake was **supposed** to be ready.

About two hundred of the most common verbs in English are **irregular.** Unfortunately, a verb's simple form does not provide a clue about whether the verb is irregular or regular. Although you can always look up the principal parts of any verb, memorizing them is much more convenient in the long run.

COMMON IRREGULAR VERBS

Simple Form	Past Tense	Past Participle
arise	arose	arisen
awake	awoke *or* awaked	awaked *or* awoken
be (is, am, are)	was, were	been
beat	beat	beaten
become	became	become
begin	began	begun
bend	bent	bent
blow	blew	blown
break	broke	broken
bring	brought	brought
build	built	built
catch	caught	caught
choose	chose	chosen
come	came	come
deal	dealt	dealt
dig	dug	dug
dive	dived *or* dove	dived
do	did	done
draw	drew	drawn
drink	drank	drunk

(continued on next page)

COMMON IRREGULAR VERBS *(continued)*

SIMPLE FORM	PAST TENSE	PAST PARTICIPLE
drive	drove	driven
eat	ate	eaten
fall	fell	fallen
fight	fought	fought
find	found	found
freeze	froze	frozen
get	got	got *or* gotten
give	gave	given
go	went	gone
grow	grew	grown
have	had	had
hear	heard	heard
hide	hid	hidden
keep	kept	kept
know	knew	known
lay	laid	laid
lead	led	led
lend	lent	lent
lie	lay	lain
lose	lost	lost
make	made	made
read	read	read
ring	rang	rung
rise	rose	risen
run	ran	run
say	said	said
see	saw	seen
send	sent	sent
shake	shook	shaken
shoot	shot	shot
sing	sang	sung
sink	sank	sunk
sit	sat	sat
sleep	slept	slept

(continued on next page)

COMMON IRREGULAR VERBS *(continued)*

SIMPLE FORM	PAST TENSE	PAST PARTICIPLE
speak	spoke	spoken
spring	sprang *or* sprung	sprung
stand	stood	stood
steal	stole	stolen
sting	stung	stung
strike	struck	struck
swear	swore	sworn
swim	swam	swum
take	took	taken
teach	taught	taught
throw	threw	thrown
wear	wore	worn
write	wrote	written

EXERCISE 9-2

In each blank, write the correct past-tense form of the verb in parentheses. Use the list of irregular verbs on pages 000–000.

EXAMPLE   The colorful butterflies (begin) **began** to arrive a few at a time in November.

1. As the month of November (wear) _____ on, millions of black, white, and orange flocks of monarch butterflies (take) _____ to the sky.

2. Scientists (know) _____ that the monarch butterfly (have) _____ been migrating between Canada and Mexico for more than ten thousand years.

3. Zoologists visiting from the University of Florida (rise) _____ early to observe the migration of these butterflies.

4. In 1975, the scientists (find) _____ evidence suggesting that monarch butterflies might be threatened by the destruction of the Mexican forests for farmland.

5. A group concerned about the monarchs asked for help from the Mexican government, which in 1980 (write) _____ laws to protect the butterflies.

9e Using auxiliary verbs

Auxiliary verbs, also called **helping verbs,** are usually forms of the verbs *be, do,* and *have.* They deserve special attention because their different forms are quite irregular, as shown in the chart below and the chart on the next page. Auxiliary verbs combine with main verbs° to make **verb phrases.**

The gym **is closing** early today. [*is* = auxiliary verb; *closing* = main verb; *is closing* = verb phrase]

❖ USAGE ALERT: Academic writing requires standard forms and uses of *be: He **is** (not **be**) driving his car to work.* ❖

THE FORMS OF THE VERB *BE*			
SIMPLE FORM	be	*-s* FORM	is
PAST TENSE	was, were	PRESENT PARTICIPLE	being
PAST PARTICIPLE	been		

PERSON	PRESENT TENSE	PAST TENSE
I	am	was
you (singular)	are	were
he, she, it	is	was
we	are	were
you (plural)	are	were
they	are	were

THE FORMS OF THE VERBS *DO* AND *HAVE*			
SIMPLE FORM	do	**SIMPLE FORM**	have
PAST TENSE	did	**PAST TENSE**	had
PAST PARTICIPLE	done	**PAST PARTICIPLE**	had
-s FORM	does	**-s FORM**	has
PRESENT PARTICIPLE	doing	**PRESENT PARTICIPLE**	having

The verb *be,* along with its various forms, is also a **linking verb.** It joins a subject° to its subject complement°. When *be* functions as a linking verb, it takes on the role of a **main verb**° rather than that of an auxiliary verb.

The gym **is** a busy place. [*gym* = subject; *is* = linking verb; *busy place* = subject complement]

The verbs *can, could, may, might, should, would, must,* and *ought to* are called **modal auxiliary verbs.** Modal auxiliary verbs have only one form.

9f Using intransitive and transitive verbs

Many verbs are both **intransitive** and **transitive;** other verbs are only one or the other. A verb is intransitive when the context in which it is used does not require an object° to complete its meaning: *I sing loudly.* A verb is transitive when the context requires an object to complete its meaning: *I sing a song.*

The verbs *lie* and *lay* are particularly confusing. *Lie* is intransitive (it does not need an object°). *Lay* is transitive (it needs an object°). Some of their forms, however, are similar. Get to know these verbs, if you do not already, so that you can use them with ease.

	LIE	**LAY**
SIMPLE FORM	lie	lay
PAST TENSE	lay	laid
PAST PARTICIPLE	lain	laid
-s FORM	lies	lays
PRESENT PARTICIPLE	lying	laying

To *lie* means to recline, to place oneself down, or to remain; to *lay* means to place something down.

INTRANSITIVE

PRESENT TENSE	The hikers **lie** down to rest.
PAST TENSE	The hikers **lay** down to rest.

TRANSITIVE

PRESENT TENSE	The hikers **lay** their backpacks on a rock.
PAST TENSE	The hikers **laid** their backpacks on a rock.

Note from the examples above that the word *lay* is both the past tense of *lie* and the present tense simple form of *lay*.

VERB TENSE

9g Understanding verb tense

Verbs use tense to express time. They do this by changing form. The chart on the next page provides a summary of verb tenses.

SUMMARY OF TENSES

SIMPLE TENSES (see 9h)

	REGULAR VERB	IRREGULAR VERB
PRESENT	I talk	I eat
PAST	I talked	I ate
FUTURE	I will talk	I will eat

PERFECT TENSES (see 9i)

PRESENT PERFECT	I have talked	I have eaten
PAST PERFECT	I had talked	I had eaten
FUTURE PERFECT	I will have talked	I will have eaten

All six tenses also have progressive forms, to show an on-going or a continuing aspect of the verb (see 9j).

9h   Using the simple present tense

The **simple present tense** uses the simple form of the verb (see 9b). It describes what is happening, what is true at the moment, and what is consistently true. It also has other special functions.

The tourists **are** here. [happening now]

Traveling on ships **makes** them seasick. [regularly occurring action]

Cruises **are** expensive vacations. [general truth]

The ship **leaves** port at midnight. [fixed-time future event]

9i Using the perfect tenses correctly

The **perfect tenses** generally describe actions or occurrences completed, or to be completed, before a more recent point in time. They use the past participle (see 9d) together with auxiliary verbs to form verb phrases.

PRESENT PERFECT	Our government **has offered** to help. [action completed but condition still in effect]
PRESENT PERFECT	The drought **has created** terrible hardship. [condition completed and still prevailing]
PRESENT PERFECT	We **have** always **believed** in freedom of speech. [condition true once and still true]
PAST PERFECT	The tornado **had** barely passed when the farm **was hit** by heavy rain. [both events occurred in the past; earlier event uses *had*]
FUTURE PERFECT	Egg production on the chicken farm **will have reached** 500 per day by next year. [event will be complete before specified or predictable time]

9j Using progressive forms

Progressive forms show action or condition is ongoing. They use the present participle (the *-ing* form) of the verb together with auxiliary verbs to form verb phrases.

PRESENT PROGRESSIVE	The smog **is making** their eyes tear. [event taking place at the time]
PAST PROGRESSIVE	Stationery made from recycled paper **was selling** well last week. [event continuing from the past within stated limits]

FUTURE PROGRESSIVE	Because more people **are starting** to recycle, we **will be expecting** more buyers to shop for recyclable products. [future event that will continue for some time and that depends on another action]
PRESENT PERFECT PROGRESSIVE	Scientists **have been warning** us about air pollution for years. [event ongoing in the past that is likely to continue in the future]
PAST PERFECT PROGRESSIVE	Our neighborhood **had been recycling** many years before yours did. [ongoing condition in the past that has been ended by something stated]
FUTURE PERFECT PROGRESSIVE	In May, the college recycling center **will have been operating** for five years. [event ongoing until some specific future time]

9k Using accurate tense sequence

When you want your sentences to deliver messages about actions, occurrences, or states that occur over time, you must depend on verb tenses in sequences. These sequences often include more than one verb. Using **accurate tense sequences** correctly—that is, showing the time relationships correctly—is important for clear communication.

SUMMARY OF SEQUENCE OF TENSES

WHEN INDEPENDENT-CLAUSE VERB IS IN THE SIMPLE PRESENT TENSE, FOR THE DEPENDENT-CLAUSE VERB:

■ Use the present tense to show same-time action.

The director **says** that the movie **is** a tribute to Chaplin.

I **avoid** shellfish because I **am** allergic to them.

SUMMARY OF SEQUENCE OF TENSES *(continued)*

■ Use the past tense to show earlier action.

> I **am** sure that I **deposited** the check.

■ Use the present perfect tense to show a period of time extending from some point in the past to the present.

> They **claim** that they **have visited** the planet Venus.

■ Use the future tense for action to come.

> The book **is** open because I **will be reading** it later.

WHEN INDEPENDENT-CLAUSE VERB IS IN THE PAST TENSE, FOR THE DEPENDENT-CLAUSE VERB:

■ Use the past tense to show earlier action.

> I **ate** dinner before you **offered** to buy me pizza.

■ Use the past perfect tense to show earlier action.

> The sprinter **knew** she **had broken** the record.

■ Use the present tense to state a general truth.

> Christopher Columbus discovered that the world **is** round.

WHEN INDEPENDENT-CLAUSE VERB IS IN THE PRESENT PERFECT OR PAST PERFECT TENSE, FOR THE DEPENDENT-CLAUSE VERB:

■ Use the past tense.

> The agar plate **has become** moldy since I **poured** it last week.

> Sugar prices **had** already **declined** when artificial sweeteners first **appeared.**

(continued on next page)

SUMMARY OF SEQUENCE OF TENSES *(continued)*

WHEN THE INDEPENDENT-CLAUSE VERB IS IN THE FUTURE TENSE, FOR THE DEPENDENT-CLAUSE VERB:

■ Use the present tense to show action happening at the same time.

> You **will be** rich if you **win** the prize.

■ Use the past tense to show earlier action.

> You **will** surely **win** the prize if you **remembered** to mail the entry form.

■ Use the present perfect tense to show future action earlier than the action of the independent-clause verb.

> The river **will flood** again next year unless we **have built** a better dam by then.

WHEN THE INDEPENDENT-CLAUSE VERB IS IN THE FUTURE PERFECT TENSE, FOR THE DEPENDENT-CLAUSE VERB:

■ Use either the present tense or the present perfect tense.

> Dr. Chang **will have delivered** 5,000 babies by the time she **retires.**
> Dr. Chang **will have delivered** 5,000 babies by the time she **has retired.**

❖ USAGE ALERT: When an independent-clause verb is in the future tense, use the present tense in the dependent clause. ❖

No   The river **will flood** again next year unless we **will build** a better dam.

YES   The river **will flood** again next year unless we **build** a better dam.

Tense sequences that include infinitives° or participles° must be correct. The **present infinitive** can name or describe an activity or occurrence coming at the same time or after the time expressed in the main verb°.

> I **hope to buy** a used car. [*To buy* comes later than the hoping. *Hope* is the main verb.]

> I **hoped to buy** a used car. [*To buy* comes at the same time as the hoping. *Hoped* is the main verb.]

> I **had hoped to buy** a used car. [The hoping came before the attempt to buy. *Hoped* is the main verb with an auxiliary verb.]

The **present participle** (a verb's *-ing* form) can describe action happening at the same time.

> **Driving** his new car, the man **smiled.** [The driving and the smiling happen at the same time.]

EXERCISE 9-3

Select the verb form in parentheses that best suits the sequence of tenses. Be prepared to explain your choices.

EXAMPLE   Over seventy-five years ago, after Albert Schweitzer left Europe, he (traveled, had traveled) up the Ogooue River in Africa.

Over seventy-five years ago, after Albert Schweitzer left Europe, he *traveled* up the Ogooue River in Africa.

1. The Ogooue is a vast, brown waterway that (stretched, stretches) across the central African wilderness.

2. Schweitzer had been traveling for many days when he (had come, came) to a small village.

3. He (had been seeing, saw) that the natives (have not been receiving, had not been receiving) proper health care.

4. Even though Schweitzer anticipated difficulties, he (establishes, established) a jungle clinic.

5. When Schweitzer died at age ninety, he (was providing, had been providing) medical treatment to the native population for over fifty years.

6. Today visitors to the clinic (learned, learn) that many changes (had been made, have been made) over the years.

7. For example, a few years ago an electrical link with the nearest city (has allowed, allowed) the staff to shut down the noisy generators that (have been providing, had been providing) all the clinic's power.

8. Impressed by Schweitzer's work, European and American donors (gave, had given) money for five new buildings, which were completed in the late 1970s.

9. Although nearly everyone admires Schweitzer, he (has been criticized, had been criticized) for ignoring preventive medicine.

10. Doctors presently at the clinic (planned, plan) to address this issue by giving workshops on nutrition and hygiene.

MOOD

91 Understanding mood

Mood refers to the ability of verbs to convey a writer's attitude toward a statement. The most common mood in English is the **indicative mood.** It is used for statements about real things, or highly likely ones, and for questions about fact.

INDICATIVE   The door to the tutoring center opened.
              She seemed to be looking for someone.
              Do you want to see a tutor?

The **imperative mood** expresses commands and direct requests. When the subject is omitted in an imperative sentence—and it often is—the subject is assumed to be either *you* or the indefinite pronouns *anybody, somebody,* or *everybody.* ❖ PUNCTUATION ALERT: A strong command is followed by an exclamation point; a mild command is followed by a period (see 28c). ❖

IMPERATIVE	Please shut the door.
	Watch out, that hinge is broken!

The **subjunctive mood** expresses conditions including wishes, recommendations, indirect requests, and speculations.

SUBJUNCTIVE	If I were you, I would ask for a tutor.

9m Using correct subjunctive forms

Various rules apply for using subjunctive forms correctly.

1 Using the subjunctive in *if* clauses and some *unless* clauses for speculations or conditions contrary to fact

In dependent clauses introduced by *if* and sometimes by *unless,* use the subjunctive to describe speculations or conditions contrary to fact.

If **it were** [not *was*] to rain, attendance at the race would be low.

In an *unless* clause, the subjunctive signals that what the clause says is very unlikely.

Unless rain **were** [not *was*] to create floods, the race will be held on Sunday.

Not every clause introduced by *if* requires the subjunctive. Use the subjunctive only when an *if* clause describes a speculation or condition contrary to fact.

INDICATIVE	If she is going to leave late, I **will** drive her to the track meet.
SUBJUNCTIVE	If she were going to leave late, I **would** drive her to the track meet.

2 Using the subjunctive for conjectures introduced by *as if* or *as though*

Use the subjunctive to express conditions that are possible but cannot be confirmed.

The runner looked as if he **were** [not *was*] winded.

The finish line looked as though it **were** [not *was*] miles away.

3 Using the subjunctive in *that* clauses for wishes, indirect requests, recommendations, and demands

Use the subjunctive for things that people wish for, ask for, or demand but that have not yet become reality.

I wish that this race **were** [not *was*] over.

It is important that the doctor **attend** [*not attends*] the race because someone is demanding that **she examine** [not examines] the runners.

4 Using the subjunctive with modal auxiliary verbs for speculations and conditions contrary to fact

The modal auxiliary verbs *would, could,* and *should* are often used with the subjunctive. These modal auxiliaries convey the notion of speculations and conditions contrary to fact.

If the runner **were** [not *was*] faster, I **would** expect stiffer competition.

When an independent clause contains *would have,* be sure to use *had* in any related *if* clause.

No   If I **would have** trained, I **would have** won the race.

Yes   If I **had** trained, I **would have** won the race.

Sometimes the word *should* appears in the *if* clause to convey speculation.

> **Should** the runners jump the starting gun, the official **would have** [not *will have*] to restart the race.

EXERCISE 9-4

Fill in the blanks with the appropriate subjunctive form of the verb in parentheses.

EXAMPLE   To improve a patient's general health, a doctor may ask that the person (diet) **diet.**

1. Suppose that George thought he (to be) _____ in good physical shape.
2. George's doctor, however, believed it important he (lose) _____ at least twenty pounds.
3. Medical experts urge that dieters (to be) _____ aware that the family may be uncooperative.
4. A jealous family member may even wish that the overweight person (gain) _____ weight.
5. For example, an insecure spouse may demand that the dieter (eat) _____ a food forbidden for that diet.

9n Understanding voice

Voice refers to verbs' ability to show whether a subject° acts or receives the action named by the verb. English has two voices: active and passive. In the **active voice**, the subject performs the action.

> Most clams live in salt water. [The subject *clams* does the acting; they *live*.]

In the **passive voice,** the subject is acted upon, and the person or thing doing the acting often appears as the object° of the preposition *by.*

> Clams have long been considered a delicacy by many people. [The subject *clams* are acted upon by *people,* the object of the preposition° *by*]

Your choices about audience and purpose for your writing greatly influence the voice that you choose for a sentence. Misusing voice usually creates problems of writing style rather than problems of incorrect grammar. To make your writing clear, use voice consistently in sentences on the same topic. (For ways to identify and correct confusing shifts in voice, see 17b.)

90   Using the active voice, not the passive voice, except to convey special types of emphasis

Because the active voice emphasizes the doer of an action, active constructions are more direct and dramatic. Most sentences in the passive voice can easily be converted to the active voice.

PASSIVE	African tribal masks are often imitated by Western sculptors.
ACTIVE	Western sculptors often imitate African tribal masks.

The passive voice, however, does have some uses. If you become familiar with them, you can use the passive to advantage.

1   Using the passive voice when the doer of the action is unknown or unimportant

When no one knows who or what did something, the passive voice is often used.

The lock **was broken** sometime last night. [Who broke the lock is unknown.]

When the doer of an action is unimportant, writers often use the passive voice.

In 1899, the year I was born, **a peace conference was held at The Hague.** [The doers of the action—holders of the conference—are unimportant to White's point.]

—E. B. WHITE, "Unity"

| 2 | Using the passive voice to focus attention on the action rather than on the doer of the action |

The passive voice emphasizes the action, while the active voice focuses on the doer of the action. In a passage about important contributions to the history of science, you might want to emphasize a doer by using the active voice.

ACTIVE   **Joseph Priestley discovered** oxygen in 1774.

But in a passage summarizing what is known about oxygen, you may want to emphasize what was done.

PASSIVE   **Oxygen was discovered** in 1774 by Joseph Priestley.

EXERCISE 9-5

First, determine whether each of these sentences is in the active or the passive voice. Second, rewrite the sentence in the other voice. Then decide which voice best suits the meaning.

EXAMPLE   Scientists were fooled by a horse and its owner about one hundred years ago. [passive voice]

               A horse and its owner fooled scientists about one hundred years ago. [active voice]

1. Around the turn of the century, Berlin newspapers carried a story about a clever horse.
2. The horse was named Clever Hans by his owner.
3. Answers to math problems were given by taps from the horse's hoofs.
4. Many people suspected some kind of fraud.
5. Two zoologists and a horse trainer were called in to investigate by the people who doubted Hans's talents.
6. Even with Hans's master out of the horse's sight, Hans still provided perfect answers to every question.
7. A young psychologist still entertained doubts.
8. People who did not know the answers to the problems were used by the psychologist to ask Hans questions.
9. The math test was failed by Clever Hans.
10. Apparently Clever Hans had been reading small, subconscious human gestures that indicated the correct answers.

10 Case of Nouns and Pronouns

Understanding case

Case refers to the different forms that nouns° and pronouns° take to deliver information. English has three cases: *subjective case, objective case,* and *possessive case.*

Personal pronouns, the most common type of pronouns, have a full range of cases that show changes in **person** (first, second, and third person) and **number** (singular and plural).

CASES OF PERSONAL PRONOUNS						
	SUBJECTIVE		**OBJECTIVE**		**POSSESSIVE**	
PERSON	SING.	PLUR.	SING.	PLUR.	SING.	PLUR.
First	I	we	me	us	my/mine	our/ours
Second	you	you	you	you	your/yours	your/yours
Third	he she it	they	him her it	them	his her/hers its	their/theirs

155

A pronoun in the **subjective case** functions as a subject°.

> **We** were going to get married. [*We* is the subject.]
>
> John and **I** wanted a one-person band to play at our wedding. [*I* is part of the compound subject° *John and I.*]

A pronoun in the **objective case** functions as a direct object°, an indirect object°, or the object of a preposition°.

> We saw **him** perform in a public park. [*Him* is the direct object.]
>
> We showed **him** our budget. [*Him* is the indirect object.]
>
> He understood and shook hands with **me** to confirm the deal. [*Me* is the object of the preposition *with.*]

A pronoun in the **possessive case** indicates possession or ownership.

> The **musician's** contract was in the mail the next day. [*Musician's,* a noun in the possessive case, indicates ownership.]
>
> **Our** signatures quickly went on the contract. [*Our,* a pronoun in the possessive case, indicates possession.]

The pronouns **who** and **whoever** also change form for case changes, as explained in 10e.

10b Using the same cases for pronouns in compound constructions as in single constructions

A compound construction contains more than one subject° or object°.

> **He** saw the eclipse of the sun. [single subject]
>
> **He and I** saw the eclipse of the sun. [compound subject]
>
> That eclipse astonished **us.** [single object]
>
> That eclipse astonished **him and me.** [compound object]

A compound construction has no effect on the choice of pronoun case. A compound subject uses the subjective case, and a compound object uses the objective case. Sometimes, however, people make the mistake of switching cases for compounds. If you sometimes are unsure which case to use, try the "drop test." Temporarily drop all of the compound elements except the pronoun in question.

EXAMPLE	**Janet and (me, I)** read that the moon has one-eightieth the mass of the earth.
DROP	Janet and
TEST	Which reads correctly: "***Me** read that the moon has one-eightieth the mass of the earth*" or "***I** read that the moon has one-eightieth the mass of the earth*"?
ANSWER	**I**

This "drop test" also works when both parts of a compound subject° are pronouns: ***She** and **I*** [not ***Her** and **me, she and me,** or **Her** and **I.***] *read that the moon has one-eightieth the mass of the earth.*

The same "drop test" works for compound objects.

EXAMPLE	The instructor told **Janet and (I, me) that the moon has one-fiftieth the volume of the earth.**
DROP	Janet and
TEST	Which reads correctly: "*The instructor told **I** that the moon has one-fiftieth the volume of the earth*" or "*The instructor told **me** that the moon has one-fiftieth the volume of the earth*"?
ANSWER	**me**

This "drop test" also works when both parts of a compound object° are pronouns: *The instructor told **her** and **me*** [not ***she** and **I***] *that the moon has one-fiftieth the volume of the earth.*

When pronouns in a prepositional phrase° occur in compound constructions, be sure to use the correct case for the pronouns. A prepositional phrase always has an object°, so any pronouns that follow words such as *to, from,* and *after* must be in the objective case.

> **No** The instructor gave an assignment **to Sam and I.** [*To* is a preposition; *I* is in the subjective case and cannot follow a preposition.]
>
> **Yes** The instructor gave an assignment **to Sam and me.** [*To* is a preposition; *me* is in the objective case, so it is correct.]

Be especially aware that *between* is a preposition that frequently leads people to pronoun error. A pronoun after *between* must always be in the objective case.

> **No** The instructor divided the work **between Sam and I.** [*Between* is a preposition; *I* is in the subjective case and cannot follow a preposition.]
>
> **Yes** The instructor divided the work **between Sam and me.** [*Between* is a preposition; *me* is in the objective case, so it is correct.]

If you are in doubt when you use pronouns in prepositional phrases use the test for compound objects above.

10c Matching noun and pronoun cases

When you use a pronoun and a noun together, be sure that they are in the same case. To check yourself, adapt the "drop test" shown in section 10b: Temporarily drop the noun following the pronoun and see which pronoun reads correctly.

EXAMPLE	**(We, Us)** tennis players practice hard.
No	**Us** practice hard.
Yes	**We** practice hard.
Yes	**We** tennis players practice hard. [*Tennis players* is the subject, so the pronoun must be in the subjective case.]

EXAMPLE	Our coach tells **(we, us)** tennis players to practice hard.
No	Our coach tells **we** to practice hard.
Yes	Our coach tells **us** to practice hard.
Yes	Our coach tells **us** tennis players to practice hard. [*Tennis players* is the object, so the pronoun must be in the objective case.]

The same principles hold when pronouns occur in an **appositive**—a word or group of words that renames the noun or noun phrase° preceding it. Again, adapt the "drop test" shown in section 10b. Drop the noun and test each pronoun separately to see if it is correct.

EXAMPLE	The winners, **(she, her)** and **(I, me)** advanced to the finals.
No	The winners, **her** and **me**, advanced to the finals. [*Her* and *me* rename the subject, *the winners,* so objective pronouns are incorrect.]
Yes	The winners, **she** and **I**, advanced to the finals. [*She* and *I* rename the subject, *the winners,* so subjective pronouns are correct.]

EXAMPLE	The crowd cheered the winners, **(she, her)** and **(I, me)**.
No	The crowd cheered the winners, **she** and **I**. [*She* and *I* rename the object, *the winners,* so subjective pronouns are incorrect.]
Yes	The crowd cheered the winners, **her** and **me**. [*Her* and *me* rename the object, *the winners,* so objective pronouns are correct.]

10d Using the subjective case after linking verbs

Because a pronoun coming after any linking verb° renames the subject, the pronoun must be in the subjective case.

The contest winner was **I.** [*I* renames *the contest winner*, the subject, so the subjective case is required.]

10e Using *who, whoever, whom,* and *whomever*

The pronouns *who* and *whoever* are in the subjective case. The pronouns *whom* and *whomever* are in the objective case. Informal spoken English tends to blur distinctions between *who* and *whom,* so you might not want to rely entirely on what sounds right.

1 Using *who, whoever, whom,* and *whomever* in dependent clauses

Pronouns such as *who, whoever, whom,* or *whomever* can start dependent clauses. see 8f.)

CASES OF RELATIVE AND INTERROGATIVE PRONOUNS		
SUBJECTIVE	**OBJECTIVE**	**POSSESSIVE**
who whoever	whom whomever	whose ————

To determine what pronoun case is correct in a dependent clause, see whether the pronoun is functioning as a subject° or an object°.

To check your choice of *who* or *whom,* try this variation of the "drop test" in section 10b. Temporarily drop everything in the sentence up to the pronoun in question, and then make substitutions. Remember that *he, she, they, who,* and *whoever* are subjects; *him, her, them, whom,* and *whomever* (the *-m* forms and *her*) are objects.

EXAMPLE	I wondered (**who, whom**) would vote.
DROP	I wondered
TEST	Substitute **he** and **him** (or *she* and *her*). Which reads correctly: "**He** *would vote*" or "**Him** *would vote*"?
ANSWER	**He.** Therefore: I wondered **who** would vote.

This "drop test" also works for *whoever.*

Voter registration drives attempt to enroll **whoever** is eligible to vote. ["*He* (not *him*) is eligible to vote" proves that the subjective case of *whoever* is needed.]

The subjective case *(who, whoever)* is called for even when expressions such as *I think* or *he says* come between the subject and verb. *She is the candidate who I think will get my vote.*

You can also use a "drop test" for the objective case.

EXAMPLE	**Volunteers go to senior citizen centers hoping to enroll people (who, whom)** others have ignored.
DROP	Volunteers . . . people.
TEST	Substitute **they** and **them.** Which reads correctly: "*Others have ignored* **they**" or "*Others have ignored* **them**"?
ANSWER	**Them.** Therefore: *Volunteers go to senior citizens centers hoping to enroll people* **whom** *others have ignored.*

This "drop test" also works for *whomever:*

> The senior citizens can vote for **whomever** they wish. ["The senior citizens can vote for *him*" proves that the objective case of *whomever* is needed.]

2   Using *who* and *whom* in questions

At the beginning of questions, use *who* if the question is about the subject° and *whom* if the question is about the object°. To determine whether the case is subjective or objective, recast the question into a statement, using *she* or *her* (or *he* or *him*) as temporary substitutions.

> **Who** watched the space shuttle liftoff? ["*She* watched the space shuttle liftoff" uses the subjective pronoun *she*. *Who* is correct.]
>
> Ann admires **whom?** ["Ann admires *her*" uses the objective pronoun *her*. *Whom* is correct.]
>
> **Whom** does Ann admire? ["Ann admires her" uses the objective pronoun *her*. *Whom* is correct.]
>
> To **whom** does Ann speak about becoming an astronaut? ["Ann speaks to *them* about becoming an astronaut" uses the objective pronoun *them*. *Whom* is correct.]

EXERCISE 10-1

Circle the correct pronoun in each pair in parentheses.

EXAMPLE   Experts say that our personal philosophies depend largely upon ((who), whom) or what has been important in our lives.

1. For example, many people vote for (whoever, whomever) their parents prefer.
2. Parents transmit to use their ideas about politics and (who, whom) to respect in government.

3. Research shows that children (who, whom) have been over-protected often become adults for (who, whom) life is difficult beyond the protective family circle.

4. Adults (who, whom) were consulted as children about some family decisions, such as (who, whom) to invite to dinner or what to name the dog, usually are more active politically than people (who, whom) had no voice in family matters.

5. In totalitarian countries, schools indoctrinate youngsters (who, whom) have learned never to question authority, so adults believe that trouble waits for (whoever, whomever) challenges the system.

10f Using the pronoun case that reflects intended meaning after *than* or *as*

A sentence of comparison often can be clear even though some of the words following *than* or *as* are implied rather than directly stated. *My two-month-old Saint Bernard is larger **than** most full-grown dogs* [the word *are* is implied].

When a pronoun follows *than* or *as,* the pronoun case carries essential information about what is being said. For example, these two sentences convey two very different messages, simply because of the choice between the words *me* and *I* after *than.*

1. My sister loved that dog more **than me.**
2. My sister loved that dog more **than I.**

Sentence 1 means "My sister loved that dog more *than she loved me.*" Sentence 2 means "My sister loved that dog more *than I loved it.*" To make sure that any sentence of comparison delivers its message clearly, either include all words in the second half of a comparison or mentally fill in the words to check that you have chosen the correct pronoun case.

10g Using the objective case when a pronoun is the subject or the object of an infinitive

An **infinitive** is the simple form° of a verb, usually, but not always, following *to: to laugh, to dance.* Objective pronouns occur as both subjects of infinitives and objects of infinitives.

> Our tennis coach expects **me to serve.** [*Me* is the subject of the infinitive *to serve,* and so it is in the objective case.]

> Our tennis coach expects **him to beat me.** [*Him* is the subject of the infinitive *to beat,* and *me* is the object of the infinitive; therefore, both pronouns are in the objective case.]

10h Using the possessive case before gerunds

A **gerund** is a verb's *-ing* form functioning as a noun. (***Brisk walking** is excellent exercise.*) When a noun or pronoun precedes a gerund, the possessive case is called for. (***Kim's brisk walking** built up her stamina. **Her brisk walking** built up her stamina.*) In contrast, a present participle—a form that also ends in *-ing*—functions as a modifier°. It does not take the possessive case. (*Kim, **walking briskly,** caught up to me.*)

The possessive case, therefore, communicates important information. Consider these two sentences, which convey two different messages, entirely as a result of the possessive:

1. The detective noticed the **man staggering.**
2. The detective noticed the **man's staggering.**

Sentence 1 means that the detective noticed the man; sentence 2 means that the detective noticed the staggering. The same distinction applies to pronouns:

1. The detective noticed **him** staggering.
2. The detective noticed **his** staggering.

In informal conversation, the distinction is often ignored, but readers of academic writing expect that information will be precise. Consider the difference in the following two examples:

GERUND (AS A SUBJECT)	The **governor's calling for a tax increase** surprised her supporters. [The act of calling for an increase surprised the supporters]
PARTICIPLE (MODIFIER)	The governor, **calling for a tax increase,** surprised her supporters. [The governor herself surprised the supporters]

10i Reserving -*self* forms of pronouns for reflexive or intensive use

Reflexive pronouns reflect back on the subject° or object°: *The detective disguised **himself**. He had to rely on **himself** to solve the mystery.* Do not use reflexive pronouns as substitutes for subjects or objects. *The detective and **I*** (not *myself*) *had a long talk. He wanted my partner and **me*** (not *myself*) *to help him.*

Intensive pronouns provide emphasis by making another word more intense in meaning: *The detective felt that his career **itself** was at stake.*

Avoid nonstandard forms of reflexive and intensive pronouns in academic writing: *hisself,* nonstandard for *himself; theirself, theirselves, themself,* and *themselfs,* nonstandard for *themselves.*

EXERCISE 10-2

Circle the correct pronoun in each pair in parentheses.

EXAMPLE   Sam Houston, leader of the drive for Texas's independence, is less well-known for ((his), him) championing of the rights of the Cherokees.

1. Houston's concern grew out of (him, his) living with the Cherokees for three years in his late teens.

2. From 1817 to 1818 he served as a government subagent helping to settle some Cherokees on a reservation, but a reprimand from Secretary of War John C. Calhoun persuaded (he, him) to resign.

3. Calhoun was angry about (Houston, Houston's) wearing Indian clothing to meet (he, him).

4. Not only as tall and energetic as Andrew Jackson, Houston was also as popular as (he, him).

5. He lived with the Cherokees, who decided to adopt (he, him) as a member of their nation, and later he went to Washington on behalf of the Cherokees to help (them, they) protest the fraud of some government agents.

Pronoun Reference

11a Understanding pronoun reference

Pronoun reference is a term that says that the meaning of a pronoun° comes from its **antecedent,** the noun° or pronoun to which the pronoun refers. For your writing to communicate its message clearly, each pronoun must relate directly to an antecedent.

> **Facts** do not cease to exist just because **they** are ignored.
>
> —ALDOUS HUXLEY

> I have found that the best way to give advice to children is to find out what **they** want and then advise **them** to do **it**.
>
> —HARRY S. TRUMAN

11b Making a pronoun refer clearly to a single antecedent

When pronoun reference is unclear, meaning gets muddled. To be understood, a pronoun must refer clearly to a single nearby antecedent. Often the same pronoun is misused to serve as a referent to more than one antecedent.

No   In 1911, **Roald Amundsen** reached the South Pole
            just thirty-five days before **Robert F. Scott** arrived.
            He [who? Amundsen or Scott?] had told people
            that he was going to sail for the Arctic but then **he**
            turned south for the Antarctic. On the journey
            home, **he** and **his** party froze to death just a few
            miles from safety.

Yes   In 1911, **Roald Amundsen** discovered the South
            Pole just thirty-five days before **Robert F. Scott** ar-
            rived. **Amundsen** had told people that **he** was
            going to sail for the Arctic but then **he** turned south
            for the Antarctic. On the journey home, **Scott** and
            his party froze to death just a few miles from safety.

You can use more than one pronoun in a sentence, but be sure
that each has a clear antecedent.

> **Robert F. Scott** used **horses** for **his** trip to the Pole, but
> **they** perished quickly because **they** were not suited for
> travel over ice and snow.

11c Placing pronouns close to their antecedents for clarity

If too much material comes between a pronoun and its
antecedent, even if they are logically related, unclear pronoun
reference results. Readers lose track of meaning if they have to
trace back too far to find the antecedent of a pronoun.

No   **Alfred Wegener,** a highly trained German meteo-
            rologist and professor of geophysics and meteorol-
            ogy at the University of Graz in Austria, was the first
            person to suggest that all the continents on earth
            were originally part of one large land mass. Accord-
            ing to this theory, the supercontinent broke up long
            ago and the fragments drifted apart. **He** named this
            supercontinent Pangaea. [Although *he* can refer
            only to *Wegener,* too much material intervenes be-
            tween the pronoun and its antecedent.]

Yes   **Alfred Wegener,** a highly trained German meteorologist and professor of geophysics and meteorology at the University of Graz in Austria, was the first person to suggest that all the continents on earth were originally part of one large land mass. According to this theory, the supercontinent broke up long ago and the fragments drifted apart. **Wegener** named this supercontinent Pangaea.

11d   Making a pronoun refer to a definite antecedent

The antecedent of a pronoun must be clear, so that your writing will deliver its intended message.

1

A noun's possessive case° cannot be the antecedent to a pronoun, unless the pronoun is also in the possessive case.

No   The **geologist's** discovery brought **him** fame. [The pronoun *him* is not possessive and therefore cannot refer to the possessive *geologist's.*]

Yes   The **geologist** became famous because of **his** discovery.

Yes   The **geologist's** discovery was **his** alone.

2

An adjective° cannot serve double duty as both a modifier° and a noun° to which a pronoun refers.

No   Dan likes to study **geological** records. **That** is his major. [*That* cannot refer to the adjective *geological.*]

Yes   Dan likes to study **geological** records. **Geology** is his major.

169

3 Using *it*, *that*, *this*, and *which* to refer to only one antecedent

When you use *it*, *that*, *this*, and *which* be sure that your readers can easily understand what each refers to.

No Comets usually fly by the earth at 100,000 m.p.h., whereas asteroids sometimes collide with the earth. **This** interests scientists. [What does *this* refer to? The speed of the comets? Comets flying by the earth? Asteroids colliding with the earth?]

Yes Comets usually fly by the earth at 100,000 m.p.h., whereas asteroids sometimes collide with the earth. **This difference** interests scientists.

4 Using *it* and *they* precisely

In speech, statements sometimes begin with *It said on the radio* or *In Washington they say*. Because such expressions are inexact and wordy, avoid them in academic writing.

The newspaper reports [not *It said in the newspaper*] that minor earthquakes occur almost daily in California.

Californians say [not *In California they say*] that no one feels a minor earthquake.

5 Not using a pronoun in the first sentence of a work to refer to the work's title

When referring to a title, repeat or reword whatever part of the title you want to use.

TITLE Geophysics as a Major

No This subject unites the sciences of physics, biology, and ancient life.

Yes Geophysics unites the sciences of physics, biology, and ancient life.

11e Not overusing *it*

It has three different uses in English.

1. *It* is a personal pronoun°: *Doug wants to visit the 18-inch Schmidt telescope, but **it** is on Mount Palomar.*
2. *It* is an expletive—a word that postpones the subject: ***It** is interesting to observe the stars.*
3. *It* is part of idiomatic expressions of weather, time, or distance: ***It** is sunny. **It** is midnight. **It** is not far to the hotel.*

All of these uses are acceptable, but combining them in the same sentence can create confusion.

> **No** Because our car was overheating, **it** came as no surprise that **it** broke down just as **it** began to rain. [*It* is overused here even though all three uses—2, 1, and 3 above, respectively—are acceptable.]
>
> **Yes** **It** came as no surprise that our overheating car broke down just as the rain began to fall.

11f Using *you* only for direct address

In academic writing, *you* is not a suitable substitute for specific words that refer to people, situations, and occurrences. Exact language is always preferable. Also, *you* used for other than direct address tends to lead to wordiness. This handbook uses *you* to address you directly as the reader.

> **No** Uprisings in prison often occur when **you allow** overcrowded conditions to continue. [Are you, the reader of this handbook, allowing the conditions to continue?]
>
> **Yes** Uprisings in prison often occur when **the authorities allow** overcrowded conditions to occur.

171

11g Using *who, which,* and *that* correctly

Who refers to people or to animals with names or special talents.

> **Theodore Roosevelt, who** served from 1901 to 1909 as the twenty-sixth President of the United States, inspired the creation of the stuffed animal called the "teddy bear."

> **Lassie, who** was known for her intelligence and courage, was actually played by a series of male collies.

Which and *that* refer to animals, things, and sometimes anonymous or collective groups of people. To choose between *which* and *that,* see whether the clause introduced by the pronoun is restrictive or nonrestrictive. Use *that* or *which* with restrictive clauses, but be consistent in each piece of writing. Use *which* with nonrestrictive clauses. Use *who,* for people, in both kinds of clauses.❖ COMMA ALERT: Set off nonrestrictive clauses with commas (see 29f). ❖

> Modern **zoos that** are being built or renovated today provide natural habitats for their animals.

> **Giant pandas, which** are native to China, are in danger of extinction.

> **Bamboo, which** is the panda's primary food source, recently has become scarce in many areas of China.

> **Children, who** nearly all like zoos, especially enjoy zoos where they can touch animals safely.

> **Children who** like animals usually grow up to be affectionate adults.

EXERCISE 11–1

Rewrite each sentence so that all pronoun references are clear. If you consider a passage correct as written, circle its number.

EXAMPLE   It is claimed that slips of the tongue are common.
> *Experts claim that slips of the tongue are common.*
> (Revision avoids imprecise use of *it*.)

1. It is interesting to note that it is thought that slips of the tongue might be the result of more than merely momentary mental lapses.

2. Sigmund Freud's theories include what he thought about the connection between slips of the tongue and unconscious thoughts.

3. Most psychologists agree, however, that a simple slip does not indicate that you are covering up deeply hidden secrets.

4. It says in research reports by psychologists and language experts that ordinary slips of the tongue provide important clues about how the brain learns information.

5. Understanding the slips and why they occur has scientific value.

6. It can also be very interesting.

7. When people are suffering from anxiety, and when people have a great deal on their minds, they tend to make more slips. This is the result of being distracted.

8. A first-time public speaker, who is particularly nervous about being inexperienced, is likely to make slips.

9. The first person to have written about slips of the tongue was the linguist Meringer, who published a book on the subject in 1895. Sigmund Freud was helped by Meringer's ideas. He developed a theory of the unconscious mind.

10. You are less likely to make slips of the tongue if you do not make other kinds of slips, such as forgetting people's names or bumping into things.

12 Subject-Verb Agreement

12a Understanding subject-verb agreement

Subject-verb agreement means that subjects° and verbs° must match in number and in person. These concepts are explained in the chart on the opposite page.

> The **firefly glows** with luminescent light. [*firefly* = singular subject in the third person; *glows* = singular verb in third person]

> **Fireflies glow** with luminescent light. [*fireflies* = plural subject in the third person; *glow* = plural verb in third person]

12b Using the final -*s* or -*es* either for plural subjects or for singular verbs

Subject-verb agreement often involves one letter: *s.* Be aware that the -*s* added to subjects and the -*s* added to verbs have very different functions.

> **REVIEW OF "NUMBER" AND "PERSON" FOR AGREEMENT**
>
> **Number,** as a concept in grammar, refers to *singular* and *plural.*
>
> ■ The **first person** is the speaker or writer. *I* (singular) and *we* (plural) are the only subjects that occur in the first person.
>
> SINGULAR   **I** see a field of fireflies.
>
> PLURAL   **We** see a field of fireflies.
>
> ■ The **second person** is the person spoken or written to. *You* (both singular and plural) is the only subject that occurs in the second person.
>
> SINGULAR   **You** see a shower of sparks.
>
> PLURAL   **You** see a shower of sparks.
>
> ■ The **third person** is the person or thing being spoken or written of. Most rules for subject–verb agreement involve the third person.
>
> SINGULAR   The **scientist sees** a cloud of cosmic dust.
>
> PLURAL   The **scientists see** a cloud of cosmic dust.

Most **plural subjects** are formed by adding an *-s* or *-es*: *lip* becomes *lips; princess* becomes *princesses.* Exceptions include most pronouns *(they, who);* a few nouns that do not change form *(deer, deer);* and a few nouns that change in other ways *(mouse, mice; child, children).* **Singular verbs** in the present tense of the third person are formed by adding *-s* or *-es* to the simple form of the verb: *laugh* becomes *laughs; kiss* becomes *kisses.* Exceptions include the verb *be (is)* and *have (has).* Even though *is* and *has* end in *-s,* they are not formed from the simple form° of the verb.

PATTERN FOR BASIC SUBJECT–VERB AGREEMENT

The **student works** long hours. ↑ ↑ SINGULAR SINGULAR SUBJECT VERB	The **students work** long hours. ↑ ↑ PLURAL PLURAL SUBJECT VERB

Here is a memory device to help you to visualize how, in most cases, the *s* works in agreement. The *-s* (or *-es*) can take only one path at a time, going either to the top or the bottom.

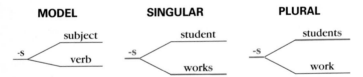

MODEL	**SINGULAR**	**PLURAL**
subject -s< verb	student -s< works	students -s< work

❖ USAGE ALERT: Do not add *-s* to a singular main verb in the third person after a modal auxiliary verb (such as *can,* and *might;* see 9e): *The coach **can walk*** (not ***can walks***) *to campus.*

12c For agreement, ignoring words that come between a subject and verb

Words that separate a subject from its verb should not influence verb agreement. The intervening material often appears as a prepositional phrase°, so eliminate all prepositional phrases from consideration for agreement.

No The **winners** in the state competition **goes** to the national finals. [*Winners* is the subject with which the verb must agree; *in the state competition* is a prepositional phrase.]

Yes The **winners** in the state competition **go** to the national finals.

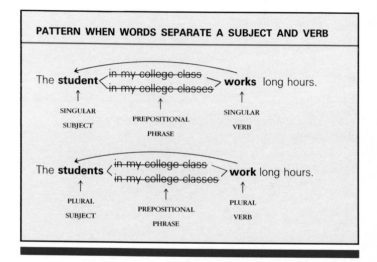

PATTERN WHEN WORDS SEPARATE A SUBJECT AND VERB

The **student** ⟨ ~~in my college class~~ / ~~in my college classes~~ ⟩ **works** long hours.

SINGULAR SUBJECT   PREPOSITIONAL PHRASE   SINGULAR VERB

The **students** ⟨ ~~in my college class~~ / ~~in my college classes~~ ⟩ **work** long hours.

PLURAL SUBJECT   PREPOSITIONAL PHRASE   PLURAL VERB

Also, to locate the subject of a sentence, eliminate phrases that start with *including, together with, along with, accompanied by, in addition to, except,* and *as well as.*

No **The moon,** as well as Venus, **are** visible in the night sky. [*The moon* is the subject with which the verb must agree; ignore *as well as Venus.*]

Yes **The moon,** as well as Venus, **is** visible in the night sky.

Be especially careful with a construction that starts with the words *one of the.* This construction takes a singular verb, to agree with the word *one*. Do not be distracted by a plural noun in the prepositional phrase.

> **No**   **One** of the problems **are** broken equipment.
>
> **Yes**   **One** of the problems **is** broken equipment.

12d Using a plural verb for subjects connected by *and*

Two or more subjects joined by *and* become plural as a group; therefore, use a plural verb.

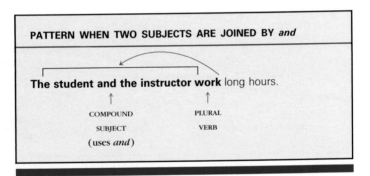

PATTERN WHEN TWO SUBJECTS ARE JOINED BY *and*

The student and the instructor work long hours.

COMPOUND SUBJECT (uses *and*)

PLURAL VERB

When *each* or *every* precedes singular subjects joined by *and,* use a singular verb.

> **Each human hand and foot leaves** a distinctive print.
>
> **Every police chief, sheriff, and federal marshal has used** these prints to identify people.

But when *each* or *every* follows subjects joined by *and,* the basic rule stands: Use a plural verb for subjects joined by *and.*

> **Memphis and St. Louis each claim** to be the birthplace of the blues.

The one exception occurs when subject parts combine to form a single thing or person: Use a singular verb.

Ham and cheese is our best-selling sandwich.

EXERCISE 12-1

Supply the correct present-tense form of the verb in parentheses.

EXAMPLE   Increased heartbeat, rapid breathing, muscular tension, and sweaty palms (to be) __**are**__ physical signs of anxiety.

1. Every adult, as well as most children, (to experience) _____ some anxiety.
2. Each man, woman, and child (to have) _____ a different reaction to feelings of anxiety.
3. When a person (to suffer) _____ from anxiety, the person might (to feel) _____ a need to escape from some imagined danger.
4. Anxiety, as expressed in behavior disorders, (to take) _____ several forms.
5. Sigmund Freud, one of the founders of modern psychoanalysis, (to be) _____ said to have been the first to call severe anxieties *neuroses*.

12e Making a verb agree with the subject closest to it

When subjects are joined with *or, nor, either . . . or, neither . . . nor,* or *not only . . . but (also),* make the verb agree with the subject closest to it. For subject-verb agreement, ignore everything before the final subject.

PATTERN WHEN SUBJECTS ARE JOINED BY *or*

~~Either the instructor or~~

~~Either the instructors or~~   the **student knows** the answer.

SINGULAR SINGULAR
SUBJECT   VERB

~~Either the instructor or~~

~~Either the instructors or~~   the **students know** the answer.

PLURAL   PLURAL
SUBJECT   VERB

12f Making a verb agree with its subject in inverted word order

In English, the subject of a sentence normally precedes its verb: *Astronomy is interesting.* Inverted word order means a change in the usual order. Most questions use inverted word order. Be sure to look *after* the verb, not before it, to check that the subject and verb agree.

Is astronomy interesting?

What **are** the **requirements** for the major?

Do John and Mary study astronomy?

Expletive constructions use inverted word order. With the use of *there* or *it,* they postpone the subject. Check ahead in such sentences to identify the subject, and be sure that the verb agrees with it. (For advice on being concise by eliminating expletives, see 20a-1.)

> **There are** nine **planets** in our solar system. **It is** astronomers who want more powerful telescopes.

Using singular verbs for most indefinite pronouns

Indefinite pronouns do not refer to any particular person, thing, or idea. In context, however, they take on very clear meanings. Indefinite pronouns are usually singular, so they take singular verbs. (For information about avoiding sexist language° with indefinite pronouns, see 13d-2.)

COMMON INDEFINITE PRONOUNS

another	each	everything	nothing
anybody	either	neither	somebody
anyone	every	nobody	someone
anything	everyone	no one	something

> Whenever **anyone says** anything, **nothing is** done.
>
> **Everything** about that intersection **is** dangerous.

A few indefinite pronouns—*none, some, more, most, any,* and *all*—may be either singular or plural, depending on the meaning of the sentence.

> **Some** of our streams **are** polluted. [*Some* refers to more than one stream, so the plural verb is used.]

> Pollution is always a threat, but **some is** easy to reverse. [*Some* refers to a portion of *pollution,* so the singular verb is used.]

12h Using singular or plural verbs in context for colletive nouns

A **collective noun** names a group of people or things, for example, *family, group, audience, class, number, committee, team.* When the group acts as one unit, use a singular verb. When the members of the group act individually, thus creating more than one action, use a plural verb.

> **The senior class** nervously **awaits** final exams. [*Class* is acting as a single unit, so the verb is singular.]

> **The senior class were fitted** for their graduation robes today. [Each member was fitted individually, but because there was more than one fitting, the verb is plural.]

> **The couple** in blue **is** engaged.

> **The couple say** their vows tomorrow.

12i Making a linking verb agree with the subject—not the subject complement

Linking verbs indicate a state of being or a condition. They connect the subject to its complement—a word that renames or describes the subject. You can think of a linking verb as an equal sign between a subject and its complement, called the **subject complement.**

> The car **looks** new. [*The car = new; the car* is the subject, *looks* is the linking verb, and *new* is the subject complement.]

When you write a sentence that contains a subject complement, remember that the verb always agrees with the subject. For the purposes of agreement, ignore the subject complement.

No   **The worst part** of owning a car **are** the bills. [The subject is *the worst part,* with which the verb *are* does not agree; the subject complement is *the bills.*]

Yes   **The worst part** of owning a car **is** the bills. [The subject *the worst part* agrees with the verb *is;* the subject complement is *the bills.*]

When the wording of a sentence is revised so that the word or words that were the subject complement become the subject, the same rule applies: the verb always agrees with the subject. For the purposes of agreement, ignore the subject complement.

No   **Bills is** the worst part of owning a car.

Yes   **Bills are** the worst part of owning a car.

12j   Using verbs that agree with the antecedents of *who, which,* and *that* as subjects

The pronouns *who, which,* and *that* have the same form in singular and plural. Before deciding whether the verb should be singular or plural, find the pronoun's antecedents.

The scientist will share the income from her new patent with the graduate **students who work** with her. [*Who* refers to *students,* so the plural verb *work* is used.]

George Jones is **the student who works** in the science lab. [*Who* refers to *student,* so the singular verb *works* is used.]

Be especially careful when you use *one of the* or *the only one of the* in a sentence before *who, which,* or *that.* If the pronoun refers to *one*, use a singular verb. If the pronoun refers to what comes after *one of the*, use a plural verb.

> Tracy is one of the students **who talk** in class. [*Who* refers to *students,* so *talk* is plural.]

> Jim is the only one of the students **who talks** in class. [*Who* refers to only *one,* so *talks* is singular.]

12k Using singular verbs with subjects that specify amounts and with singular subjects that are in plural form

Subjects that refer to sums of money, distance, or measurement are considered singular and take singular verbs.

> **Ninety cents is** the current bus fare.

> **Three-quarters of an inch is** all we need.

> **Two miles is** a short sprint for a serious jogger.

Some words that end in *-s* or *-ics* are singular in meaning and therefore need singular verbs, despite their plural appearance. These words include *news, ethics,* and *measles*—and when they refer to a course of study—they include *economics, mathematics, physics,* and *statistics.*

> **Statistics is** required of science majors. [*Statistics* is a course of study, so it agrees with the singular verb *is.*]

> **Statistics show** that a recession is coming. [*Statistics* refers to separate pieces of information, so it agrees with the plural verb *show.*]

Some nouns are singular in some contexts but not in others. These include *politics* and *sports.* Such words agree with singular or plural verbs, depending on the meaning of the sentence.

> Some people think that **politics is** a noble profession.

> Corrupt **politics are** behind the new law.

Some words are treated as plural, even though they refer to one thing: *jeans, scissors, eyeglasses,* and *riches.* If, however, the words *pair of* are used in conjunction with such words, the verb is singular, because it agrees with *pair.*

> The **scissors need** sharpening.
> The **pair of scissors needs** sharpening.

Series and *means* have the same form in singular and plural, so the meaning determines whether the verb is singular or plural.

> **The new television series is** beginning on Sunday night.
> **Those series of disasters** plaguing the production are expensive for the producers.

121 Using singular verbs for titles of written works, companies, and words as terms

When plural nouns° occur in a title, the title itself signifies one work or entity and thus always takes a singular verb.

> *Cats* **is** a successful Broadway musical.

Even if a word is plural, when you refer to it as a term, it takes a singular verb.

> *Our* implies that I am included.
> During the Vietnam War, ***protective reaction strikes* was** a euphemism used by the government to mean *bombing.*

EXERCISE 12-2

Supply the correct present-tense form of the verb in parentheses.

EXAMPLE   In the United States, most business cards (to show) **show** a person's name, address, and telephone number.

1. In Japan, a company often (to require) _____ people to carry business cards.
2. There (to be) _____ many different styles of business cards.
3. In Japan, every business person, as well as most people in professions, (to need) _____ to carry a carefully designed card.
4. Everyone who (to use) _____ business cards must (to observe) _____ certain rules of etiquette and tradition.
5. The *Tokyo Times* (to publish) _____ articles on international business customs.
6. One of the most important parts of offering someone a business card (to be) _____ to exchange slight bows.
7. People also (to explain) _____ that a male visiting Japan should not (to use) _____ business cards with rounded corners, which (to be) _____ reserved for females.
8. Malaysian business people, however, (to believe) _____ that anyone, male or female, (to be) _____ free to carry a round-cornered card.
9. The European community of countries (to be) _____ less strict in business card etiquette.
10. Throughout the world, the most important part of handling business cards (to be) _____ the customs of the country the person is visiting.

Focus on Revising

The case study at the end of Chapter 13 offers you the chance to observe and particpate in revisions that eliminate errors in subject-verb agreement this chapter and pronoun-antecedent agreement (Chapter 13).

13 Pronoun-Antecedent Agreement

13a Understanding pronoun-antecedent agreement

The form of most **pronouns** depends on **antecedents:** nouns°, noun phrases°, or other pronouns to which the pronouns refer. For your writing to deliver its intended meaning,

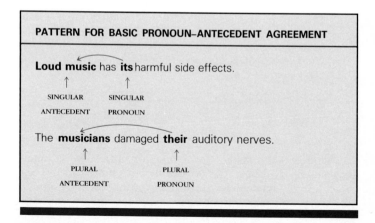

PATTERN FOR BASIC PRONOUN–ANTECEDENT AGREEMENT

Loud music has **its** harmful side effects.

↑ ↑
SINGULAR   SINGULAR
ANTECEDENT   PRONOUN

The **musicians** damaged **their** auditory nerves.

↑ ↑
PLURAL   PLURAL
ANTECEDENT   PRONOUN

the connection between a pronoun and its antecedent must be clear. Pronouns and antecedents must match in number (singular pronouns refer to singular antecedents, and plural pronouns to plural antecedents).

13b Using a plural pronoun when its antecedents are joined by *and*

Two or more antecedents joined by *and* require a plural pronoun, even if the antecedents are singular.

The United States and Canada maintain **their** border as the longest open frontier in the world.

When *each* or *every* precedes singular nouns joined by *and,* use a singular pronoun.

Each car and truck that comes through the border station has **its** contents inspected.

The one exception occurs when singular nouns are joined by *and* but refer to a single person or thing: Use a singular pronoun.

Our guide and translator told us to watch out for scorpions as **she** took us into the ancient tomb. [The guide is the same person as the translator. If the guide and translator were two people, *our* would appear before *translator* and *she* would be *they.*]

13c Making a pronoun agree with the antecedent closest to it

Antecedents joined by *or, nor,* or correlative conjunctions° (such as *either . . . or, neither . . . nor),* can mix the masculine and feminine or singular and plural. For the purposes of agreement, however, ignore everything before the final antecedent.

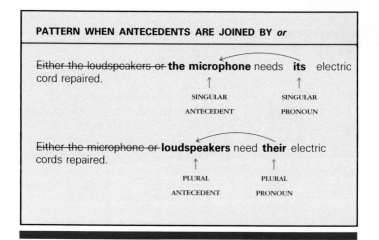

PATTERN WHEN ANTECEDENTS ARE JOINED BY *or*

~~Either the loudspeakers or~~ **the microphone** needs **its** electric cord repaired.

SINGULAR ANTECEDENT — SINGULAR PRONOUN

~~Either the microphone or~~ **loudspeakers** need **their** electric cords repaired.

PLURAL ANTECEDENT — PLURAL PRONOUN

13d Using a singular pronoun to refer to most indefinite-pronoun antecedents

Indefinite pronouns (for a list, see 12g) do not refer to any particular person, thing, or idea. In context, however, they take on very clear meanings. Indefinite pronouns are usually singular, so the pronouns that refer to them should also be singular: ***Anyone*** *who knows the answer should raise **his or her** hand.*

1

Some indefinite pronouns can be singular or plural *(none, some, more, most, any, all)*, depending on the meaning of the sentence. When an indefinite pronoun is plural, the pronouns that refer to it should be plural.

None are confident that **they** will pass. [The entire group does not expect to pass, so the plural pronoun *they is used.*]

None is confident that **he or she** will pass. [No one individual expects to pass, so the singular pronouns *he or she* are used.]

Be especially careful when you use the words *this* (singular) and *these* (plural). Make sure that they agree with their antecedent, and with any other pronoun in the same sentence: ***This kind*** *of hard work has **its** advantages.* ***These kinds*** *of difficult jobs have **their** advantages.*

2   Avoiding sexist pronoun use

In the past, grammatical convention specified using masculine pronouns to refer to indefinite pronouns: "*Everyone*

HOW TO AVOID USING ONLY THE MASCULINE PRONOUN TO REFER TO MALES AND FEMALES TOGETHER

Solution 1: Use a pair—but try to avoid a pair more than once in a sentence or in many sentences in a row. When you use a *he or she* construction, remember that it acts as a singular pronoun.

Everyone hopes that **he or she** will win the scholarship.

Solution 2: Revise into the plural.

Many people hope that **they** will win the scholarship.

Solution 3: Recast the sentence.

Everyone hopes to win the scholarship.

---

should admit *his* mistakes." Today people are more conscious that the pronouns *he, his, him,* and *himself* exclude women, who make up over half the population. Many experienced writers try to avoid using masculine pronouns to refer to the entire population. (For advice on how to avoid other types of sexist language, see 25b.)

13e With collective-noun antecedents, using singular or plural pronouns according to context

A **collective noun** names a group of people or things, such as *family, group, audience, class, number, committee, team.* When the group acts as one unit, use a singular pronoun to refer to it. When the members of the group act individually, thus creating more than one action, use a plural pronoun.

> **The audience** was cheering as **it** stood to applaud the performers. [The audience is acting as one unit, so the pronoun is singular.]

> **The audience** put on **their** coats and walked out. [The audience is acting as individuals, so the pronoun is plural.]

EXERCISE 13-1

Revise each sentence so that all pronouns agree with their antecedents. When necessary, change verbs and other words to maintain subject-verb agreement. Some sentences have more than one solution.

EXAMPLE   Many people wonder what gives rainbows its colors.
          Many people wonder what gives rainbows *their* colors.

1. A raindrop acts as a prism when sunlight enters them.

2. For people to see a rainbow, he must have their back to the sun and the raindrops in front of him.

3. Rays of light come over the observer's head, and it then enters into the raindrops.

4. A rainbow looks like an arch, but actually they are part of a circle.

5. If two people are looking at a rainbow, each sees their own version.

6. Because their angles of viewing are different, both observers see a rainbow that is unique to his or her eyes.

7. When people see one rainbow inside another, the outside rainbow has their colors in reverse order.

8. A third and even a fourth rainbow may form, but it is usually too faint to be seen.

9. A garden hose or lawn sprinklers can create its own small rainbows.

10. To view a homemade rainbow, people must stand with his or her back to the sun and the spray in front.

Focus on Revising

REVISING YOUR WRITING

If you make errors in agreement, go back to your writing and locate the errors. Revise your writing to eliminate errors in subject-verb agreement (Chapter 12) and pronoun-antecedent agreement (this chapter).

CASE STUDY: REVISING FOR AGREEMENT

This case study lets you observe a student writer revising. It also gives you the chance to revise some student writing on your own.

Observation

A student wrote the following draft for a course for students training as rehabilitation therapists. The assignment was to discuss the main idea of a film about handicapped athletes. The material offers a good summary of the film, but the draft's effectiveness is diminished by errors in subject-verb agreement and in pronoun-antecedent agreement.

Read through the draft. The errors are highlighted and explained. Before you look at how the student revised to eliminate the errors, revise the material yourself. Then compare what you and the student did.

singular verb needed for this collective noun: 12h

Last week students training as physical therapists saw a film about severely handicapped people participating actively in sports. The class know now that doing the impossible is becoming normal for many handicapped people. General fitness and eagerness to

verb should be plural for subjects joined by *and*: 12d

(continued on next page)

compete is among the reasons that a handicapped person might want to develop their skill in sports. All that is needed is a minimum of mobility and the will to train very hard. Either artificial limbs—called *prostheses*—or a wheelchair allow many severely handicapped people to become athletes. Advances in design and material have led to better athletic equipment for the handicapped.

Barriers are broken daily. Rafting, rock climbing, and basketball have found enthusiasts among the handicapped. Marathon racing, along with skiing and cycling, also have great appeal. Many has tried their skill at these sports. One competitive event for the handicapped was the eighth Paralympic Games, which was held in Seoul, South Korea, the site of the 1988 Olympics.

Every disabled athlete needs to train somewhat differently to accommodate their particular handicap. One of the most versatile athletes known today compete in a triathlon event by wearing one kind of prosthesis for cycling, another for running, and none for swimming.

singular pronoun needed: 13d

verb should agree with subject closest to it: 12e

singular verb needed to agree with indefinite pronoun many: 12g

plural verb needed to agree with this use of which: 12j

singular pronoun needed: 13d

the linking verb should agree with the subject: 12i

verb should agree with subject, not with words between subject and verb: 12c

singular verb needed to agree with one: 12c

Here is how the student revised the paragraph to correct the agreement errors. In a few places, the student had alternatives for the revision, so your revision might not match this one exactly. Your revision should, however, deal with each error highlighted on the draft.

Last week students training as physical therapists saw a film about severely handicapped people participating actively in sports. The class knows now that doing the impossible is becoming normal for many handicapped people.

General fitness and eagerness to compete are among the reasons that a handicapped person might want to develop his or her skill in sports. All that is needed are a minimum of mobility and the will to train very hard. Either artificial limbs—called *prostheses*—or a wheelchair allows many severely handicapped people to become athletes. Advances in design and material have led to better athletic equipment for the handicapped.

Barriers are broken daily. Rafting, rock climbing, and basketball have found enthusiasts among the handicapped. Marathon racing, along with skiing and cycling, also has great appeal. Many have tried their skill at these sports. One competitive event for the handicapped was the eighth Paralympic Games, which were held in Seoul, South Korea, the site of the 1988 Olympics.

Every disabled athlete needs to train somewhat differently to accommodate his or her particular handicap. One of the most versatile athletes known today competes in a triathlon event by wearing one kind of prosthesis for cycling, another for running, and none for swimming.

Participation

A student wrote the following draft for a course called Introduction to Health Sciences. The assignment was to write about a function of the body. The material is concisely written and explains the material clearly, but the draft's effectiveness is diminished by pronoun–antecedent agreement errors and by subject-verb agreement errors.

Read through the draft. Then revise it to eliminate the errors. Also, make any additional revisions you think would improve the content, organization, and style of the material.

Without kidney function, the body's ability to regulate fluids, blood pressure, red-cell production, protein levels, and blood chemistry are destroyed. If the kidneys no longer function, the standard prescription are dialysis treatments. Two or three times a week are the norm for the treatments, which sometimes continues for months or even years. Dialysis, though, does not do everything that healthy kidneys does.

Regulating the amount of water in the blood and tissues are the best-known function of the kidney. Therefore, someone without functioning kidneys must be careful to keep their fluid intake within limits set by the doctor. Dialysis help to remove excess fluid. Reducing salt and controlling fluid intake also helps. Neither medical procedures nor diet are effective, however, without cooperation from the patient.

The whole family are affected, so it is important that the medical team discuss the functions of a healthy kidney with the patient and the family so that he better understand the problems involved. Once the team makes their treatment recommendations known, everyone can work together with greater patience and understanding.

14 Using Adjectives and Adverbs

14a Distinguishing between adjectives and adverbs

Both adjectives and adverbs are **modifiers**—words or groups of words that describe other words.

SUMMARY OF DIFFERENCES BETWEEN ADJECTIVES AND ADVERBS

WHAT ADJECTIVES MODIFY

nouns°	The **busy** *lawyer* rested.
pronouns°	*She* felt **triumphant.**

WHAT ADVERBS MODIFY

verbs°	The lawyer *spoke* **quickly.**
adverbs°	The lawyer spoke **very** *quickly*.
adjectives°	The lawyer was **extremely** *busy*.
independent clauses°	**Therefore,** *the lawyer rested.*

The key to distinguishing between adjectives and adverbs is understanding that they modify different words or groups of words. The chart on the previous page explains these distinctions.

ADJECTIVE	The ***brisk** wind* blew.
ADVERB	The wind *blew **briskly***.

Inexperienced writers sometimes interchange adjectives and adverbs because of the *-ly* ending. Even though many adverbs° do end in *-ly* (eat, *swiftly,* eat *frequently,* eat *hungrily*), some do not (eat *fast,* eat *often,* eat *little*). To complicate matters further, some adjectives end in *-ly* (*lovely* flower, *friendly* dog). The *-ly* ending, therefore, is not a reliable way to identify adverbs.

14b Using adverbs—not adjectives—to modify verbs, adjectives, and other adverbs

Using adjectives as adverbs creates nonstandard structures.

No   The chauffeur drove **careless.** [Adjective *careless* cannot modify verb *drove.*]

YES   The chauffeur drove **carelessly.** [Adverb *carelessly* modifies verb *drove.*]

No   The candidate felt **unusual** energetic today. [Adjective *unusual* cannot modify adjective *energetic.*]

YES   The candidate felt **unusually energetic** today. [Adverb *unusually* modifies adjective *energetic.*]

No   The candidate spoke **exceptional forcefully** today. [Adjective *exceptional* cannot modify adverb *forcefully.*]

YES   The candidate spoke **exceptionally forcefully** today. [Adverb *exceptionally* modifies adverb *forcefully.*]

14c Not using double negatives

A **double negative** is a statement that contains two negative modifiers. Negative modifiers include *no, never, not, none, nothing, hardly, scarcely,* and *barely.*

No	The union members did **not** have **no** money in the reserve fund.
Yes	The union members did **not** have **any** money in the reserve fund.
Yes	The union members have **no** money in the reserve fund.

No	The supervisor did **not** hear **nothing.**
Yes	The supervisor did **not** hear **anything.**

14d Using adjectives—not adverbs—as complements after linking verbs

Linking verbs indicate a state of being or a condition. They include *be (am, is, are, was, were)*; verbs related to the senses, including *look, smell, taste, sound,* and *feel*; and verbs such as *appear, seem, become, grow, turn, remain,* and *prove.* Linking verbs connect the subject° to a complement—a word that renames or describes the subject. You can think of a linking verb as an equal sign between a subject and its complement.

> The guests looked **happy.** [The subject *guests* = The adjective *happy.*]

Problems can arise with verbs that are sometimes linking verbs and sometimes action verbs, depending on the sentence. As linking verbs, these verbs use adjectives in complements. As action verbs, these verbs use adverbs.

Anne **looks happy.** [*looks* = linking verb; *happy* = adjective]

Anne **looks happily** at the sunset. [*looks* = action verb; *happily* = adverb]

Bad—Badly

The words *bad* (adjective) and *badly* (adverb) are particularly prone to misuse with linking verbs such as *feel, grow, smell, sound, taste.* Only the adjective *bad* is correct when a verb is functioning as a linking verb.

FOR DESCRIBING A FEELING

No   The student felt **badly.**
YES   The student felt **bad.**

FOR DESCRIBING A SMELL

No   The food smelled **badly.**
YES   The food smelled **bad.**

Good—Well

Well functions both as an adverb and as an adjective. *Good* is always an adjective. *Well* is an adjective when it is referring to good health. When it is describing anything other than good health, *well* is an adverb.

You look **well.** = You look in good health. [*well* = adjective]

You write **well.** = You write skillfully. [*well* = adverb]

Except when *well* is an adjective referring to health, use *good* only as an adjective and *well* only as an adverb: *She sang **well*** [not *good*] tonight.

14e   Using correct comparative and superlative forms of adjectives and adverbs

When comparisons are made, descriptive adjectives and adverbs often carry the message. Adjectives and adverbs, therefore, have forms that communicate relative degrees of intensity.

1   Using correct forms of comparison for regular adjectives and adverbs

Most adjectives and adverbs show degrees of intensity by adding *-er* and *-est* endings or by combining with the words *more; less, least.* A few adjectives and adverbs are irregular, as explained in 14e-2.

POSITIVE	COMPARATIVE	SUPERLATIVE
green	greener	greenest
happy	happier	happiest
selfish	less selfish	least selfish
beautiful	more beautiful	most beautiful

Her tree is **green.**

Her tree is **greener** than his tree.

Her tree is the **greenest** tree on the block.

The choice of whether to use *-er, -est* or *more, most* depends largely on the number of syllables in the adjective or adverb. With **one-syllable words,** the *-er, -est* endings are most common: *large, larger, largest* (adjective); *far, farther, farthest* (adverb). With **three-syllable words,** *more, most* are used. With **adverbs of two or more syllables,** *more, most* are used: *easily, more easily, most easily.* With **adjectives of two syllables,** practice varies: some take the *-er, -est* endings; others combine with *more* and *most.*

Do not use a **double comparative** or **double superlative.** The words *more* or *most* cannot be used if the *-er* or *-est* ending has been used.

The band played **louder** [not *more louder*] later on.

Her music was the **snappiest** [not *more snappiest*] on the radio.

People danced **more easily** [not *more easier*] to her music.

> **2** | Using correct forms of comparison for irregular adjectives and adverbs

Some comparative and superlative forms are irregular. The list, in the chart below, is short, so you can memorize it easily.

IRREGULAR COMPARATIVES AND SUPERLATIVES		
POSITIVE [1]	**COMPARATIVE [2]**	**SUPERLATIVE [3+]**
good (adjective)	better	best
well (adjective and adverb)	better	best
bad (adjective)	worse	worst
badly (adverb)	worse	worst
many	more	most
much	more	most
some	more	most
little	less	least

❖ USAGE ALERT: Do not use *less* and *fewer* interchangeably. Use *less* with non-countable items. Use *fewer* to refer to numbers or anything that can be counted. *They consumed **fewer** calories; the sweetener had **less** aftertaste.* ❖

14f Avoiding too many nouns as modifiers

Sometimes nouns° can modify° other nouns: *truck driver, train track, security system.* When, however, nouns pile up in a sequence of modifiers°, it can be difficult to know which nouns are being modified and which nouns are doing the modifying. As a result, the reader finds it hard to understand the writer's message.

No   I asked my advisor to write **two college recommendation** letters for me.

Yes   I asked my advisor to write **letters of recommendation** to **two colleges** for me.

EXERCISE 14-1

Revise the following sentences so that they are suitable for academic writing.

EXAMPLE   Increasing in recent years, bankrupt businesses are being rescued by their employees who are willing to think creative.

Increasingly in recent years, bankrupt businesses are being rescued by their employees who are willing to think *creatively.*

1. Workers who want bad to keep their jobs pool their money careful and become worker-owners who buy shares in the business and participate democratic in its operations.
2. The resulting "cooperative" often has unusual enthusiastic workers and the most happiest customers.
3. The worker-owners have to work more harder because they have to do their original jobs good and at the same time not do nothing wrong as managers.

203

4. Collective decision making does not never work good unless the worker-owners number less than four hundred, so in large cooperatives the worker-owners elect managers about whom they feel well.

5. Cooperative managed businesses are considered by some experts as the better hope for the future of small, local owned businesses.

Three

WRITING CORRECT SENTENCES

When you write correct sentences, you have a better chance of communicating clearly with your readers. Part Three offers you practical advice about how to avoid the most common sentence errors that interfere with the delivery of meaning. As you use Chapters 15 through 19, keep in mind that correct sentences give you a foundation. On it you can build an effective, graceful, and memorable style.

15 Sentence Fragments

A **sentence fragment** is a portion of a sentence that is punctuated as though it were a complete sentence. Sentence fragments distract readers by intruding on the clarity of the message that you want your material to deliver.

> **No**   **Because** the telephone rang loudly.
>
> **Yes**   Because the telephone rang loudly, the family was awakened.

15a Testing for sentence completeness

If you write sentence fragments frequently, you need a system to check that your sentences are complete. Here is a test to use if you suspect that you have written a sentence fragment.

TEST FOR SENTENCE COMPLETENESS

1. **Is there a verb°?** If no, there is a sentence fragment.
2. **Is there a subject°?** If no, there is a sentence fragment.
3. **Do the subject and verb start with a subordinating word—and lack an independent clause to complete the thought?** If yes, there is a sentence fragment.

QUESTION 1: Is there a verb?

If there is no verb, you are looking at a sentence fragment. Verbs convey information about what is happening, what has happened, or what will happen. In testing for sentence completeness, find a verb that can change form to communicate a change in time.

Yesterday, the telephone **rang.**

Now the telephone **rings.**

When you check your writing to locate verbs do not mistake a verbal°* for a verb. Verbals are gerunds (*-ing* forms as nouns°), present participles (*-ing* forms as modifiers°), past participles (*-ed* or irregular past forms), and infinitives (*to* forms).

Fragment	Yesterday, the students registering for classes.
Revised	Yesterday, the students **were** registering for classes.
Revised	Yesterday, the students **registered** for classes.
Fragment	Now the students registering for classes.
Revised	Now the students **are** registering for classes.
Fragment	Yesterday, told about an excellent teacher.
Revised	Yesterday, I **was** told about an excellent teacher.
Fragment	Now the students to register for classes.
Revised	Now the students **want** to register for classes.

QUESTION 2: Is there a subject?

If there is no subject, you are looking at a sentence fragment. To find a subject, ask the verb "who?" or "what?"

---

*Throughout this book a degree mark (°) indicates a term that is defined in the book's Glossary.

FRAGMENT	Studied hard for class. [Who studied? unknown]
REVISED	The students studied hard for class. [Who studied? students]
FRAGMENT	Contained some difficult questions. [What contained? unknown]
REVISED	The test contained some difficult questions. [What contained? the test]

Every sentence must have its own subject. A sentence fragment without a subject often occurs when the missing subject is the same as the subject in the preceding sentence.

NO	The students formed a study group to prepare for the test. **Decided** to study together for the rest of the course.
YES	The students formed a study group to prepare for the test. **They decided** to study together for the rest of the course.

Imperative statements—commands and some requests—are an exception. They are not sentence fragments. Imperative statements imply the word "you" as the subject.

Run! = (You) run!

Think fast. = (You) think fast.

QUESTION 3: Do the subject and verb start with a subordinating word—and lack an independent clause to complete the thought?

If the answer to Question 3 is "yes," you are looking at a sentence fragment. Clauses that begin with subordinating words are called **dependent clauses** (see 8f). They cannot stand alone as independent units. A dependent clause must be joined to an independent clause in order to be part of a complete sentence. One type of subordinating word is a **subordinating conjunction** (for a list, see 7g).

❖ PUNCTUATION ALERT: When a dependent clause starting with a subordinating conjunction comes before an independent clause, a comma usually separates the clauses. ❖

| FRAGMENT | **Because** she returned my books. |
| REVISED | **Because** she returned my books, I can study. |

| FRAGMENT | **When** I study. |
| REVISED | I have to concentrate **when** I study. |

Another type of subordinating word is a **relative pronoun.** The most frequently used relative pronouns are *that, which, who, what, whichever, whoever,* and *whatever.*

| FRAGMENT | The test **that** we worried about all week. |
| REVISED | The test **that** we worried about all week was cancelled. |

| FRAGMENT | **Whoever** was assigned to register early in the week. |
| REVISED | **Whoever** was assigned to register early in the week got a good schedule. |

HOW TO CORRECT SENTENCE FRAGMENTS

■ If the sentence fragment is a dependent clause, join it to an adjacent independent clause. (15b)
■ If the sentence fragment is a dependent clause, revise it into an independent clause. (15b)
■ If the sentence fragment is a phrase, join it to an adjacent independent clause. (15c)
■ If the sentence fragment is a phrase, revise it into an independent clause. (15c)

EXERCISE 15-1

Check each word group according to the Test for Sentence Completeness on page 206. If a word group is a sentence fragment, explain what makes it incomplete. If a word group is a complete sentence, circle its number.

EXAMPLE   The rescue of thousands of whales. [no verb; Question 1 on the Test]

1. A Soviet icebreaker trying to rescue the whales.
2. Thousands of ten-foot-long whales struggling for air in the thick ice.
3. In the Arctic Ocean in the winter.
4. Raced to reach the whales.
5. The icebreaker arrived in time.
6. Because the whales were afraid of the ship.
7. Although the ship wanted to cut a path through the ice.
8. A crew member who found a solution.
9. Classical music which he played over the ship's loudspeaker.
10. The whales then followed the ship to the open sea.

15b Revising dependent clauses punctuated as sentences

A **dependent clause** starts with a subordinating word and therefore cannot stand on its own as a sentence (8f).

To revise a dependent clause punctuated as a sentence, you can do one of two things. (1) You can join the dependent clause to an independent clause that comes directly before or after; sometimes you will need to add words so that the combined sentence makes sense. (2) You can drop the subordinating word and, if necessary, add words to create an independent clause.

FRAGMENT	Many people over twenty-five years of age are deciding to get college degrees. **Because they want the benefits of an advanced education.**
REVISED	Many people over twenty-five years of age are deciding to get college degrees because they want the benefits of an advanced education. [joined into one sentence]
REVISED	Many people over twenty-five years of age are deciding to get college degrees. They want the benefits of an advanced education. [subordinating conjunction dropped to create an independent clause]

15c Revising phrases punctuated as sentences

A **phrase** is a group of words that lacks a subject°, a verb°, or both. A phrase, therefore, is not a sentence. To revise a phrase into a complete sentence you can do one of two things. (1) You can rewrite it to become an independent clause. (2) You can join it to an independent clause that comes directly before or after.

FRAGMENT	The mayor called a news conference on the first day of winter. **Hoping for strong public support** for her plan to care for the homeless.
REVISED	The mayor called a news conference on the first day of winter, hoping for strong public support for her plan to care for the homeless. [joined into one sentence]
REVISED	The mayor called a news conference on the first day of winter. She hoped for strong public support for her plan to care for the homeless. [rewritten]

A **prepositional phrase**° by itself is not a sentence (see 8e).

> **FRAGMENT** Cigarette smoke made the conference room seem airless. **During the long news conference.**
>
> **REVISED** Cigarette smoke made the conference room seem airless during the long news conference. [joined into one sentence]
>
> **REVISED** Cigarette smoke made the conference room seem airless. It was hard to breathe during the long news conference. [rewritten]

An **appositive** by itself is not a sentence.

> **FRAGMENT** Most people respected the mayor. **A politician with fresh ideas and practical solutions.**
>
> **REVISED** Most people respected the mayor, a politician with fresh ideas and practical solutions. [joined into one sentence]
>
> **REVISED** Most people respected the mayor. She seemed to be a politician with fresh ideas and practical solutions. [rewritten]

To be part of a complete sentence, a predicate must have a subject. Half of a **compound predicate** is not a sentence.

> **FRAGMENT** The reporters asked the mayor many questions about the details of her program. **And then discussed her answers thoroughly among themselves.**
>
> **REVISED** The reporters asked the mayor many questions about the details of her program and discussed her answers thoroughly among themselves. [joined into one sentence]
>
> **REVISED** The reporters asked the mayor many questions about the details of her program. Then they discussed her answers thoroughly among themselves. [rewritten]

15d Recognizing intentional fragments

Professional writers sometimes intentionally use fragments, sparingly, for emphasis and effect.

> What is right at one stage may be restricting at another or too soft. During the passage from one stage to another, we will be between two chairs. **Wobbling no doubt, but developing.**
>
> —GAIL SHEEHY, *Passages*

The ability to judge the difference between an acceptable and unacceptable sentence fragment comes from much exposure to reading the work of skilled writers. Many instructors, therefore, often do not accept sentence fragments in student writing until a student can demonstrate the firm ability to write complete, well-constructed sentences.

EXERCISE 15–2

Revise this paragraph to eliminate any sentence fragments. In some cases you can join word groups to create complete sentences; in other cases, you have to revise the word groups into complete sentences. In the final version, check not only the individual sentences but also the clarity of the whole paragraph.

(1) Students looking for jobs need more than the "Help Wanted" section of a newspaper. (2) One major tool, a carefully written résumé. (3) A résumé should be written in a standard form. (4) And proofread carefully to eliminate errors in spelling, punctuation, or grammar. (5) For the content of the résumé. (6) Students should analyze all types of experiences. (7) A résumé including not only paid jobs but also volunteer positions and extracurricular activities. (8) Students have a better chance of getting a job. (9) If they have supervised other people, handled money,

or taken on highly responsible tasks. (10) Such as participating in political campaigns or chairing major committees at school. (11) Many employers will consider student résumés. (12) Especially when the résumés include names of the students' supervisors.

EXERCISE 15–3

Revise this paragraph to eliminate any sentence fragments. In some cases you can join word groups to create complete sentences; in other cases, you have to revise the word groups into complete sentences. In the final version, check not only the individual sentences but also the clarity of the whole paragraph.

(1) Telemarketing, which is the selling of goods and services over the phone. (2) A business practice growing at a very fast rate. (3) United States companies generated $56 billion through telephone sales in 1983. (4) According to current estimates by a major telemarketing company. (5) By the late 1980s, the figure skyrocketed. (6) And reached over $163 billion. (7) In the early 1980s, only 1,650 telemarketing companies employing approximately 4,500 people. (8) While today more than 142,000 companies employ over 2,000,000 telesales workers. (9) Telemarketing is highly effective, but ethical questions arise. (10) For instance, intruding on the privacy of prospective buyers. (11) In addition, cases of fraud are increasing. (12) A 1982 U.S. Senate subcommittee estimating that phone fraud cost unwary buyers of financial investments more than $200 million.

> # *Focus on Revising*

REVISING YOUR WRITING

If you write sentence fragments, go back to your writing and locate them. Then figure out why each is a sentence fragment by using the Test for Sentence Completeness in 15a. Next, revise each sentence fragment into a complete sentence using the explanations in 15a, 15b, and 15c.

CASE STUDIES: REVISING TO AVOID SENTENCE FRAGMENTS

In these case studies, you can observe a student writer revising. Then you have the chance to revise other student writing on your own.

Observation

A student wrote the following draft for a course called Introduction to the Novel. The assignment was to compose a paragraph about the childhood of a major novelist. This material is well organized as a narrative and tells an interesting story, but the draft's effectiveness is diminished by the presence of sentence fragments.

Read through the draft. The sentence fragments are highlighted. Before you look at how the student revised to eliminate the sentence fragments, revise the material yourself. Then compare what you and the student did.

> The creative imagination of Victorian novelist Charlotte Brontë got an early start. When she was a child. —— Her father brought her brother,

dependent clause punctuated as a sentence: 15b

(continued on next page)

Branford, a set of wooden soldiers. Her father who was a clergyman and who wrote poetry and a novel as well as sermons. After he gave Branford the set. He told Charlotte and her sisters, Emily and Anne, to each pick one of the toy soldiers. And give it a name. Each sister then made up a history of her soldier. Soon creating tales of heroism. Inspired by the pleasure of telling stories. Charlotte, together with her brother, invented an imaginary kingdom. With Angria as its name. Because she treasured her fantasies and wanted to remember them. Charlotte began to write them in notebooks. Wanting them to look like miniature editions of books. She printed in a tiny, almost microscopically small handwriting. Those notebooks stand as a reminder of how early in life Charlotte Brontë expressed her creativity.

dependent clause punctuated as a sentence: 15b

phrase—using *-ing* form of verb—punctuated as a sentence: 15c

prepositional phrase punctuated as a sentence: 15c

dependent clause punctuated as a sentence: 15b

phrase—part of compound predicate—punctuated as a sentence: 15c

phrase—with past participle of verb—punctuated as a sentence: 15c

phrase—with *-ing* form of verb—punctuated as a sentence: 15c

Here is how the student revised the paragraph. In many cases, the student had alternatives for correcting the errors. Your revision, therefore, might not be exactly like this one, but it should not contain any sentence fragments.

The creative imagination of Victorian novelist Charlotte Brontë got an early start. When she was a child, her father brought her brother, Branford, a set of wooden soldiers. Her father was a clergyman who wrote poetry and a novel as well as sermons. After he gave Branford the set, he told Charlotte and her sisters, Emily and Anne, to each pick one of the toy soldiers and give it a name. Each sister then made up a history of her soldier, and each soon was creating tales of heroism. Inspired by the pleasure of telling stories, Charlotte, together with her brother, invented an imaginary kingdom with Angria

(continued on next page)

as its name. Because she treasured her fantasies and wanted to remember them, Charlotte began to write them in notebooks. Wanting her notebooks to look like miniature editions of books, she printed in a tiny, almost microscopically small handwriting. Those notebooks stand as a reminder of how early in life Charlotte Brontë expressed her creativity.

Participation

A student wrote the following draft for a course called European History. The assignment was to discuss the political atmosphere of a European nation during the seventeenth century. This material is effectively organized for chronological presentation of information, and it uses specific details well. The draft's effectiveness, however, is diminished by the presence of sentence fragments.

Read through the draft. Then revise it to eliminate the sentence fragments. Also, make any additional revisions that you think would improve the content, organization, and style of the material.

In seventeenth-century England, from the death of Elizabeth I in 1603 to William of Orange's ascension to the throne in 1689. The monarchy of England was the cause of unrest and uncertainty.

Queen Elizabeth I died single and childless in 1603. Because she did not have a direct descendant. The throne passed to the Queen's cousin. Who was crowned James I. Discord over the relative power of Parliament and the crown emerged under James I. And erupted during the reign of James' son, Charles I. Incapable of resolving the conflicts, Charles I lost both the throne and his head to Oliver Cromwell's Puritan Revolution in 1649.

Holding fast to his anti-monarchy sentiments and refusing a crown. Oliver Cromwell did not establish a new line of English monarchs. Instead, he became Lord Protector of England. When Cromwell died, his son Richard lacked the

(continued on next page)

charisma and political astuteness to hold on to power. As a result, the son of Charles I was recalled from France. Where he had fled to live in safety. He was crowned Charles II in 1660. And had very limited power, according to new laws passed by Parliament. Charles II sired no legitimate heirs, so the succession passed to his brother, James. An apparently able man with one serious political handicap in seventeenth-century England. He was Catholic, at a time when the English feared that the Pope was plotting to reclaim England and rule it from Rome. When the second wife of James baptized her newborn son Catholic. Unease over James' rule escalated rapidly. To ensure the safety of his wife and new son. James sent them to France and followed soon after. James's Protestant daughter Mary took the throne. With her husband William of Orange. A Dutchman who was a staunch supporter of Protestantism. Their union was so popular with the English that William continued to rule after Mary's death in 1694. Thus, the century that saw much upheaval and instability in England ended in relative calm.

16 Comma Splices and Fused Sentences

A **comma splice** (also called a *comma fault*) is an error that occurs when a comma by itself joins independent clauses°. The only time that a comma is correct between two independent clauses is when the comma is followed by a coordinating conjunction *(and, but, for, or, nor, yet,* and *so).* The word *splice* means "to fasten ends together." The end of one independent clause and the beginning of another should not be fastened together with a comma alone.

COMMA SPLICE   The hurricane suddenly intensified, it turned toward land.

A **fused sentence** is an error that occurs when two independent clauses° are not separated by punctuation or joined by a comma with a coordinating conjunction *(and, but, for, or, nor, yet,* and *so).* The word *fuse* means "to unite as if by melting together." Two independent clauses cannot be united as if melted together. A fused sentence is also known as a *run-on sentence* or a *run-together sentence.*

FUSED SENTENCE   The hurricane suddenly intensified it turned toward land.

Comma splices and fused sentences are two versions of the same problem: incorrect joining of two independent clauses°. A fused sentence, however, reveals less awareness of the need for a separation between the independent clauses.

HOW TO CORRECT COMMA SPLICES AND FUSED SENTENCES

- ■ Use a period (16b and 16e).
- ■ Use a semicolon (16b and 16e).
- ■ Use a comma and a coordinating conjunction (16c).
- ■ Revise one of two independent clauses into a dependent clause (16d).
- ■ Use a semicolon and a conjunctive adverb (16e).

16a Recognizing comma splices and fused sentences

Comma splices and fused sentences distract readers from the meaning you want your material to deliver. To recognize comma splices and fused sentences, you need to be able to recognize an independent clause (see 8f).

SUBJECT   PREDICATE

Thomas Edison was an American inventor.

You can avoid writing comma splices and fused sentences by becoming aware that the majority of such errors occur for the reasons listed in the chart that starts on the opposite page. If you tend to write comma splices, try this technique for proofreading your work. Cover all the words on one side of the comma and see if the words on the other side of the comma are an independent clause. If they are, cover that clause and uncover the words that had been covered. If the second side of the comma is also an independent clause, you have written a comma splice. To further help yourself avoid writing comma splices, become familiar with correct uses for commas, explained in Chapter 29.

Experienced writers sometimes use a comma to join very brief independent clauses that use parallelism°: *Mosquitos do not bite, they stab.* Many instructors consider this form an error in student writing; therefore, use a semicolon or period.

MAJOR CAUSES OF COMMA SPLICES AND FUSED SENTENCES

1. **Pronouns.** A comma splice or fused sentence often occurs when the second independent clause° starts with a pronoun°.

    No   Thomas Edison was a productive inventor, **he** held over 1,300 U.S. and foreign patents.

    Yes   Thomas Edison was a productive inventor. **He** held over 1,300 U.S. and foreign patents.

2. **Conjunctive adverbs and other transitional expressions.** A comma splice or fused sentence often occurs when the second independent clause° starts with a conjunctive adverb (for a list, see 7g) or other transitional expression (for a list, see 5c). Remember that these words are *not* coordinating conjunctions *(and, but, or, nor, for, so,* and *yet),* so they cannot work in concert with a comma to join two independent clauses.

    No   Thomas Edison was a brilliant scientist, **however,** his schooling was limited to only three months of his life.

    Yes   Thomas Edison was a brilliant scientist. **However,** his schooling was limited to only three months of his life.

(continued on next page)

MAJOR CAUSES OF COMMA SPLICES AND FUSED SENTENCES
(continued)

---

3. **Explanations or examples.** A comma splice or fused
   sentence often occurs when the second independent
   clause° explains or gives an example of the information in
   the first independent clause°.

   No Thomas Edison was the genius behind many
          inventions, the phonograph and the incandescent
          lamp are among the best known.

   Yes Thomas Edison was the genius behind many
          inventions. The phonograph and the incandescent
          lamp are among the best known.

16b Using a period or semicolon to correct comma splices and fused sentences

You can use a period or semicolon to correct comma
splices and fused sentences. Do not always choose punctuation
to correct this type of error, (however, see 16c and 16d).

A **period** can separate the independent clauses° in a
comma splice or fused sentence.

COMMA SPLICE	The Muir Woods National Monument is located in northern **California, its** dominant tree is the coast redwood.
FUSED SENTENCE	The Muir Woods National Monument is located in northern **California its** dominant tree is the coast redwood.
REVISED	The Muir Woods National Monument is located in northern **California. Its** dominant tree is the coast redwood.

A **semicolon** can separate independent clauses° that are closely related in meaning (see 30).

COMMA SPLICE	The coast redwood is named "Sequoia" after a Cherokee **Indian, he** developed the first alphabet used by that tribe.
FUSED SENTENCE	The coast redwood is named "Sequoia" after a Cherokee **Indian he** developed the first alphabet used by that tribe.
REVISED	The coast redwood is named "Sequoia" after a Cherokee **Indian; he** developed the first alphabet used by that tribe.

16c Using coordinating conjunctions to correct comma splices and fused sentences

When ideas in independent clauses° are closely related and grammatically equivalent, you can connect them with a co-ordinating conjunction *(and, but, or, nor, for, so,* and *yet)* that fits the meaning of your material. To correct a comma splice, insert a coordinating conjunction and retain the comma. To correct a fused sentence, insert a comma followed by a con-junction. ❖ PUNCTUATION ALERT: Use a comma before a coordinating conjunction that links independent clauses (see 29b). ❖

COMMA SPLICE	Redwood trees can grow to over 300 feet in height and up to 16 feet in di-ameter, their seeds are only a sixteenth of an inch long.
FUSED SENTENCE	Redwood trees can grow to over 300 feet in height and up to 16 feet in di-ameter their seeds are only a sixteenth of an inch long.
REVISED	Redwood trees can grow to over 300 feet in height and up to 16 feet in di-ameter, **but** their seeds are only a six-teenth of an inch long.

16d

Revising one of two independent clauses into a dependent clause to correct comma splices and fused sentences

You can revise a comma splice or fused sentence by changing one of two independent clauses° into a dependent clause°. This method is suitable when one idea can be logically subordinated to the other (see 21d–21h).

One way you can create a dependent clause is to use a subordinating conjunction (for a list, see 7g) before the subject and verb. ❖ PUNCTUATION ALERTS: (1) Do not put a period after a dependent clause that is not attached to an independent clause. If you do you will create the error called a sentence fragment; see Chapter 15. (2) Generally, use a comma after an introductory dependent clause that starts with a subordinating conjunction; see 29c-1. ❖

COMMA SPLICE	Gertrude Stein wrote many novels, short stories, essays, poems, plays, and one opera, she is better known for her art collection.
FUSED SENTENCE	Gertrude Stein wrote many novels, short stories, essays, poems, plays, and one opera she is better known for her art collection.
REVISED	Gertrude Stein wrote many novels, short stories, essays, poems, plays, and one opera **although she is better known for her art collection.**

Another way you can create a dependent clause is to use a relative pronoun°. Common relative pronouns are *who, which,* and *that.* ❖ PUNCTUATION ALERT: When an adjective clause is nonrestrictive°, use commas to separate it from the independent clause; see 29f. ❖

COMMA SPLICE	Gertrude Stein moved from America to Paris in 1902, she quickly became fascinated by impressionist painting and painters.
FUSED SENTENCE	Gertrude Stein moved from America to Paris in 1902 she quickly became fascinated by impressionist painting and painters.
REVISED	Gertrude Stein, **who moved from America to Paris in 1902,** quickly became fascinated by impressionist painting and painters.

16e Using a semicolon or a period before a conjunctive adverb or other transitional expression between two independent clauses

Conjunctive adverbs and other transitional expressions link ideas between sentences. When conjunctive adverbs and other transitional expressions fall between sentences, they must be immediately preceded by a period or semicolon.

Conjunctive adverbs include such words as *however, therefore, also,* and *nevertheless* (for a complete list, see 7g).

COMMA SPLICE	Car theft has increased alarmingly in most major cities, **however,** one city has decided to fight back.
FUSED SENTENCE	Car theft has increased alarmingly in most major cities **however,** one city has decided to fight back.
REVISED	Car theft has increased alarmingly in most cities; **however,** one city has decided to fight back.
REVISED	Car theft has increased alarmingly in most major cities. **However,** one city has decided to fight back.

Transitional expressions include *for example, in addition, of course,* and *in fact* (for a complete list, see 5c).

COMMA SPLICE	In Boston stolen car reports are broadcast over the radio, **in fact,** a police officer "deputizes" about 500,000 listeners to be on the alert for stolen vehicles.
FUSED SENTENCE	In Boston stolen car reports are broadcast over the radio **in fact,** a police officer "deputizes" about 500,000 listeners to be on the alert for stolen vehicles.
REVISED	In Boston stolen car reports are broadcast over the radio; **in fact,** a police officer "deputizes" about 500,000 listeners to be on the alert for stolen vehicles.
REVISED	In Boston stolen car reports are broadcast over the radio. **In fact,** a police officer "deputizes" about 500,000 listeners to be on the alert for stolen vehicles.

EXERCISE 16-1

Revise all comma splices or fused sentences, using a different method of correction for each one. If an item is correct, circle its number.

EXAMPLE   Cro-Magnon people lived between 35,000 and 12,000 years ago, these ancient humans cared about status symbols.

Cro-Magnon people lived between 35,000 and 12,000 years ago. These ancient humans cared about status symbols.

1. Some Cro-Magnon people were buried with many valuable possessions, we can assume, therefore, that Cro-Magnons had a society based on class distinctions, also they probably believed in an afterlife.
2. In one 24,000-year-old grave that was found in Russia, for example, a man was buried in clothing decorated with over 3,000 ivory beads.
3. A young boy and girl were buried together with many rings, ivory spears, and 8,000 ivory beads, these possessions indicated their high rank.
4. The living Cro-Magnons also wore jewelry, this practice indicates that they were not simply struggling to survive.
5. People who were worried about mere subsistence would not have had the time and energy to spend hundreds of hours stringing beads they would have had to devote every waking minute to securing food and shelter.

EXERCISE 16-2

Revise any comma splices and fused sentences, using as many different methods explained in this chapter as you can.

(1) During the nineteenth century, a number of fearless women traveled long distances from their homes, they visited places far more exotic than their native France or England. (2) Isabella Bird, for example, a British clergyman's daughter, began traveling and writing when she was in her forties, she often wrote by the light of a portable oil lamp and with a gun in her pocket. (3) In 1896, she celebrated her sixty-fourth birthday that same year she crossed northwest China, she hoped to reach Tibet. (4) While she was traveling, her guides collapsed with fever, then her rice supply grew dangerously low. (5) Only when tribal warfare broke out, however, and the bridges were torn down did she turn around. (6) Like Isabella Bird, Flora Tristan, a native of France,

proved her adventurous spirit, she sailed from France to Peru, a trip that inspired her to write a book. (7) The book was published in 1838, however, its title, *Peregrinations of a Pariah,* meaning "travels of an outcast," suggests that not everyone admired its courageous author.

EXERCISE 16-3

Revise any comma splices and fused sentences, using as many different methods explained in this chapter as you can.

(1) Most baseball fans know many amusing stories and wild tales about Casey Stengel, he could be a clown on the ball field but a great strategist behind the scenes. (2) Stengel was born in Kansas City, Missouri, in 1890 he died in Glendale, California, in 1975, he had eighty-five years in between to devote to baseball, (3) He claimed that he did not play golf or go to the movies, baseball was all that was left. (4) In 1929 he was managing a last-place team called the Toledo Mud Hens, he was not, of course, very happy with their performance. (5) He told the players that they should all get interested in the stock market; in fact, he told them to invest in Pennsylvania Railroad stock. (6) He told the team that they had to improve, otherwise they would be riding trains out of town. (7) The railroad would get many new customers, therefore, Stengel reasoned, the stock would go up. (8) Baseball history does not reveal whether the players bought the stock, they did start playing better.

Focus on Revising

REVISING YOUR WRITING

If you write comma splices or fused sentences, go back to your writing and locate them. Then figure out why each is an error by using the chart on Leading Causes of Comma Splices and Fused Sentences in 16a. Next, using the explanations in 16b through 16e, revise your writing to eliminate the errors.

CASE STUDIES: REVISING TO AVOID COMMA SPLICES AND FUSED SENTENCES

In these case studies, you can observe a student writer revising. Then you have the chance to revise other student writing on your own.

Observation

A student wrote the following draft for a course called Introduction to Criminal Justice. The assignment was to discuss a current controversy in trial law. This material is well organized and presents its information clearly and fully. However, the draft's effectiveness is diminished by comma splices and fused sentences.

Read through the draft. The errors are highlighted and explained. Before you look at how the student revised to eliminate the errors, revise the material yourself. Then compare what you and the student did.

> When fingerprinting was first introduced in the late nineteenth century, many judges hesitated to accept fingerprints as legal evidence. Recently, a similar controversy has arisen, it involves hypnosis. During this

comma splice with pronoun *it:* 16a, Cause 1

(continued on next page)

century, various state and federal courts have issued contradictory rulings on the admissibility of testimony obtained under hypnosis, however, in 1987 the United States Supreme Court ruled that such evidence is admissible. This ruling is a major new development, but the public should not look to hypnosis as a miracle technique, because testimony obtained under hypnosis is no more reliable than that obtained when witnesses search their memories.

comma splice with conjunctive adverb *however:* 16a, Cause 2

fused sentence with pronoun *it;* 16a, Cause 1

There is one major advantage of hypnosis it usually allows witnesses to recall incidents in far greater detail than they would otherwise. Hypnotized people will still recall what they think they saw or what they wished they had seen. In fact, it is possible for people to lie when hypnotized furthermore, a hypnotist can unintentionally lead witnesses to give certain responses.

comma splice with conjunctive adverb *furthermore;* 16a, Cause 2

comma splice with explanation in second independent clause: 16a, Cause 3

fused sentence with explanation in second independent clause: 16a, Cause 3

One thing is certain, lively legal debates lie ahead. Hypnotists are not licensed professionals, they can be circus entertainers or serious practitioners. It would be up to a jury to decide on the competence of a hypnotist most people who sit on juries have no idea of what standards to apply.

comma splice with pronoun *they:* 16a, Cause 1

Here is how the student revised the paragraph to correct comma splices and fused sentences. The student had alternatives for correcting the errors. Your revision, therefore, might not be exactly like this one, but it should deal with each error highlighted on the draft.

When fingerprinting was first introduced in the late nineteenth century, many judges hesitated to accept fingerprints as legal evidence. Recently, a similar controversy has arisen. It involves hypnosis. During this century, various state and federal courts have issued contradictory rulings on the admissibility of testimony obtained under hypnosis. However, in 1987 the United States Supreme Court ruled that such evidence is admissible. This ruling is a major new development, but the public should not look to hypnosis as a miracle technique, because testimony obtained under hypnosis is no more reliable than that obtained when witnesses search their memories.

There is one major advantage of hypnosis; it usually allows witnesses to recall incidents in far greater detail than they would otherwise. Hypnotized people will still recall what they think they saw or what they wished they had seen. In fact, it is possible for people to lie when hypnotized; furthermore, a hypnotist can unintentionally lead witnesses to give certain responses.

One thing is certain. Lively legal debates lie ahead. Hypnotists are not licensed professionals. They can be circus entertainers or serious practitioners. It would be up to a jury to decide on the competence of a hypnotist, but most people who sit on juries have no idea of what standards to apply.

Participation

A student wrote the following draft for a course called Introduction to Fashion Design. The assignment was to describe characteristics of fabric. This material is well organized and uses specific examples well, but the draft's effectiveness is diminished by comma splices and fused sentences.

Read through the draft. Then revise it to eliminate the comma splices and fused sentences. Also, make any additional revisions that you think would improve the content, organization, and style of the material.

(continued on next page)

As consumers, when we buy clothes, we often make choices on the basis of the fabric of an article of clothing, therefore, fashion designers always pay attention to matters of composition and design in fabrics.

Fabric is composed of natural fibers, synthetic fibers, and blends of the two. Natural fibers include cotton, linen, and wool, they offer the advantages of durability and absorbency. Synthetic fibers include rayon, polyester, acrylic, or combinations of them and other synthetic fibers they resist wrinkling and retain their color well. Fiber blends combine natural and synthetic fibers to create combinations such as cotton and polyester, which offer the advantages of each but have their own problems, such as retaining stains.

The design of fabric is affected by the way that the fabric is produced, for example, a fabric can be produced on a loom to create woven fabrics such as crepe and denim, conversely, a fabric can be produced on a knitting machine to create fabrics such as jersey and velour. Once the basic fabric is being produced, special patterns can be woven or knit into it, for instance, diagonal patterns can be woven into cotton fabrics for a geometric effect, and vertical patterns can be woven into a cable-stitched fabric for a thicker look and feel. Various finishes can further alter a fabric's appearance stone washing, for example, gives denim a worn look, and brushing gives flannel a softer look. Puckers or wrinkles can be set into a fabric, these features characterize fabrics such as seersucker and crinkle gauze.

These many options, and others, in fabrics permit fashion designers to satisfy the needs of many different types of people, some consumers care more about being in style than building a long-lasting wardrobe, while others place a high priority on ease of care or on comfortable fit.

17 Unnecessary Shifts

Shifts within sentences blur meaning quickly. Unless the meaning or grammatical structure of a sentence requires it, avoid shifting between person and number (see 17a), subject and voice (see 17b), and tense and mood (see 17c). Also, do not shift from indirect to direct discourse within a sentence without using punctuation and grammar to make the changes clear (see 17d).

17a Staying consistent in person and number

Do not shift **person** within a sentence or a longer passage unless the meaning calls for a shift. (For a chart that explains the grammatical term "person," see page 175.)

No   **They** enjoy feeling productive, but when a job is unsatisfying, **you** usually become depressed. [*They* switches to *you*.]

Yes   **They** enjoy feeling productive, but when a job is unsatisfying, **they** usually become depressed.

Number refers to one (singular) and more than one (plural). Do not start to write in one number and then shift suddenly to another.

No   By the year 2000, most **people** will live longer, and **an employed person** will retire later. [The plural *people* shifts to the singular *person*.]

Yes   By the year 2000, most **people** will live longer, and **employed people** will retire later.

A common cause of inconsistency in person and number is shifts to the second-person *you* from the first-person *I* or from a third-person noun such as *person, the public,* or *people.* Reserve *you* for sentences that directly address the reader.

No   I enjoy reading forecasts of the future, but **you** wonder which will turn out to be correct. [*I,* which is first person, shifts to *you,* which is second person.]

Yes   I enjoy reading forecasts of the future, but **I** wonder which will turn out to be correct.

No   By the year 2000, **Americans** will pay twice today's price for a car, and **you** will get twice the gas mileage. [*Americans,* which is third person, shifts to *you,* which is second person.]

Yes   In 2000, **Americans** will pay twice today's price for a car, and **they** will get twice the gas mileage.

Another common cause of inconsistency in person and number is shifts from singular to plural in the third person.

No   When a **person** is treated with respect at work, **they** usually feel more fulfilled. [The singular *person* shifts to the plural *they*.]

Yes   When **a person** is treated with respect at work, **he or she** usually feels more fulfilled.

Yes   When **people** are treated with respect at work, **they** usually feel more fulfilled.

Words such as *someone, everyone,* and other indefinite pronouns (for a complete list, see 12g) are sometimes troublesome for writers who want to avoid using sexist language. For advice on handling pronouns in such situations, see 13d-2 and especially 25b.

17b Staying consistent in subject and voice

A **subject°** **shift** within a sentence should be made only when the meaning justifies the shift.

People look forward to the future, but **the future** holds many secrets.

Shifts in subjects are rarely justified when they are accompanied by a shift in voice. For more about voice, see 9n–9o.) Unnecessary shifts in subject and voice cause a sentence or longer stretch of writing to drift out of focus.

No	Most of **the people polled expect** major improvements by the year 2000, but some **hardships are anticipated.** [The subject shifts from *people* to *hardships,* and the voice shifts from active to passive.]
Yes	Most of **the people polled expect** major improvements by the year 2000, but **they anticipate** some hardships.

17c Staying consistent in verb tense and mood

Changes in verb tense° are required when time movement is described. If **tense shifts** are illogical, clarity suffers. (For more about accurate sequences of tenses, see 9k.)

No   The campaign in the United States to clean up the movies **began** in the 1920s as civic and religious groups **try** to ban sex and violence from the screen. [The tense shifts from the past *began* to the present *try*.]

Yes   The campaign in the United States to clean up the movies **began** in the 1920s as civic and religious groups **tried** to ban sex and violence from the screen.

No   Producers and distributors **created** a film Production Code in the 1930s. At first, violating its guidelines **carried** no penalty. Eventually, however, films that **fail** to get the board's Seal of Approval **are not distributed** widely. [This shift occurs between sentences: the past tense *created* and *carried* shift to the present tense *fail* and *are not distributed*.]

Yes   Producers and distributors **created** a film Production Code in the 1930s. At first, violating its guidelines **carried** no penalty. Eventually, however, films that **failed** to get the board's Seal of Approval **were not distributed** widely.

Shifts among **moods** blur your message. (For more about mood, see 9l-m.) The most common error is between the imperative° and indicative°, though others sometimes occur.

No   The Production code included two guidelines about violence. **Do not show** the details of brutal killings, and **movies should not be** explicit about how to commit crimes. [The verbs shift from the imperative mood *do not show* to the indicative mood *movies should not be*.]

Yes   The Production code included two guidelines about violence. **Do not show** the details of brutal killings, and **do not be** explicit about how to commit crimes.

Yes   The Production code included two guidelines about violence. **Movies should not show** the details of brutal killings and **should not be** explicit about how to commit crimes.

17d Avoiding unmarked shifts between indirect and direct discourse

Indirect discourse reports speech or conversation and is not enclosed in quotation marks. **Direct discourse** repeats speech or conversation exactly and encloses the spoken words in quotation marks (see 33a). Sentences that merge **indirect discourse** and **direct discourse** without quotation marks and other markers confuse readers and distort the message you want to deliver.

No The movie reviewer praised the quality of new movies but **why are no minorities cast in major roles.** [The first clause is indirect discourse; the second clause shifts to unmarked direct discourse.]

Yes The movie reviewer praised the quality of new movies but **asked why no minorities were cast in major roles.** [This revision consistently uses indirect discourse.]

Yes The movie reviewer praised the quality of new movies but then **asked "Why are no minorities cast in major roles?"** [This revision uses direct and indirect discourse correctly because the quotation marks and grammatical structures clearly signal which is which.]

EXERCISE 17-1

Revise this paragraph to eliminate incorrect shifts. Be alert to shifts between, as well as within, sentences.

(1) The robots of today can perform many more tasks than its earlier counterpart. (2) Twenty years ago, a robot remained stationary and welded a car body or lifted heavy steel bars. (3) Today's robot, on the other hand, performs work that included

cleaning offices, guarding a hotel room, and inspecting automobiles. (4) At California's Memorial Medical Center of Long Beach, a doctor has performed brain surgery using a robot arm that allows them to drill into a person's skull and reach your brain more accurately. (5) A robot recently joined the police force in Dallas, and a suspect was forced into surrendering by the robot. (6) When the robot broke a window, the suspect shouted "Help," and asked what is that? (7) Many people do not realize that service robots often prepare your fast food or sort the packages you brought to the post office. (8) In the near future, robots selling for about $20,000 will work without human assistance, and you will be able to buy a robot costing $50,000 that will do household chores.

Focus on Revising

The case study at the end of Chapter 19 offers you the chance to observe and participate in revisions that eliminate unnecessary shifts (this chapter), misplaced and dangling modifiers (Chapter 18), and mixed and incomplete sentences (Chapter 19).

18 Misplaced and Dangling Modifiers

18a Avoiding misplaced modifiers

A modifier is a word, phrase°, or clause° that describes other words, phrases, or clauses. A **misplaced modifier** is a modifier that is incorrectly positioned in a sentence, so that the meaning is distorted. As you revise your writing, always check to see that your modifiers are placed as close as possible to what they describe so that your reader will attach the meaning where you intend it to be.

1 Avoiding ambiguous placements

With **ambiguous placement** of a modifier, it is not clear which of two or more words in a sentence is being modified. Words such as *only, just, almost, hardly, nearly, even, exactly, merely, scarcely, simply* can change meaning according to where they are placed. When you use such words, position them precisely. Consider how different placements of *only* change the meaning of this sentence: *Professional coaches say that high salaries motivate players.*

Only professional coaches say that high salaries motivate players. [No one else says this.]

Professional coaches say that **only** high salaries motivate players. [Nothing except high salaries motivates players.]

Professional coaches say that high salaries motivate **only** players. [No others on the team, such as coaches and managers, are motivated by high salaries.]

Squinting modifiers also cause ambiguity. A squinting modifier is one that can describe both what precedes and what follows it. Because a modifier cannot do double duty, either move the modifier to a position where its meaning will be precise or revise the sentence.

No   The high school's football star being recruited **actively** believed each successive offer would be better. [What was active—the recruitment or the star's belief?]

Yes   The high school's football star being recruited believed **actively** that each successive offer would be better.

Yes   The **actively** recruited high school's football star believed each successive offer would be better.

2   Avoiding wrong placements

With **wrong placement,** modifying words are misplaced in a sentence, thus garbling the meaning.

No   The history of college athletics sheds light on current policies and practices of college football **beginning in the nineteenth century.** [This sentence says that current policies and practices, not the history, started in the nineteenth century.]

Yes   The history of college athletics, **beginning in the nineteenth century,** sheds light on current policies and practices of college football.

3 | Avoiding awkward placements

Awkward placements are interruptions that seriously break the flow of a message and thereby distract your reader from understanding your material.

A **split infinitive** is one type of awkward placement. An **infinitive** is a verb form that starts with *to,* such as *to create.* When words come between *to* and its verb, meaning can be interrupted. This often happens when the intervening material could easily go before or after the infinitive.

> **No**   Orson Welles's radio drama "War of the Worlds" managed **to,** on October 30, 1938, **convince** listeners that they were hearing an invasion by Martians.
>
> **Yes**   On October 30, 1938, Orson Welles's radio drama "War of the Worlds" managed **to convince** listeners that they were hearing an invasion by Martians.

Interruptions of subjects° and verbs° by highly complex phrases or clauses disturb the smooth flow of a sentence.

> **No**   **The announcer,** because the script, which Welles himself wrote, called for perfect imitations of emergency announcements, **opened** with a warning that included a description of the "invasion."
>
> **Yes**   Because the script, which Welles himself wrote, called for perfect imitations of emergency announcements, **the announcer opened** with a warning that included a description of the "invasion."

Interruptions of a verb phrase (a group of words that functions as a verb in a sentence: *was kissed, had been kissed*) by words unrelated to the time sequence of the verb, makes the sentence lurche instead of flow. Your reader has to work too hard to understand the message you want your sentence to deliver.

No   People who tuned in late to "The War of the Worlds" believed that New Jersey **had,** by Martians bent on destruction, **been invaded.**

Yes   People who tuned in late to "The War of the Worlds" believed that New Jersey **had been invaded** by Martians bent on destruction.

Interruptions of a verb° and its object° by words that should modify both those elements often makes clarity suffer.

No   Many churches **held** for their frightened communities **"end of the world" prayer services.**

Yes   Many churches **held "end of the world" prayer services** for their frightened communities.

EXERCISE 18-1

Revise these sentences to correct any ambiguous, wrong, or awkward placements. If a sentence is correct, circle its number.

EXAMPLE   One of the greatest accomplishments in history took place in 1885, the invention of the first car.

One of the greatest accomplishments in history, *the invention of the first car, took place in 1885.*

1. The origins of the automobile can, if we look back in history, be found in 1769 in France.

2. The Frenchman Nicholas Cugnot, because of his determination to travel without the assistance of animals, built the first self-propelled vehicle.

3. Cugnot's invention only was powered by steam.

4. During a trial drive, the vehicle, which was run by a huge steam boiler that hung in front of its single front wheel and which was difficult to steer and hard to stop, knocked over a rock wall.

5. The invention, beginning in 1860, of various types of gas-combustion engines provided an alternative to clumsy steam power.

6. Two other inventors, Karl Benz and Gottlieb Daimler, were, in Germany, trying to invent a gas-driven vehicle.

7. Only they lived sixty miles apart, but they did not know each other.

8. Benz is finally the man who produced the first car and was given credit for the invention of the automobile.

9. The first car rolled, after the finishing touches had been added, out of a workshop in a small German town.

10. It rattled and banged down the street to loudly and dramatically announce a revolution in transportation.

18b Avoiding dangling modifiers

A **dangling modifier** confuses meaning. It describes or limits what is implied but not stated in a sentence. Dangling modifiers can be hard for a writer to spot. Because the writer knows the intended meaning, the writer's brain tends to supply the missing material. The writer might not notice the error, but readers usually do see it.

> **No**   **Reading Faulkner's short story "A Rose for Emily,"** the ending surprised us.

The No sentence says that the story's ending is doing the reading. The implied subject of the modifier is *we,* but nowhere is that subject stated—thus the modifier dangles. You can correct a dangling modifier by revising the sentence so that the intended subject is stated.

> **Yes**   **Having read Faulkner's short story "A Rose for Emily,"** **we** were surprised by the ending.
>
> **Yes**   We read Faulkner's short story "A Rose for Emily" and were surprised by the ending.

Dangling modifiers sometimes result from unnecessary use of the passive voice. (For more about passive voice, see 9n–9o.)

> **No**   **To earn money, china-painting lessons** were of-fered by Emily to wealthy young women. [*China-painting lessons* cannot earn money.]
>
> **Yes**   **To earn money, Emily** offered china-painting les-sons to wealthy young women.

EXERCISE 18–2

Identify and correct any dangling modifiers in these sentences. If a sentence is correct, circle its number.

EXAMPLE   Assigned to interview an unfriendly person, the ex-perience can be instructive to a student journalist.

            Assigned to interview an unfriendly person, *a student journalist can find the experience instructive.*

1. To be successful, careful plans must be made by the student journalist.
2. Being tense, the interview might begin on the wrong note for an inexperienced journalist.
3. Until relaxed, questions should mention only neutral topics.
4. After the journalist is more at ease, the person being inter-viewed might also relax.
5. With a list of questions, the interview process goes more smoothly for everyone involved.
6. Although easy to answer, mistakes are sometimes made on factual questions by a hostile interviewee.
7. By being analytic and evaluative, those mistakes can reveal a great deal to an experienced journalist.

8. Knowing how to pace an interview, the hard questions are more likely to be answered honestly after the interviewee has been caught off guard.

9. Until an interview is complete, the seasoned journalist always remains alert.

10. Essential information might be revealed when leaving.

Focus on Revising

The case study at the end of Chapter 19 offers you the chance to observe and participate in revisions that eliminate unnecessary shifts (Chapter 17), misplaced and dangling modifiers (this chapter), and mixed and incomplete sentences (Chapter 19).

19 Mixed and Incomplete Sentences

19a Avoiding mixed sentences

A **mixed sentence** has two or more parts that do not make sense together. This problem usually occurs when the writer loses track of the beginning of a sentence while writing the end of the sentence. Careful proofreading, including reading aloud, can help you avoid this error (see 3e).

1 Revising mixed constructions

A **mixed construction** starts out taking one grammatical form and then changes, derailing the meaning of the sentence.

No   Because television's first transmissions in the 1920s included news programs became popular with the public. [The opening subordinate clause° starts off on one track, but the independent clause° goes off in another direction. What does the writer want to emphasize—the first transmissions or the popularity of news programs?]

| Yes | Television's first transmissions in the 1920s included news programs, which quickly became popular with the public. [The idea of the first transmissions is now emphasized. *Because* has been dropped, making the first clause independent; and *which* has been added, making the second clause subordinate and logically related to the first.] |

No	By doubling the time allotment for network news to thirty minutes increased the prestige of network news programs. [A prepositional phrase°, such as *by doubling,* cannot be the subject of a sentence.]
Yes	Doubling the time allotment for network news to thirty minutes increased the prestige of network news programs. [Dropping the preposition *by* clears up the problem.]
Yes	By doubling the time allotment for network news to thirty minutes, the network executives increased the prestige of network news programs. [Inserting a logical subject, *the network executives,* clears up the problem; an independent clause° is now preceded by a modifying prepositional phrase°.]

2 Revising faulty predication

Faulty predication, sometimes called *illogical predication,* occurs when a subject° and its predicate° do not make sense together.

No	The **purpose** of television **was invented** to entertain people.
Yes	The **purpose** of television **was** to entertain people.
Yes	**Television was invented** to entertain people.

One key cause of faulty predication is a breakdown in the connection between a subject° and its complement°.

> **No**   Walter Cronkite's outstanding characteristic as a newscaster was credible.

The subject of the sentence above is *characteristic.* While *credible* can rename (and would complement) a person, it cannot rename (or complement) a characteristic. A suitable renaming of a characteristic is *credibility.*

> **Yes**   Walter Cronkite's outstanding characteristic as a newscaster was credibility.

Faulty predication is the problem in most constructions that begin *is when* or *is where.* Avoid these constructions in academic writing.

> **No**   A disaster **is when** television news shows get some of their highest ratings.
>
> **Yes**   Television news shows get some of their highest ratings during a disaster.

Similarly, avoid *reason . . . is because* in academic writing.

> **No**   **One reason** that television news captured national attention **is because** it covered the Vietnam War thoroughly.
>
> **Yes**   **One reason** that television news captured national attention **is that** it covered the Vietnam War thoroughly.
>
> **Yes**   Television news captured national attention **because** it covered the Vietnam War thoroughly.

EXERCISE 19-1

Revise the mixed sentences below so that the beginning of each sentence fits logically with its end. If a sentence is correct, circle its number.

EXAMPLE   As a result of the increasing amount of sewage in the United States is a crisis in disposing of these wastes.

The increasing amount of sewage in the United States is creating a crisis in waste disposal.

1. The fact that millions of gallons of raw sewage are being dumped into the nation's waters are becoming unfit for use.

2. The reason that ecologists are extremely concerned is because waste disposal problems will get worse in the future.

3. Because of multiple sewage spills in San Diego transformed a wildlife refuge into a public health hazard.

4. Also, when hospital waste and other sewage created a fifty-mile-long slick closed beaches in New Jersey and New York.

5. This situation is similar to what happened in the nineteenth century, when sewage in overexpanded cities led to outbreaks of typhoid and cholera.

19b   **Avoiding incomplete sentences**

An **incomplete sentence** has missing words, phrases, or clauses necessary for grammatical correctness or sensible meaning. Such omissions blur your meaning, and your reader has to work too hard to understand your message.

1   **Using elliptical constructions carefully**

An **elliptical construction** deliberately leaves out words that have already appeared in the sentence: *I have my book* *and Joan's* [*book*]. For an elliptical construction to be correct, the words that are left out must be exactly the same as the words that do appear in the sentence.

> **No**   During the 1920s in Chicago, the cornetist Manuel Perez **was leading** one outstanding jazz group, Tommy and Jimmy Dorsey another. [The words *was leading* cannot take the place of *were leading,* needed in the second clause°.]

> **Yes**   During the 1920s in Chicago, the cornetist Manuel Perez **was leading** one outstanding jazz group; Tommy and Jimmy Dorsey **were leading** another.

> **Yes**   During the 1920s in Chicago, the cornetist Manuel Perez **led** one outstanding jazz group; Tommy and Jimmy Dorsey another. [The verb *led* works in both clauses, so it can be omitted from the second clause.]

2   Making comparisons complete, unambiguous, and logical

In writing a comparison, be sure to include all words needed to make clear the relationship between the items or ideas being compared.

> **No**   Individuals with high concern for achievement make better business executives. [*Better* indicates a comparison, but none is stated.]

> **Yes**   Individuals with high concern for personal achievement make better business executives than do people with little interest in getting ahead.

> **No**   Most personnel officers value high achievers more than risk takers. [Not clear: more than risk takers value high achievers, or more than personnel officers value high achievers?]

> **Yes**   Most personnel officers value high achievers more than they value risk takers.

> **Yes**   Most personnel officers value high achievers more than risk takers do.

No   An achiever's chance of success in business is greater than a gambler. [*Chance* is compared with *a gambler;* a thing cannot be compared logically to a person.]

Yes   An achiever's chance of success in business is greater than a gambler's. [A correct elliptical construction, with the word *chance* omitted]

3   **Proofreading carefully to catch inadvertently omitted articles, pronouns, conjunctions, and prepositions**

Small words—articles°, pronouns°, conjunctions°, and prepositions°—are often needed to make sentences complete and meaning clear. If you have a tendency to omit such words, proofread your work an extra time exclusively to discover words left out.

No   On May 2, 1808, citizens Madrid rioted against French soldiers.

Yes   On May 2, 1808, **the** citizens **of** Madrid rioted against French soldiers.

EXERCISE 19-2

Revise this paragraph to create correct elliptical constructions and to complete comparisons. Also, insert any missing words.

(1) Engineering students use practical thinking to solve difficult problems as much as academic training. (2) One group students at the University California Berkeley received challenging assignment. (3) These students had to create a package that would allow an egg to be dropped as much, but not more than eighty feet onto cement without breaking. (4) This complex problem was considered and possible solutions analyzed by fourth-year chemical engineering student, Carla St. Laurent. (5) She gave so much thought to professor's challenge. (6) She created a mother hen made papier-mâché that kept safe egg she dropped from fourth-floor window.

251

> # *Focus on Revising*

REVISING YOUR WRITING

If you write sentences that contain the problems covered in Chapters 17-19, go back to your writing and locate the errors. Revise your writing to eliminate unnecessary shifts (17a), misplaced modifiers (18a), dangling modifiers (18b), mixed sentences (19a), and incomplete sentences (19b).

CASE STUDY: REVISING TO CORRECT UNNECESSARY SHIFTS, MISPLACED MODIFIERS, DANGLING MODIFIERS, MIXED SENTENCES, AND INCOMPLETE SENTENCES

This case study lets you observe a student writer revising. It also gives you the opportunity to revise some student writing on your own.

Observation

A student wrote the following draft for a course called Freshman Composition. The assignment was to compose a narrative of a personal experience with which other students in the class might sympathize. This narrative explains the experience clearly, uses specific examples well to illustrate the story, and draws on the writer's voice effectively. The draft's effectiveness is diminished, however, by the presence of unnecessary shifts, misplaced modifiers, dangling modifiers, and mixed and incomplete sentences.

Read through the draft. The problems are highlighted and explained. Before you look at how the student revised to eliminate the errors, revise the material yourself. Then compare what you and the student did.

Moving to a different part of the United States was one of the most difficult experiences of my life.

dangling
modifier: 18b

Looking forward to my senior year in high school, my father's company informed him that he had been transferred to Colorado Springs, and would we be ready to move in a month? I liked Boston much better than my father, so I was less than thrilled about having to leave. But after days of arguing and talking to my parents, I knew that the decision was final.

ambiguous comparison: 19b-2

incorrect elliptical construction: 19b-1

shift from direct to indirect discourse: 17d

When our family arrived in Colorado Springs, I was depressed. Our house was comfortable, about twice the size of our Boston apartment, but you had the feeling that it was in the middle of nowhere. Living in the outskirts of the city, I couldn't go anywhere without car. In Boston, all I have to do is hop on the "T" to go anywhere in the city.

unnecessary shift in person and number: 17a-1

omitted word: 19b-3

unnecessary shift in tense: 17c

Also, by discovering that the expressions for some everyday things were different than in Boston was the place that I wanted to be. When I asked for a submarine, a thick sandwich on a long roll, the convenience store clerk said she didn't have kits for making model ships with a confused look. When buying something in Colorado, salespeople offered me what they called "a sack" instead of a bag. As far as I knew, a sack means that the quarterback has been tackled in football game.

mixed construction: 19a-1

dangling modifier: 18b

misplaced modifier; wrong placement: 18a-2

Slowly, however, I began to realize that in Colorado even there are movies, fast-food restaurants, and

omitted word: 19b-3

misplaced modifier; ambiguous placement: 18a-1

(continued on next page)

shopping malls. Mostly, the people made the big difference for me. It didn't happily take long for me to get to know some students in my high school, and to, much to my surprise, find that most were eager to make me feel at home. By now, I can't imagine a better place to live than Colorado Springs.

misplaced modifier; ambiguous placement: 18a-1

Here is how the student revised the draft to correct the errors. In a few places, the student had alternatives for correcting the errors. Your revision, therefore, might not be exactly like this one, but it should deal with each error highlighted on the draft.

Moving to a different part of the United States was one of the most difficult experiences of my life. At the time that I was looking forward to my senior year in high school, my father's company informed him that he had been transferred to Colorado Springs, and we would need to be ready to move in a month. I liked Boston much better than my father did, so I was less than thrilled about having to leave. But after days of arguing with and talking to my parents, I knew that the decision was final.

When our family arrived in Colorado Springs, I was depressed. Our house was comfortable, about twice the size of our Boston apartment, but I had the feeling that it was in the middle of nowhere. Living in the outskirts of the city, I couldn't go anywhere without a car. In Boston, all I had to do was hop on the "T" to go anywhere in the city.

Also, when I discovered that the expressions for some everyday things were different, Boston was the place that I wanted to be. When I asked for submarine, a thick sandwich on a long roll, the convenience store clerk looked confused and said she didn't have kits for making model ships. When I would buy something in Colorado, salespeople offered me "a

(continued on next page)

sack" instead of a bag. As far as I knew, a sack means that the quarterback has been tackled in a football game.

Slowly, however, I began to realize that even in Colorado there are movies, fast-food restaurants, and shopping malls. Mostly, the people made the big difference for me. Happily, it didn't take long for me get to know some students in my high school, and to find, much to my surprise, that most were eager to make me feel at home. By now, I can't imagine a better place to live than Colorado Springs.

Participation

A student working in the college peer counseling program for job hunters wrote the followng draft for an article in the campus newspaper. This material shows a very good awareness of audience, and it contains well-organized, useful information. The draft's effectiveness is diminished, however, by the presence of unnecessary shifts, misplaced modifiers, dangling modifiers, mixed sentences, and incomplete sentences.

Read through the draft. Then revise it to eliminate the errors. Also, make any additional revisions that you think would improve the content, organization, and style of the material.

Most job hunters enter business world through a door labeled "Job Interviews." Regardless of training and experience, the interview is the occasion when an employer gets an impression of the candidate. What can a person do so that you perform successfully at what is likely to be a fifteen-minute interview?

By understanding the objectives of the interview will help an applicant prepare. An applicant who knows the company's needs is better equipped. Most businesses with a position to fill interview with three basic questions in mind: Is this applicant qualified to do the job? Will this applicant perform if hired? Will you fit into the work environment?

A job applicant can use a well-prepared résumé to present information about experience and training. At the interview, applicants should be prepared to talk about courses taken, jobs held, and capabilities demonstrated. Probing for specific details, the applicant's abilities will be judged by the employer. Job applicants should be aware that personal questions about marital status or plans to have children are illegal; however, such matters might be raised by some interviewers anyway. By preparing an answer like "Those areas of my life are personal," or "I make it a rule never to let my personal life interfere with business" will help an applicant's confidence.

A major concern of an interviewer is focused on whether the applicant would fit into the company. An applicant who plays merely a role to impress an interviewer is making a mistake, particularly if you are offered a job that you are not suited for. Present a natural image. Use the interview to find out how well the company's work environment will fit your personal style.

Four

WRITING EFFECTIVE SENTENCES

20 Conciseness

21 Coordination and Subordination

22 Parallelism

23 Variety and Emphasis

 When you write effective sentences, you move beyond correctness to writing characterized by style and grace. Part Four shows you how to employ various techniques of writing style that enhance the delivery of your message to your readers. As you use Chapters 20 through 23, remember that writers have many choices for making form and content work in concert to create memorable prose.

20 Conciseness

Conciseness describes writing that is direct and to the point. Wordy writing is not concise. It irritates readers because it forces them to clear away excess words before sentences can deliver their messages.

20a Eliminating wordy sentence structures

Wordy sentence structures can make writing seem abstract and uninteresting.

1 Revising unnecessary expletive constructions

An **expletive construction** postpones the subject°* by using *it* or *there* plus a form of the verb *be* before the subject. If you remove the expletive and revise slightly, you give the subject—and the entire sentence—greater power.

---

*Throughout this book a degree mark (°) indicates a term that is defined in the book's Glossary.

No   **It is** necessary for students to fill out both registration forms.

YES   Students must fill out both registration forms.

No   **There are** three majors offered by the computer science department.

YES   Three majors are offered by the computer science department.

YES   The computer science department offers three majors.

2   Revising unnecessary passive constructions

In the **active voice**, the subject° of a sentence *does* the action named by the verb. In the **passive voice**, the subject of a sentence *receives* the action named by the verb (see 9n). For most writing, the active voice adds liveliness as well as conciseness. One way to revise from the passive to the active voice is to make the doer of the action the subject of the sentence.

No   Volunteer work **was done by the students** for credit in sociology. [The students are doers of the action, but they are not the subject of the sentence.]

YES   The **students did** volunteer work for credit in sociology.

Sometimes you can revise a sentence from passive voice to active voice by using a new verb. This works especially well when you want to keep the same subject.

PASSIVE   Britain **was defeated** by the United States in the war of 1812.

ACTIVE   Britain **lost** the war of 1812 to the United States.

Writers can use the passive voice when the doer of an action is unknown or when naming the doer would disrupt the focus of a sentence. Such situations are discussed in 9o.

| 3 | Combining sentences, reducing clauses to phrases, and reducing phrases to words |

Clarity is among your main concerns during revision. When you see the need for conciseness, often you can combine sentences or reduce a clause to a phrase or reduce a phrase to a single word, making your writing clearer.

Combining sentences

When you revise, look carefully at sets of sentences in your draft. You may be able to reduce the information in one sentence to a group of words that you can include in another sentence.

TWO SENTENCES

The *Titanic* was discovered seventy-three years after being sunk by an iceberg. The wreck was located in the Atlantic by a team of French and American scientists.

COMBINED SENTENCE

Seventy-three years after being sunk by an iceberg, the *Titanic* was located in the Atlantic by a team of French and American scientists.

Reducing clauses

You can often reduce adjective clauses° to phrases°, sometimes just by dropping the opening relative pronoun° and its verb°.

The *Titanic,* **which was a huge ocean liner,** sank in 1912.
The *Titanic,* **a huge ocean liner,** sank in 1912.

Sometimes you can reduce a clause° to a single word.

> The scientists held a memorial service for the passengers and crew members **who had died.**

> The scientists held a memorial service for the **dead** passengers and crew members.

Creating elliptical constructions° is another way you can reduce clauses. Be sure to omit only words that are clearly implied (see 19b-1).

> **When they were confronted with disaster,** some passengers behaved heroically, **while others behaved selfishly.**

> **Confronted with disaster,** some passengers behaved heroically, **others selfishly.**

Reducing phrases

Sometimes you can reduce phrases° to shorter phrases or to single words.

> **Although loaded with luxuries,** the liner was thought to be unsinkable.

> The **luxury** liner was thought to be unsinkable.

4	Using strong verbs and avoiding nouns formed from verbs

Your writing will have more impact when you choose strong verbs—verbs that directly convey an action. *Be* and *have* are not strong verbs, and they tend to create wordy structures. When you revise weak verbs to strong ones, you often can reduce the number of words in your sentences.

WEAK VERB

The proposal before the city council **has to do with** locating the sewage treatment plant outside city limits.

STRONGER VERB

The proposal before the city council **suggests** locating the sewage treatment plant outside city limits.

When you look for weak verbs to revise, look also for nouns° derived from verbs with suffixes added (such as *-ance, -ment,* or *-tion*). To achieve conciseness, turn such words back into verbs, thus reducing words and gaining impact.

No	The building **had the appearance of** being renovated.
Yes	The building **appeared** to be renovated.

20b Eliminating unneeded words

Unneeded words clutter your writing. Always eliminate them to achieve conciseness. When a writer tries to write very formally or tries to reach an assigned word limit, **padding** usually results. Sentences are loaded down with **deadwood**— empty words and phrases that increase the word count but lack meaning.

Padded	<u>In fact</u>, the television station <u>which was situated in the local area</u> had won <u>a great</u> many awards as <u>a result of its having been involved in the</u> coverage of <u>all kinds of</u> controversial issues.
Concise	The local television station had won many awards for its coverage of controversial issues.

The chart that starts on the opposite page lists typical wordy examples and suggests possible revisions.

20c Revising redundancies

Planned repetition can create a powerful rhythmic effect. Unplanned repetition, however, can bore a reader with its dull drone. Unplanned repetition—called **redundancy**—gives the

(continued on page 264)

GUIDE FOR ELIMINATING UNNEEDED WORDS

Empty Word or Phrase	Wordy Example	Revision
as a matter of fact	As a matter of fact, statistics show that many marriages end in divorce.	Statistics show that many marriages end in divorce.
because of the fact that	Because of the fact that a special exhibit is scheduled, the museum will be open until ten P.M.	Because of a special exhibit, the museum will be open until ten P.M.
factor	The project's final cost was an essential factor to consider.	The project's final cost was essential to consider.
for the purpose of	Work crews arrived for the purpose of fixing the potholes.	Work crews arrived to fix the potholes.
in a very real sense	In a very real sense, the drainage problems caused the house to collapse.	The drainage problems caused the house to collapse.

(continued on next page)

GUIDE FOR ELIMINATING UNNEEDED WORDS *(continued)*		
in the case of	*In the case of* the proposed water tax, residents were very angry.	Residents were very angry about the proposed water tax.
manner	The child touched the snake in a reluctant *manner*.	The child touched the snake reluctantly.
nature	His comment was of an offensive *nature*.	His comment was offensive.
type of	Gordon took a relaxing *type of* vacation.	Gordon took a relaxing vacation.
what I mean to say	*What I mean to say* is that I expect a bonus.	I expect a bonus.

same message more than once and deadens the sentence's impact on a reader.

> **No**   Bringing the project to **final completion** three weeks early, the new manager earned our **respectful regard.**
>
> **Yes**   **Completing** the project three weeks early, the new manager earned our **respect.**
>
> **No**   The package, **rectangular in shape,** lay on the counter.
>
> **Yes**   The rectangular package lay on the counter.

rep **20c**

EXERCISE 20-1

Eliminate redundant words and phrases. Then revise the paragraph so that it is concise.

EXAMPLE   Many people will be surprised to learn that, amazingly enough, labor-saving household devices that are intended to save people from working hard as a matter of fact often do not accomplish their aim or goal.

Many people will be surprised to learn that labor-saving household devices often fail to accomplish their goal.

(1) Why would people pay good money and spend hard-earned dollars to buy labor-saving household appliances unless the devices really and truly lived up to their promise and saved work hours? (2) Think of the fact that time is saved because of the fact that clothes are now washed in a washing machine instead of being washed on a washboard. (3) Today the vacuum cleaner now cleans floors in place of the broom doing all the sweeping and cleaning. (4) Instead of the manual egg beater people have the electric mixer. (5) Nevertheless, regardless of these inventions, homemakers in the United States spend about the same number of hours doing housework, laundry, and cleaning as people did in the year of 1910. (6) How could this situation and state of affairs come to be? (7) The reasons are because labor-saving household devices, in a very real sense, have not saved much labor nor have they lessened the time devoted to housework. (8) Surprisingly, it is amazing to note that people's wealth today is one essential factor to consider as a reason. (9) As a matter of fact, more people in this day and age compared with the year of 1910 can afford the expense of larger apartments or houses. (10) In addition, the level of cleanliness people expect of themselves has increased at about the same rate of speed as the advances in inventions.

Focus on Revising

REVISING YOUR WRITING

If you need to write more concisely, go back to your writing and locate wordy material. Using this chapter as a resource, revise your writing to eliminate wordy sentence structures (20a) and to avoid unneeded words (20b) and redundancy (20c).

CASE STUDY: REVISING FOR CONCISENESS

This case study lets you observe a student writer revising. It also gives you the opportunity to revise some student writing on your own.

Observation

A student wrote the following draft for a course called Business Management. The assignment was to write a summary of a research study related to the course. This material summarizes the source material thoroughly, but the draft's effectiveness is diminished by a lack of conciseness.

Read through the draft. The wordy material is highlighted and explained. Before you look at how the student revised to eliminate the wordiness, revise the material yourself. Then compare what you and the student did.

unnecessary passive construction: 20a-2

clause can be reduced to phrase: 20a-3

Researchers in business management interviewed and talked to over two hundred people who have experienced important, major career defeats. The study was undertaken by the researchers for the purpose of discovering why some smart people fail at their careers while there are others who generally do not fail. The

redundant: 20c

unneeded words: 20b

unnecessary expletive construction: 20a-1; and clause can be reduced to word: 20a-3 ——

weak verb: 20a-4

weak verb: 20a-4

noun formed from verb: 20a-4

unnecessary passive construction: 20a-2

results show that in a very real sense many people lack the recognition that most careers involve getting along well with other people. It is often claimed by many employees who fail that "office politics" was the cause of the problems. In point of fact, however, those employees often have no ability to listen to others sensitively and to give and take criticism constructively. The researchers also found that some people fail to have success because they have an absence of commitment to their work. Sometimes the underlying reason is a fear. That fear is the fear of failure, which has the manifestation of being a lack of motivation. When people do not attempt to try to succeed, they do not expose themselves to the risk of failure. Finally, it was discovered by the researchers that the fact of the matter is that luck sometimes has a role, as when a change in management means that the new people bring in their own team.

—— unneeded words: 20b

noun formed from verb: 20a-4

unneeded words: 20b

redundant: 20c

sentences can be combined: 20a-3

redundant: 20c

unneeded words: 20b

weak verb: 20a-4

Here is how the student revised the paragraph to achieve conciseness. In a few places, the student had alternatives for correcting the errors. Your revision, therefore, might not be exactly like this one, but it should eliminate the wordy material highlighted on the draft.

Researchers in business management interviewed over two hundred people who have experienced major career defeats. The researchers wanted to discover why some smart people fail at their careers while others do not. The results show that many people do not recognize that most careers

(continued on next page)

involve getting along well with other people. Many employees who fail claim that "office politics" caused the problem. However, those employees often do not listen to others sensitively and do not give and take criticism constructively. The researchers also found that some people fail because they are not committed to their work. Sometimes the underlying reason is a fear of failure, which manifests itself as a lack of motivation. When people do not try to succeed, they do not risk failure. Finally, the researchers discovered that luck sometimes plays a role, as when a change in management means that the new people bring in their own team.

Participation

A student wrote the following draft for a journalism class called Feature Writing. The material is logically presented and informative, but the draft's effectiveness is diminished by wordy constructions, padding, and redundancies.

Read through the draft. Then revise it to eliminate the errors. Also, make any additional revisions you think would improve the content, organization, and style of the material.

College students seeking alternatives to dormitories, young adults moving out on their own, and newcomers to an area often rent apartments or houses. All of these potential renters should keep in mind that renting or leasing involves a legal agreement between landlord and tenant. It is recommended that anyone preparing to rent conduct careful and extensive evaluations of the entire situation before making any decisions. One major area to investigate is the evaluation of the type of landlord. It is also recommended that renters carefully examine the condition and nature of the premises before any lease is signed by them.

An initial step in the rent process is the investigation of the landlord. A list of current and former tenants of the facility can be requested from the landlord. Renters should not hesitate to contact a reasonable number of parties on the list.

Renters should ask all of those with whom they come in contact whether the management of the property, in particular the landlord, is easy to contact if problems should arise and whether the landlord is willing to handle such problems without delay. If anyone is of the opinion that the landlord has a poor reputation for handling problems properly, it is better to find out before signing a lease or deposit check.

Also, for the purpose of being protected in the event of future disagreements, it is recommended that renters inspect the premises carefully. If there is any type of damage in the apartment, the details should be written down in a written inventory by the renters, and it should be signed and dated by the renters and the landlord. If any damages are to be repaired by the landlord, those promises should also be put in writing. In the event that any damage is present when renters leave the property, it is the renters who will probably be held legally liable for repairs since the landlord would be able to claim that the damage was done during the term of the renters' lease.

In short, only after careful consideration should the renter even consider signing a lease or leaving a deposit or signing anything that might be legally binding.

21 Coordination and Subordination

The techniques of **coordination** and **subordination** help writers communicate relationships between two or more ideas. These techniques can help your writing style work in concert with the meaning that you want your sentences to deliver.

TWO IDEAS	The sky became dark gray. The air stilled ominously.
COORDINATED VERSION	The sky turned dark gray, and the air stilled ominously.
SUBORDINATED VERSION	As the sky turned dark gray, the air stilled ominously. [The *air* is the focus.]
SUBORDINATED VERSION	As the air stilled ominously, the sky turned dark gray. [The *sky* is the focus.]

21a Understanding coordination

Coordination can produce harmony by bringing together related but separate elements to function smoothly in unison. Coordination uses grammatical equivalency to communicate a balance or sequence in ideas. A **coordinate sentence**—also known as a compound sentence—has two features. It contains grammatically equivalent independent clauses, and those independent clauses are joined either by a semicolon or by a coordinating conjunction *(and, but, for, or, nor, yet,* or *so).* The compounding of a sentence must be justified by its meaning, for coordinate sentences communicate balance or sequence in the ideas that they contain.

The sky became dark gray, **and** the air stilled ominously.

Each coordinating conjunction has a specific meaning that communicates the relationship between the ideas in a coordinate sentence. ❖ PUNCTUATION ALERT: Always use a comma before a coordinating conjunction that joins two independent clauses°; see 29b. ❖

You can also coordinate ideas within a sentence by using correlative conjunctions (such as *either . . . or, not only . . . but also;* for a complete list, see 7g).

People chose **either** to ignore the signs **or** to prepare for a storm. [correlative conjunctions joining phrases°]

The blizzard brought **not only** gale-force winds that ripped off roofs **but also** twelve feet of snow that crippled the area for days. [correlative conjunctions joining dependent clauses°]

21b **Using coordinate sentences to show relationships**

Some writers like to use a string of short sentences for the impact of the style (see 23a). In most cases, however, a series of short sentences does not communicate well the relationships among the ideas. Coordination can help you avoid writing a series of short sentences that have unclear relationships.

UNCLEAR RELATIONSHIPS

We decided not to go to class. We planned to get the notes. Everyone else had the same plan. Most of us ended up failing the quiz.

CLEAR RELATIONSHIPS

We decided not to go to class, **but** we planned to get the notes. Everyone else had the same plan, **so** most of us ended up failing the quiz.

21c Avoiding the misuse of coordination

Illogical coordination occurs when ideas in compounded independent clauses are not related.

> **No** Computers came into common use in the 1970s, and they sometimes make costly errors.

In the No example, the statement in each independent clause is true, but the ideas are not closely enough related. The years in which computers became commonly used is not related to their making errors. The two ideas therefore should not be coordinated. Here are two ideas that do coordinate logically.

> **YES** Computers came into common use in the 1970s, and they are now indispensible for conducting business.

> **YES** Modern computer systems are often very complex, and they sometimes make costly errors.

Overused coordination creates writing that reads as if it were whatever came into the writer's head. Readers become impatient with "babble" and quickly lose interest. When you are revising, be sure to check that your intended meaning justifies the use of coordination.

| No | Dinosaurs could have disappeared for many reasons, and one theory holds that the climate suddenly became cold, and another theory suggests that a sudden shower of meteors and asteroids hit the earth, so the impact created a huge dust cloud that caused a false winter. The winter lasted for years, and the dinosaurs died, for most of the vegetation they lived on died out. |
| YES | Dinosaurs could have disappeared for many reasons. One theory holds that the climate suddenly became cold, and another suggests that a sudden shower of meteors and asteroids hit the earth. The impact created a huge dust cloud that caused a false winter. The winter lasted for years, killing most of the vegetation that dinosaurs used for food. |

21d Understanding subordination

Subordination expresses the relative importance of ideas through where these ideas are placed in the sentence. The more important idea appears in the independent clause—a group of words that can stand alone as a grammatical unit. The subordinated idea or ideas appear in the dependent clause—a group of words that cannot stand alone as a grammatical unit. What information you choose to subordinate depends on the meaning you want a sentence to deliver.

The major patterns of subordination with dependent clauses are shown in the chart on the next page. For information about using commas in subordination patterns, see 29f.

You can use subordination by writing sentences that contain an adverb clause or an adjective clause, two types of dependent clauses. An **adverb clause** is a dependent clause that starts

(continued on page 275)

PATTERNS OF SUBORDINATION WITH DEPENDENT CLAUSES

SENTENCES WITH ADVERB CLAUSES

■ **Adverb clause,** independent clause.

   After the sky grew dark, the air stilled ominously.

■ Independent clause, **adverb clause.**

   Birds stopped singing, **as they do during an eclipse.**

■ Independent clause **adverb clause.**

   The shops closed **before the storm began.**

SENTENCES WITH ADJECTIVE CLAUSES

■ Independent clause **restrictive (essential)* adjective clause.**

   The weather forecasts warned of a storm **that might bring a thirty-inch snowfall.**

■ Independent clause, **nonrestrictive (nonessential)* adjective clause.**

   Spring is the season for tornados, **which rapidly whirl their destructive columns of air.**

■ Beginning of independent clause **restrictive (essential)* adjective clause** end of independent clause.

   Anyone **who lives through a tornado** recalls the experience.

■ Beginning of independent clause, **nonrestrictive (nonessential)* adjective clause,** end of independent clause.

   The sky, **which had been clear,** was turning gray.

*For an explanation of restrictive and nonrestrictive elements, see 29f.

with a subordinating conjunction (such as *after, if,* and *although;* for a complete list, see 7g). Each subordinating conjunction has a specific meaning that expresses a relationship between the dependent clause and the independent clause; see 8f.

An **adjective clause** is a dependent clause that starts with a relative pronoun, (such as *who, whom, which, that*). ❖ USAGE ALERT: Use *which* to begin a nonrestrictive adjective clause°. Use either *which* or *that* to begin a restrictive adjective clause°. ❖

21e Using subordination to show relationships

Subordination directs your reader's attention to the idea in the independent clause while at the same time using the idea in the dependent clause to provide context and support. Consider this example (the dependent clause is in boldface).

> **As soon as I saw the elephant,** I knew with perfect certainty that I ought not to shoot it.
>
> —GEORGE ORWELL, "Shooting an Elephant"

Subordination usually communicates relationships among ideas more effectively than does a group of separate sentences. (You may want to use an occasional string of short sentences for impact. See 23a.)

UNCLEAR RELATIONSHIPS

In 1888, two cowboys had to fight a dangerous Colorado snowstorm. They were looking for cattle. They came to a canyon. They saw outlines of buildings through the snow. Survival then seemed certain.

CLEAR RELATIONSHIPS

In 1888, two cowboys had to fight a dangerous Colorado snowstorm **while they were looking for cattle. When they came to a canyon,** they saw outlines of buildings through the snow. Survival then seemed certain.

In the clearer version, the first four short sentences have been combined into two subordinate sentences. The last sentence is left short for dramatic impact.

21f Choosing the subordinate conjunction appropriate to your meaning

Subordinating conjunctions are your allies in communicating the relationship between major and minor ideas in sentences. (For a list of subordinating conjunctions and the relationships they express, see 7g.) Consider the influence of the subordinating conjunction in each of the following sentences.

After you have handed it in, you cannot make any changes in your report. [time limit]

Because you have handed it in, you cannot ask me to discuss your report. [reason]

Unless you have handed it in, you cannot make any changes in your report. [condition]

Although you have handed it in, you can make changes in your report. [contrast]

I want to read your report **so that I can evaluate it.** [purpose]

21g Avoiding the misuse of subordination

Illogical subordination occurs when the subordinating conjunction does not make clear the relationship between the independent clause° and dependent clause°.

> **No** Because he was deaf when he wrote them, Beethoven's final symphonies were masterpieces.

This sentence is illogical because Beethoven's deafness did not lead to his writing symphonic masterpieces.

> **YES** Although Beethoven was deaf when he wrote his final symphonies, they are musical masterpieces.

Overused subordination occurs when too many images or ideas crowd together, making readers lose track of the message. If you have used more than two subordinating conjunctions or relative pronouns in a sentence, check carefully to see if your meaning is clear.

> **No** A new technique for eye surgery, which is supposed to correct nearsightedness, which previously could be corrected only by glasses, has been developed, although many doctors do not approve of it because it can create unstable eyesight.
>
> **YES** A new technique for eye surgery, which is supposed to correct nearsightedness, has been developed. Previously, nearsightedness could be corrected only by glasses. Because it can create unstable eyesight, many doctors do not approve of it, however.

In the revised version the first sentence has a relative clause°, the second is a simple sentence°, and the third has a dependent clause° starting *Because.* Some words have been moved to new positions. The revision communicates its message more clearly because it provides a variety of sentence structures (see 23a) while avoiding the clutter of overused subordination.

21h Achieving a balance between subordination and coordination

Coordination and subordination can sometimes be used in concert with each other. Varying sentence types improves a writer's ability to emphasize key points in his or her writing. Consider the following paragraph, which demonstrates a good balance in the use of coordination and subordination.

When I was growing up, I lived on a farm just across the field from my grandmother. My parents were busy trying to raise six children and to establish their struggling dairy farm. It was nice to have Grandma so close. **While my parents were providing the necessities of life,** my patient grandmother gave her time to her shy, young granddaughter. I always enjoyed going with Grandma and collecting the eggs **that her chickens had just laid.** Usually she knew which chickens would peck, **and** she was careful to let me gather the eggs from the less hostile ones.

—Patricia Mapes, student

EXERCISE 21-1

Using subordination and coordination, combine these sets of short, choppy sentences.

EXAMPLE Some people love their cars. Some people give their cars pet names.

Because some people love their cars, they like to give them pet names.

1. Five-figure prices are for new cars. The prices are shocking. The prices may keep you away from the showrooms.

2. Perhaps you should lease your next car. You may pay less as a down payment. You may pay less each month.

3. You are a potential customer. Potential customers should shop carefully. You may find a particularly good arrangement. The arrangement might save you money.

4. Ten years ago only one in every ten private cars was leased. In 1984, one of every six private cars was leased. By now many more drivers favor car leasing.

5. Leasing has become popular with many drivers. It is particularly popular with young professionals. They want to save their money for necessities or luxuries.

22 Parallelism

This chapter advises you how to avoid **faulty parallelism** (22b and 22c) and how to use the grace and power of **parallelism** to strengthen your writing (22d and 22e).

22a Understanding parallelism

Parallelism in writing, related to the concept of parallel lines in geometry, calls for the use of equivalent grammatical forms to express equivalent ideas. An **equivalent grammatical form** is a word or group of words that matches—is parallel to—the structure of a corresponding word or group of words. When you are expressing similar information or ideas in your writing, parallel sentence structures echo that fact and offer you a writing style that uses balance and rhythm to help deliver your meaning. For illustrations of parallel structures, see the chart on the next page as well as the example below.

> **The deer** often come **to eat their grain, the wolves to destroy their sheep, the bears to kill their hogs, the foxes to catch their poultry.** [The message of the multiple, accumulating assaults is echoed by the parallel structures.]
>
> —J. HECTOR ST. JEAN DE CREVECOEUR
> Letters from an American Farmer

PARALLEL STRUCTURES

PARALLEL WORDS

Recommended exercise includes

running,
swimming,
and
cycling.

The -*ing* words are parallel in structure and equal in importance.

PARALLEL PHRASES

Exercise helps people
to maintain healthy bodies
and
to handle mental pressures.

The phrases are parallel in structure and equal in importance.

PARALLEL CLAUSES

Many people begin to exercise
because they want to look healthy,
because they need to have stamina,
and
because they hope to live longer.

The clauses are parallel in structure and equal in importance.

22b Using words in parallel form

To avoid faulty parallelism, be sure that words in parallel structures occur in the same grammatical form.

> **No**   The strikers had tried **pleading, threats,** and **shouting.**

YES   The strikers had tried **pleading, threatening,** and **shouting.**

YES   The strikers had tried **pleas, threats,** and **shouts.**

22c Using phrases and clauses in parallel form

To avoid faulty parallelism, be sure that phrases° and clauses° in parallel structures occur in the same grammatical form.

No   The committee members **read the petition, were discussing its arguments,** and **the unanimous decision was to ignore it.**

YES   The committee members **read the petition, discussed its arguments,** and unanimously **decided to ignore it.**

22d Being aware that certain words call for parallel structures

Whenever you join words, phrases, or clauses with **coordinating conjunctions** *(and, but, for, or, nor, yet, so),* be sure to use parallel forms.

> You come to understand what to expect when you **tease a cat, or toss a pebble** in a pool, **or touch a hot stove.**
>
> —ANN E. BERTHOFF, *Forming, Thinking, and Writing*

Use parallel form when you link elements of a sentence with **correlative conjunctions** (such as *either . . . or, not only . . . but also;* for a complete list, see 7g).

> Differences between classical and modern style in ballet affect **both** dance **and** dancer.
>
> —LISA LANG, student

To enhance the effect of parallelism, you can intentionally repeat certain words that begin parallel phrases or clauses. Such words include prepositions (see 7f), articles *(a, an, the),* and the *to* of the infinitive°. Consider how Didion uses the infinitive form to reinforce her message with the impact and grace of parallelism.

> **To assign** unanswered letters their proper weight, **to free us** from the expectations of others, **to give us** back to ourselves—here lies the great, the singular power of self-respect.
>
> —JOAN DIDION, "On Self-Respect"

Because repetition can create dull prose, the technique has to be used carefully. The Didion passage avoids monotony by mixing parallel repetition with much variety in her other word choices.

Be sure to use parallel clauses beginning with *and who, and whom, and which,* or *and that* when they follow clauses beginning with *who, whom, which,* or *that.*

> I have in my own life a precious friend, a woman of 65 **who has** lived very hard, **who is** wise, **who listens** well, **who has** been where I am and can help me understand it, **and who represents** not only an ultimate ideal mother to me but also the person I'd like to be when I grow up.
>
> JUDITH VIORST, "Friends, Good Friends—and Such Good Friends"

22e Using parallel structures for impact

Deliberate repetition of word forms, word groups, and sounds creates a rhythm that underlines the message your sentence delivers. This technique can be highly effective if not overused.

> Go back to Mississippi, go back to Alabama, go back to South Carolina, go back to Georgia, go back to Louisiana, go back to the slums and ghettos of our northern cities, knowing that somehow this situation can and will be changed.
>
> —MARTIN LUTHER KING, JR., "I Have a Dream"

Climatic order arranges elements from least to most important so that the material builds to a climax. Parallel structures in climactic order are particularly effective.

> You can fool some of the people all of the time, and all of the people some of the time, but you cannot fool all of the people all of the time.
>
> —ABRAHAM LINCOLN

Balanced sentences use parallel structures to enhance the message of ideas that are compared or contrasted.

> Ask not what your country can do for you, ask what you can do for your country.
>
> —JOHN F. KENNEDY

EXERCISE 22-1

Revise these sentences to eliminate errors in parallel structure.

EXAMPLE   Widely known as the sick-building syndrome, indoor air pollution causes office workers to suffer from burning eyes, from breathing that has become difficult, rashes that cause severe pain, and from throbbing headaches.

Widely known as the sick-building syndrome, indoor air pollution causes office workers to suffer *from burning eyes, difficult breathing, severely painful rashes, and throbbing headaches.*

1. In many new office buildings today not only are the windows sealed shut but also the problem is that internal ventilation systems are inadequate and filthy.

2. Indoor pollutants include tobacco smoke, the fumes that come from copy machines, the gas that is released from carbonless paper when it is written on, cleaning chemicals, and even fibers from rugs and draperies.

3. Other pollutants come from outdoors when the intake ducts for air into a ventilation system are located right over loading docks where trucks spew out exhaust fumes, or streets and highways filled with truck and car traffic are located right next to air-intake ducts of buildings.

4. Environmental experts have studied sick buildings and made recommendations that are easy to implement, and that do not cost very much, and they would be able to solve most of the problems that contribute to the indoor air pollution.

5. Some of the simpler remedies range from frequently cleaning air ducts and the replacement of air filters to the rearrangement of office partitions so that the air can flow more freely.

EXERCISE 22-2

Using topics of your choosing, imitate the writing style of three different passages shown in this chapter. Choose from DeCrevecoeur, King, Lincoln, Didion, or Viorst.

23 Variety and Emphasis

Your writing style has **variety** when your sentence lengths and patterns vary. Your writing style is characterized by **emphasis** when your sentences are constructed to communicate the relative importance of their ideas. This chapter shows you how variety and emphasis work in concert to create graceful, memorable writing.

23a Varying sentence length

When you use a variety of sentence lengths, you communicate clear distinctions among ideas. Such a style can help your

---

HOW TO ACHIEVE VARIETY AND EMPHASIS

- Vary sentence length to achieve a more interesting, lively writing style (23a).
- Choose the subject of a sentence according to your intended meaning (23b).
- Add modifiers to basic sentences (23c).
- Invert standard word order (23d).

---

readers understand the focus of your material. Also, such a style avoids the unbroken rhythm of monotonous sentence length that can lull your reader into inattention.

1 Revising strings of too many short sentences

Strings of too many short sentences rarely establish relationships and levels of importance among ideas. Readers cannot easily make distinctions between major and minor points. Such strings, unless deliberately planned in a longer piece of writing for occasional impact, suggest that the writer has not thought through the material and decided what to emphasize. The style tends to read like that of young children.

No There is a legend. This legend is about a seventeenth-century Algonquin Indian. It says that he was inspired. He had an idea about popcorn. He transformed it into a gift. It was the first gift to a hostess in American history. He was invited to the Pilgrims' harvest meal. He brought along a bag of popcorn. This was a demonstration of good will. The occasion is honored to this day with Thanksgiving dinner.

Yes According to legend, in the seventeenth century an inspired Algonquin transformed popcorn into the first hostess gift in history. Invited to the Pilgrims' harvest meal, the Indian brought along a bag of popcorn as a demonstration of good will. The occasion is honored today with Thanksgiving dinner.

—Patricia Linden, "Popcorn"

2 Revising a string of too many compound sentences

A **compound sentence** consists of two or more independent clauses° that are grammatically equivalent (see 8f). The compounding of a sentence must be justified by its meaning. Too often, compound sentences are short sentences only strung together with *and* or *but,* without consideration of the relationships among the ideas.

> **No**   Science fiction writers are often thinkers, and they are often dreamers, so they let their imaginations wander. Jules Verne was such a writer, and he predicted space ships and atomic submarines, but most people did not believe airplanes were possible.

> **Yes**   Science fiction writers are often thinkers and dreamers who let their imaginations wander. Jules Verne was one such writer. He predicted space ships and atomic submarines before most people believed airplanes were possible.

3	Revising for a suitable mix of sentence lengths

To emphasize one idea among many others, you can express it in a sentence noticeably different in length or structure from the sentences surrounding it. Depending on the message of your material, you can decide to write one short sentence among longer ones, as shown in the following passage. A long sentence among shorter ones is equally effective.

> Today is one of those excellent January partly cloudies in which light chooses an unexpected landscape to trick out in gilt, and then shadow sweeps it away. **You know you are alive.** You take huge steps, trying to feel the planet's roundness arc between your feet. Kazantzakis says that when he was young he had a canary and a globe. When he freed the canary, it would perch on the globe and sing. All his life, wandering the earth, he felt as though he had a canary on top of his mind, singing.

> —Annie Dillard, *Pilgrim at Tinker Creek*

23b Choosing the subject of a sentence according to your intended emphasis

The subject° of a sentence establishes the focus for that sentence. The subject you choose should correspond to the emphasis you want to communicate to your reader.

Each of the following sentences, all of which are correct grammatically, contains the same information. Consider, however, how changes of the subject (and its verb) influence meaning and impact.

1. **Our study showed** that 25 percent of college students' time is spent eating or sleeping. [Focus is on the study.]

2. **College students eat or sleep** 25 percent of the time, according to our study. [Focus is on the student.]

3. **Eating or sleeping occupies** 25 percent of college students' time, according to our study. [Focus is on eating and sleeping.]

4. **Twenty-five percent** of college students' time **is spent** eating or sleeping, according to our study. [Focus is on the percentage of time.]

23c Adding modifiers to basic sentences for variety and emphasis

Adding modifiers° to basic sentences provides you with a rich variety of sentence patterns. Consult the chart on the opposite page. Your decision to expand a basic sentence will depend on the focus of each sentence and how it works in concert with its surrounding sentences to deliver its intended meaning. As you add modifiers°, be sure to position them according to the emphasis you want to achieve. (Be sure, however, to place them precisely and thereby avoid the error of misplaced modifiers°; see 18a).

WAYS TO EXPAND A BASIC SENTENCE	
BASIC SENTENCE	The river rose.
ADJECTIVE°	The **swollen** river rose.
ADVERB°	The river rose **dangerously.**
PREPOSITIONAL PHRASE°	**In April,** the river rose **above its banks.**
PARTICIPIAL PHRASES°	**Swollen by melting snow,** the river rose, **flooding the farmland.**
ABSOLUTE PHRASE°	**Trees swirling away in the current,** the river rose.
ADVERB CLAUSE°	**Because the snows had been heavy that winter,** the river rose.
ADJECTIVE CLAUSE°	The river, **which runs through vital farmland,** rose.

A **cumulative sentence** starts with a subject° and verb°. It is called "cumulative" because information accumulates after the subject and verb.

CUMULATIVE   **The driver, killed instantly,** was very young and apparently drunk.

Although most sentences in English are cumulative, they sometimes lack impact, so experienced writers try to use an occasional periodic sentence. A periodic sentence (sometimes called a *climactic sentence*) is highly emphatic. It builds up to the period of the sentence, reserving the main idea for the end. It therefore draws in the reader as it builds to its climax.

PERIODIC   **The driver,** very young and apparently drunk, **was killed instantly.**

—JOAN DIDION, "On Morality"

While periodic sentences can be very effective, if you overuse them they can lose their punch.

23d   Inverting standard word order

Standard word order in the English sentence places the subject before the verb: *The **mayor walked** into the room.* Because this pattern is so common, it is set in people's minds. Any variation from the pattern creates emphasis. Inverted word order places the verb before the subject. *Into the room **walked the mayor.*** Used too often, inverted word order can be distracting, but used sparingly, it can be very effective.

EXERCISE 23-1

Using the techniques of variety and emphasis discussed in this chapter, revise the following paragraph.

Many amazing events in bathtubs have taken place. Three different women died by drowning in the bathtub while they were married to George Joseph Smith of England. There was great surprise at Mr. Smith's trial when the fact that he now had a fourth wife, Edith, was revealed. Edith testified at the trial that she remembered George's taking only one bath during the whole time they were married. Other things besides gory murders, however, happen in the bathtub. For example, French author Edmond Rostand took baths while he was writing plays like *Cyrano de Bergerac* to escape interruptions from friends. Also, many people know that the discovery of the scientific theory of displacement by Archimedes took place in the bathtub. Archimedes shouted "Eureka!" jumped out of his bath, and ran through the streets in the nude because he was so excited by his discovery. A modern example of the importance of the bathtub is illustrated by what happened to astronaut John Glenn. There was going to be an election for senator in Ohio, but Glenn had to withdraw from the race because he hurt himself when he fell in a bathtub. He recovered completely and was later elected to the Senate.

Five

USING EFFECTIVE WORDS

 When you use words effectively, you choose words that communicate your message precisely. Part Five alerts you to the meanings that reside in words and the effect that words have on your reader. As you use Chapter 24-27, keep in mind that words work in concert with effective sentence structures and paragraphs to create good writing.

24 Understanding the Meaning of Words

American English, evolving over centuries into a rich language, reflects the many cultures that have merged in our melting-pot society. Because American English is a growing, changing language, you want to stay informed about it. To use American English effectively, you need to be familiar with the kinds of information that dictionaries offer (see 24a), and to know how to choose exact words (see 24b).

24a Using dictionaries

Good dictionaries show how language has been used and is currently being used. Such dictionaries give at each entry not only the word's meaning but also much additional important information. Here is the entry for *celebrate,* taken from *Webster's New World Dictionary,* Third College Edition. Below you will also find a list of what a dictionary entry usually includes (items 1 through 11, and sometimes items 12 and 13).

1. **Spelling.** If more than one spelling is shown, the first is the most commonly used, and the others are acceptable.
2. **Word Division.** The dots (or bars, in some dictionaries) show a word's syllables. In *Webster's New World Dictio-*

nary, Third College Edition, a hairline (a thin vertical line) indicates a syllable where the break should not be used for hyphenating.

3. **Pronunciation.** The symbols in parentheses show how the word is pronounced. If more than one pronunciation is given, the first is the most common, and others are acceptable. A guide to the pronunciation of the symbols appears in the front of most dictionaries, and some dictionaries provide a brief guide to the most common symbols at the bottom of pages.

4. **Part of Speech Labels.** Abbreviations, explained in the front of the dictionary, indicate parts of speech. Many words can function as more than one part of speech.

5. **Grammatical Forms.** This information tells of variations in grammar: for a verb, its principal parts and form variations; for a noun, its plural when the spelling demands other than the addition of *s;* for an adjective or adverb, its comparative form° and superlative form°*.

6. **Etymology.** Etymology is a word's history that tells how the word evolved through different languages to the definition in current use.

7. **Definitions.** If a word has more than one meaning, the definitions are numbered in most dictionaries from the oldest to the newest meaning. A few dictionaries start with the most common use.

8. **Usage Labels.** Usage labels indicate how a word is used. The chart on page 295 explains the most common usage labels in dictionaries.

9. **Field Labels.** A field label identifies a specialized area of study, such as chemistry or law. Abbreviations signal that a word has a specialized meaning within a field of study.

10. **Related Words.** Words based on the defined word appear, with their part of speech, at the end of the definitions.

---

*Throughout this book a degree mark (°) indicates a term that is defined in the book's Glossary.

11. **Synonyms and Antonyms.** Synonyms—words close in meaning—are listed, and their subtle differences explained. Also, for each word in the list of synonyms, a cross-reference appears at that word's entry so that the reader can tell where to find the complete list. Antonyms—words opposite in meaning to the word defined—are given, if any, after the synonyms.
12. **Idioms.** Common expressions that use the defined word in slightly different ways are idioms. Idioms are shown with usage labels (see 8 above), so that a writer can decide when their use is appropriate.
13. **Examples.** Some definitions provide an example sentence that illustrates the defined word in use.

   Usage refers to the customary manner of using particular words or phrases. As a writer, you can refer to the **usage labels** in a dictionary to help you decide when a word is appropriate for use. For a list of usage labels and their meanings, see the chart on the opposite page.

   Unabridged dictionaries are comprehensive, complete, and accurate. Most libraries have them. *Webster's Third New International Dictionary of the English Language* is a highly respected, one-volume work that has more than 470,000 entries and is especially strong in new scientific and technical terms. It uses quotations to show various meanings, and its definitions are given in order of their appearance in the language. *Random House Dictionary of the English Language,* second edition, is another one-volume work. It has more than 315,000 entries, along with an atlas with color maps and appendixes that list reference books.

   Abridged dictionaries, which contain most commonly used words, are convenient in size and economical to buy. For most college students, abridged dictionaries are practical reference books. Many good abridged dictionaries are referred to as "college" editions because they serve the needs of most college writers and readers. *Webster's New World Dictionary of Amer-*

USAGE LABELS

LABEL	DEFINITION	EXAMPLE
COLLOQUIAL	Characteristic of conversation and informal writing	**pa** [father] **ma** [mother]
SLANG	Not considered part of standard language, but sometimes used in informal conversation	**whirlybird** [helicopter]
OBSOLETE	No longer used; occurred in earlier writing	**betimes** [promptly, quickly]
POETIC	Found in poetry or poetic prose	**o'er** [*over*]
DIALECT	Used only in some geographical areas	**poke** [South: a bag or sack]

---

ican English, Third College Edition, is an abridged dictionary, but it has more than 170,000 entries and gives detailed etymologies. Definitions appear in chronological order of their acceptance into the language. Its introductory material includes essays on the English language and etymology. *The American Heritage Dictonary of the English Language* has more than 200,000 entries and 3,000 photographs, illustrations, and maps. This dictonary lists a word's most common meaning first, departing from the usual practice of listing the oldest meaning first.

24b
Choosing exact words

The English language offers you a wealth of words from which to choose as a writer. **Diction**—choice of words—affects the clarity and impact of the message your sentences deliver. To be successful at choosing exact words for each particular context in your writing, you need to understand the denotation and connotation of words (24b-1). You must also understand the relation between specific, concrete language and general, abstract language (24b-2).

1   Understanding denotation and connotation

Denotation is the explicit dictionary meaning of a word —its definition. When you look up a word in the dictionary to find out what it means, you are looking for its denotation.

Readers expect writers to use words according to established meanings for established functions. Exactness is essential. Dangers, as well as benefits and pleasures, arise when you use a thesaurus or dictionary of synonyms. Be aware that subtle shades of meaning differentiate words with the same general definitions. These small differences in meaning allow you to be very precise in choosing the word you want. Such subtleties, however, oblige you to be sure of the exact meanings your words convey. For example, you would be wrong to describe a person famous for praiseworthy achievements in public life as *notorious.* Although *notorious* means "well-known" and "publicly discussed"—which famous people usually are—*notorious* also carries the meaning "unfavorably known or talked about." George Washington is *famous,* not *notorious.* Al Capone, on the other hand, is *notorious.*

Connotation refers to ideas implied, but not directly indicated, by a word. Connotations convey associations as emotional overtones beyond a word's direct, explicit definition. For example, the word *home* probably evokes more emotion than does its denotation, "a dwelling place," or its synonym *house*. *Home* may have very pleasant connotations of warmth, security, and the love of family. Or *home* may have unpleasant connotations of a mismanaged institution for elderly or physically disabled people. Experienced writers and readers are aware of the additional layer of meaning connotations deliver. Connotations are never completely fixed, for the associations to a word often are individual. Most words, however, have relatively stable connotations and denotations in most contexts.

> **2** Using specific and concrete language to bring life to general and abstract language

Specific words identify individual items in a group *(Oldsmobile, Honda, Ford)*. **General** words relate to an overall group *(car)*. **Concrete** words identify persons and things that can be perceived by the senses—seen, heard, tasted, felt, smelled (the *black padded vinyl dashboard* of my car). **Abstract** words denote qualities, concepts, relationships, acts, conditions, ideas *(transportation)*.

Usually, specific and concrete words bring life to general and abstract words. When you choose general and abstract words, be sure to supply enough specific, concrete details and examples to illustrate your generalizations and abstractions. As you make choices, keep in mind your purpose (see 1b) for writing and the audience (see 1c) that will read your writing. Sentences with general words often come to life when they are revised to contain words that refer to specifics.

Remember, however, specific language is not always preferable to general language, and concrete language is not always preferable to abstract language. Effective writing usually combines them.

GENERAL		SPECIFIC	SPECIFIC		ABSTRACT

My car, a **220-horsepower Trans Am,** is **quick.**

	SPECIFIC		SPECIFIC

It accelerates from **0 to 50** miles per hour in **6 seconds**—

SPECIFIC		SPECIFIC

but it gets only **18 miles** per gallon. The **Dodge Lancer,** on

ABSTRACT	GENERAL	SPECIFIC

the other hand, gets **very good** gas **mileage:** about **35 mpg**

GENERAL		SPECIFIC		SPECIFIC

in **highway driving** and **30 mpg** in **stop-and-go**

GENERAL

driving conditions.

In being specific and concrete, do not overdo it. If you want to inform a nonspecialist reader about possible automobile fuels other than gasoline, *do* name the fuels and be very specific about their advantages and drawbacks. *Do not,* however, go into a detailed, highly technical discussion of the chemical profiles of the fuels. Always base your choices on an awareness of your purpose (see 1b) and audience (see 1c).

EXERCISE 24-1

Revise the following paragraph by providing specific and concrete words to explain and enliven the general and abstract words.

I enjoy good food. I do not like to eat greasy foods or foods made with more artificial ingredients than real ones. To me, good food starts with sweet, delicious desserts. I am also fond of many ethnic dishes. Bread is one of my other favorites. As long as I watch my weight, I can look forward to years of pleasure from good food.

25 Understanding the Effect of Words

As words communicate meaning, they have an effect on the people reading or hearing them. As a writer, you want to choose words carefully. Sometimes the choices available to you are either right or wrong but often the choices are subtle.

GUIDELINES FOR EFFECTIVE USE OF LANGUAGE

- Use proper level of formality (25a-1).
- Use edited American English (25a-2).
- Avoid slang or inappropriate colloquial words or regional words (25a-3).
- Avoid slanted language (25a-4).
- Avoid sexist language (25b).
- Use figurative language appropriately (25c).
- Avoid clichés (25d).
- Avoid artificial language (25e).

25a Using appropriate language

As a writer, you need to pay special attention to tone (see 1d) and **diction** (see 24b). You need to make certain that the words you use will communicate your meaning as clearly and effectively as possible. As you choose your words, be aware of their connotations as well as their denotations (see 24b). Also, your word choice should be appropriate for your purpose (see 1b) and audience (see 1c).

1 Using appropriate levels of formality

Tone in writing is established by what you say and how you say it. The level of formality of your language directly affects tone. The level of your language can be highly formal, informal, or somewhere in between.

Informal language, which creates an informal tone, may include slang, colloquialisms, and regionalisms (see 25a-3). In addition, informal writing often includes sentence fragments, contractions, and other forms that approximate casual speech. **Medium** language level uses general English—not too casual, not too scholarly. Unlike informal language, medium-level language is acceptable for academic writing. This level uses standard vocabulary, (for example, *learn* instead of *wise up*), conventional sentence structure, and few or no contractions. A **highly formal** language level uses a multisyllabic Latinate vocabulary (*edify* for *learn*) and often stylistic flourishes. Academic writing, as for most writing for general audiences, should range from medium to somewhat formal levels of language.

INFORMAL	Ya know stars? They're a gas!
MEDIUM	Gas clouds slowly changed into stars.
FORMAL	The condensations of gas spun their slow gravitational pirouettes, slowly transmogrifying gas cloud into star.

—CARL SAGAN, "Starfolk: A Fable"

2	Using edited American English for academic writing

The language standards you are expected to use in academic writing are those of **edited American English**—the accepted written language of a book like this handbook or a magazine like *Newsweek.* Such language conforms to widely established rules of grammar, sentence structure, punctuation, and spelling. Because advertising language and other language intended to reach and sway a large audience often ignore conventional usage, readers often encounter English that varies from the standard. As a writer, do not let these published departures from edited American English influence you into believing they are acceptable in academic writing.

Edited English is not a fancy dialect for the elite. It is a practical form of the language that most people expect in academic writing. As a student writer, you might find that early drafts of your essays contain language that departs from edited American English. Do not revise your words too early in the writing process. First get your ideas down on paper. Then revise so that your final drafts are in edited American English.

3	Avoiding slang and colloquial or regional language for most academic writing

Slang consists of words that are new or have extended meanings attached to them. Slang is used only in very informal situations. Sometimes slang terms are inventions: *hippie* from the 1960s and its 1990s counterpart *yuppie* are examples. Sometimes slang terms are redefinitions of existing words. For example, *awesome* has been used informally for "excellent" or "wonderful" as has *wired* for "nervous." **Colloquial** language is characteristic of casual conversation and informal writing: *The student flunked chemistry* instead of *the student failed chemistry.* **Regional** (also called *dialectal*) **language** is specific to some geographic areas: *They have nary a cent.* Slang and colloquial and regional language are neither substandard nor illiterate, but they are usually not appropriate for academic writing.

301

4

To communicate clearly, you need to choose words that convince your audience of your fairness as a writer. When you are writing about a subject on which you hold strong opinions, it is easy to slip into biased or emotionally loaded language. Such **slanted language** usually does not convince a careful reader to agree with your point. Instead, it makes the reader wary or hostile. For example, suppose you are arguing against the practice of experiments on animals. If you use language such as "laboratory Frankensteins" who "routinely maim helpless puppies," you are using slanted language. You want to use words that make your side of an issue the more convincing one. Once you start using slanted, biased language, readers feel manipulated rather than reasoned with.

25b Avoiding sexist language

Sexist language assigns roles or characteristics to people on the basis of gender. Most women *and* men today feel that sexist language unfairly discriminates against both sexes. Sexist language inaccurately assumes all nurses and homemakers are female (and therefore refers to them as "she") and all physicians and wage earners are male (and therefore refers to them as "he"). Avoid such practices.

One of the most widespread occurrences of sexist language is the use of the pronoun *he* to refer to someone of unidentified sex. Although tradition holds that *he* is correct in such situations, using only masculine pronouns to represent the human species is a distortion of reality. You can avoid sexism by not lapsing into demeaning, out dated stereotypes, such as *women are bad drivers* or *men are bad cooks*.

To help yourself to avoid sexist language in your writing, use the guidelines in the chart on the next page.

HOW TO AVOID SEXIST LANGUAGE

---

1. Avoid using only the masculine pronoun to refer to males and females together. Use a pair of pronouns.

   No   A doctor has little time to read outside **his** specialty.

   Yes   A doctor has little time to read outside **his or her** specialty.

   Try to avoid having to use the "he or she" construction in several consecutive sentences. Revising into the plural may be a better solution.

   No   A successful doctor knows that **he** has to work long hours.

   Yes   Successful doctors know that **they** have to work long hours.

   Another choice is to recast a sentence to omit the gender-specific pronoun.

   No   Everyone hopes that **he** will win the scholarship.

   Yes   Everyone hopes to win the scholarship.

2. Avoid the use of *man* when men and women are clearly intended in the meaning.

   No   **Man** is a social animal.

   Yes   **People** are social animals.

3. Avoid stereotyping jobs and roles by gender when men and women are included.

No	Yes
policeman	police officer
businessman	businessperson, business executive

(continued on next page)

HOW TO AVOID SEXIST LANGUAGE *(continued)*

4. Avoid expressions that exclude one sex.

No	**YES**
mankind	humanity
the common man	the average person
old wives' tale	superstition

5. Avoid using demeaning and patronizing labels.

No	**YES**
male nurse	nurse
career girl	professional woman

No My **girl** will help you.

YES My **secretary** will help you.

  Heidi Moore will help you.

25c Using figurative language

Figurative language uses words for more than their literal meanings.

TYPES OF FIGURATIVE LANGUAGE

Analogy: a comparison of similar traits between dissimilar things (An analogy may extend for several sentences.)

  A cheetah sprinting across the dry plains after its prey, the base runner dashed for home plate, his cleats kicking up dust.

TYPES OF FIGURATIVE LANGUAGE *(continued)*

Irony: the use of words to suggest the opposite of their usual sense

> Told that the car repair would cost $2,000 and take at least two weeks, she said, "Oh, that would be wonderful!"

Metaphor: a comparison between otherwise dissimilar things without using the word *like* or *as* (Be alert to avoid the error of a mixed metaphor, explained following this chart.)

> The rush-hour traffic bled out of all the city's major arteries.

Overstatement (also called *hyperbole*): deliberate exaggeration for emphasis

> If I don't get this paper in on time, the professor is going to kill me.

Personification: the assignment of a human trait to a nonhuman thing

> The book begged to be read.

Simile: a direct comparison between otherwise dissimilar things, using the word *like* or *as*

> Langston Hughes says that a deferred dream dries up like a raisin in the sun.

Understatement: deliberate restraint for emphasis

> It gets a little warm when the temperature reaches 105 degrees.

A **mixed metaphor** is an error. It confuses readers by combining images that do not work well together. Consider this sentence, for example: *Milking the migrant workers for all they were worth, the supervisors barked orders at them.* Here the initial image is of taking milk from a cow, but the final image has supervisors barking, an action suggesting dogs.

25d Avoiding clichés

A **cliché** is an overused, worn-out expression that has lost its capacity to communicate effectively. Some comparisons, once clever, have grown trite: *dead as a doornail, gentle as a lamb, straight as an arrow.* If you have heard words over and over again, so has your reader. If you cannot think of a way to rephrase a cliché, delete the phrase entirely.

25e Avoiding artificial language

As a writer, you need to avoid using **artificial language:** pretentious word choice, unnecessary jargon, and euphemisms. Experienced writers work hard to communicate as clearly and directly as they can. As a student writer, avoid spending time looking for long, fancy words to explain a point. Instead, try to make what you write as accessible as possible to your readers. Extremely complex ideas or subject areas may require complex terms or phrases to explain them, but in general the simpler the language, the more likely it is to be understood.

1 Avoiding pretentious language

Pretentious language is too showy, calling undue attention to itself with complex sentences and polysyllabic words.

Academic writing does not call for big words used for their own sake. Overblown words are likely to obscure your message.

No   The raison d'etre for my matriculation in this institution of higher learning is the acquisition of a better education.

Yes   The reason that I am in college is to get a better education.

<hr>

2

Avoiding unnecessary jargon

Jargon is specialized vocabulary of a particular group: words that an outsider unfamiliar with this field might not understand. As you write, consider your purpose (see 1b) and audience (see 1c) to decide whether a word is jargon in the context of your material. Specialized language evolves in every field: professions, academic disciplines commerce, and even hobbies. However, using jargon unnecessarily may shut readers out. Therefore, when you need to use jargon for a general audience, be sure to explain the specialized meanings.

ACCEPTABLE SPECIALIZED LANGUAGE

As the lake eutrophicates, it gradually fills until the entire lake will be converted into a terrestrial community. Eutrophic changes (or eutrophication) is the nutritional enrichment of the water, promoting the growth of aquatic plants.

—DAVIS AND SOLOMON, *The World of Biology*

<hr>

3

Avoiding euphemisms

Euphemisms attempt to avoid the harsh reality of truth by using more pleasant-sounding, "tactful" words. Euphemisms are sometimes necessary for tact in social situations (using *passed away* instead of *died* when offering condolences, for example). Most of the time, however, euphemisms drain meaning from truthful writing. Some people use unnecessary euphemisms to hide unpleasant facts: "She is between assignments" instead of "She lost her job."

EXERCISE 25-1

Revise the following sentences to make the language more effective. Apply all the material covered in this chapter.

1. The lady doctor had to perform an emergency operation.
2. If you want to make a sale, you have to take the bull by the horns.
3. I recall the time in my past when the school I matriculated at was razed by an incendiary event.
4. She came within the venue of the law enforcement establishment.
5. She is on maternity leave awaiting a little bundle of joy from heaven.
6. An effective businessman understands the needs of his staff members.
7. To make customers happy as larks, give them a good product and good service.
8. The administrative assisant typed an epistle for the company's president.
9. Her occupation is domestic engineering.
10. Man likes to learn and master new skills.

26 Spelling

Good spellers do not always remember how to spell every word, but most good spellers know when to consult the dictionary for help. If you are unsure of how to spell a word but you know how it starts, look it up in the dictionary (see 24a). The various origins of English words and the various ways English-speaking people pronounce words make it almost impossible to rely on pronunciation in spelling a word. What you *can* rely on, however, is a system of proofreading and learning spelling rules.

26a Eliminating spelling careless errors

Many spelling errors are the result of illegible handwriting, slips of the pen, or typographical errors. Catching "typos" requires careful proofreading. Try the techniques in the chart below. For information on how to correct typos by using proofreaders' marks, see Appendix B, Using Correct Manuscript Format.

TECHNIQUES FOR PROOFREADING FOR SPELLING

1. Slow down your reading speed so that you can concentrate on individual letters of words rather than on the meaning of the words.

(continued on next page)

TECHNIQUES FOR PROOFREADING FOR SPELLING *(continued)*

2. Stay within your "visual span," the number of letters you can identify with a single glance. Most people have a visual span of about six letters.

3. Put a ruler or large index card under each line as you proofread, to focus your concentration and vision.

4. Read each paragraph *backwards,* from the last sentence to the first. This method helps to prevent your being distracted by the meaning of the material.

26b Spelling homonyms and commonly confused words

Homonyms are words that sound exactly like others *(its, it's; instead of, morning, mourning).* Many other words sound so much alike that they are often confused with each other. The best way to distinguish between homonyms or between other commonly confused words is to use memory devices. For example, if you have trouble with the homonyms *stationary* and *stationery* try this: *Stationary* means standing (*a* is in both) still while *stationery* is written (*e* is in both) on. Make up similar memory devices for words you often misspell.

HOMONYMS AND COMMONLY CONFUSED WORDS

accept	to receive
except	with the exclusion of
advice	recommendation
advise	to recommend
affect	to produce an influence on *(verb);* an emotional response *(noun)*
effect	result *(noun);* to bring about or to cause *(verb)*

Homonyms and Commonly Confused Words *(continued)*

already	by this time
all ready	fully prepared
altar	sacred platform or place
alter	to change
altogether	thoroughly
all together	everyone or everything in one place
are	plural form of *to be*
hour	sixty minutes
our	plural form of *my*
breath	air taken in
breathe	to take in air
brake	device for stopping
break	to destroy, to make into pieces
buy	to purchase
by	next to, through the agency of
capital	major city
capitol	government building
choose	to pick
chose	past tense of *to choose*
cite	to point out
sight	vision
site	a place
complement	something that completes
compliment	praise, flattery
dessert	final, sweet course in a meal
desert	to abandon; dry, sandy area
formally	conventionally, with ceremony
formerly	previously
its	possessive form of *it*
it's	contraction for *it is*
lead	heavy metal substance; to guide
led	past tense of *to lead*
loose	unbound, not tightly fastened
lose	to misplace

(continued on next page)

HOMONYMS AND COMMONLY CONFUSED WORDS *(continued)*

passed	past tense of *to pass*
past	at a previous time
presence	attendance at a place or in something
presents	gifts
principal	foremost *(adjective);* administrator of a school *(noun)*
principle	moral conviction, basic truth
raise	to lift up
raze	to tear down
stationary	standing still
stationery	writing paper
than	besides
then	at that time; next; therefore
their	possessive form of *they*
there	in that place
they're	contraction for *they are*
to	toward
too	also
two	number following one
weather	climatic condition
whether	if
whose	possessive form of *who*
who's	contraction for *who is*
your	possessive form of *you*
you're	contraction for *you are*
yore	long past

26c Spelling plurals

Plurals in English are formed in different ways. The rules are relatively easy to learn because they are consistent.

Most **plurals** are formed by adding *-s: leg, legs, shoe, shoes.* If the word ends in -ch, -s, -sh, -x, or -z, the plural is formed by adding *-es* to the singular: *beach, beaches tax, taxes.*

Plurals of words ending with -o are formed by adding *-s* if the **-o** is preceded by a vowel *(radio, radios)* and *-es* if the **-o** is preceded by a consonant *(potato, potatoes)*.

Plurals of words ending with a -f or -fe are either formed by adding *-s (belief, beliefs)* or changing the *-f* or *-fe* to *-ves (wife, wives)*.

Plurals of compound words are formed by adding *-s* or *-es* to the end of a whole compound word *(checkbooks)* or to the end of the most important word in a noun combination *(mothers-in-law, nurse-midwives)*.

Plurals formed by internal changes do not use the added *-s* or *-es*: *foot, feet; mouse, mice.*

Plurals of foreign words are formed according to the rules of the language: *alumnus, alumni.*

Plurals that retain their singular form are spelled the same for both singular and plural: *deer, fish, rice.*

26d Spelling words with prefixes

Prefixes are syllables placed in front of words, either changing or adding to the word's meaning. For example, the prefixes *un-* and *in-* turn a word into its opposite *(**un**coopera-tive, **in**admissible)*; *re-* adds the meaning "again" to a word *(**re**create, **re**incarnation)*; and *pre-* adds the meaning "before" to a word *(**pre**cook, **pre**destination)*. A prefix does not alter the spelling of the word to which it is added: for example, *un + reliable = unreliable; re + locate = relocate.* Some prefixes, however, do require hyphens (see Chapter 27).

26e Spelling words with suffixes

A **suffix** is a word ending added to the basic (root) form of a word. A suffix cannot stand alone as a word. Often spelling is affected when a suffix is added to a word. Even though they have many exceptions, rules and other guidelines about suffixes can help you.

1 Using spelling rules for suffixes

Three spelling rules can help you add suffixes to words correctly. Whenever you are unsure, check your dictionary.

When to change a final Y to I

Check the letter before the final *y* in the word. If a consonant, change the *y* to *i,* unless the suffix begins with an *i* (for example, *-ing*). If the letter before the *y* is a vowel, keep the final *y*.

fry, fried, frying
employ, emplo**yed**, emplo**ying**

When to drop a final E

Drop the final *e* when the suffix begins with a vowel (for example, *-ing*). Do not, however, drop the *e* if doing so would cause confusion; for example, the final *e* is needed to avoid confusing *dyeing* and *dying* (in *dying* the *y* to *i* rule also operates). Major exceptions are *argument, judgment,* and *truly.*

require, requiring, requirement
like, liking, likely
guide, guiding, guidance

When to double a final letter

Check the final letter of a word. If it is a consonant, double it when adding a suffix—but only if it passes these three tests: (1) the last two letters of a word are a vowel followed by a consonant; (2) the word has one syllable or is accented on the last syllable; (3) the suffix beings with a vowel.

drop, dropped
begin, beginning
forget, forgetful, forgettable
happen, happened

2 **Using other guidelines about suffixes**

The *-ble* suffixes *(-able* and *-ible)* have no consistent rules for their use. More words end in *-able: advisable, comfortable.* Still, some common words end in *-ible: audible, forcible.* The best rule is "When in doubt, look it up."

The *-nce* and *-nt* suffixes have no rules for their use. Some words end in *-ance: compliance, defiance.* Other words end in *-ence: confidence, convenience.* If a noun ends in *-ance,* its adjective° form ends in *-ant: defiance, defiant.* If a noun ends in *-ence,* the adjective form ends in *-ent: confidence, confident.*

The -cede, -ceed, and -sede suffixes have very dependable rules. Only one word ends in -sede: *supersede.* Three words end in -ceed: *exceed, proceed,* and *succeed.* All other words whose endings sound like these suffixes end in -cede: *concede, intercede, precede.*

26f Using the *ie, ei* rule

The old rhyme for *ie* and *ei* is usually true: *"I* before *e,* except after *c,* or when sounded like *ay,* as in **neighbor** and **weigh**."

I Before E
believe, field, grief
Except After C
ceiling, conceit
Except When Sounds Like *AY*
eight, vein, neighbor

Because there are few major exceptions, they are worth memorizing.

IE   conscience, financier, science, species

EI   counterfeit, either, foreign, forfeit, height, leisure, neither, seize, sleight, weird

EXERCISE 26-1

This paragraph contains eleven misspelled words. Circle the words, correct them, and match them to the appropriate section of this handbook. If the error does not fall under any particular section, describe the cause of the error in your own words.

Among the most effective voices for nonviolent resistance and civil disobediance in the twentieth century have been

Mohandas Gandhi and Martin Luther King, Jr. Both were educated, middle-class men who found themselfs the objects of discrimination because of they're race. Gandhi first encountered racism when he visited South Africa around the turn of the century. After forcing the goverment to modify parts of the racial code in that country, he returned to his homeland, India, were he began a long quest to rid it of British rule. His succeses as well as his failures influenced a young minister from Georgia, Martin Luther King, Jr., who fiercely opposed segregation in the United States. King embraced Gandhi's warning that oppressed people must resist the temptation to answer violence with violence. They both beleived that once the oppressed resort to violence they become no better than their oppressors. King's success in eliminateing legally sanctioned segregation in the South, like Gandhi's success in freeing India from the British, is testamony to the effectiveness of non-violent resistence. It is ironic that these two apostles of peace died in the same way: victims of assassins' bullets.

27 Hyphens

27a Hyphenating a word at the end of a line

Unless the last word on a line would use up most of the right margin of your paper, do not divide it. If you must divide

---

CHECKLIST FOR HYPHENATING WORDS

Never divide single syllable or very short words.

  No we-alth, en-vy   **YES** wealth, envy

Always divide words only between syllables.

  No end-orse   **YES** en-dorse

Never leave or carry over only one or two letters.

  No a-live, he-li-cop-ter   **YES** alive, heli-copter

Always follow rules for double consonants.

  No ful-lness, omitt-ing   **YES** full-ness, omit-ting

---

a word, do not divide the last word on the first line of a paper, the last word in a paragraph, or the last word on a page.

27b Dividing words with prefixes

You can hyphenate a word with a prefix of three or more letters after the prefix rather than between other syllables. Some prefixes are always separated from the base word with a hyphen, whether or not they are divided at the end of a line.

CHECKLIST FOR USING HYPHENS TO ATTACH PREFIXES TO BASE WORDS

Always use hyphens when using the prefixes *all-, ex-, quasi-,* and *self-*.

all-inclusive   ex-husband

Always use hyphens when the main word is a proper name or number.

all-American   pre-1950

Always use hyphens when the main word is a compound.

anti-gun control

Always use hyphens when confusion in meaning or pronunciation can occur.

re-dress (meaning "dress again") rather than redress (meaning "set right")

27c Spelling compound words

A **compound word** consists of two or more words used together to form one word.

CHECKLIST FOR USING HYPHENS IN COMPOUND WORDS

Never use hyphens in open compounds that are written as two words.

cedar shingles, night shift

Never use hyphens in closed compounds that are written as one word.

handbook, toothache

Always use hyphens in hyphenated compounds.

tractor-trailer   nurse-practitioner

Always use hyphens in combined units of measurement.

light-years   kilowatt-hours

27d Using hyphens with spelled out numbers

Follow these guidelines for using hyphens with numbers.

CHECKLIST FOR USING HYPHENS IN NUMBERS

Always use a hyphen between the numerator and denominator of fractions.

three-hundredths (3/100)

Always use a hyphen between the two digits of double digit numbers from twenty-one through ninety-nine only.

thirty-five   two hundred thirty-five

EXERCISE 27-1

Write the correct form of the word in parentheses according to the way it is used in the sentence.

1. In (pre World War I) _____ America, a "red scare" gripped the nation.
2. Americans grew suspicious of foreigners, especially Slavs and (Eastern Europeans) _____.
3. (Anti Soviet) _____ feelings influenced every facet of American life.
4. The red scare coincided with the rise of (labor unions) _____.
5. Many people viewed the unions as part of a (Bolshevik inspired) _____ plot to (over throw) _____ the U.S. government.
6. While some of the unions were (semi independent) _____, many were branches of the Industrial Workers of the World, a socialist organization.
7. Often (pro and anti union) _____ forces met in violent confrontations.
8. Americans found themselves injuring and killing their (fellow citizens) _____.
9. During the Lawrence, Massachusetts, Bread and Roses strike in 1912, more than (twenty five) _____ people were injured in street fighting.
10. After the strike was over, the people of Lawrence organized a parade "for God and country," to show the world that they were patriotic, (God fearing) _____ Americans.

Six

USING
PUNCTUATION
AND
MECHANICS

When you use punctuation and mechanics according to currently accepted practice, you avoid errors that interfere with written communication. Part Six presents and explains the rules and conventions that readers have come to expect. As you use Chapters 28 through 38, remember that punctuation and mechanics are tools that help you deliver your meaning clearly to your readers.

28 End Punctuation

End punctuation consists of the **period,** (28a) the **question mark,** (28b) and the **exclamation point** (28c).

28a Using a period

Unless a sentence asks a direct question (28b) or issues a strong command or emphatic declaration (28c), it ends with a period.

STATEMENT	A journey of a thousand leagues begins with a single step.
	—Lao-Tsu
MILD COMMAND	Put a gram of boldness into everything you do.
	—Baltasar Gracían
INDIRECT QUESTION	They wondered how many attempts have been made to climb Mt. Everest. [A direct question would end in a question mark: *How many attempts have been made to climb Mt. Everest?*]

Most **abbreviations** call for periods, but some do not. See Chapter 37 for more information on abbreviations.

28b Using a question mark

Use a **question mark** after a direct question. A **direct question** asks a straightforward question. In contrast, an indirect question reports a question and ends with a period.

> How many attempts have been made to climb Mt. Everest? [An indirect question would be: *They wondered how many attempts had been made to climb Mt. Everest.*]

❖ PUNCTUATION ALERT: Do not combine a question mark with a comma, a period, or an exclamation point. ❖

> **No**   She asked, "How are you?."
> **Yes**   She asked, "How are you?"

Questions in a series are each followed by a question mark, whether or not each question is a complete sentence.
❖ CAPITALIZATION ALERT: When questions in a series are not complete sentences, you can choose whether or not to capitalize the first letter, as long as you are consistent in each piece of writing. ❖

> After the fierce storm had passed, the mountain climbers debated what to do next. Turn back? Move on? Rest for a while?

When a request is phrased as a question, it does not always require a question mark: *Would you please send me a copy.*

Always use words, not a question mark within parentheses (?) to communicate irony or sarcasm.

> **No**   Having the flu is a delightful (?) experience.
> **Yes**   Having the flu is as pleasant as almost drowning.

28c   Using an exclamation point

Use an **exclamation point** for a strong command or an emphatic declaration. A strong command gives a very firm order: *Look out behind you!* An emphatic declaration makes a shocking or surprising statement: *There's been an accident!*
❧ PUNCTUATION ALERT: Do not combine an exclamation point with a comma, a period, or a question mark. ❧

> **No**   "There's been an accident!," cried my mother.
>
> **Yes**   "There's been an accident!" cried my mother.

Avoid overusing exclamation points. Your choice of words should communicate the strength of your message. Reserve exclamation points for dialogue or—very rarely—for a short declaration within a longer passage.

> **No**   When we were in Nepal, we tried each day to see Mt. Everest! Each day, however, we failed to see it completely! Clouds defeated us! The summit never emerged from a heavy overcast!
>
> **Yes**   When we were in Nepal, we tried each day to see Mt. Everest, the world's highest mountain. But each day we failed to see it completely. Clouds defeated us! The summit never emerged from a heavy overcast.

Always use words, not an exclamation point in parentheses (!) to communicate amazement or sarcasm,

> **No**   At 29,141 feet (!), Mt. Everest is the world's highest mountain.
>
> **Yes**   At a majestically staggering 29,141 feet, Mt. Everest is the world's highest mountain.

EXERCISE 28-1

Insert needed periods and question marks. Consider inserting one exclamation point, if it seems appropriate to you. Delete any incorrect question marks or exclamation points.

During World War II, United States solders' mail was censored Specially trained people read the mail Many people wanted to know why this was necessary? The censors had to make sure that no military information was disclosed Return addresses often read "Somewhere in the Pacific Area" to keep strategic (!) positions secret Have you ever heard the story about the soldier who could not write his sweetheart for many months but finally had time He wrote he a long letter explaining the delay and telling her that he loved her very much All the woman received, however, was a tiny slip of paper that read: "Your boyfried is fine He loves you He also talks too much Sincerely, The Censor."

29 The Comma

29a Understanding the comma

The comma is the most frequently used mark of punctuation, occurring twice as often as all other marks of punctuation combined. Rules for comma use are many because the comma *must* be used in certain places, it *must not* be used in other places, and it is *optional* in still other places. The role of the comma is to group and separate sentence parts, helping to create clarity for readers. To help you sort through the various rules, a summary of the material in this chapter appears in the chart on the opposite page.

You might want to wait to check for your commas until you are revising (see 3c) and editing (see 3d). If as you are drafting you are in doubt about a comma, insert and circle it clearly so that you can go back to it later and think through whether it is correct.

Be wary of two practices that get inexperienced writers into trouble with commas: (1) As you are writing, do not insert a comma simply because you happen to pause to think before moving on. (2) As you reread your writing, do not insert commas according to your personal habits of pausing. Although a comma communicates a slight pause (except in dates and other conventional material), pausing is not a reliable guide for writ-

USES OF THE COMMA	
Comma before coordinating conjunction°* linking independent clauses°	Section 29b
Comma after an introductory clause°, phrase°, or word	Section 29c
Commas to separate items in a series	Section 29d
Commas to separate coordinate adjectives°	Section 29e
Commas to set off nonrestrictive° (nonessential) elements	Section 29f
Commas to set off parenthetical and transitional expressions°, contrasts, words of direct address°, and tag questions°	Section 29g
Commas with quoted words	Section 29h
Commas in dates, names, addresses, and numbers	Section 29i
Commas to clarify meaning	Section 29j
Commas misused or overused	Section 29k

ers, because people's breathing rhythms, accents, and thinking spans vary greatly.

29b
Using a comma before a coordinating conjunction that links independent clauses

The **coordinating conjunctions** *(and, but, or, nor, for, so,* and *yet)* can link independent clauses° to create **compound**

*Throughout this book, a degree mark (°) indicates a term that is defined in the book's Glossary.

sentences°. Use a comma before this use of a coordinating conjunction.

PATTERN FOR COMMAS WHEN COORDINATING CONJUNCTIONS LINK INDEPENDENT CLAUSES

	and	
	but	
	for	
Independent clause,	**or**	independent clause.
	nor	
	so	
	yet	

The sky was dark gray, **and** the air stilled ominously.

The March morning had just begun, **but** it looked like dusk.

Shopkeepers closed their stores early, **for** they wanted to get home.

When each independent clause contains only a few words, professional writers sometimes omit the comma before the co-ordinating conjunction: *The storm ended **and** life returned to normal.* You will never be wrong, and you avoid the risk of error, if you use a comma. ❖ COMMA CAUTION: Do not put a comma *after* a coordinating conjunction that links independent clauses. ❖

No	The sky was dark gray **and,** the air stilled ominously.
Yes	The sky was dark gray, **and** the air stilled ominously.

❖ COMMA CAUTION: To avoid creating a comma splice (see 16a), do not use a comma to separate independent clauses unless they are linked by a coordinating conjunction. ❖

No   Five inches of snow fell in two hours, one inch of ice built up when the snow turned to freezing rain.

YES   Five inches of snow fell in two hours, **and** one inch of ice built up when the snow turned to freezing rain.

When independent clauses° containing other commas are linked by a coordinating conjunction, you may use a semicolon before the coordinating conjunction (see 30b).

Because temperatures remained low all winter, the snow did not melt; **and** some people wondered when they would see grass again.

EXERCISE 29-1

Insert commas before coordinating conjunctions that link independent clauses. If a sentence is correct, circle its number.

EXAMPLE   Opinions of what constitutes good business management differ but most experts agree that the ability to make clear-cut decisions is crucial.

Opinions of what constitutes good business management differ, but most experts agree that the ability to make clear-cut decisions is crucial.

1. Harbridge House is a Boston-based firm that trains business managers but it also surveys management practices.

2. Harbridge House conducted a study of managers from large, blue-chip corporations and from small, lesser-known companies so the research results deserve close attention.

3. The 6,500 managers in the study came from over 100 diverse companies yet they shared an interest in improving not only themselves but also their firms.

4. Harbridge House used the innovative technique of soliciting opinions from the managers as well as from the managers' associates and subordinates.

5. The researchers felt that each manager would provide useful information and they also believed that the people working with each manager would contribute to a more complex yet more objective picture.

29c Using a comma after an introductory clause, phrase, or word

Use a comma to signal the end of an introductory element and the beginning of an independent clause°.

PATTERN FOR COMMAS WITH INTRODUCTORY ELEMENTS

■ Introductory clause,

■ Introductory phrase, ——————→ independent clause.

■ Introductory word,

Some professional writers omit the comma when an introductory element is very short, if they feel that the sentence is clear without a comma. This practice is not recommended for academic writing, however. You will never be wrong, and you avoid the risk of error, if you use a comma.

1 Using a comma after an introductory adverb clause

An **adverb clause** is a dependent clause (see 8f). It cannot stand alone as an independent unit because it starts with a subordinating conjunction° (for example, *although* and *be-*

cause; see 7g). When an adverb clause precedes an independent clause°, many writers separate the clauses with a comma.

> **When it comes to eating,** you can sometimes help yourself more by helping yourself less.
>
> —RICHARD ARMOUR

2 Using a comma after an introductory phrase

A **phrase** is a group of words that cannot stand alone as an independent unit (see 8e). When a phrase introduces an independent clause°, many writers separate the phrase from the clause with a comma.

> **Between 1544 and 1689,** sugar refineries appeared in London and New York. [prepositional phrase°]
>
> **Beginning in infancy,** we develop lifelong tastes for sweet and salty foods. [participial phrase°]

3 Using a comma after introductory words

Transitional expressions carry messages of a relationship between ideas in sentences and paragraphs. Transitional expressions include *for example* and *in addition* (for a complete list, see 5b-1). Conjunctive adverbs are transitional expressions that connect independent clauses. Conjunctive adverbs include *therefore* and *however* (for a complete list, see 7e). When these introductory words appear at the beginning of a sentence, many writers follow them with a comma.

> **For example,** fructose is fruit sugar, lactose is milk sugar, and maltose is malt sugar.

Interjections are introductory words that convey surprise or other emotions: *Oh, we did not realize that you are allergic to cats. Yes! Your sneezing worries me.*

EXERCISE 29-2

Insert commas where needed after introductory words, phrases, and clauses. If a sentence is correct, circle its number.

EXAMPLE   Although many people have seen Gilbert Stuart's paintings of George Washington few know the story behind this famous portrait.

Although many people have seen Gilbert Stuart's paintings of George Washington, few know the story behind this famous portrait.

(1) Called the "Athenaeum" portrait this painting of George Washington by Gilbert Stuart has appeared in many history textbooks as well as biographies of Washington. (2) In addition copies have hung on hundreds of classroom walls. (3) To see the original painting art lovers must go to the Museum of Fine Arts in Boston. (4) Noted for his choice of color and his skill in painting Gilbert Stuart is particularly admired for his understanding of human nature. (5) The "Athenaeum" is famous, but it was never officially finished by the artist. (6) In 1796 the portrait was commissioned by Martha Washington. (7) After Stuart painted it he decided not to deliver it to the president's wife. (8) In hopes of getting rich Stuart kept the picture and copied it repeatedly. (9) While he carried out his scheme Stuart never finished the background of the portrait. (10) Whenever Martha Washington inquired about the portrait Stuart could truthfully tell her that it was incomplete.

29d   Using commas to separate items in a series

A **series** is a group of three or more elements—words, phrases°, or clauses°—that match in grammatical form and in importance within the same sentence.

Marriage requires **sexual, financial, and emotional** discipline.

—ANNE ROIPHE, "Why Marriages Fail"

My love of flying goes back to those early days **of roller skates, of swings, of bicycles.**

—TERESA WIGGINS, student

We have been taught **that children develop by ages and stages, that the steps are pretty much the same for everybody, and that to grow out of the limited behavior of childhood,** we must climb them all.

—GAIL SHEEHY, *Passages*

Some professional writers omit the comma before the coordinating conjunction between the last two items of a series, but this practice is not recommended for academic writing. The absence of the comma can distort meaning and confuse a reader. If you never omit the comma, you will have more of a chance of avoiding an error.

When the items in a series contain commas or other punctuation, or when the items are long and complex, separate them with semicolons instead of commas (see 30d). This practice ensures that your sentence will deliver the meaning you intend.

If it's a bakery, they have to sell cake; if it's a photography shop, they have to develop films**; and** if it's a dry-goods store, they have to sell warm underwear.

—ART BUCHWALD, "Birth Control for Banks"

Numbered or lettered lists within a sentence are items in a series. Use commas (or semicolons if the items are long) to separate the items when the sentence contains three or more.

To file your insurance claim, please enclose (1) a letter requesting payment, (2) a police report about the robbery, and (3) proof of purchase of the items you say are missing.

❖ COMMA CAUTION: Do not use a comma before the first item or after the last item in a series unless a different rule makes it necessary. ❖

No	Many artists, writers, and composers, have indulged in daydreaming and reverie.
Yes	Many artists, writers, and composers have indulged in daydreaming and reverie.
No	Such dreamers include, Miró, Debussy, Dostoevsky, and Dickinson.
Yes	Such dreamers include Miró, Debussy, Dostoevsky, and Dickinson.

29e Using a comma to separate coordinate adjectives

Coordinate adjectives are two or more adjectives that equally modify a noun. Separate coordinate adjectives with commas (unless the coordinate adjectives are joined by a coordinating conjunction such as *and* or *but*). ✤ COMMA CAUTIONS: (1) Do not put a comma after a final coordinate adjective and the noun it modifies. (2) Do not put a comma between adjectives that are not coordinate. ✤

COORDINATE ADJECTIVES

The **large, restless** crowd waited for the concert to begin.

NONCOORDINATE ADJECTIVES

The concert featured **several new** bands.

If you are not sure whether adjectives need a comma between them, use the "Test for Coordinate Adjectives" below.

TEST FOR COORDINATE ADJECTIVES

1. Can the order of the adjectives be reversed without changing the meaning or creating nonsense? If yes, use a comma.

(continued on next page)

TEST FOR COORDINATE ADJECTIVES *(continued)*

> **No** The concert featured **new several** bands. (Only *several new* makes sense.)
>
> **Yes** The **large, restless** (or *restless, large*) crowd waited for the concert to begin.

2. Can the word *and* be inserted between the adjectives? If yes, use a comma.

> **No** The concert featured **new and several** bands.
>
> **Yes** The **large and restless** crowd waited.

EXERCISE 29-3

Insert commas to separate coordinate adjectives and items in a series. If a sentence needs no commas, circle its number.

EXAMPLE   A lively bright chimpanzee named Kanzi can communicate with humans.

A lively, bright chimpanzee named Kanzi can communicate with humans.

1. Kanzi communicates using a specially designed keyboard that is filled with complex geometric colorful symbols.
2. Kanzi was not taught how to use the sophisticated intricate system.
3. The bright curious young chimp quickly and efficiently learned on his own by watching his mother being taught.
4. Kanzi is an ideal subject because he has the most advanced linguistic abilities of any animal on record he is a cheerful alert student and he has a remarkable unending desire to learn.

5. Kanzi sometimes can be an exasperating stubborn student who teases his teachers by doing exactlu the opposite of what is asked, and he is not above giving his infant half-sister a sharp startling pinch if she is getting too much attention.

29f Using commas to set off nonrestrictive (nonessential) elements. Not setting off restrictive (essential) elements

Restrictive elements (also called *essential elements*) and **nonrestrictive elements** (also called *nonessential elements*) function as modifiers in sentences. Nonrestrictive (nonessential) elements are set off by commas.

PATTERN FOR COMMAS WITH NONRESTRICTIVE ELEMENTS

■ **Nonrestrictive element,** independent clause.
■ Beginning of independent clause, **nonrestrictive element,** end of independent clause.
■ Independent clause, **nonrestrictive element.**

Determining which sentence elements are nonrestrictive (nonessential) and therefore need commas, takes close rereading of your writing and patient analysis of the meaning of the material. The first step is to grasp the concept underlying nonrestrictive (nonessential). A nonrestrictive (nonessential) element provides information that is "extra." Although the extra information adds texture to the meaning of a sentence, a reader could still understand the meaning if the extra information were dropped. The next step is to know the patterns for commas with nonrestrictive (nonessential) elements.

Consider the following three sentences, each of which contains a nonrestrictive (nonessential) element.

> **An energetic man,** John Jones enjoys cooking. [Without knowing that John Jones is an energetic man, the reader can understand that John Jones enjoys cooking.]

> John Jones, **who raises his own vegetables,** enjoys cooking. [Without knowing that John Jones raises his own vegetables, the reader can understand that John Jones enjoys cooking.]

> John Jones enjoys cooking, **which his family appreciates.** [Without knowing about his family's appreciation, the reader can understand that John Jones enjoys cooking.]

You might wonder whether you should delete from a sentence any element that is not essential. No, many elements in sentences add texture to meaning and should be retained. Texture is added when the reader is told that John Jones is energetic, raises his own vegetables, and has a family that appreciates his enjoyment of cooking. Those pieces of information, therefore, should be retained. However, because they are not essential to the basic message of the sentence—John Jones enjoys cooking—they are nonrestrictive (nonessential) and therefore are set off by commas.

In contrast, a **restrictive element** is essential to meaning. ❖ COMMA CAUTION: A restrictive element is essential, not extra. Do not set it off with commas from the rest of the sentence. ❖

> Our neighbor **who raises his own vegetables** enjoys cooking. [The information about raising his own vegetables is essential because it identifies which of many neighbors is being discussed. The words *who raises his own vegetables* are restrictive and are not set off by commas.]

Vegetables **stir-fried in a wok** are uniquely crisp and flavorful. [The information about being stir-fried in a wok is essential because it identifies what is done to the vegetables to make them unique. The words *stir-fried in a wok* are restrictive and are not set off by commas.]

| 1 | Using commas to set off nonrestrictive (nonessential) clauses and phrases |

When **adjective clauses** are nonrestrictive (nonessential), set them off with commas. Adjective clauses usually begin with *who, whom, that,* or *which.*

NONRESTRICTIVE CLAUSE

Farming, **which is a major source of food production,** may not always be dependent on the weather. [*Farming* in this sentence is not meant to be limited by *which is a major source of food production,* so the information is not essential and commas are used.]

RESTRICTIVE CLAUSES

Much food **that is canned or frozen** is grown by the same large companies **that process it for consumption.** [The first restrictive clause limits the general word *food* to only food that is canned or frozen; the second one limits the large companies to only those that process the food for consumption. The information in both cases is essential, and so commas are not used.]

When **phrases** are nonrestrictive (nonessential), set them off with commas. A phrase is a group of related words without a subject, a predicate, or both.

NONRESTRICTIVE PHRASE

Farmers, **using pesticides and fertilizers,** try to enhance their crops' growth. [*Farmers* in this sentence is not meant to be limited by the phrase *using pesticides and fertilizers,* so the information is not essential and commas are used.]

RESTRICTIVE PHRASE

Farmers **retaining complete control over their land** are very hard to find these days. [The *farmers* in this sentence is meant to be limited to only those retaining complete control over their land, so the information is essential, and commas are not used.]

2	Using commas to set off nonrestrictive appositives

An **appositive** is a word or group of words that renames the noun or noun group preceding it. A **nonrestrictive appositive** is not essential for the identification of what it is renaming, so set it off by commas.

NONRESTRICTIVE APPOSITIVE

The agricultural scientist, **a new breed of farmer,** controls the farming environment.

Most appositives are nonrestrictive (nonessential). Once the name of something is given, words doing the renaming usually are not necessary to specify or limit the name even more. In some cases, however, appositives are restrictive (essential) and are not set off with commas.

341

Restrictive Appositive

The agricultural scientist Wendy Singh has helped develop a new fertilization technique. [The appositive *Wendy Singh* is essential for identifying which agricultural scientist from among all agricultural scientists. The information is essential, so the appositive is restrictive and is not set off with commas.]

EXERCISE 29-4

Using your knowledge of restrictive and nonrestrictive clauses and phrases, insert commas as needed.

EXAMPLE   Elena Piscopia who began to study Aristotle at the age of seven took the examination for her doctoral degree.

Elena Piscopia, who began to study Aristotle at the age of seven, took the examination for her doctoral degree.

1. Elena Piscopia a resident of Venice was the first woman to receive a doctoral degree.
2. Many university officials reflecting the beliefs of their time opposed Elena's goal of higher education.
3. The doctoral examination of a woman a unique phenomenon in 1678 drew crowds of curious spectators.
4. Elena Piscopia who had prepared carefully for her questioners completed the examination easily.
5. Her replies which were given entirely in Latin amazed her examiners with their clarity and brilliance.
6. Elena Piscopia's father who was an exceptionally enlightened man for his time supported and encouraged his daughter's education.
7. Other women who lived in the 1600s were not so lucky.
8. Christine de Pisane widowed at twenty-five turned to writing to support herself and her three children.

9. She found herself unprepared and taught herself a complete course of study which included Latin, history, philosophy, and literature.

10. She later wrote a book *The City of Ladies* about women leading creative lives.

29g Using commas to set off transitional and parenthetical expressions, contrasts, words of direct address, and tag questions

Conjunctive adverbs such as *however* and *therefore* (For a complete list, see 7g) and **transitional expressions** such as *for example* and *in addition* (for a complete list, see 5c-1) sometimes express connections within sentences. When they do, they are usually set off with commas.

> The American midwest, **therefore,** is the world's bread-basket.
>
> California and Florida are important food producers, **for example.**

Parenthetical expressions are "asides" They are additions to sentences that the writer thinks of as extra.

> A major drought, **sad to say,** reduces wheat crops drastically.

Expressions of contrast describe something by stating what it is not. They are set off with commas.

> We must work against world hunger continuously, **not only when emergencies develop.**

Words of **direct address** indicate the person or group spoken to. They are set off by commas.

> Join me, **brothers and sisters,** to end hunger.

Tag questions consist of a helping verb, a pronoun, and often the word *not,* generally contracted. Tag questions are set off by commas.

> Worldwide response to the Ethiopian famine was impressive, **wasn't it?**

29h Using commas to set off quoted words from explanatory words

Use a comma to set off quoted words from short explanations in the same sentence. This rule holds whether the explanatory words come before, between, or after the quoted words. ❖ CAPITALIZATION ALERT: Use a capital letter to start a quotation. When you interrupt a quotation in the middle of its sentence, do not resume the quotation with a capital letter (see 35c). ❖

PATTERNS FOR COMMAS WITH QUOTED WORDS

■ Explanatory words, "Quoted words."

■ "Quoted words," explanatory words.

■ "Quoted words begin," explanatory words, "quoted words continue."

> The poet William Blake wrote, "Love seeketh not itself to please."
>
> "My love is a fever," said William Shakespeare.
>
> "I love no love," proclaimed poet Mary Coleridge, "but thee."

❖ COMMA CAUTIONS (1) If explanatory words end with *that* immediately before quoted words, do not use a comma after *that*.

Shakespeare wrote that "My love is a fever."

(2) If you use indirect discourse° to paraphrase material, do not use a comma after *that*. ❖

Shakespeare wrote that his love felt like a fever.

29i Using commas in dates, names, addresses, and numbers according to accepted practice

---

RULES FOR COMMAS WITH DATES

1. Use a comma between the date and the year:
   July 20, 1969.
2. Use a comma between the day and the date:
   Sunday, July 20, 1969.
3. Within a sentence, use commas after the date *and* the year in a full date.

   > Everyone wanted to be near a television set on **July 20, 1969,** to watch Armstrong emerge from the lunar landing module.

4. Do not use a comma in a date that contains the month with only a day or the month with only a year. Also, do not use a comma in a date that contains only the season and year.

   > The major news story during **July 1969** was the moon landing; news coverage was especially heavy on **July 21.**

(continued on next page)

> **RULES FOR COMMAS WITH DATES** *(continued)*
>
> 5. An inverted date takes no commas within it or after it:
> **20 July 1969.**
>
>> On **20 July 1969** every TV station showed the landing.

> **RULES FOR COMMAS WITH NAMES, PLACES, AND ADDRESSES**
>
> 1. When an abbreviated title (Jr., M.D., Ph.D.) comes after a person's name, use a comma between the name and the title—**Rosa Gonzales, M.D.**—and also after the title if it is followed by the rest of the sentence:
>
>> The jury listened closely to the expert testimony of **Rosa Gonzales, M.D.,** last week.
>
> 2. When you invert a person's name, use a comma to separate the last name from the first: **Troyka, David.**
>
> 3. Use a comma between a city and state: **Philadelphia, Pennsylvania.** Within a sentence, use a comma after the state, as well:
>
>> The Liberty Bell has been on display in **Philadelphia, Pennsylvania,** for many years.
>
> 4. When you write a complete address as part of a sentence, use a comma to separate all the items, with the exception of the zip code. The zip code follows the state after a space without a comma, and the zip code is not followed by a comma.
>
>> I wrote to **Mr. U. Lern, 10-01 Rule Road, Englewood Cliffs, New Jersey 07632** for the instruction manual.

RULES FOR COMMAS WITH LETTERS

1. For the opening of an informal letter, use a comma. (The opening of a business or formal letter takes a colon.)
   Dear Betty,
2. For the close of a letter, use a comma:
   Sincerely yours,   **Love,**

RULES FOR COMMAS WITH NUMBERS

1. Counting from the right, put a comma after every three digits in numbers over four digits: **72,867**   **156,567,066**
2. In a number with four digits, a comma is optional for money, distance, amounts and most other measurements, as long as you are consistent within a piece of writing.
   $1776   **$1,776**
   1776 miles   **1,776 miles**
   1776 potatoes   **1,776 potatoes**
3. Do not use a comma for a four-digit year: **1990** (a year of five digits or more gets a comma: **25,000 B.C.**); in an address of four digits or more: **12161 Dean Drive;** or in a page number of four digits or more: **see page 1338.**
4. Use a comma to separate related measurements written as words: **five feet, four inches.**
5. Use a comma to separate a scene from an act in a play: **Act II, scene iv.**
6. Use a comma to separate a reference to a page from a reference to a line: **page 10, line 6.**

Using commas to clarify meaning

A comma is sometimes needed to clarify the meaning of a sentence, even though no other rule calls for one.

No   Those who can practice many hours a day.
Yes   Those who can, practice many hours a day.

No   George dressed and performed in front of the sellout crowd.
Yes   George dressed, and performed in front of the sellout crowd.

29k Avoiding misuse of the comma

1 Avoiding misuse or a comma with coordinating conjunctions

Section 29b discusses the correct use of commas with sentences joined by coordinating conjunctions°. Do not put a comma *after* a coordinating conjunction that joins two independent clauses°.

No   The sky was dark gray **and,** it looked like dusk.
Yes   The sky was dark gray, **and** it looked like dusk.

2 Avoiding misuse of commas to separate items

Section 29d discusses the correct use of commas with items in a series. Do not use a comma *before* the first or *after* the last item in a series, unless another rule makes it necessary.

Also, do not use commas to separate only two items joined with a coordinating conjunction.

> **No** The gymnasium was decorated with, **red, white, and blue** ribbons for the Fourth of July.
>
> **No** The gymnasium was decorated with **red, white, and blue,** ribbons for the Fourth of July.
>
> **Yes** The gymnasium was decorated with **red, white, and blue** ribbons for the Fourth of July.
>
> **No** **The moon, and the stars** were shining last night.
>
> **Yes** **The moon and the stars** were shining last night.

Section 29e discusses the correct use of commas with co-ordinate adjectives°. Do not put a comma after the final coordinate adjective and the noun it modifies. Also, do not use a comma between noncoordinate adjectives.

> **No** The **large, restless,** crowd waited.
>
> **Yes** The **large, restless** crowd waited.
>
> **No** The concert featured **several, new** bands.
>
> **Yes** The concert featured **several new** bands.

| 3 | Avoiding misuse of commas with restrictive elements |

Section 29f discusses the correct use of commas with restrictive (essential) and nonrestrictive (nonessential) elements. Do not use a comma to set off a restrictive (essential) element from the rest of a sentence.

> **No** Vegetables, **stir-fried in a wok,** are uniquely crisp and flavorful. [The information about being stir-fried in a wok is essential. It should not be set off with commas.]
>
> **Yes** Vegetables **stir-fried in a wok** are uniquely crisp and flavorful.

4 — Avoiding misuse of commas with quotations

Section 29h discusses the correct use of commas with quoted material. Do not use a comma to set off an indirect quotation.

No	John **said that, he likes stir-fried vegetables.**
Yes	John **said that he likes stir-fried vegetables.**
Yes	John **said, "I like stir-fried vegetables."**

5 — Avoiding use of a comma to separate a subject from its verb, a verb from its object, a verb from its complement, and a preposition from its object

No	**Orville and Wilbur Wright, made** their first successful airplane flights on December 17, 1903. [As a rule, do not let a comma separate a subject from its verb.]
Yes	**Orville and Wilbur Wright made** their first successful airplane flights on December 17, 1903.

No	These inventors enthusiastically **tackled, the problems** of powered flight and aerodynamics. [As a rule, do not let a comma separate a verb from its object°.]
Yes	These inventors enthusiastically **tackled the problems** of powered flight and aerodynamics.

No	Flying has **become, both** an important industry and a popular hobby. [As a rule, do not let a comma separate a verb from its complement°.]
Yes	Flying has **become both** an important industry and a popular hobby.

,

29k

No	Airplane hobbyists travel to Kitty Hawk's flight museum **from, all over the world.** [As a rule, do not let a comma separate a preposition° from its object.]
Yes	Airplane hobbyists travel to Kitty Hawk's flight museum **from all over the world.**

Because the comma occurs so frequently, advice against overusing it sometimes clashes with a rule requiring it. In such cases, follow the rule that calls for the comma.

The town of Kitty Hawk, North Carolina, attracts thousands of tourists each year. [Although the comma after *North Carolina* separates the subject and verb, it is required because a state is set off from a city and from the rest of the sentence; see 29j.]

EXERCISE 29-5

Insert commas where they are needed. If a sentence is correct, circle its number.

(1) Millard Fuller, executive director of Habitat for Humanity, believes that all people have a right to decent housing. (2) Habitat for Humanity an organization that depends on volunteer labor and donations of money and materials builds modest sturdy homes that are sold at cost to low-income families. (3) Previously these families had rented substandard housing without plumbing or heat. (4) The full cost of each Habitat home is approximately $28000. (5) To buy a home each family has to make a small down payment and support a mortgage. (6) The monthly mortgage payment is usually about $150 an amount less than the monthly rent that the family had been paying for their substandard housing. (7) Nevertheless Habitat for Humanity is not a charitable organization. (8) The families offered the homes must be able to take on the financial responsibility involved participate in the labor of building their house and donate time to help build other houses. (9) When

Fuller asks people to help he says "It's not your blue blood your pedigree or your college degree. (10) It's what you do with your life that counts." (11) One famous volunteer recruited to take on a yearly assignment is Jimmy Carter former President of the United States. (12) The concept of Habitat for Humanity is catching on for the number of new Habitat U.S. affiliates increased from 11 to 171 between 1980 and 1986. (13) Such a concept seems like an excellent way to fight poverty housing doesn't it?

30 The Semicolon

30a Using a semicolon between closely related independent clauses

When independent clauses are related in meaning, you can separate them with a semicolon instead of a period. A period signals complete separation between independent clauses; a semicolon tells readers that the separation is softer.

> This is my husband's second marriage; it's the first for me.
>
> —RUTH SIDEL, "Marion Deluca"

One or more of the clauses joined by a semicolon may contain a comma.

> It is rare for us to leave wild animals alive; when we do, we often do not leave them wild.
>
> —BRIGID BROPHY, "The Rights of Animals"

✤ COMMA CAUTION: Do not use only a comma between independent clauses, or you will create a comma splice (see Chapter 16). ✤

30b Using a semicolon before a coordinating conjunction joining independent clauses containing commas

When independent clauses are linked by a coordinating conjunction *(and, but, or, nor, for, yet, so),* you can use a comma. When one or more of the independent clauses contains a comma or commas, you can make your message clearer by using a semicolon before the coordinating conjunction.

> When the male peacock has presented his back, the spectator will usually begin to walk around him to get a front view; but the peacock will continue to turn so that no front view is possible.
>
> —FLANNERY O'CONNOR, "The King of the Birds"

30c Using a semicolon when conjunctive adverbs or other transitional expressions connect independent clauses

Use a semicolon between two independent clauses when the second clause begins with a conjunctive adverb (for a complete list, see 7e) or other transitional expression (for a complete list, see 5c-1).

> The average annual rainfall in Death Valley is about two inches; **nevertheless,** hundreds of plant and animal species survive and even thrive there.

❖ COMMA ALERTS: (1) Do not use only a comma between independent clauses connected by a conjunctive adverb or other words of transition, or you will create a comma splice; see 16a. (2) Use a comma *after* a conjunctive adverb or a transitional expression that begins an independent clause. (3) When you position a conjunctive adverb or a transitional expression somewhere after the first word in an independent clause, set it off with commas. ✤

30d Using a semicolon between long or comma-containing items in a series

When a sentence contains series of words, phrases°, or clauses°, commas usually separate the items from each other. When the items are long and contain commas for other purposes, use semicolons instead of commas to separate items.

> Functioning as assistant chefs, the students chopped onions, green peppers, and parsley; sliced chicken and duck meat into strips; started a delicious-smelling broth simmering; and filled a large, low, long-handled pan with oil before the head chef moved up to the stove.

30e Avoiding misuse of the semicolon

Do not use a semicolon between a dependent clause and an independent clause.

> Although the new computers had arrived at the college, the computer lab was still being built.

Use a colon, not a semicolon, to introduce a list (see 31a).

> The newscast featured three major stories: the latest pictures of Uranus, a speech by the president, and a series of brush fires in Nevada.

355

EXERCISE 30–1

Insert needed semicolons in the following sentences, and delete unnecessary ones.

1. The sound of Muzak has invaded our banks, supermarkets, and elevators, furthermore, it often assaults our ears when we are placed on hold on a busy telephone line.

2. Muzak plays in government offices, in the White House, in the Pentagon, in Congress, it played during the Olympics, and it even played in the Apollo XI spaceship that carried Neil Armstrong to the moon.

3. Not all listeners appreciate Muzak novelist Vladimir Nabokov, artist Ben Shann, and composer Philip Glass have used adjectives such as "horrible," "abominable," "offensive," and "tormenting" to describe it.

4. The Muzak system was the creation of an unusual general, George Owen Squier; a West Pointer who devoted much of his army career to science.

5. During World War I, Squier invented a system for transmitting several messages simultaneously over electric power lines, in the era following the war; he took his ideas and patents to the North American Company, a utilities combine.

EXERCISE 30–2

Combine each set of sentences into one sentence containing two independent clauses. Use a semicolon between the independent clauses. You may omit, add, revise, or rearrange words. More than one revision may be correct, so be ready to explain the reasoning behind your decisions.

EXAMPLE   Some people live by the clock on the wall. All of us are governed by internal clocks. These clocks regulate hundreds of biological functions.

Some people live by the clock on the wall; however, all of us are governed by internal clocks which regulate hundreds of biological functions.

1. Our inner clocks help determine our times of elation and depression. They also regulate our times of patience and irritability. Our inner clocks also regulate our precision and carelessness.

2. We need to understand how these clocks work. We need to know what they are. We need to know how they interact. We also need to know how they can be thrown off schedule.

3. Understanding these principles can help us to organize our lives. We will be able to maximize performance and pleasure. We will not waste energy fighting the body's natural inclinations.

4. Some valuable facts about the internal time clocks are already known. People are least likely to be alert, for example, after they have eaten lunch. In addition, calories consumed at breakfast are less likely to turn to body fat than those eaten at supper.

5. Many people find certain other facts useful. A high-protein breakfast enhances alertness. A high-carbohydrate supper helps induce sleep.

31 The Colon

31a Using a colon after an independent clause to introduce a list, an appositive, or a quotation

A colon can introduce a list, but only when the words before the colon are an independent clause°.

INTRODUCING LISTED ITEMS

If you really want to lose weight, you need give up only three things: breakfast, lunch, and dinner.

With phrases like *the following* or *as follows,* a colon is usually required. A colon is not called for with the words *such as* or *including* (see 31d).

The students' demands included the following: an expanded menu in the cafeteria, improved janitorial services, and more up-to-date textbooks.

INTRODUCING AN APPOSITIVE°

Nathan's in New York City sells the most delicious hot dogs: those world famous "Red-hots." [*"Red-hots"* renames *hot dogs.*]

INTRODUCING A QUOTATION

A colon can introduce a quotation, but only if the introductory words are an independent clause. Use a comma, not a colon, if the introductory words are not an independent clause°. (see 29c).

> E. B. White writes of his annual surge of interest in gardening: "We are hooked and are making an attempt to kick the habit."
>
> —MARIE WINN, *The Plug-In-Drug*

31b Using a colon between two independent clauses

When the first independent clause° explains or summarizes the second independent clause, a colon can separate them.

 CAPITALIZATION ALERT: You can use a capital letter or a lowercase letter for the first word of an independent clause° that follows a colon. Whichever you choose, be consistent in each piece of writing. ✤

> We will never forget the first time we made dinner at home together: He got stomach poisoning and was too sick to go to work for four days.
>
> —LISA BALADENDRUM, student

31c Using a colon to separate standard material

TITLE AND SUBTITLE

A Brief History of Time: From the Big Bang to Black Holes

HOURS, MINUTES, AND SECONDS

The track star passed the halfway point at 1:23:02.

CHAPTERS AND VERSES OF THE BIBLE

Psalms 23:1–3   Luke 3:13

MEMO FORM
To: Dean Kristen Olivero
From: Professor Daniel Black
Re: Student Work-Study Program

SALUTATION OF FORMAL OR BUSINESS LETTER
Dear Ms. Morgan:

For the use of colons in documenting sources, see 41c-41d.

31d Avoiding misuse of the colon

A complete independent clause° *must* precede a colon, except with standard material (see 31c). When you have not written an independent clause, do not use a colon.

No   The cook bought: eggs, milk, cheese, and bread.
YES   The cook bought eggs, milk, cheese, and bread.

The words *such as, including, like,* and *consists of* can be tricky: Do not let them lure you into using a colon incorrectly.

No   The health board discussed a number of problems, **such as:** poor water quality, an aging sewage treatment system, and the lack of an alternate water supply.
YES   The health board discussed a number of problems, **such as** poor water quality, an aging sewage treatment system, and the lack of an alternate water supply.
YES   The health board discussed a number of problems: poor water quality, an aging of the sewage treatment system, and the lack of an alternate water supply.

Do not use a colon to separate a dependent clause° from an independent clause.

No   After the drought ended: the farmers relaxed.
YES   After the drought ended, the farmers relaxed.

EXERCISE 31-1

Insert colons where they are needed. If a sentence is correct, circle its number.

EXAMPLE   Two characteristics aided Einstein in his work, his curiosity and his ability to concentrate.

Two characteristics aided Einstein in his work: his curiosity and his ability to concentrate.

1. One of Coney Island's greatest attractions is the Double Loop, among the world's largest roller coasters.

2. Among the forgers who have committed these crimes for hundreds of years, three continue to interest experts, William Henry Ireland, who forged a series of letters he claimed were written by Shakespeare; Hans Van Meegeren, who produced amazingly accurate copies of Jan Vermeer's paintings; and Clifford Irving, who convinced a New York publisher that he had been hired to ghost-write Howard Hughes's autobiography.

3. Writing about the problems of leadership, the historian Barbara Tuchman reaches this conclusion "As witnesses of the twentieth century's record, comparable to the worst in history, we have little confidence in our species."

4. The worst insurance risks in the United States include astronauts, drivers of hydroplanes, race drivers in the Indianapolis 500, and drivers in Grand Prix auto races.

5. Halley's comet made its predicted return in 1986, passing nearest to the sun on February 9, just before 1100 a.m. Greenwich mean time.

32 The Apostrophe

32a Using an apostrophe to form the possessive case of nouns and indefinite pronouns

The **possessive case** serves to communicate ownership or close relationship.

OWNERSHIP the writer's pen

CLOSE RELATIONSHIP the writer's mother

Possession in nouns° and certain indefinite pronouns° can be communicated in two ways: by phrases beginning with *of the* (*the comments of the instructor*) or by an apostrophe in combination with an *-s (the instructor's comments)*. Some writers prefer to avoid the possessive case with inanimate objects.

1 Adding *-'s* to show possession when nouns and indefinite pronouns do not end in *-s*

In one more year I will receive my **bachelor's** degree. [*bachelor* = singular noun° not ending in -s]

They care about their **children's** futures. [*children* = plural noun° not ending in -*s*]

The accident was really **no one's** fault. [*no one* = indefinite pronoun° not ending in -*s*]

| 2 | Adding -*'s* to show possession when singular nouns end in -*s* |

That **business's** system for handling complaints is inefficient.

Lee **Jones's** insurance is expensive.

When adding -*'s* leads to tongue-twisting pronunciation, practice varies. All writers use the apostrophe, but some writers do not add the -*s*. Other writers prefer to use the -*'s* for consistency with other possessives; the result is pronounced as it sounds in its singular form. This handbook uses -*'s*.

> Charles Dickens's story "A Christmas Carol" is a classic tale. [*Dickens's* is pronounced *Dickens,* without any attempt at two *z* sounds in a row.]

| 3 | Not adding -*'s* to show possession |

When a plural noun ends in -*s,* only the apostrophe is needed to show possesion.

> The **boys'** statements were printed in the newspaper.
> Three **months'** maternity leave is in the **workers'** contract.
> The newspapers have publicized several **medicines'** severe side effects.

| 4 | Adding -*'s* to the last word in compound words and phrases |

His **mother-in-law's** corporation is very successful.

They wanted to hear **someone else's** version of the story.

| 5 | Adding -'s to each noun in individual possession |

Olga's and Joanne's books are valuable. [Olga and Joanne each own valuable books, but they do not own the books together.]

| 6 | Adding -'s to only the last noun in joint or group possession |

Olga and Joanne's books are valuable. [Olga and Joanne own the books together.]

32b Not using an apostrophe with the possessive forms of personal pronouns

Some pronouns have specific possessive forms. Do not use an apostrophe with these forms.

PRONOUN	POSSESSIVE FORM(S)
he	his
she	her, hers
it	its [not *it's*]
we	our, ours
you	your, yours
they	their, theirs
who	whose [not *who's*]

32c Using an apostrophe to stand for omitted letters, numbers, or words in contractions

A **contraction** is a word in which an apostrophe signals that one or more letters have been omitted. Many readers dislike contractions in academic writing. To choose between a contraction and the full phrase, consider your audience and the level of formality you want.

SOME COMMON CONTRACTIONS

aren't = are not	*let's* = let us
can't = cannot	*there's* = there is
didn't = did not	*they're* = they are
don't = do not	*wasn't* = was not
it's = it is	*we're* = we are
I'd = I would, I had	*who's* = who is
I'm = I am	*won't* = will not
isn't = is not	*you're* = you are

32d Using an apostrophe to form plurals of letters, numerals, symbols, and words used as terms

Billie always has trouble printing **W**'s.

The address includes six **6**'s.

The *for*'s in the paper were all misspelled as *four*'s.

In some computer programs, a series of **&**'s on the monitor screen indicates a keyboard jam.

❖ UNDERLINING ALERT: Always underline letters as letters and words as words in typewritten or handwritten material. In printed material, they are set in italic type. ❖

```
Many first-graders have trouble making 8's.
```

For the plural form of years, two styles are acceptable: with an apostrophe (1990's) or without (1990s). Whichever form you prefer, use it consistently in each piece of writing. This handbook uses the form without the apostrophe.

32e   Avoiding misuse of the apostrophe

Do not overuse apostrophes by inserting them where they do not belong. This chart lists the major causes for apostrophe errors.

LEADING CAUSES OF APOSTROPHE ERRORS

1. Do not use an apostrophe with a present-tense° verb.

    No   Cholesterol **plays'** an key role in how long we live.
    Yes Cholesterol **plays** an key role in how long we live.

2. Do not add an apostrophe at the end of a nonpossessive noun° ending in -s.

    No   Medical **studies'** reveal that cholesterol is the primary cause of coronary heart disease.
    Yes Medical **studies** reveal that cholesterol is the primary cause of coronary heart disease.

3. Do not use an apostrophe before the -s in the possessive plural of a noun.

    No   Medical workers want to learn more from those **doctor's** investigations into heart disease.
    Yes Medical workers want to learn more from those **doctors'** investigations into heart disease.

4. Do not use an apostrophe to form a nonpossessive plural.

    No   **Team's** of doctors are trying to predict who might be most harmed by cholesterol.
    Yes **Teams** of doctors are trying to predict who might be most harmed by cholesterol.

EXERCISE 32-1

Correct any errors in the use of apostrophes in the paragraph below.

(1) One of Albert Einsteins biographers tells about the famous physicists encounter with a little girl in his' neighborhood. (2) The little girl stared at Einstein's soaking wet feet and said, "Mr. Einstein, youve come out without you'r boots again!" (3) Einstein laughed and, pulling up his trousers, replied, "Yes, and Ive forgotten my socks, too. (4) Most people arent as forgetful as Einstein, but sometimes our memories' let all of us down. (5) We may not be able to remember if our first job started in '81 or 82; we may forget whether our employers' husband spells his name with two *t*s or with one. (6) No one is absolutely sure how memory works. (7) Dr. Barbara Jones study of memory suggests that personality style's affect memory. (8) People with rigid personalities who's livelihoods depend on facts tend to have good memories. (9) Mr. Harry Lorayne and Dr. Laird Cermak's studies of memory each provide a different approach to improving that useful faculty. (10) Mr. Lorayne suggest's relating what you want to remember to something verbal or visual. (11) For instance, if you want to remember that your sister's-in-law's name is Rose, you would picture her wearing a rose corsage. (12) Dr. Cermaks suggestions include consideration of physiological factors. (13) He notes that doctors' are currently developing drugs that will prevent older people from losing the memories that are rightfully their's.

33 Quotation Marks

33a

33a Using quotation marks to enclose direct quotations of not more than four lines

Direct quotations are exact words copied from a print source or transcribed from a nonprint source.

When you quote the words of others in your writing, be sure to incorporate the quotations smoothly into your writing (see 39e) and avoid plagiarism (see 39a).

1 Using quotation marks to enclose short quotations

A quotation is considered "short" if it can be typed or handwritten to occupy no more than four lines on a page. Short quotations are enclosed in quotation marks. Longer quotations are not enclosed in quotation marks—they are **displayed.** A displayed quotation starts on a new line. In MLA style°, all type-written lines indent ten spaces; in APA style° typewritten lines indent five spaces. (In this chapter, MLA style for parenthetical documentation is used; see 41b.)

SHORT QUOTATIONS

Edward T. Hall explains the practicality of close
conversational distances: "If you are interested in
something, your pupils dilate; if I say something you
don't like, they tend to contract" (47).

Personal space "moves with us, expanding and
contracting according to the situation in which we
find ourselves" (Fisher, Bell, and Baum 149).

LONG QUOTATION

Robert Sommer, an environmental psychologist, uses
literary and personal analogies to describe personal
space:

> Like the porcupines in Schopenhauer's fable,
> people like to be close enough to obtain
> warmth and comradeship but far enough away to
> avoid pricking one another. Personal space
> . . . has been likened to a snail shell, a
> soap bubble, an aura, and "breathing room." (26)

| 2 | **Using single quotation marks for quotations within quotations** |

When you want to quote four lines or less and the original
words already contain quotation marks, use quotation marks at
the start and end of the directly quoted words. Then, substitute
single quotation marks ('   ') wherever double quotation
marks ("   ") occur in the original source.

ORIGINAL SOURCE

Personal space . . . has been likened to a snail shell, a soap bubble, an aura, and "breathing room."

—ROBERT SOMMER, *Personal Space*
The Behavioral Bases of Design, page 26

SINGLE QUOTATION MARKS WITHIN DOUBLE QUOTATION MARKS

Robert Sommer, an environmental psychologist, compares personal space to "a snail shell, a soap bubble, an aura, and 'breathing room' " (26).

If there are quotation marks in a quotation of more than four lines, display the quotation without enclosing it in quotation marks.

| 3 | Using quotation marks correctly for short quotations of poetry and for direct discourse |

A quotation of poetry is "short" if it is no more than three lines of the poem. Use quotation marks to enclose the material. If you quote more than one line of poetry, use a slash with one space on each side to indicate where each line ends (see 34e). ❖ CAPITALIZATION ALERT: When you quote lines of poetry, follow the capitalization of your source. ❖

As W. H. Auden wittily defined personal space, "some thirty inches from my nose / The frontier of my person goes."

When you write **direct discourse°**, use quotation marks at the beginning and end of a speaker's words. Start a new paragraph each time the speaker changes.

"I don't know how you can see to drive," she said.
"Maybe you should put on your glasses."
"Putting on my glasses would help you to see?"
"Not me; you," Macon said. "You're focused on the windshield instead of the road."

—ANNE TYLER, *The Accidental Tourist*

Do not to enclose indirect discourse in quotation marks.

DIRECT DISCOURSE

The mayor said, "I cannot attend the conference."

INDIRECT DISCOURSE

The mayor said that he could not attend the conference.

33b Using quotation marks to enclose certain titles

Use quotation marks around the titles of short published works, such as poems, short stories, essays, articles from periodicals, pamphlets, and brochures. Also use them around song titles and individual episodes of a television or radio series. ❖ ITALICS ALERT: Use underlining (for italics) for titles of longer works, such as books and plays, (see 36a). ❖

For the title of your own paper, do not use quotation marks on a title page, at the top of a page, or if you refer to the title within your paper (see 33d).

"Shooting an Elephant" describes George Orwell's experience in Burma. [essay]

33c Using quotation marks for words used in special senses or for special purposes

Technical terms can be put in quotation marks—and defined—the first time they are used. No quotation marks are needed once such terms have been introduced and defined.

"Plagiarism"—the unacknowledged use of another person's words or ideas—can result in expulsion. Plagiarism is a serious offense.

The translation of a word or phrase can be enclosed in quotation marks. (Underline all words or phrases that require translation.)

> My grandfather usually ended arguments with *de gustibus non disputandum est* ("there is no disputing about tastes").

Words referred to as words can be either enclosed in quotation marks or underlined. Follow consistent practice throughout each piece of writing. This handbook uses italics to indicate underlining.

> **Yes** Many people confuse "affect" and "effect."
>
> **Yes** Many people confuse *affect* and *effect.*

Words or phrases meant ironically or in another nonliteral sense can be enclosed in quotation marks.

> The proposed tax "reform" is actually a tax increase.

33d Avoiding misuse of quotation marks

Do not use quotation marks around language you sense is inappropriate to your audience (see 1c) or your purpose (see 1b). Take the time to revise so that you have accurate, appropriate, and fresh words.

> **No** They "eat like birds" in public, but they "stuff their faces" in private.
>
> **Yes** They hardly eat anything in public, but they feast on enormous amounts of food in private.

Do not enclose a word in quotation marks merely to call attention to it.

> **No** "Plagiarism" can result in expulsion.
>
> **Yes** Plagiarism can result in expulsion.

Do not use quotation marks to enclose the title of your paper at the top of a page or on a title page. The only exception is if the title of your paper refers to another title.

No   "The Elderly in Nursing Homes: A Case Study"

Yes   The Elderly in Nursing Homes: A Case Study

No   Character Development in Shirley Jackson's story The Lottery

Yes   Character Development in Shirley Jackson's story "The Lottery"

33e Using accepted practices for other punctuation with quotation marks

1 Placing commas and periods inside closing quotation marks

Because the class enjoyed F. Scott Fitzgerald's "The Freshest Boy," they were looking forward to his longer works.

Edward T. Hall coined the word "proxemics."

2 Placing colons and semicolons outside closing quotation marks

Aerobic instructors have to know "how much is too much": overexertion can be dangerous.

Some health clubs offer "low-impact aerobics"; others do not.

3 Placing question marks, exclamation points, and dashes inside or outside closing quotation marks, according to the context

If a question mark, exclamation point, or dash belongs

with the words enclosed in quotation marks, put that punctuation mark *inside* the closing quotation mark.

"Did I Hear You Call My Name?" was the winning song.

"I've won the lottery!" he shouted.

If a question mark, exclamation point, or dash belongs with words that are *not* included in quotation marks, put the punctuation *outside* the closing quotation mark.

Have you read Nikki Giovanni's poem "Knoxville, Tennessee"?

EXERCISE 33-1

Make the use of quotation marks correct in the following sentences.

1. Don't let anyone convince you that you can't fulfill your ambitions, warned the speaker, or you surely won't.
2. Almost everyone who has had to make a difficult choice in life can relate to Robert Frost's poem The Road Not Taken.
3. A snake gives Sherlock Holmes the clue that he needs to solve a puzzling murder in the mystery story The Speckled Band.
4. "Accept" and *except* sound enough alike to confuse many listeners.
5. The words that Emma Lazarus wrote, "Give me your tired, your poor, your huddled masses yearning to breathe Free", open the inscription on the Statue of Liberty.

34 Other Marks of Punctuation

This chapter explains the uses of the **dash** (see 34a), **parentheses** (see 34b), **brackets** (see 34c), **ellipsis** (see 34d), and the **slash** (see 34e).

34a Using the dash

The dash, or a pair of dashes, lets you interrupt a sentence's structure to add information. Such interruptions can fall in the middle or at the end of a sentence. Use dashes sparingly—if you do use them—so that their impact is not diluted by overexposure.

In typed papers, make a dash by hitting the hyphen key twice (--). Do not put a space before, between, or after the hyphens. In print, the dash is an unbroken line that is approximately the length of two hyphens joined together (—). In handwritten papers, make a dash slightly longer than a hyphen, using one unbroken line (— —).

 1 Using a dash or dashes to emphasize an example, a definition, an appositive, or a contrast

EXAMPLE

The care-takers—those who are helpers, nurturers, teachers, mothers—are still systematically devalued.

—ELLEN GOODMAN, "Just Woman's Work?"

DEFINITION

Although the emphasis at the school was mainly language—speaking, reading, writing—the lessons always began with an exercise in politeness.

—ELIZABETH WONG, *Fifth Chinese Daughter*

APPOSITIVE°

Two of the strongest animals in the jungle are vegetarians—the elephant and the gorilla.

—DICK GREGORY, *The Shadow that Scares Me*

CONTRAST

Tampering with time brought most of the house tumbling down, and it was this that made Einstein's work so important—and controversial.

—BANESH HOFFMANN, "My Friend, Albert Einstein"

2 Using a dash or dashes to emphasize an "aside"

"Asides" are writers' comments within the structure of a sentence or a paragraph. In writing meant to seem objective, asides help writers convey their personal views. Consider your purpose (see 1b) and audience (see 1c) when deciding whether to insert an aside.

Television showed us the war. It showed us the war in a way that was—if you chose to watch television, at least—unavoidable.

—NORA EPHRON, *Scribble Scrabble*

❖ PUNCTUATION ALERTS: (1) If the words within a pair of dashes would take a question mark or an exclamation point if they were a separate sentence, use that punctuation before the second dash. *A first date—do you remember?—stays in the memory forever.* (2) Do not use commas, semicolons, or periods next to dashes. When such a possibility comes up, revise to avoid it. ❖

 Using parentheses

Parentheses allow writers to interrupt a sentence's structure to add information of many kinds. Parentheses are like dashes in this function of setting off extra or interrupting words. Unlike dashes, which tend to make interruptions stand out, parentheses tend to deemphasize what they enclose.

Use parentheses sparingly, because their overuse can be very distracting for readers.

> The books and journals (and tapes, filmstrips, even the people you want to interview) are all too often unavailable when you are ready.

1 | Using parentheses to enclose interrupting words

EXPLANATION

In *division* (also known as *partition*) a subject commonly thought of as a single unit is reduced to its separate parts.

—DAVID SKWIRE, *Writing with a Thesis*

EXAMPLE

Though other cities (Dresden, for instance) had been utterly destroyed in World War II, never before had a single weapon been responsible for such destruction.

—LAURENCE BEHRENS and LEONARD J. ROSEN,
Writing and Reading Across the Curriculum

ASIDE

A great number of students suffer from "math anxiety" (although most of these students earn high grades in math).

—AILEEN MARY MORGAN, student

2 Using parentheses for certain numbers and letters of listed items

When you number listed items within a sentence, enclose the numbers (or letters) in parentheses. ❖ PUNCTUATION ALERTS: (1) Use a colon before a list only if the list is preceded by an independent clause; see 31b. (2) You can use commas or semicolons to separate items in a list that falls within a sentence as long as you are consistent within a piece of writing. ❖

> Four items are on the agenda for tonight's meeting: (1) current membership figures, (2) current treasury figures, (3) the budget for renovations, and (4) the campaign for soliciting additional public contributions.

3 Using other punctuation with parentheses

Do not put a **comma** before an opening parenthesis even if what comes before the parenthetical material requires a comma.

No   Although clearly different from my favorite film, *(The Wizard of Oz) Gone with the Wind* is an important film and one worth studying.

Yes   Although clearly different from my favorite film *(The Wizard of Oz), Gone with the Wind* is an important film and one worth studying.

You can use a **question mark** or an **exclamation point** with parenthetical words that occur within the structure of a sentence.

> Looking for clues (what did we expect to find?) wasted four days.

A complete sentence enclosed in parentheses sometimes stands alone and sometimes falls within the structure of another sentence. Those that stand alone start with a capital and end with a period. Those that fall within the structure of another sentence do not start with a capital and do not end with a period.

No   Looking for his car keys (he had left them at my sister's house.) wasted an entire hour.

Yes   Looking for his car keys wasted an entire hour. (He had left them at my sister's house.)

Yes   Looking for his car keys (he had left them at my sister's house) wasted an entire hour.

34c Using brackets

Use brackets to enclose words you insert into quotations. To blend quoted words smoothly into a sentence (see 39e), you may have to change a word or two in the quotation to fit it into the structure of your sentence. Enclose any changes you make in square brackets. (In the examples, MLA style of parenthetical documentation is used; see 41b.)

ORIGINAL SOURCE

Surprisingly, this trend is almost reversed in Italy, where males interact closer and display significantly more contact than do male/female dyads and female couples.

—ROBERT SHUTER, "A Field Study of Nonverbal Communication in Germany, Italy, and the United States," page 305

QUOTATION WITH BRACKETS

Although German and American men stand farthest apart and touch each other the least, Shuter reported "this trend [to be] almost reversed in Italy" (305).

Enclose your words in brackets if you need to add explanations and clarifications to quoted material.

ORIGINAL SOURCE

This sort of information seems trivial, but it does affect international understanding. Imagine, for example, a business conference between an American and an Arab.

—CHARLES G. MORRIS, *Psychology: An Introduction,* page 516

QUOTATION WITH BRACKETS

"This sort of information [about personal space] seems trivial, but it does affect international understanding" (Morris 516).

Now and then you may find that an author or a typesetter has made a mistake in something you want to quote—a wrong date, a misspelled word, an error of fact. You cannot change another writer's words, but you want your readers to know that you did not make the error. To show that you see the error, insert the Latin word *sic* in brackets, right after the error. Meaning "so" or "thus," *sic* in brackets says to a reader, "It is thus in the original."

The construction supervisor points out one unintended consequence of doubling the amount of floor space: "With that much extra room per person, the tennants [*sic*] would sublet."

34d Using the ellipsis

An **ellipsis** is a set of three spaced dots (use the period key when typing). Its most important function is to show that you have left out some of the original writer's words in material you are quoting. When an ellipsis takes the place of one or more sentences, use four dots to show the period and then the ellipsis.

ORIGINAL SOURCE

Personal space is not necessarily spherical in shape, nor does it extend equally in all directions. (People are able to tolerate closer presence of a stranger at their sides than directly in front.) It has been likened to a snail shell, a soap bubble, an aura, and "breathing room."

—ROBERT SOMMER, *Personal Space:*
The Behavioral Bases of Design, page 26

QUOTATION WITH WORDS IN A SENTENCE OMITTED

Sommer says, "It has been likened to . . . 'breathing room.' "

QUOTATION WITH SENTENCE OMITTED

Sommer uses similes to define its dimensions: "Personal space is not necessarily spherical in shape. . . . It has been likened to a snail shell, a soap bubble, an aura, and 'breathing room' " (26).

34e Using the slash

1 Using the slash to separate lines of quoted poetry

To quote more than three lines of a poem, display the poetry as you would a prose quotation of more than four lines (see 33a). For three lines or less of poetry, use a sentence format and enclose the lines in quotation marks, with a slash to divide one line of poetry from the next. Leave a space on each side of the slash.

Consider the beginning of Anne Sexton's poem "Words": "Be careful of words, / even the miraculous ones."

2 **Typing the slash for numerical fractions**

If you have to type numerical fractions that are not on your keyboard, do this: Use the slash to separate the numerator and denominator and use a hyphen to tie a whole number to its fraction: *1/16, 1-2/3* (for using spelled-out and numerical forms of numbers, see Chapter 38).

3 **Using the slash for *and/or***

Try not to use word combinations like *and/or* for writing in the humanities. In academic disciplines where their use is acceptable, separate the words with a slash. Leave no space before or after the slash.

EXERCISE 34-1

Supply needed dashes, parentheses, brackets, and slashes as they should appear in written form. In some sentences you can choose between dashes and parentheses; when you make your choice, be ready to explain it.

EXAMPLE   Every year in the United States, four times the amount of money spent on baby food is spent on pet food $1.5 billion.

Every year in the United States, four times the amount of money spent on baby food is spent on pet food ($1.5 billion).

1. Albert Einstein's last words they were spoken in his native German will never be known because his attending nurse spoke only English.

2. During one five-week span in 1841, three different men served as President of the United States: 1 Martin Van Buren finished his term on March 3; 2 William Henry Harrison Van Buren's successor was inaugurated on March 4; and 3 John Tyler assumed the Presidency when Harrison died on April 6 after only thirty-two days in office.

3. We are required to memorize Shakespeare's sonnet that begins with these two lines: "Shall I compare thee to a summer's day? Thou art more lovely and more temperate."

4. The American portrait artist Charles Wilson Peale made George Washington an innovative set of dentures elks' teeth set in lead.

5. The letter from the factory's Personnel Department said, "Your *sic* requested to report to work next Monday."

35 Capitals

35a Capitalizing the first word of a sentence

Always capitalize the first letter of the first word in a sentence: *Records show that four inches of snow fell last year.* Practice varies for using a capital letter to start each question in a series of questions. Whichever practice you choose, be consistent throughout a piece of writing. Of course, if the questions are complete sentences, start each with a capital letter.

YES   What facial feature would most people change if they could? Their eyes? Their ears? Their mouth?

YES   What facial feature would most people change if they could? their eyes? their ears? their mouth?

Practice also varies for using a capital letter for a complete sentence following a colon (see 31b). Whichever practice you choose, be consistent throughout a piece of writing. This handbook uses a capital letter.

A complete sentence enclosed in parentheses sometimes stands alone and sometimes falls within the structure of another sentence. Those that stand alone start with a capital letter and end with a period. Those that fall within the structure of another sentence do not start with a capital letter and do not end with a period.

> I did not know till years later that they called it the Cuban Missile Crisis. But I remember Castro. (We called him Castor Oil and were awed by his beard.) We might not have worried so much (what would the Communists want with our small New Hampshire town?) except that we lived 10 miles from an air base.

To use capital letters when you quote lines of poetry, follow the practice of the version you are quoting from. (For advice on formats for quoted poetry, see 33a-1.)

35b Capitalizing listed items correctly

When the items in a run-in list are complete sentences, capitalize the first letter of each item. When the items in a run-in list are not complete sentences, do not begin them with capital letters. (For capitals in a formal outline, see 2n.)

> We found three reasons for the delay: (1) Bad weather held up delivery of raw materials. (2) Poor scheduling created confusion and slowdowns. (3) Lack of proper machine maintenance caused an equipment failure.

> The reasons for the delay were (1) bad weather, (2) poor scheduling, and (3) equipment failure.

35c Capitalizing the first letter of an introduced quotation

If you have made quoted words part of the structure of your own sentence, do not capitalize the first quoted word.

Mrs. Cousteau says that when students visit a country whose language they are trying to learn, they "absorb a good accent with the food."

If the words in your sentence serve only to introduce quoted words or if you are directly quoting speech, capitalize the first letter of the quoted words if it is capitalized in the original.

Mrs. Cousteau says, "Students should always visit a country when they want to learn its language. They'll absorb a good accent with the food."

Do not capitalize a one-sentence quotation that you continue within your sentence, and do not capitalize a partial quotation.

"Persistence," says my supervisor, "is more important than quickness for this task."

Winking, she encouraged me nevertheless to try "very speedy persistence."

For full coverage of quotation marks, see Chapter 33.

35d Capitalizing nouns and adjectives according to standard practice

Capitalize **proper nouns** *(Mexico, Rome)*. Also capitalize **proper adjectives** *(a Mexican festival, the Roman legions)*. Do not capitalize articles *(the, a, an)* in front of proper nouns or proper adjectives. ✤ CAPITALIZATION ALERT: A proper noun or adjective sometimes takes on a "common" meaning, losing its very specific "proper" associations. When this happens, the word loses its capital letter as well. Examples include *french fries, italics, pasteurize.* ✤

Many common nouns are capitalized when names or titles are added to them. For example, *lake* is not ordinarily capitalized, but when a specific name is added, it is: *Lake Ontario.*

Here is a Capitalization Guide to consult. Apply what you find in it to similar items not listed.

CAPITALIZATION GUIDE

	CAPITALS	**LOWER-CASE LETTERS**
NAMES	Mother Teresa	my mother (*relationship*)
TITLES	President Truman	a president
	the President (*now in office*)	
	Democrat (*a party member*)	democrat (*a believer in democracy*)
	Representative Jane Doe	the congressional representative
	Senator Dole	the senator
	Professor Roberts	the professor
	Queen Elizabeth II	the queen
GROUPS OF HUMANITY	Caucasian (*race*)	white (*also* White)
	Negro (*race*)	black (*also* Black)
	Oriental (*race*)	
	Muslim	
	Jewish	
ORGANIZATIONS	Congress	congressional
	the Ohio State Supreme Court	the state supreme court
	the Republican Party	the party
	Wang Corporation	the corporation
PLACES	Los Angeles	
	India	
	the South (*a region*)	turn south (*a direction*)
	Main Street	the street
	Atlantic Ocean	the ocean
	Orinoco River	the river

(continued on next page)

CAPITALIZATION GUIDE *(continued)*

	CAPITALS	LOWER-CASE LETTERS
BUILDINGS	Lee High School China West Cafe the Capitol (in Washington, D.C.)	the high school the restaurant the state capitol
SCIENTIFIC TERMS	Earth (*the planet*) the Milky Way *Streptococcus aureus* Newton's law	the earth (*where we live*) the moon the sun the galaxy a streptococcal infection the theory of gravity
LANGUAGES, NATIONALITIES	Spanish Chinese	
SCHOOL COURSES	Chemistry 342 my English class	a chemistry course a literature course
NAMES OF THINGS	the *St. Louis Post-Dispatch* *Time* Purdue University Heinz Ketchup the Dodge Colt	the newspaper the magazine the university ketchup the car
SEASONS AND TIME NAMES	Friday August	spring, summer, fall, autumn, winter

(continued on next page)

CAPITALIZATION GUIDE *(continued)*

	CAPITALS	**LOWER-CASE LETTERS**

HISTORICAL PERIODS	World War II
	the Great
	    Depression (*in
	    the 1930s*)
	the Reformation
		the war
		the depression
		    (*any economic
		    downturn*)
		an era, an age
		the eighteenth
		    century
		fifth-century
		    manuscripts
		the civil rights
		    movement

RELIGIOUS TERMS	God Buddhism the Torah the Koran the Bible	a god, a goddess
LETTER PARTS	Dear Ms. Tauber: Sincerely yours,	
TITLES OF WORKS	"The Lottery" *Grapes of Wrath*	the play the novel
COMPOUND WORDS	post-Victorian Italian-American Indo-European	
ACRONYMS AND INITIALISMS	IRS FBI AFL-CIO IBM NAACP CUNY	

EXERCISE 35-1

Add, retain, or delete capital letters as needed.

1. What is the most common item in a family medicine chest? Is it aspirin? adhesive bandages? A thermometer? an antibacterial agent?

2. "I don't care what you do, my dear," the actress mrs. Patrick Campbell is supposed to have said, "as long as you don't do it in the street and frighten the horses!"

3. The book that has sold the most copies of any book throughout the world is the bible.

4. I registered for biology 101 and history 121, but the courses I wanted in psychology and in art were filled.

5. Researchers at the institute for policy studies of harvard university discovered that the following jobs are considered most boring by those who hold them: (1) assembly line workers, (2) elevator operator, (3) pool typist, (4) Bank Guard, (5) Housewife.

36 Italics

In printed material, **roman type** is the standard; type that slants to the right is called **italic.** Words in italics indicate material that is underlined when typewritten or written by hand.

HANDWRITTEN *Catch 22*

TYPED Catch 22

TYPESET *Catch 22*

36a Using standard practice for underlining titles and other words, letters, or numbers

Use the following chart as a guide to underlining.

GUIDE TO UNDERLINING

TITLES	
UNDERLINE	**DO NOT UNDERLINE**
The Bell Jar [a novel]	
Death of a Salesman [a play]	

(continued on next page)

GUIDE TO UNDERLINING *(continued)*

UNDERLINE	**DO NOT UNDERLINE**
<u>Collected Works of</u> <u>O. Henry</u> [a book]	"The Last Leaf" [one story in the book]
<u>Simon & Schuster</u> <u>Handbook Concise</u> [a book]	"Writing Paragraphs" [one chapter in the book]
<u>Contexts for</u> <u>Composition</u> [a collection of essays]	"Science and Ethics" [one essay in the collection]
<u>The Iliad</u> [a long poem]	"Nothing Gold Can Stay" [a short poem]
<u>The African Queen</u> [a film]	

the <u>Los Angeles Times</u> [a newspaper. Note: Even if *The* is part of the title printed on a newspaper, do not use a capital letter and do not underline it in your paper. In documentation°, omit the word *The*.]

<u>Scientific American</u> [a magazine]	"The Molecules of Life" [an article in a magazine]
<u>The Barber of Seville</u> [title of an opera]	Concerto in B–flat Minor
<u>Symphonie Fantastique</u> [title of a long musical work]	[identification of a musical work by form, number, and key. Use neither quotation marks *nor* underlining.]
<u>Twilight Zone</u> [a television series]	"Terror at 30,000 Feet" [an episode of a television series]
<u>The Best of Bob Dylan</u> [a record album or a tape]	"Mr. Tambourine Man" [a song or a single selection on an album or a tape]

(continued on next page)

GUIDE TO UNDERLINING *(continued)*

OTHER WORDS

UNDERLINE	DO NOT UNDERLINE
the <u>Intrepid</u> [a ship; don't underline preceding initials like U.S.S. or H.M.S.] <u>Voyager 2</u> [names of specific aircraft, spacecraft, and satellites]	aircraft carrier [a general class of ship] Boeing 747 [general names shared by classes of aircraft, spacecraft, and satellites]
<u>summa cum laude</u> [term in a language other than English]	burrito, chutzpah [widely used and commonly understood words from languages other than English]
What does <u>our</u> imply? [a word referred to as such]	
the <u>abc</u>'s; confusing <u>3</u>'s and <u>8</u>'s [letters and numbers referred to as themselves]	

36b Underlining sparingly for special emphasis

Professional writers sometimes use italics to clarify a meaning or stress a point.

Many people we *think* are powerful turn out on closer examination to be merely frightened and anxious.

—MICHAEL KORDA, *Power!*

Try not to rely on underlining to deliver impact. In academic writing, rely on your choice of word and sentence structures to convey emphasis.

EXERCISE 36-1

Cross out unneeded underlining and quotation marks and add needed underlining.

1. The first rule in an old book about <u>rules of etiquette</u> reads, "Do not eat in mittens."
2. When he originated the role of <u>Fonzie</u> in the television series "Happy Days," Henry Winkler earned about $750 per episode.
3. The Monitor and the Merrimac were the first iron-hulled ships to engage in battle.
4. <u>Iowa's</u> name comes from the Indian word <u>ayuhwa</u>, which means "sleepy ones."
5. The New York Times does not carry comic strips.
6. Judy Garland was the second-lowest-paid star in the film classic The Wizard of Oz; only the dog who portrayed <u>Toto</u> was paid less.
7. For distinguished accomplishments of people over age 70, we should look to Verdi, who wrote the song "<u>Ave Maria</u>" at age 85, and Tennyson, who wrote the short poem "<u>Crossing the Bar</u>" at age 80.
8. Handwriting experts say personality traits affect the way an individual dots an i and crosses a t.
9. The <u>Italian</u> word <u>ciao</u> is both a greeting and a farewell.
10. A sense of danger develops slowly in Shirley Jackson's short story <u>The Lottery</u>.

37 Abbreviations

37a Using abbreviations with numbers and symbols

Some abbreviations are standard in all writing circumstances. In some situations, you can choose whether to abbreviate or spell out a word. When choosing, consider your purpose for writing (see 1b) and your audience (see 1c). Then be consistent in each piece of writing. ❖ PUNCTUATION ALERT: When the period of an abbreviation falls at the end of a sentence, the period serves also to end the sentence. ❖

TIME

The abbreviations a.m. (A.M.) and p.m. (P.M.) can be used only with exact times, such as *7:15 A.M., 7:15 a.m.; 3:47 P.M., 3:47 p.m.* You can use capital or lower case letters, but be consistent in each piece of writing. ❖ USAGE ALERT: Use *a.m.* and *p.m.* only with numbers indicating time. Do not use them instead of *morning, evening,* and *night.* ❖

In abbreviations for years, A.D. precedes the year: *A.D. 977.* Conversely, B.C. (or B.C.E.) follows the year: *12 B.C.*

SYMBOLS

Symbols are seldom used in the body of papers written for courses in the humanities. You can use a percent symbol (%) or a cent sign (¢) in a table, graph, or other illustration, but in the body of the paper spell out *percent* and *cent.* You can use a dollar sign with specific dollar amounts: *$23 billion, $7.85.* When choosing, let common sense and your readers' needs guide you. If you mention temperatures once or twice in a paper, spell them out: *ninety degrees, minus twenty-six degrees.* If you mention temperatures throughout a paper, use figures and symbols: *90°, −26°.*

37b Using abbreviations with titles, names and terms, and addresses

TITLES

Use either a title of address before a name: *Dr. Daniel Gooden* or an academic degree after a name: *Daniel Gooden, Ph.D.* Do not use both.

NAMES AND TERMS

If you use a long name or term frequently in a paper, you can abbreviate it using these guidelines: The first time, give the full term, with the abbreviation in parentheses immediately after the spelled-out form. After that you can use the abbreviation alone.

> Spain voted to continue as a member of the North Atlantic Treaty Organization (NATO), to the surprise of other NATO members.

You can abbreviate *U.S.* as a modifier *(the U.S. ski team),* but spell out *United States* when you use it as a noun.

| **No** | The U.S. has many different climates. |
| **YES** | The United States has many different climates. |

ADDRESSES

If you include a full address—street, city, and state—in the body of a paper, you can use the state abbreviation for the state name, but spell out any other combination of a city and a state or a state by itself. (Use a comma before *and* after the state.)

No   The Center for Disease Control in **Atlanta, GA,** sometimes quarantines livestock.

YES   The Center for Disease Control in **Atlanta, Georgia,** sometimes quarantines livestock.

EXERCISE 37-1

Make needed changes so that abbreviations are used correctly.

1. The first swim across the Eng. Channel took twenty-one hrs., forty-five mins.

2. According to most drs., the best places in the U.S. for allergy sufferers to live in are the deserts of AZ.

3. Many coll. students today are required to take courses in lit., soc. sci., and lang.

4. It seems ironic that the paintings of Vincent van Gogh, who died penniless, now sell for millions of $.

5. At fifty mins. before the liftoff, the Sat. launch was postponed for the next a.m.

38 Numbers

38a Using spelled-out numbers

Depending on how often numbers occur in a paper and what they refer to, you will sometimes express the numbers in words and sometimes in figures. The guidelines here, like those in the *MLA Handbook for Writers of Research Papers,* Third Edition, are suitable for writing in the humanities. For the guidelines other disciplines follow, consult other style manuals (see 41g).

If conveying numerical exactness to your readers is not a prime purpose in your paper, and if you mention numbers only a few times, spell out numbers that can be expressed in one or two words: *Iceland's population increases by more than **one** percent a year, but that gain translates into fewer than **three thousand** individuals.* ❖ HYPHENATION ALERT: Use a hyphen between spelled-out two-word numbers from *twenty-one* through *ninety-nine.* (see 27d) ❖

If you use numbers fairly frequently in a paper, spell out numbers from *one* to *nine* and use figures for numbers *10* and above. Never start a sentence with a figure. If a sentence starts *num* 38b

with a number, spell it out. In practice, you can usually revise a sentence so that the number does not come first.

> Three hundred seventy-five dollars per credit is the tuition rate for nonresidents.
>
> The tuition rate for nonresidents is $375 per credit.

Do not mix spelled-out numbers and figures in a paper when they both refer to the same thing. Use figures for all the numbers.

No   In four days, our volunteers increased from five to eight to 17 to 233.

Yes   In four days, our volunteers increased from 5 to 8 to 17 to 233. [All the numbers referring to volunteers are given in figures, but *four* is still spelled out because it refers to a different quantity—days.]

38b Using numbers according to standard practice

Standard practice requires figures for numbers in the cases covered in the chart below.

GUIDE FOR USING SPECIFIC NUMBERS	
DATES	August 6, 1941 1732–1845 34 B.C. to A.D. 230
ADDRESSES	10 Downing Street 237 North 8th Street Export Falls, MN 92025
TIMES	8:09 A.M.; 10:20 A.M. 3:30 p.m.; 6:00 P.M.; *six o'clock,* not *6 o'clock;* 4 P.M. or four in the afternoon, not four P.M.

(continued on next page)

GUIDE FOR USING SPECIFIC NUMBERS *(continued)*

DECIMALS AND FRACTIONS	5.55; 98.6; 3.1416; 7/8; 12-1/4 three quarters, not 3 quarters
CHAPTERS AND PAGES	Chapter 27, page 245
SCORES AND STATISTICS	a 6–0 score; a 5 to 3 ratio; 29 percent
IDENTIFICATION NUMBERS	94.4 on the FM dial; call 1-212-555-XXXX
MEASUREMENTS	2 feet; 67.8 miles per hour; 1.5 gallons; 8-1/2″ × 11″ paper or 8-1/2 × 11-inch paper
ACT, SCENE, AND LINE NUMBERS	act II, scene 2, lines 75–79
TEMPERATURES	43° F; 4° Celsius
MONEY	$1.2 billion; $3.41; 25 cents or 25¢

EXERCISE 38-1

Revise so that numbers are in correct form—spelled out or in figures.

1. The film *Quo Vadis* used thirty thousand extras and 63 lions.
2. The best time to use insecticides is four p.m. because that is when insects are most susceptible.
3. People in the United States spend six hundred million dollars a year on hot dogs.
4. 4/5 of everything alive on this earth is in the sea.

5. The earliest baseball game on record was played in 1846 on June nineteenth for a final score of 23 to one in 4 innings.

6. Aaron Montgomery Ward started the first mail order company in the United States in 1872 at eight hundred twenty-five North Clark Street in Chicago.

7. The record for a human's broad jump is about twenty-eight feet, one-quarter inch, and the record for a frog's broad jump is 13 feet, 5 inches.

8. 250 words per minute is the reading speed of the typical reader.

9. The yearly income of the average family in the United States in nineteen fifteen was six hundred and eighty-seven dollars.

10. 3 out of 4 people who wear contact lenses are between 12 and 23 years of age.

Seven

WRITING
RESEARCH

 When you write research, you engage in two processes: doing research and writing a research paper. Part Seven explains how to find and write from sources, how to conduct research and write a paper based on your findings, and how to document your sources completely and accurately. As you use Chapters 39 through 42, be aware that the activities of research writing foster habits of mind that will serve you well throughout your life.

39 Paraphrasing, Summarizing, and Quoting Sources

The core of every writing project is its content. In many writing assignments, the source of that content is expected to be your own thinking. For many other assignments, however, you are expected to draw upon outside sources—such as books, articles, films, and interviews—to explain and support your ideas. **Paraphrasing** (see 39c), **summarizing** (see 39d), and **quoting** (see 39e) are three techniques you can use to incorporate information from sources. Along with these techniques you are always expected to **document your sources** (see 39b) and **avoid plagiarism** (see 39a).

GUIDELINES FOR USING OUTSIDE SOURCES IN YOUR WRITING

---

1. Avoid plagiarism by always attributing ideas and words that are not yours to their source.

2. Document sources accurately and completely.

3. Know how and when to use the techniques of **paraphrase, summary,** and **quotation.**

39a   Avoiding plagiarism

To **plagiarize** is to present another person's words or ideas as if they were your own. Plagiarism is like stealing. It is a serious offense that can be grounds for failure of a course or expulsion from a college. Plagiarism can be intentional, as when you deliberately incorporate the work of other people in your writing without mentioning and documenting the source. Plagiarism can also be unintentional—but no less serious an offense—if you are unaware of what must be acknowledged and how to go about documenting. All college students are expected to know what plagiarism is and how to avoid it.

What do you *not* have to document? When you write a paper that draws on outside sources, you are not expected to document common knowledge (if there is any on your topic) or your own thinking.

What should you document? Everything that you get from an outside source. Writing the words of others in your own words does not release you from the obligation to document.

Common knowledge

You do not have to document **common knowledge.** Common knowledge is information that most educated people know, although they might need to remind themselves of certain facts by looking up information in a reference book. For example, every educated person knows that the U.S. space program included moon landings. Some people might have to look in a reference book to remind themselves that Neil Armstrong, the first man to set foot on the moon, landed on July 20, 1969. That fact is common knowledge and does not have to be documented. You move into *the realm of research and the need to document* as soon as you get into less commonly known details about the moon landing, such as the duration of the stay on the moon. If you feel that you are walking a thin line between knowledge held in common and knowledge learned from research, be safe and document.

Your own thinking

You do not have to document **your own thinking.** As you conduct your research, you learn new material by building on what you already know. You are expected to think about the new material, formulate a thesis, and organize a paper. In the research paper in Chapter 42, examples of Amy Brown's own thinking include her thesis statement°* (paragraph 1), her organizing sentences (paragraph 3), and her conclusion (paragraph 11).

Be particularly careful about plagiarism slipping into a thesis statement°. It is plagiarism to put a source's main idea into your words and pass that off as your thesis. Similarly, it is plagiarism to combine the main ideas of several sources, put them into your own words, and pass that off as your thesis.

To prevent plagiarism in your writing, take careful notes as you conduct research using outside sources. Here are practices that help researchers avoid plagiarism.

1. **Record complete documentation information.** Become entirely familiar with the documentation style you intend to use in your paper (see 39b). Make a master list of the documentation facts required for each source, and write down all the facts on a bibliography card (see 41a).

2. **Record documentation information as you go along.** Never forget to write down complete documentation facts. As you take notes, use clear handwriting. *When you write your research paper, your chances of unintentional plagiarism increase sharply if you have to recreate your research process. Do not expect to be able to relocate your sources or to reconstruct what came from the source and what was your own thinking.*

3. **Use a consistent note-taking system.** Always use different colors of ink or a code system to keep three things sep-

*Throughout this book a degree mark (°) indicates a term that is defined in the book's Glossary.

arate: (1) material paraphrased or summarized from a source; (2) quotations from a source; and (3) your own thoughts triggered by what you are reading. For quotations, always write clear, perhaps oversize, quotation marks that you have no chance of missing later.

39b Understanding the concept of documentation

Documentation means acknowledging your sources by giving full and accurate information about the author, title, date of publication, and related facts. Whenever you paraphrase (see 39c), summarize (see 39d), or quote (see 39e), you must document your source according to correct documentation style.

Documentation styles vary among the academic disciplines. In courses for which you write using outside sources, find out what documentation style you are expected to use. Chapter 41 explains and illustrates the various documentation styles in academic disciplines.

39c Paraphrasing accurately

When you **paraphrase,** you precisely restate in your own words a passage written by another author (or spoken by someone interviewed, or heard on a film). Your paraphrasings offer an account of what various authorities have to say, not in their words but in yours. The ideas of authorities can give substance and credibility to your message, and they can offer support for your material. Guidelines for writing a paraphrase are in the chart on page 408.

Select for paraphrase only the passages that carry ideas you need to reproduce in detail. Because paraphrase calls for very close approximation of a source, avoid trying to paraphrase whole chapters—or indeed much more than a page. Usually,

---

GUIDELINES FOR WRITING A PARAPHRASE

1. Say what the source says, but no more.
2. Reproduce the source's order of ideas and emphases.
3. Use your own words, phrasing, and sentence structure to restate the message. If certain synonyms are awkward, quote the material—but resort to this very sparingly.
4. Read over your sentences to make sure that they do not distort the source's meaning.
5. Expect your material to be as long as, and possibly longer than, the original.
6. Avoid plagiarism.
7. As you take notes, record all documentation facts about your source so that you can prevent plagiarism°.

---

two or three paragraphs are the most you should attempt to translate in the detail required by paraphrase. Use summary (see 39d) for the rest.

To avoid plagiarism when you paraphrase, you must use documentation° to credit your source. Also, when you paraphrase, be sure to reword your source material. Compare these three passages:

SOURCE

Morris, Desmond. *Manwatching.* New York: Abrams, 1977. 131.*

ORIGINAL

Unfortunately, different countries have different ideas about exactly how close is close. It is easy enough to test your own "space reaction": when you are talking to someone in the street or in any open space, reach out with your arm

*Source information throughout this chapter is in MLA style (see Chapter 41).

and see where the nearest point on his body comes. If you hail from western Europe, you will find that he is at roughly fingertip distance from you. In other words, as you reach out, your fingertips will just about make contact with his shoulder. If you come from eastern Europe, you will find you are standing at "wrist distance." If you come from the Mediterranean region, you will find that you are much closer to your companion, at little more than "elbow distance."

UNACCEPTABLE PARAPHRASE (UNDERLINED WORDS ARE PLAGIARIZED)

Regrettably, different nations think differently about exactly how close is close. Test yourself: when you are talking to someone in the street or in any open space, stretch your arm out to measure how close that person is to you. If you are from western Europe, you will find that your fingertips will just about make contact with the person's shoulder. If you are from eastern Europe, your wrist will reach the person's shoulder. If you are from the Mediterranean region, you will find that you are much closer to your companion, when your elbow will reach that person's shoulder (Morris 131).†

ACCEPTABLE PARAPHRASE

People from different nations think that "close" means different things. You can easily see what your reaction is to how close to you people stand by reaching out the length of your arm to measure how close someone is as the two of you talk. When people from western Europe stand on the street and talk together, the space between them is the distance it would take one person's fingertips to reach to the other person's shoulder. People from eastern Europe converse at a wrist-to-shoulder distance. People from the Mediterranean, however, prefer an elbow-to-shoulder distance (Morris 131).

The first attempt to paraphrase fails because the writer has changed only a few words of the original source. Even though it documents its sources, the passage contains plagiarism because it keeps most of the original's language and sentence

---

†Parenthetical references throughout this chapter are in MLA style (see Chapter 41).

structure. Quotation marks around the original language would
have helped the plagiarism problem, but the use of quotation
marks would not have satisfied the criteria for using quotations
(see 39e).

The second paraphrase is acceptable. It captures the essence of the original in the student's own words.

EXERCISE 39-1

Read the original material. Then read the paraphrase that is unacceptable because it plagiarizes. Find each example of plagiarism. Then write your own paraphrase. Be sure to end it with
(Jacobs 141) before the final period, which is correct MLA documentation style°.

ORIGINAL MATERIAL

This paragraph is from *The Death and Life of Great American
Cities* by Jane Jacobs, published by Random House in 1961, page
141.

A good street neighborhood achieves a marvel of balance
between its people's determination to have essential privacy and
their simultaneous wish for differing degrees of contact, enjoyment, or help from the people around. This balance is largely
made up of small, sensibly managed details, practiced and accepted so casually that they normally seem taken for granted.

UNACCEPTABLE PARAPHRASE (PLAGIARIZES)

A good neighborhood maintains an impressive balance between the people being determined to have privacy and wishing
for varying degrees of contact, pleasure, or assistance from others nearby. People managed this with small details that are normally taken for granted (Jacobs 141).

39d Summarizing accurately

When you write a **summary,** you condense the essentials
of someone else's ideas in a few general statements. Guidelines
for writing a summary appear in a chart on the opposite page.

GUIDELINES FOR WRITING A SUMMARY

1. Identify the main points and condense them without losing the essence of the material.
2. Use your own words to condense the message.
3. Keep your summary short.
4. Avoid plagiarism.
5. As you take notes, record all documentation facts about your source, so that you can prevent plagiarism°.

Summaries differ from paraphrases in one important way. A paraphrase restates the original material completely; a summary is much shorter and provides only the main point of the original source. Summarizing is probably the most frequently used technique for taking notes and for incorporating sources into one's own writing.

SOURCE

Raudsepp, Eugene. "Daydreaming," *Success Unlimited* Nov. 1975: 64.

ORIGINAL

During times of stress, daydreaming erects a temporary shield against reality, in much the same way that building a house protects our bodies from the elements. Both may be seen as forms of escapism, but no one wants to spend life in unrelieved battle for survival. We are entitled to occasional strategic withdrawals to regroup our forces.

SUMMARY

Our minds create daydreams to protect us from pressure (Raudsepp 64).

411

As you summarize, you trace a line of thought. Doing this involves deleting less central ideas and sometimes transposing certain points into an order more suited to summary. A summary should reduce the original by at least half. In summarizing a longer original—about ten pages or more—you may find it helpful to first divide the original into subsections. These subsections may fall under a main heading, or they may be a few pages of text that has no heading. Group your subsection summaries, and use them as the basis for further condensing the material into a final summary.

As you summarize, you may be tempted to interpret something the author says or make some judgment about the value of the argument. Your own opinions do not belong in a summary, but try to jot down your ideas immediately. *Always be sure to use a different color ink or a code in your notes so that they are physically separate from your summary.*

To avoid plagiarism when you write summaries, you must use documentation to credit your source (see Chapter 41). Also, when you summarize, use your own language. If you have no alternative but to use a source's key terms because synonyms would distort the material, use quotation marks.

When a paraphrase (see 38c) becomes too long and involved to use in your paper, condense your paraphrase by summarizing it. Here is a summary written from the paraphrase of the Desmond Morris material in 39c.

> People from different nations have differing perceptions of what "close" means.

EXERCISE 39-2

Read the original material at the top of the opposite page. Then read the summary that is unacceptable because it plagiarizes. Find each example of plagiarism. Then write your own summary. Be sure to end it with (Friedman 69) before the final period, which is correct MLA documentation style°.

ORIGINAL MATERIAL

This is from *Overcoming the Fear of Success* by Martha Friedman, published by Seaview Books in 1980, page 69.

> The manner in which we respond to negative criticism is a clue to the level of our self-esteem, which in turn is a good index to the degree of our fear of success. If we harbor a feeling of inadequacy, as many of us do, about something, no matter how slight, negative criticism can wipe us out. Many of us carry too many internalized low-esteem messages from the past, negative things our parents or siblings or teachers or schoolday peers said to us.

UNACCEPTABLE SUMMARY (PLAGIARIZES)

> Many people harbor feelings of low self-esteem as a result of internalized negative messages from the past, and if people respond badly to negative criticism, no matter how slight, it indicates a low level of self-esteem, which is also an excellent index of their fear of success (Friedman 69).

39e   Using quotations effectively

Quotations are the exact words of a source set off in quotation marks (see 33a). Whereas paraphrase (see 39c) and summary (see 39d) distance your reader one step from your source, quotations give your reader the chance to encounter directly the words of your source.

Two conflicting demands confront you when you use quotations in your writing. Along with the effect and support of quotations, you also want your writing to be coherent and readable. You might seem to gain authority by quoting experts on your topic, but if you use too many quotations, you lose coherence, as well as control of your own paper. As a general rule, if more than a quarter of your paper consists of quotations, you have written what some people call a "scotch tape special." Having too many quotations may give readers—including instructors—the impression that you have not developed your own thinking and you are letting other people do your talking. Use quotations sparingly, therefore. Guidelines for working quotations into your paper appear below.

GUIDELINES FOR USING QUOTATIONS

1. Use quotations from authorities in your subject to *support* what you say, not to present your thesis° or main points.
2. Select quotations that fit your message.
3. Choose a quotation only if
   a. its language is particularly appropriate or distinctive
   b. its idea is particularly hard to paraphrase accurately
   c. the authority of the source is especially important to support your thesis° or main points
   d. the source's words are open to interpretation.
4. Do not use quotations in more than a quarter of your paper; rely mostly on paraphrase and summary to report information from sources.
5. Quote accurately.
6. Work quotations smoothly into your writing.
7. Document your source. Set off quotations with quotations marks—otherwise you will be plagiarizing.

When you do use quotations, be very careful not to misquote a source. Always check your quotations against the originals—and then recheck. If you photocopy material, be sure to mark off on the copy the exact place that caught your attention.

Otherwise, you might forget your impressions and will have to spend time trying to reconstruct your thought processes.

If you have to add a word or two to a quotation so that it fits in with your prose, put those words in brackets (see 34c). Make sure that your additions do not distort the meaning of the quotation. Similarly, if for the sake of conciseness and focus, you delete a portion of a quotation, indicate the omission with an ellipsis (see 34d). When using an ellipsis, make sure that the remaining words accurately reflect the source's meaning, and that the sentence structure has not become awkward.

The greatest risk you take when you use quotations is that you will end up with choppy, incoherent sentences. In such cases, problems arise because the quoted portions do not mesh with the style, grammar, or logic of your prose. Read the material aloud and try to hear whether the language flows smoothly and gracefully.

No   Sommer says personal space for people "like the porcupines in Schopenhauer's fable, people like to be close enough to obtain warmth and comradeship but far enough away to avoid pricking one another" (26). [problem with grammar]

Yes   Sommer says concerning personal space that "like the porcupines in Schopenhauer's fable, people like to be close enough to obtain warmth and comradeship but far enough away to avoid pricking one another" (26).

You can make sure that your reader is prepared for a quotation by mentioning the author's name as you introduce a quotation. If the flow of language is not seriously interrupted, also give the title of the source you are quoting. Moreover, if the source is a noteworthy figure, you can give additional authority to your material if you refer to his or her credentials, as in the example below.

Author's Name, Credentials, and Source Title

Edward T. Hall, an anthropologist who has studied personal space, claims in *The Hidden Dimension* that "people from different cultures, when interpreting each other's behavior, often misinterpret the relationship, the activity, or the emotions" (171).

Work quotations smoothly into your writing by using well-chosen verbs. Some of these useful verbs are listed in the chart below. To see many of these verbs in use, read the research paper by Amy Brown in Chapter 42. Note expecially annotation Z, which goes with paragraph 8. As you use this list of verbs, note that some have rather specific meanings while others are general enough to use in most situations. Choose them according to the meaning that you want your sentences to deliver.

VERBS USEFUL FOR PARAPHRASING, SUMMARIZING, AND QUOTING

analyze	complain	find	offer	show
argue	concede	illustrate	point out	speculate
ask	conclude	insist	report	suggest
assert	consider	maintain	reveal	suppose
claim	describe	note	say	think
comment	explain	observe	see	write

EXERCISE 39-3

For a paper describing how and why twins make important contributions to scientific research, write a three- to four-sentence passage that includes your own words and a quotation from this material. After the quoted words, use (Begley 84) before the final period, which is correct MLA documentation style°.

ORIGINAL MATERIAL

This is from "Twins," by Sharon Begley, published in *Newsweek*, November 23, 1987, page 84.

For over a century twins have been used to study how genes make people what they are. Because they share precisely the same genes but live in different surroundings under different influences, identical twins reared apart are helping science sort out which qualities of body and mind are shaped by our genes, and which by upbringing. Researchers needn't worry about running out of subjects: according to the Twins Foundation, there are approximately 4.5 million twin individuals in the United States alone, and about 70,000 more are born each year.

40 The Process of Research Writing

40a Understanding research writing

Research writing involves two processes: conducting research and writing the paper based upon it. The processes of researching and writing are interwoven throughout a research project. The **writing process** for a research paper is much like the writing process for all academic papers (Chapters 1-4). The **research process** adds a new dimension throughout your writing process. In planning, you choose a suitable topic, refine it into a research question, use a search strategy to find and evaluate sources, and take notes. In drafting and revising, you integrate sources into your paper by paraphrasing, summarizing, and quoting (see Chapter 39).

Research writing seeks to answer a question. Seeing research as a quest for an answer makes clear that you cannot know whether you have found something unless you know what you are looking for. Few research assignments are stated as questions, but all assignments imply that you will need to search for answers. To attempt to find these answers, you must track down information from varied sources. *Attempt* is an important word in relation to research. Some research questions lead to a final, definitive answer; some do not, especially when an assignment asks that you argue an issue.

Research can be an engrossing, creative activity. By gathering information and composing a synthesis of it, you come to know your subject deeply. As you write, you can make fresh connections and gain unexpected insights. Equally important, you sample the pleasures of being an independent learner with the self-discipline and intellectual resources to locate and learn information on your own.

If you are among those who feel overwhelmed by the prospect of research writing, you are not alone. Once, however, you break research writing into a series of steps, the project will seem far less intimidating. This chapter explains these steps.

40b Scheduling for research writing

Research writing takes time. Once you are aware of what is involved, you can plan ahead and budget your time intelligently. Try using or adapting the schedule below.

RESEARCH PAPER SCHEDULE

Assignment received (date) _____   **FINISH BY**

1. Choose a suitable topic (40d).   _____
2. Prepare to conduct research (40e).
3. Keep a research log (40c).   _____
4. Review how to evaluate sources (40f).   _____
5. Determine documentation style (40f-4) and
   make bibliographic cards (40m).   _____
6. Locate sources (40e-40l).   _____
7. Compile a working list of sources (41a).   _____
8. Take notes (40m).   _____
9. Draft a thesis statement (40n).   _____

(continued on next page)

RESEARCH PAPER SCHEDULE *(Continued)*

10. Draft paper (40p).   _____
11. Use documentation style correctly (41).   _____
12. Revise paper (40p).   _____
13. Edit and proofread paper.   _____

Assignment due (date) _____

40c Starting a research log

A **research log** is like a diary. Keep it in a notebook re-

> *Nov. 15:* Found Sommer and made a biblio. card. Excellent source. He is an environmental psychologist. Tone is calm, seems to be unbiased. I now realize that I was overlapping two concepts: territory and personal space. Territory refers to the places we carve out as "our own" — a chair in a classroom, a room in a house. Personal space is the "bubble" of space we carry around with us. We don't like intrusions in our bubbles. Sommer's description on page 26 is the best I've seen. I photocopied the page and marked off the part I will probably quote in my paper.

Excerpt from Amy Brown's Research Log

served exclusively for your research project. A thorough research log helps you think about your evolving material. Your log is a history of your search strategy and of ideas that occur to you during the research process. It keeps you from having to retrace your steps or reconstruct your thoughts unnecessarily. It is *not* for notes about the content of sources: put your notes on index cards, as explained in 40m. Rereading your log can help you make decisions about the next research step or about the content of your paper. Although much of your log will not find its way into your paper, its entries become valuable aids when you move from gathering material to organizing information to writing the paper. An excerpt of an entry from Amy Brown's log written for the research paper in Chapter 42 is shown on the opposite page.

40d Choosing and narrowing a topic for research writing

WAYS TO GET AN OVERVIEW

1. Confer briefly with a **professor** in your general area of interest (psychology, biology, literature, and so on). Inquire about the names of major books and authorities on your topic. Ask for advice in narrowing your topic.

2. Browse through a **textbook** in your area of interest. Look for material that might suggest how to narrow your topic. Consult the table of contents and the major headings. Look for names of major books and experts on your topic.

3. Read an **encyclopedia article** about your area of interest or subcategories of that area. Get basic information that might help you narrow your topic. *Do not, however, stop with the encyclopedia.* College-level research demands a thorough search of a variety of sources.

Except when you are assigned a specific topic for a research paper, your first step in the process of research writing is to **choose your topic.** Whether you are expected to choose a topic of your own or to narrow an assigned subject into a researchable topic, first decide on your general area of interest. Then get an overview of that area by using the suggestions in the chart on the previous page.

Once you have an overview of your general area of interest, you are ready to choose a topic. The chart below gives you guidelines to use.

GUIDELINES FOR CHOOSING A RESEARCH TOPIC

1. **Expect to think through various topics before making your final choice.** Avoid rushing. Keep your mind open to flashes of insight and to alternative ideas. Conversely, do not allow indecision to use up too much time.

2. **Be practical.** Plan to do the work within the established time limit and paper length. Be sure that sufficient resources on your topic are available and accessible in your college's library.

3. **Narrow the topic sufficiently.** Avoid topics that are too broad, such as *communication* or even *nonverbal communication.* At the same time, avoid topics that are too narrow.

4. **Choose a topic worth researching.** Avoid trivial subjects. Such topics prevent you from doing what you as a student researcher are expected to do: investigate related ideas, think about them critically and create a synthesis of complex and/or conflicting concepts.

5. **Try to select a topic that interests you.** Know that your topic will be a companion for quite a while, sometimes most of a semester. Select a topic that arouses your interest and allows you to sample the pleasure of satisfying your intellectual curiosity.

Communication was the general topic assigned to Amy Brown, the student who wrote the paper in Chapter 42. Her instructor required a paper of 1800 to 2000 words to be written in five weeks based on about twelve secondary sources. To get started, Brown borrowed two textbooks from a friend, one an introduction to psychology and the other an introduction to business communications. Browsing through the textbooks helped Brown make her first major choice. She decided to focus on *nonverbal communication.* To narrow her focus, Brown read a book that a psychology professor recommended during an interview. She then began to concentrate on *personal space,* a topic that particularly caught her interest. She was fascinated to learn that cultures have unspoken standards for the accepted distances between people who are conversing and interacting. Brown also liked the topic of personal space because her college had many sources to which she could refer. As she began to read closely on the topic, Brown evolved her research question: "How do standards for personal space differ among cultures?"

40e Equipping yourself for research

Before you start your research, you need to prepare. You need to have the proper equipment at hand in order to facilitate your work.

Experienced researchers use equipment that helps them work efficiently. Gather the materials listed on the next page. Keep them separate from your regular books and materials so that you can locate them easily.

Color coding is an option many researchers find helpful in establishing categories for information. For example, you might use one color of index cards or colored clips for notes and another for bibliographic information. You might use one color ink for summarized information, another for quotations taken from sources, and a third for your own comments on a source.

BASIC EQUIPMENT FOR CONDUCTING RESEARCH

1. A copy of your assignment.

2. A separate notebook to use for a research log (see 40c).

3. Pens—several different colors—for taking notes. Writing in pencil tends to blur when notes are shuffled and handled often.

4. Index cards for taking notes and recording bibliographic data (see 41a).

5. Whatever coins are needed for the library's copying machines. (See 40m about the uses and limitations of photocopying.)

6. Paper clips, a small stapler, or rubber bands to help you organize index cards and other papers, and a book bag if you intend to check out books from the library.

40f Using a search strategy to conduct research

A **search strategy** is an organized procedure for locating sources for your research. Using the library as a resource for a research paper project takes time, so plan accordingly. You usually need to locate and evaluate many more sources than you eventually use in your paper. Get to know the physical layout of your library. Also, become aware fo the breadth and depth of your library's resources. Locate and carefully read any written guides to your library's resources. At times your most important resource is the librarian. Do not hesitate to ask the librarian questions about how best to locate information.

40g Evaluating sources for research

As you conduct research, you are expected to locate **sources.** A source can be a book, article, videotape, or any other form of communication. Sources are not, however, equally valuable. Always evaluate any sources you find. Use the criteria explained in the chart below.

CRITERIA FOR EVALUATING SOURCES FOR RESEARCH

1. **Authoritative:** Check encyclopedias, textbooks, articles in academic journals, and ask experts. If a particular name or a specific work is mentioned often, that source is probably recognized as an authoritative one on your topic. Also, to find out if the author of a source has a background that makes him or her an authority, consult one of the biographical references listed in 40i.

2. **Reliable:** Check different sources. If the same information appears, the material is likely to be reliable.

3. **Well supported:** Check that each source supports assertions or information with sufficient evidence (see 40F). If the material expresses the source's point of view but offers little to back up that position, turn to another source.

4. **Balanced tone:** Read a source critically (see 6b through 6f). If the tone is unbiased and if the reasoning is logical, chances are that the source is balanced.

5. **Current:** Check that the information is up-to-date. Sometimes long-accepted information is replaced or modified by new research. Check the library's book catalog indexes to journals to see if anything more recent has come along.

| 1 | Understanding the difference between primary and secondary sources. |

Primary sources include original works of an author—novels, poems, short stories, autobiographies, diaries, first-hand reports of observations and of research, and so on. When you use primary sources, no one comes between you and your direct exposure to the author's own words. Also, you can conduct primary research such as a scientific experiment, a survey, or an interview. The data from such research becomes a primary source.

Secondary sources present someone else's original work. The information comes to you second-hand, influenced by the intermediary between you and the primary source. Secondary sources explain events, analyze information, and draw conclusions. Consulting secondary sources gives you the opportunity to read closely (and listen closely, if you interview authorities) and thereby work to understand what scholars and other experts know about your subject. As you work, combine your intellectual curiosity with caution. Evaluate critically as you read (see 6b-3), use evidence to think critically (see 6d), and remember to recognize logical fallacies (see 6f).

| 2 | Compiling a list of headings or key words |

Researchers use headings and key words to look up information. **Headings** are subject categories in books and periodicals. **Key words** (sometimes called *descriptors* or *identifiers*) identify subject categories in periodicals and computerized databases. Knowing how to locate headings and key words is central to the research process. Reference books and library catalogs and indexes group information into logical categories. Then you have to locate the headings and key words that lead you to books and articles on your topic. Keep an ongoing list in your research log of these headings and key words. Also record any false leads, so that you can avoid repeating the error later on.

3 Determining your documentation style

The term **documentation style** refers to a system for providing information about each source you have used in a research paper. Documentation styles vary among the disciplines. The **Modern Language Association** (MLA) has developed the style often used in the humanities (see 41b-1, 41c-1, and 41d). The **American Psychological Association** has developed the style often used in the social sciences (see 41b-2, 41c-2, and 41d).

Before you start consulting sources, know what documentation style you need to use. If your assignment does not specify a documentation style, ask your instructor which to use. As you take notes on each source, keep a record of that information so that you can document your sources correctly and fully.

40h Using general reference books

General reference books usually contain summaries of vast amounts of information. As you conduct your research, you will likely have to use general reference books as well as specialized reference books (see 40i). The *Guide to Reference Books* is a valuable resource. It covers reference works in all fields, describing general ones first, and then specialized ones. This book, or another like it, is worth getting to know well.

Encyclopedias

Articles in general encyclopedias such as *Collier's Encyclopedia* and *Encyclopedia Brittanica* summarize information about a wide variety of subjects. The articles can be useful for a broad overview but not as major sources for college-level research. They are written by specialists for nonspecialist readers. Many articles end with a brief bibliography of major works on the subject. Because encyclopedias take a long time to write and publish, some kinds of information in them quickly become outdated. Look for up-to-date editions and annual supplements. To locate the information you want, start with the Index volume. If you cannot find what you are looking for, try alternate headings or key words (see 40f). General encyclopedias are not the place to look for reports on recent events or current research. Specialized encyclopedias exist in many fields. See the list (pages 430–431) of specialized reference works arranged by academic discipline.

Almanacs, yearbooks, fact books

Almanacs—books such as *The World Almanac* and *Book of Facts*—briefly present a year's events and data in government, politics, sports, economics, demographics, and many other categories. *Facts on File* covers world events in a weekly digest and in an annual one-volume *Yearbook.*

Congressional Record and *Statistical Abstract* contain a wealth of data about the United States. *Demographic Yearbook* and *United Nations Statistical Yearbook* carry worldwide data. Other specialized yearbooks and handbooks are named in the list of reference works below, arranged by academic discipline.

Atlases

Atlases contain maps. Seas and skies and even other planets have been mapped. These comprehensive books contain many kinds of geographic information: topography, climates, populations, natural resources, crops, and so on.

Dictionaries

Dictionaries define words and terms. The dictionaries described in section 24a define words in the English language and give various other information about these words. Specialized dictionaries exist in many academic disciplines. Such books define words and phrases specific to a field. For a list, see section 40i.

Biographies

Biographical reference books give brief information about the major events in many famous people's lives. Various *Who's Who* series cover noteworthy people, male or female, living or dead. *Current Biography: Who's News and Why* is published monthly, with six-month and annual cumulative editions. *Dictionary of American Biography* and *Webster's Biographical Dictionary* are very widely available.

Specialized biographical reference books focus on artists, musicians, important people of various historical periods or nationalities, and so on. For a list, see 40i.

Bibliographies

Bibliographies list books. *Books in Print* lists all books available through their publishers and sometimes other sources in the United States. This multivolume work classifies its entries by author name, title, and general subject headings, but it does not describe a book's content in any way.

The *Book Review Digest* excerpts book reviews in major newspapers and magazines. These excerpts of critics' opinions can help you evaluate a source (see 40g). This digest is published every year. The reviews appear in the volume that corresponds either to the year a book was published or to the one immediately following.

40i Using specialized reference books

As you work into a research topic and use general reference books (see 40h), you will need increasingly specific information. Here are selected titles, grouped by general academic disciplines. This list can only hint at the wide variety available at many libraries.

BUSINESS AND ECONOMICS

A Dictionary of Economics
Encyclopedia of Advertising
Encyclopedia of Banking and Finance
Handbook of Modern Marketing

FINE ARTS

Crowells' Handbook of World Opera
International Cyclopedia of Music and Musicians
Oxford Companion to Art

HISTORY AND POLITICAL SCIENCE

Encyclopedia of American History
An Encyclopedia of World History
New Cambridge Modern History

LITERATURE

Cassell's Encyclopedia of World Literature
Dictionary of Literary Biography
A Dictionary of Literary Terms
MLA International Bibliography of Books and Articles on the Modern Languages and Literature
The Oxford Companion to American Literature
The Oxford Companion to English Literature

PHILOSOPHY AND RELIGION

Dictionary of the Bible
Eastern Definitions: A Short Encyclopedia of Religions of the Orient
Encyclopedia of Philosophy

SCIENCE AND TECHNOLOGY

Encyclopedia of Chemistry
Encyclopedia of Physics
The Encyclopedia of the Biological Sciences
The Larousse Encyclopedia of Animal Life
The McGraw-Hill Encyclopedia of Science and Technology

SOCIAL SCIENCES

Dictionary of Anthropology
Dictionary of Education
Encyclopedia of Psychology
International Encyclopedia of the Social Sciences

40j Using periodicals

Periodicals are magazines and journals published at set periods during a year. The key to using periodicals is to locate **indexes to periodicals.** These indexes list articles written between the dates on the cover on each edition. Many indexes are kept up-to-date with supplements between editions. Some but not all indexes include abstracts—brief summaries—of each article. Classification systems vary among indexes, so take time to learn how to decipher the codes and abbreviations in the index you need. Most indexes include a guide for readers in the front or back of each volume and supplement, and the guide is usually also in a computerized database, if available. As you learn to use an index, update your list of headings and key words (see 40g) for future reference.

Indexes are packaged in a variety of ways. Some indexes are in yearly bound volumes and interim paperback updates. Depending on the systems at your library, some indexes may be on microfilm or microfiche. These may have to be accessed through computer terminals. Before you start using periodicals, get to know the systems at your library.

1   Using general indexes to periodicals

General indexes list articles in magazines and newspapers. Headings and key words on the same subject vary among indexes, so think of every possible way to look up the information you seek. Large libraries have many general indexes. Almost all libraries have these two major indexes:

> The *New York Times Index* catalogs all articles that have been printed in this encyclopedic newspaper since 1851. Supplements are published every two weeks in paperbound volumes. The supplements are organized into volumes (bound, in computerized databases, or on microfilm) periodically.

> The *Readers' Guide to Periodical Literature* is the most widely used index to over 100 magazines and journals for general (rather than specialized) readers. Paperback supplements are published every two weeks. These supplements are organized into volumes (bound, in computerized databases, or on microfilm) periodically. This index does not include scholarly journals, so its uses are often limited for college-level research. It can be useful, however, for getting a broad overview and for

COMMUNICATION, Nonverbal ———————— Subject heading
  Does your body *parle francais*? French body —— Title of article
  language; teaching methods of L. Wylie. pors ———— Author
  Time 113:107+ My 14 '79 ———————————— Periodical title
  Watching your every move: what you reveal
  about yourself without saying a word. J.
  Marks. Teen 23:36+ Jl '79 ———————————— Vol. 23, p. 36+, July 1979
  When tensions talk—listen! Subtle motion tells
  a story. E. Hamilton. por Sci Digest 85:30–2+ —— Has portrait
  Ap '79
  Women smile less for success; study of job
  success by Wendy McKenna and Florence
  Denmark. M. B. Parlee. Psychol Today 12:16
  Mr '79
    See also
  Eye—Movements
  Gesture ————————————————————— Related subject
  Sign language   headings
  Touch

Annotated Excerpt from *Readers' Guide to Periodical Literature*

ways to narrow a subject. Illustrated is an entry from *Readers' Guide* showing listings for Communication, the subject of Amy Brown's research paper assignment.

---

2 Using specialized indexes to periodicals

Specialized indexes list articles published in academic and professional periodicals. When researching a college-level paper, you will often find the material in specialized indexes more appropriate than that in general indexes. Many specialized indexes carry an abstract (a summary) of each listed article.

Depending on their resources, libraries stock many or few specialized indexes in book form and in paperback supplements. Some libraries make available a computerized database that includes many different, specialized indexes. Commonly available specialized indexes include *America: History and Life, Applied Science and Technology Index, Art Index, Biological Abstracts, Biological and Agricultural Index, Business Periodicals Index, Education Index, General Science Index, Humanities Index, MLA International Bibliography of Books and Articles in the Modern Languages and Literatures, Music Index, Psychological Abstracts,* and *Social Science Index.*

Here is an entry from the *Humanities Index* that Amy Brown used in her research for the paper in Chapter 34. The

> Nonverbal communication
> *See also*
> Expression
> Gesture
> Background to kinesics. R. L. Birdwhistell. *Etc* 40:352-61
> Fall '83
> Mediated interpersonal communication: toward a new
> typology. R. Cathcart and G. Gumpert. *Q J Speech*
> 69:267-77 Ag '83

Excerpt from *Humanities Index*

abbreviations have the same meaning as those in the excerpt from the *Readers' Guide to Periodical Literature* on page 432.

40k Using a book catalog

A **book catalog** is a list of all books in a library. Years ago, all libraries used a **card catalog** for their record of holdings. In recent years, many libraries have transferred their cards onto a **microfiche catalog** and/or a **computerized catalog** that can be accessed at a terminal.

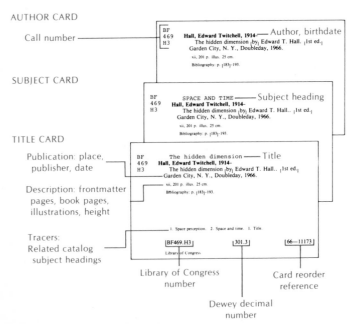

AUTHOR CARD

Call number ——— BF 469 H3   **Hall, Edward Twitchell, 1914-** —— Author, birthdate
The hidden dimension ₍by₎ Edward T. Hall. ₍1st ed.₎ Garden City, N. Y., Doubleday, 1966.
xii, 201 p. illus. 25 cm.
Bibliography: p. ₍183₎-193.

SUBJECT CARD

BF 469 H3   SPACE AND TIME —— Subject heading
Hall, Edward Twitchell, 1914-
The hidden dimension ₍by₎ Edward T. Hall. ₍1st ed.₎ Garden City, N. Y., Doubleday, 1966.
xii, 201 p. illus. 25 cm.
Bibliography: p. ₍183₎-193.

TITLE CARD

Publication: place, publisher, date

Description: frontmatter pages, book pages, illustrations, height

BF 469 H3   The hidden dimension —— Title
Hall, Edward Twitchell, 1914-
The hidden dimension ₍by₎ Edward T. Hall.. ₍1st ed.₎ Garden City, N. Y., Doubleday, 1966.
xii, 201 p. illus. 25 cm.
Bibliography: p. ₍183₎-193.

Tracers: Related catalog subject headings

I. Space perception. 2. Space and time. I. Title.

₍BF469.H3₎   ₍301.3₎   ₍66—11173₎
Library of Congress

Library of Congress number

Dewey decimal number

Card reorder reference

Library of Congress Catalog Cards

Catalog information is organized alphabetically in three categories: author names, book titles, and subjects. In some libraries, authors and titles are in one file, subjects in another. In other libraries, the three types of information are filed together.

Each card in the catalog contains much useful information. The **call number** is most important. Be sure to copy it down *exactly* as it appears, with all numbers, letters, and decimal points. The call number tells where the book is located in the stacks. If you are working in a library with open stacks (one where you can go into the book collection yourself), the call number leads you to the area in the library where all books on the same subject can be found. The call number is also crucial in a library with closed stacks. To get a book, you have to use the system at your library (such as fill in a call slip and wait for the book to arrive).

Libraries classify books according to one of two systems. You can tell what system a particular library uses from the call numbers in the catalog. Call numbers in the **Library of Congress system** have call numbers that start with a letter. Cards in the **Dewey Decimal system** start with numbers. Find out what system your library uses, and ask a librarian for a complete list of the classifications so that you can use the system efficiently.

Tracers are another important feature of cards in the card catalog. Tracers are words, numbered and in fine print, below a book's publication data. Tracers give other headings used to classify information related to the same subject. They are valuable hints when you want to find more about a subject. As you find tracers, be sure to add them to your list of headings and key words (see 40g-3).

At libraries that use the Library of Congress cataloging systems, the multi-volume *Library of Congress Subject Headings (LCSH)* is an excellent guide. Available in the reference or reserve section of a library, it is a catalog of the subject headings (not title or author) used in the library's catalog (see the *Library of Congress Subject Headings* example on page 436).

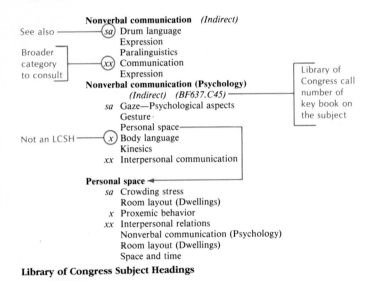

See also ———— (sa) **Nonverbal communication** *(Indirect)*
Drum language
Expression

Broader
category ———— (xx) Paralinguistics
to consult Communication
Expression

Nonverbal communication (Psychology)
(Indirect) *(BF637.C45)* ———— Library of
Congress call
sa Gaze—Psychological aspects number of
Gesture · key book on
Personal space ———— the subject

Not an LCSH ———— (x) Body language
Kinesics
xx Interpersonal communication

Personal space ◄
sa Crowding stress
Room layout (Dwellings)
x Proxemic behavior
xx Interpersonal relations
Nonverbal communication (Psychology)
Room layout (Dwellings)
Space and time

Library of Congress Subject Headings

401 Using computerized databases

Computerized databases vary in format and coverage. Indexes to periodicals (see 40j) and book catalogs (see 40k) are available as computerized databases at some libraries. Each item in a computerized database provides information about title, author, and publisher. If the database lists articles from scholarly journals, the entry might also provide a summary—called an *abstract*—of the material. Once you locate an item that seems promising for your research, you must then locate the source itself. An abstract is only the beginning.

Amy Brown, the student who wrote the research paper in Chapter 42, used the DIALOG Information System to search for sources. DIALOG contains over 100 million references—mostly journal articles and reports—combined from over 200 smaller databases in the humanities, the social sciences, business, the sciences and technology, medicine, economics, and current events. (Some libraries have systems with other names, but the principle is the same.)

A librarian helped Brown choose key words (see 40g-3). Brown's topic was *personal space,* an area of nonverbal communication. Brown started with *nonverbal communication,* but the term was too general. It would have yielded 1,486 citations. To reduce the number to manageable size, Brown crossed *nonverbal communication* with other key words such as *conversation, personal space, social perception,* and *ethnic values.* One of those citations is illustrated below, with an explanation of its parts.

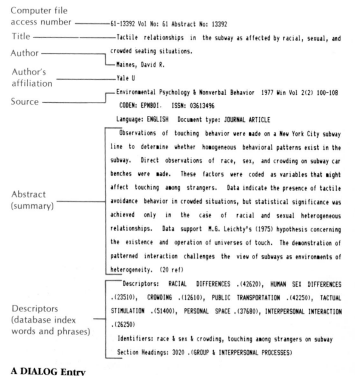

Computer file access number ———— 61-13392 Vol No: 61 Abstract No: 13392

Title ———————— Tactile relationships in the subway as affected by racial, sexual, and crowded seating situations.

Author ———— Maines, David R.

Author's affiliation ———— Yale U

Source ———— Environmental Psychology & Nonverbal Behavior 1977 Win Vol 2(2) 100-108
CODEN: EPNBDI. ISSN: 03613496

Language: ENGLISH Document type: JOURNAL ARTICLE

Abstract (summary) ————
Observations of touching behavior were made on a New York City subway line to determine whether homogeneous behavioral patterns exist in the subway. Direct observations of race, sex, and crowding on subway car benches were made. These factors were coded as variables that might affect touching among strangers. Data indicate the presence of tactile avoidance behavior in crowded situations, but statistical significance was achieved only in the case of racial and sexual heterogeneous relationships. Data support M.G. Leichty's (1975) hypothesis concerning the existence and operation of universes of touch. The demonstration of patterned interaction challenges the view of subways as environments of heterogeneity. (20 ref)

Descriptors (database index words and phrases) ————
Descriptors: RACIAL DIFFERENCES .(42620), HUMAN SEX DIFFERENCES .(23510), CROWDING .(12610), PUBLIC TRANSPORTATION .(42250), TACTUAL STIMULATION .(51400), PERSONAL SPACE .(37680), INTERPERSONAL INTERACTION .(26250)

Identifiers: race & sex & crowding, touching among strangers on subway
Section Headings: 3020 .(GROUP & INTERPERSONAL PROCESSES)

A DIALOG Entry

40m Taking useful notes

Your research process includes taking notes as you consult sources and recording your ideas as you move through the process. Taking good notes is the key to using sources well in your research paper. Together with your research log and bibliography cards, your notes give you a complete record of your research and the information you found.

Note-taking is a decision-making process. The first decision concerns whether a source related to your topic is worth taking notes on. To decide, evaluate it according to the guidelines in 40f. If it seems to be a good source, take notes. If it does not, record its title and location in your research log—along with a message to yourself about why you rejected it. What seems useless one day might have potential if you revise your focus or narrow your topic.

The second decision concerns what to put into your notes. Knowing how to select material for notes comes with experience. Use critical reading skills (see 6b) to sort major information from minor information as it relates to your topic. Do not get bogged down in unimportant details. At the same time, do not overlook important material. Try for a reasonable balance. When you begin, if you have only a general sense of your topic, read and take notes widely. Stay alert for ways to narrow your topic (see 40d). Use your research log to keep track of your thoughts; ideas tend to pop in and out of mind during a selection process. Once you have narrowed your subject, take notes focused within the boundaries of your choice.

The third decision in the notetaking process concerns the form of your notes. **You must use procedures that prevent plagiarism.** This matter is so important that Chapter 39 is devoted to avoiding plagiarism and to the skills of paraphrasing, summarizing, and quoting. To plagiarize is to steal someone else's words and pass them off as your own. To avoid the risk of plagiarism, take notes in such a way that you will always be able to tell from your notes what is yours and what belongs to a source. You might want to use one color ink for your thoughts and ideas and another color ink for words that are paraphrases, summaries, or quotations.

Use index cards for your notes. Cards provide flexibility for organizing information to write your paper. Never put notes from more than one source on the same index card. If your notes on a source require more than one card, be sue to number the cards sequentially. If you take notes on more than one idea or topic from a particular source, start a new card for each new area of information. Head each index card with identifying information that clearly relates to one of your bibliographic cards. Include the source's title and the number of the page or pages from which you are taking notes. Also, clearly identify the *type* of note on the card: paraphrase, summary, or quotation. A note card written by Amy Brown, the student whose paper is in Chapter 42, is shown below.

Photocopying can save you time if you want a word-for-word record of a source. Photocopying, however, can be a

> Hall, <u>Hidden</u>, p. 109
>
> <u>Awareness of personal space</u>
>
> <u>Summary</u>: Most people are unaware
> that interpersonal distances exist
> and contribute to peoples'
> reactions to one another.

A Note Card Summarizing a Source

waste of time and money if you photocopy everything you come across. Write your paraphrases and summaries as you go along. When you do photocopy, always mark the paper with identifying information and notations about what you consider important and why. A photocopy Amy Brown made and annotated is shown below.

Sommer, p. 26

The best way to learn the location of invisible boundaries is to keep walking until somebody complains. Personal space refers to an area with invisible boundaries surrounding a person's body into which intruders may not come. [Like the porcupines in Schopenhauer's fable, people like to be close enough to obtain warmth and comradeship but far enough away to avoid pricking one another. Personal space ~~is not necessarily spherical in shape, nor does it extend equally in all directions. (People are able to tolerate closer presence of a stranger at their sides than directly in front.) It~~ has been likened to a snail shell, a soap bubble, an aura, and "breathing room."] There are major differences between cultures in the distances that people maintain—Englishmen keep further apart than Frenchmen or South Americans. Reports

I'll paraphrase this

I'll quote this with ellipses

Photocopy of Source, with Annotations

40n Drafting a thesis statement

Drafting a **thesis statement** for a research paper is the beginning of the transition between the research process and the writing process. A thesis statement in a research paper is like the thesis statement in any essay: it tells the central message (see 2m). Any paper must fulfill the promise of its thesis statement. Because readers expect unified material, the theme of the thesis must be sustained throughout a research paper.

Most researchers draft a **preliminary thesis statement** before or during their research process. They expect that they will revise the thesis somewhat after their research, because they know that the sources they will consult will enlarge their knowledge of a subject. Other researchers draft a thesis statement after the research process.

As you draft a thesis statement, remember that one of your major responsibilities in a research paper is to support the thesis. Be sure that the material gathered during the research process offers effective support. If it does not, revise your thesis statement, or conduct further research, or both.

No matter when you draft your thesis statement, expect to write many alternatives. Your goal is to draft the thesis carefully so that it delivers the message you intend. In writing a **revised thesis statement,** take charge of your material. Reread your research log and your notes. Look for categories of information. Try to rearrange your note cards into logical groupings. Begin to impose a structure on your material.

Amy Brown, whose research paper appears in Chapter 42, drafted two different preliminary thesis statements before she composed one that worked well with her material.

FIRST PRELIMINARY VERSION	Standards for personal space vary among cultures.
NEXT PRELIMINARY VERSION	These different norms can lead to intercultural misunderstandings when people from different countries come together unaware of how their expectations concerning interpersonal distances can affect their reactions to each other.
FINAL VERSION	Everyone has expectations concerning the use of personal space, but accepted distances for that space are determined by each person's culture.

40o   Outlining a research paper

Some instructors require an outline of a research paper. To begin organizing your material for an outline, you might write an **informal outline.** Group the subcategories in your material until you are ready to write a formal outline.

A formal outline should be in the form discussed in Section 2n. Head it with the paper's thesis statement. You can use a **topic outline** (a format that requires words or phrases for each item) or a **sentence outline** (a format that requires full sentences for each item). Do not mix the two types. For a sentence outline of Amy Brown's research paper on personal space, see Chapter 42.

40p Drafting and revising a research paper

Drafting and revising a research paper have much in common with the writing processes for writing any type of paper. (See Chapter 3.) But more is demanded. You must demonstrate that you have followed the research steps in this chapter. You must demonstrate an understanding of the information you have located. You must organize for effective presentation. You must integrate sources into your writing without plagiarizing, by properly using the techniques of paraphrase, summary, and quotation (see Chapter 39). Also, you must document your sources (see Chapter 41). These special demands take extra time for drafting, thinking, redrafting, and rethinking.

Expect to write a number of drafts of your research paper. Successive drafts help you to gain authority over the information you learn from your research. The **first draft** is your initial attempt to structure your notes into a unified whole. It is also a chance to discover new insights and fresh connections. Only the act of writing makes such discovery possible. A first draft is a rough draft, a prelude to later work at revising and polishing. Some researchers work with their notes in front of them. They use their organized piles for drafting a thesis statement (see 40n) and for outlining (see 40o), and they proceed from one pile to the next. Other researchers quickly write a **partial first draft,** without using their notes, to get a broad view of their material. They then go back and write a **complete first draft** with their notes at hand, correcting and inserting information and adding documentation (see Chapter 41).

Your **second and subsequent drafts** are the results of reading your first draft critically and revising it. If at all possible, get some distance from your material by taking a break of a few days. Then reread your first draft and think how it can be improved. You also might ask other people to read it and react.

As you work, pay attention to any uneasy feelings you have that hint at the need to rethink or rework your material. Experienced writers expect to revise; they know that writing is really rewriting. Research papers are among the most demanding composing assignments, and most writers have to revise

---

REVISION CHECKLIST FOR A RESEARCH PAPER

If the answer to any question in the list is "no," revise your draft.

1. Does the introductory paragraph lead effectively into the material (see 5e)?
2. Are you fulfilling the promise of the thesis statement?
3. Do the ideas follow from one another?
4. Do you stay on the topic?
5. Are important questions answered?
6. Do you avoid bogging down the paper with irrelevent or insignificant information?
7. Do you avoid leaving gaps in information?
8. Have you integrated source material without plagiarizing?
9. Have you used paraphrases, summaries, and quotations well?
10. Does the concluding paragraph end the material effectively (see 5e)?

---

their drafts more than a few times. As you revise, consult the Revision Checklists in 3c to remind yourself of general principles of writing. Also, consult the special revision checklist on page 443 for a research paper.

The **final draft** shows that you have revised well. It shows also that you have edited and proofread for correct grammar, spelling, and punctuation. No amount of careful research and good writing can make up for a sloppy manuscript. Strive to make the paper easy to read. If any page is messy with corrections, retype it. If your instructor accepts handwritten papers, use ruled white paper that has *not* been torn out of a spiral notebook. (Typed work is always preferable because it presents itself better.) Use black or blue ink and write very legibly.

For an example of the writing process for research writing in action, and for a sample research paper, see Chapter 42.

41 Documenting Sources for Research Writing

When you write a research paper, you always have to **document** your sources. Documenting involves creating a working bibliography on cards (see 41a) so that you can keep careful track of all the sources on which you take notes. In your research paper itself, you are expected to document your sources in two separate but equally important ways.

1. Within the body of the paper, use **parenthetical references** (see 41b). Some courses might require endnotes or footnotes instead of parenthetical references (see 41f).
2. At the end of the paper, provide a **list of sources** (see 41c and 41d).

Two different documentation styles are featured in this chapter. The most frequently used style in the humanities was developed by the Modern Language Association (MLA). Another style used in some humanities and most social sciences was developed by the American Psychological Association (APA). The MLA style and APA style for parenthetical references are given in 41b. The MLA style and APA style for listing sources are given in 41c and 41d. Content notes are explained in 41e. Use *only* MLA style, *only* APA style, or *only* a different style required by your instructor. Never mix documentation styles.

If you are expected to use a note system (footnotes or endnotes) of documentation, consult 41f.

41a   Creating a working bibliography

To create a working bibliography, write out a bibliographic card for every source on which you take notes. Include on each card all the bibliographic information you need to fulfill the requirements of the documentation style you are using. Also, for each card on a library source, write the call number in the upper left-hand corner, being careful to copy it exactly. When the time comes to compile a final list of sources for your research paper, you can easily arrange bibliographic cards in correct order. A bibliographic card is shown here for Amy Brown's research paper, which appears in Chapter 42.

HM
285
H3

Hall, Edward T. The Hidden Dimension. New York: Doubleday, 1969.

As you organize and write your paper, you may find that you have not drawn on certain sources at all, even though you took notes on them. In both MLA and APA documentation styles, list only the sources you mention in your paper. In MLA style, the list is called Works Cited; in APA style, the list is called References.

41b Documenting sources with parenthetical references

As you draft and revise your research paper, be sure to use **parenthetical references.** The purpose of parenthetical references is to lead your readers to the sources for your paraphrases (see 39c), summaries (see 39d), and quotations (see 39e). In the past, you may have used footnotes or endnotes to document your sources, but current practice in some of the humanities and most of the social sciences calls for parenthetical references. When you need to use footnotes or endnotes for documentation, refer to section 41f.

Make parenthetical references brief and accurate. When you are deciding what information to include in a reference, you need to consider what information about the source already appears in the sentence or the immediate context.

MLA style permits underlining of a title of two or more words with either an unbroken or a broken line. (Some widely used word processing programs permit underlining only with a broken line.) Whatever your choice, be consistent in each piece of writing. This handbook uses an unbroken line. APA style does not specify either type of underline, but the examples of APA style in this handbook are shown with an unbroken line.

1 Understanding the MLA system of parenthetical references

Paraphrased, summarized, and quoted material requires documentation in MLA style. MLA parenthetical references direct a reader to the full citation list on a separate page, called Works Cited, at the end of a paper.

In the first example below, the author's name and the page number appear in parentheses. The author's name, which a reader needs to find an entry for the Works Cited list, is presented in parentheses because it does not appear elsewhere in the sentence. No punctuation separates the author's name from the page number. In the second example, the author's name is mentioned in the sentence, so only the page number appears in parentheses. In the third example, the author's name and the title of the work appear in the sentence, so only the page number is given in parentheses.

PARAPHRASES

> People from the Mediterranean prefer an elbow-to-shoulder distance (Morris 131).

> Desmond Morris notes that people from the Mediterranean prefer an elbow-to-shoulder distance (131).

> In <u>Manwatching: A Field Guide to Human Behavior</u>, Desmond Morris notes that people from the Mediterranean prefer an elbow-to-shoulder distance (131).

When you are documenting a short quotation, the parenthetical reference is placed at the end of the quotation and *before* the final period. When you are documenting a long, indented quotation, the parenthetical reference appears *after* the final period. (See 33a-1 for more on using quotation marks with quotations; see 39e for a discussion of how to work quotations smoothly into your own prose.)

Additional examples of parenthetical references in MLA style start on the next page. To avoid lengthy parenthetical references, get in the habit of putting reference information into your sentence. Whether you put documentation information in a parenthetical reference or a sentence, remember that your reader must be able to find an entry in the Works Cited list for each reference to a source in your paper. If you have further questions about *parenthetical references* using MLA style, consult Joseph Gibaldi and Walter S. Achtert, *MLA Handbook for Writers of Research Papers,* 3rd ed., New York: MLA, 1988.

Work by one author—MLA

The examples of paraphrase on page 448 illustrate parenthetical references to a work by one author.

Work by two or more authors—MLA

If you use a source written by more than one author, you have the option of providing the names and page number in the parenthetical reference—(Leghorn and Parker 115)—or providing the names in the sentence itself, followed by just the page number in parentheses. If a book is by two or three authors, give all the names. If a book is by more than three authors, you can use the first author's name plus *et al.* either in the parenthetical reference—(Moore et al. 275)—or in the sentence.

One author with two or more works—MLA

If you use two sources by the same author, when you refer to one of the sources, supply the author's last name, an abbreviated title of the work, and the relevant page numbers—(Morris, Manwatching 95). Notice that a comma separates the author and underlined title, but no punctuation separates the title and page number. To shorten the parenthetical reference, use the author's name and the title of the work in your sentence and give only the page number in parentheses.

Two or more authors with the same last name—MLA

If you use sources that include works by different authors with the same name, you must supply the author's first and last names—(Charles G. Morris 516). Notice that no comma separates the author from the page numbers. To shorten the parenthetical reference, you can include the author's complete name in your sentence and give only the page numbers in parentheses.

Corporate author—MLA

If the author of a source is the name of the corporation, a parenthetical reference might use the corporate author's name and relevant page number—(Boston Women's Health Collective 11). Whenever possible, incorporate long names in your sentence to avoid a long parenthetical reference. The parentheses would then contain only the page number.

Work cited by title—MLA

If you use a source with no author given, substitute the title or an abbreviated title for the author's name in the parenthetical reference—(Chicago 305)—or in the text itself. Notice that the title is underlined. If you use an abbreviated version of the title, be sure it starts with the word by which you alphabetize the source in your Works Cited list.

Multivolume work—MLA

Suppose you have used both volumes of a work by John Herman Randall, Jr. To cite a reference from one volume, indicate the volume number as well as the page number in the parenthetical reference—(Randall 1:64). Notice that a colon separates the volume number and the page number. If the entry in the Works Cited list refers only to one volume of a multivolume work, give only the page number, not volume number too, in the parenthetical citation—(Ernest 130). If you include the author's name in your sentence, supply only the page number, or the volume and page number, in the parenthetical reference.

Literary work—MLA

If you use an edition of a classic novel, play, or poem, give more information than a page reference. (Readers might be using other editions.) For prose works, in addition to a page number to your edition, give additional information about parts, sections, or chapters—(3; pt. 1, ch. 1). Notice that a semicolon separates the page number from other information. Use standard abbreviations, such as *pt.* (part); *sec.* (section); and *ch.*

(chapter). For classic verse, plays, and poems, the MLA recommends that you omit page references altogether and cite divisions (canto, book, part, act, or scene and line), using periods to separate the various numbers: (<u>King Lear</u> 4.1.5–6). This means act 4, scene 1, lines 5–6 of Shakespeare's *King Lear.* Some instructors still prefer roman numerals for citing acts and scenes—(<u>King Lear</u> IV.i).

Reference to more than one source—MLA

If more than one source has contributed to an idea or opinion in your paper, acknowledge multiple sources by putting all necessary information for each source in the parenthetical reference. Separate the sources with a semicolon—(Morris, <u>Intimate</u> 193; Mead 33).

Article in a book—MLA

If you use an article that appears in an edited book, give the name of the author of the article, not the editor of the book. If you were quoting from Ernesto Galarza's "The Roots of Migration," which appears in a book edited by Luis Valdez and Stan Steiner, you would use the following citation form: (Galarza 127).

An indirect source—MLA

If you are quoting an author who has been quoted by another author, indicate both names: (Cather qtd. in McClave). This form tells the reader that you are quoting the words of Willa Cather, that you found them in McClave's work, and that the Works Cited entry is in McClave's name.

2	Understanding the APA system of parenthetical references

In the APA style of documentation, any quotation shorter than forty words is considered short, and any quotation forty words or longer is considered long. Integrate short quotations into your own material (see 39e). Set off and indent long quotations five spaces from the left margin.

When you quote material, always include the page number with *p.* for one page or *pp.* for more than one page. Give the page number immediately after the end of the quotation, even in mid-sentence. If you do not mention the name of the author or the year in your sentence, include all three pieces of information in the parenthetical reference—(Morris, 1977, p. 131). Use a comma after the author and after the year. If your sentence includes the author's name, give the year of publication immediately after the name, even if the page number falls at a different place in the sentence—Morris (1977) found "elbow-to-shoulder distance" (p. 131) is preferred. If your sentence includes the author's name and the date of publication, then give only the page—(p. 131).

When you paraphrase (see 39d) or summarize (see 39e) material, APA practice is that the writer can decide whether or not to give a page number, depending on whether the reader is likely to want to know the specific location of information. As a student writer, you might be required to give the page number so that your instructor can verify your information. Check with your instructor to find out the requirements in any class that calls for APA documentation style.

If you refer to a work more than once in a paper, give the author and date the first time that you mention the work, and then give only the author in subsequent mentions.

Additional examples of parenthetical references in APA style start on the next page. Whether you put documentation information in a parenthetical reference or in a sentence, remember that your reader must be able to find an entry in the References list for each reference to a source in your paper. If you have further questions about parenthetical references using APA style, consult American Psychological Association, *Publication Manual of the American Psychological Association,* 3rd ed., Washington, D.C.: APA, 1984.

Work by one author—APA

The examples discussed above illustrate parenthetical references to a work by one author, Morris.

Work by two or more authors—APA

If you are citing a source that has two authors, always use both last names. If the authors' last names appear in your sentence, only the year appears in parentheses. If the authors' last names do not appear in your writing, the reference includes them and the year—(Worchel & Cooper, 1983). Note that APA style permits the use of the ampersand—&—to stand for the word *and.*

If a work has more than two authors but fewer than six, use all the authors' last names in the first reference but use only the last name of the first author followed by *et al.* for subsequent references. In the actual reference, do not underline any item—(Peat et al., 1987).

If a work has six or more authors, use only the last name of the first author and et al. for each citation.

Author(s) with two or more works—APA

If you use more than one source written in the *same year* by the same author(s), alphabetize the works and assign letters (*a, b,* etc.) to them. Then use the letters next to the year for works in the References list and in the parenthetical references—(Jones, 1989a).

Two or more authors with the same last name—APA

If you use sources that include works by different authors with the same last name, use first- and middle-name initials in all text citations—(A. J. Jones, 1988).

Corporate author—APA

If the author of a source is the name of a corporation, a parenthetical reference usually does not abbreviate the name.

An abbreviation can be used, as long as a reader could easily identify the work in your References list—(National Aeronautics and Space Administration [NASA], 1990). Note that brackets enclose the abbreviation. Subsequent citations would have this form: (NASA, 1990).

Work cited by title—APA

If you use a source that gives no author, substitute the title or the first two or three words of the title and the year—(Chicago Manual, 1982). The title is underlined because the source is a book. An article title appears in quotation marks.

Reference to more than one source—APA

If more than one source has contributed to an idea or opinion in your paper, cite the sources alphabetically in a single reference and separate them with a semicolon—(Morris, 1977; Worchel & Cooper, 1983).

41c   Documenting sources with a list of sources

In both MLA and APA documentation styles, you must present a final list of sources. Use *only* MLA style or *only* APA style. Never mix them. In MLA style, the list is called Works Cited. In APA style, the list is called References. Whichever style you follow, list all sources referred to in your paper. Include only the sources from which you paraphrase, summarize, or quote. Do not include sources that you consulted but do not refer to in the paper. Begin the list on a new page that is numbered sequentially with the rest of your paper. Arrange entries alphabetically by author name. If the author's name is unknown, alphabetize the entry by the first significant word of the title (not by *A, An,* or *The*).

For citing books, you may find most of the information you need on the title page or the copyright page (the reverse of the title page). For citing articles, the information you need usually appears on the cover, title page, contents page, or sometimes the first page of the article.

The MLA documentation style for Works Cited is illustrated and explained in section 41c-1. The APA documentation style for References is illustrated and explained in section 41c-2. Then on the red-bordered pages of 41d is a directory of forms, followed by an example of each form in MLA style and in APA style.

---

1 | Using MLA documentation style: the Works Cited list

Citing books—MLA

Citations for books have three main parts: author, title, and publication information (place of publication, publisher, and date of publication). Each part is followed by a period and two spaces.

NAME	TITLE	PUBLISHING INFORMATION
Didion, Joan.	Salvador.	New York: Simon, 1983.

Many sources need additional information included in the citation. Indent all lines after the first line five spaces. In the title, capitalize all major words. If several cities are listed for the place of publication, give only the first. If a foreign city might be unfamiliar to a reader, add an abbreviation of the province (if Canadian) or country. You can shorten the publisher's name as long as the shortened version is easily identifiable. *(Prentice Hall can be Prentice; Oxford University Press can be Oxford UP; Simon & Schuster can be Simon.)* Give the latest copyright date for the edition you are using. If the book has had several printings (rather than editions), use the publication year, not the reprint year. See 41d for a directory of forms followed by an example of each form in MLA style.

Citing articles—MLA

Citations for articles in periodicals (such as journals, magazines, and newspapers) contain three major parts: author, title of article, and publication information. The publication information usually includes the periodical title, volume number, year of publication, and inclusive page numbers.

NAME   ARTICLE TITLE

    Shuter, Robert.   "A Field Study of Nonverbal Communication

    in Germany, Italy, and the United States."

PERIODICAL TITLE   VOLUME NUMBER   PUBLICATION YEAR

    Communication.Monographs 44 (1977): 298–305.

PAGE. NUMBERS

Additional information may be required depending on the source. Indent all lines after the first line five spaces. In the citation for an article, each part is followed by a period and two spaces. Within each part, use one space between each word and after punctuation. In the title, capitalize all major words. ✤ NUMBER ALERT: In citing inclusive page numbers, give the second number in full for numbers through 99 (for example, 23–24). For numbers 100 and above, give only the last two digits unless this would create confusion (for example, 103–04 and 2234–67; however, 567–602.) ✤

See 41d for a directory of forms followed by an example of each form in MLA style. If you have further questions about citations using MLA style, consult Joseph Gibaldi and Walter S. Achtert, *MLA Handbook for Writers of Research Papers,* 3rd ed., New York: MLA, 1988.

> **2** **Using APA documentation style: the References list**

Citing books—APA

Citations for books have four main parts: author, date, title, and publication information. Indent all lines after the first line three spaces.

456

Didion, J.   (1977).   A book of common prayer. New York.

Simon & Schuster.

Give the last name first and then the initial of the first and, if any, middle name. In the title, capitalize only the first word and any word after a colon. If several cities are listed for place of publication, give only the first. If the city might be unfamiliar to a reader, add an abbreviation of the state (use U.S. Postal Service abbreviations), province, or country. Do not use a shortened form of the publisher's name, but you may omit terms such as *Publishers, Co.,* and *Inc.* Give the latest copyright date for the edition you are using.

Citing articles—APA

Citations for articles in periodicals (such as journals, magazines, and newspapers) contain four major parts: author, date, title of article, and publication information. For articles, the publication information usually includes the periodical title, volume number, and inclusive page numbers.

NAME   DATE   ARTICLE TITLE
Shuter, R.   (1977).   A field study of nonverbal

communication in Germany, Italy, and the United

States. Communication Monographs, 44, 298–305.

In the citation for an article, each part is followed by a period and two spaces. Within each part, use one space between words and after punctuation. In the title, capitalize only the first word and any word after a colon. Additional items of information may be required, depending on the source.

❖ NUMBER ALERT: Use complete inclusive page numbers (for example, 103–104, 344–347, 2334–2367). ❖

If you have further questions about citations using APA style, consult American Psychological Association, *Publication Manual of the American Psychological Association,* 3rd ed., Washington, D.C.: APA, 1984.

41d Using MLA forms or APA forms for a list of sources

The following directory presents a numbered list of the forms shown in the examples in this section. The MLA style and the APA style appear together for each pattern so that you can compare them easily. Use *only* MLA style or *only* APA style. Never mix them.

Not every possible documentation model is given. You may find that you have to combine features of more than one model to document a particular source.

DIRECTORY

1. Book by one author
2. Book by two or three authors
3. Two or more books by same author (s)
4. Book by group or corporate author
5. Book with no author named
6. Translation
7. Work in several volumes or parts
8. One selection from an anthology or an edited book
9. Edition
10. Anthology or edited book
11. Books with a title within a title
12. Government publication
13. Article from a daily newspaper

14. Editorial, letter to the editor, review
15. Unsigned article from a daily newspaper
16. Article from a weekly or biweekly magazine or newspaper
17. Article in a monthly or bimonthly periodical
18. Unsigned article from a weekly or monthly periodical
19. Article in a journal with continuous pagination
20. Article in a journal that pages each issue separately
21. Interview
22. Lectures, speeches, and addresses
23. Films and videotapes
24. Recordings
25. Live performance
26. Radio and television programs
27. Computer software

1. BOOK BY ONE AUTHOR

MLA   Welty, Eudora. <u>One Writer's Beginnings</u>.
Cambridge: Harvard UP, 1984.

APA   Welty, E. (1984). <u>One writer's beginnings</u>.
Cambridge: Harvard University Press.

2. BOOK BY TWO OR THREE AUTHORS

MLA   Leghorn, Lisa, and Katherine Parker. <u>Woman's
Worth</u>. Boston: Routledge, 1981.

MLA   Kelly, Alfred H., Winfred A. Harbison, and Herman
Belz. <u>The American Constitution: Its Origins
and Development</u>. New York: Norton, 1983.

Give only the first author's name in reversed order; give other authors' names in normal order. Use commas to separate authors' names, including a comma before the *and* preceding the last name in the series. Give the names in the order in which they appear on the title page of the book.

APA   Leghorn, L, & Parker, K. (1981). <u>Woman's worth</u>.
           Boston: Routledge & Kegan Paul.

APA   Kelly, A. H., Harbison, W. A., & Belz, H. (1983).
           <u>The American constitution: Its origins and</u>
           <u>development</u>. New York: Norton.

Give each author's name in reversed order. Use initials for first
and middle names. Use commas to separate authors' names, including a comma before the ampersand (the symbol &) with
more than two authors. Give the names in the order in which
they appear on the title page of the book.

3. TWO OR MORE BOOKS BY SAME AUTHOR(S)

MLA   Morris, Desmond. <u>Manwatching: A Field Guide to</u>
           <u>Human Behavior</u>. New York: Abrams, 1977.
           ---, ed. <u>Primate Ethology</u>. London: Wiedenfeld,
           1967.

When citing two or more books by the same author(s), give the
name(s) in the first entry only. In the second and subsequent
entries, use three hyphens and a period to stand for exactly the
same name(s). If the person served as editor or translator, put
a comma and the appropriate abbreviation *(ed.* or *trans.)* following the three hyphens. Alphabetize the works listed according to book title, regardless of such labels as *ed.* or *trans.,* and
regardless of the chronological order in which they were
published.

APA   Morris, Desmond. (1977). <u>Manwatching: A field</u>
           <u>guide to human behavior</u>. New York: Henry N.
           Abrams.

APA   Morris, Desmond, ed. (1967). <u>Primate ethology</u>.
           London: Wiedenfeld.

Give the author's name in full in all entries.

4. Book by Group of Corporate Author

MLA   The Boston Women's Health Collective. <u>Our Bodies,</u>
            <u>Ourselves</u>. New York: Simon, 1986.

Cite the full name of the corporate author first.

APA   The Boston Women's Health Collective. (1986). <u>Our</u>
            <u>bodies, ourselves</u>. New York: Simon & Schuster.

Cite the full name of the corporate author first. If the author is also the publisher, use the word *Author* as the name of the publisher.

5. Book with No Author Named

MLA   <u>The Chicago Manual of Style</u>. 13th ed. Chicago: U
            of Chicago P, 1982.

If there is no author's name on the title page, begin the citation with the title. Alphabetize the entry according to the first significant word of the title (not *A, An,* or *The*).

APA   <u>The Chicago manual of style</u> (13th ed.). (1982).
            Chicago: University of Chicago Press.

If there is no author's name on the title page, begin the citation with the title. Alphabetize the entry according to the first significant word of the title (not *A, An,* or *The*).

6. Translation

MLA   Freire, Paulo. <u>Pedagogy of the Oppressed</u>. Trans.
            Myra Bergman Ramos. New York: Seabury, 1970.

APA   Freire, P. (1970). <u>Pedagogy of the oppressed</u> (M.
            B. Ramos, Trans.). New York: Seabury Press.

7. Work in Several Volumes or Parts

MLA   Jones, Ernest. <u>The Last Phase</u>. New York: Basic,
            1957. Vol. 3 of <u>The Life and Work of Sigmund
            Freud</u>. 3 vols.

MLA   Randall, John Herman, Jr. <u>The Career of
            Philosophy</u>. 2 vols. New York: Columbia UP,
            1962.

If you are citing only one volume of a multivolume work, place
this information after the publication date. You may end the
entry giving the total number of volumes. MLA recommends
using arabic numerals, even if the source uses roman numerals
(Vol. 6 for *Vol. VI).* If you have drawn from two or more volumes of a multivolume work, give the total number of volumes.

APA   Randall, J. H., Jr. (1962). <u>The career of
            philosophy</u> (Vols. 1–2). New York: Columbia
            University Press.

8. ANTHOLOGY OR EDITED BOOK

MLA   Valdez, Luis, and Stan Steiner, eds. <u>Aztlan: An
            Anthology of Mexican American Literature</u>. New
            York: Knopf, 1972.

APA   Valdez, L., & Steiner, S. (Eds.). (1972). <u>Aztlan:
            An anthology of Mexican American literature</u>.
            New York: Alfred A. Knopf.

9. ONE SELECTION FROM AN ANTHOLOGY OR AN EDITED BOOK

MLA   Galarza, Ernest. "The Roots of Migration."
            <u>Aztlan: An Anthology of Mexican American
            Literature</u>. Ed. Luis Valdez and Stan Steiner.
            New York: Knopf, 1972. 127–132.

Give the author and title of the selection first. Place titles of essays, short stories, or short poems in quotation marks. Underline the title of a book or a play. Then give the full title of the anthology. Follow it with the name or names of the editor(s). Precede the name(s) by *Ed.* whether there is one or many editors. Give the first name before the last. End the citation with the inclusive page number of the selection; do not use the abbreviation *p.* or *pp.*

APA   Galarza, E. (1972). The roots of migration.   In

L. Valdez and S. Steiner (Eds.), <u>Aztlan: An</u>

<u>anthology of Mexican American literature</u>

(pp. 127—132). New York: Alfred A. Knopf.

The word *In* introduces the larger work from which the selection is taken. Use *Ed.* for one edition, and use *Eds.* for two or more editors.

10. EDITION

MLA   Mandell, Maurice I. <u>Advertising</u>.   4th ed.

Englewood Cliffs: Prentice, 1984.

When a book is not the first edition, the edition number appears on the title page. Place this information between the title and the publication information.

APA   Mandell, M. I. (1984). <u>Advertising</u> (4th ed.).

Englewood Cliffs, NJ: Prentice Hall.

11. BOOK WITH A TITLE WITHIN A TITLE

MLA   Lumiansky, Robert M., and Herschel Baker, eds.

<u>Critical Approaches to Six Major English</u>

<u>Works</u>: Beowulf <u>Through</u> Paradise Lost.

Philadelphia: U of Pennsylvania P, 1968.

When a book title includes the title of another work that is usually underlined (such as a novel, play, or long poem), do *not* underline the incorporated title. If the incorporated title is usually enclosed in quotation marks (such as a short story or short poem), keep the quotation marks and underline the complete title of the book. The word *through* is underlined in this subtitle because it is not part of the incorporated titles.

APA   Lumiansky, R. M., & Baker, H. (Eds.). (1968).

            Critical approaches to six major English works:

            Beowulf through Paradise Lost. Philadelphia:

            University of Pennsylvania Press.

12. GOVERNMENT PUBLICATION

MLA   United States. Cong. House. Committee on the

            Judiciary. Immigration and Nationality with

            Amendments and Notes on Related Laws. 7th ed.

            Washington: GPO, 1980.

If a government publication has no stated author, use the government, governmental body, and/or government agency as the author, with periods and two spaces separating the parts. *GPO* is the standard abbreviation for Government Printing Office.

APA   United States Congressional House Committee on the

            Judiciary. (1980). Immigration and nationality

            with amendments and notes on related laws (7th

            ed.). Washington, D.C.: U.S. Government

            Printing Office.

13. ARTICLE FROM A DAILY NEWSPAPER

MLA   Dullea, Georgia. "Literary Folk Look for Solid

            Comfort." New York Times 6 Apr. 1986: C14.

Cite the title of the newspaper exactly as it appears on the masthead, omitting any introductory *A* or *The*. If the city of publication is not in the title of the periodical, add it in square

brackets after the title, not underlined: for example, Patriot
Ledger [Quincy, MA]. Give the day, month, and year of the issue.
Be sure to give the section letter as well as the page number, if
appropriate: C14. If an article does not run on consecutive
pages (if, for example, it starts on 23 and continues on 42), give
the first page number and add a plus sign (23+).

APA   Dullea, G. (1986, April 16). Literary folk look
             for solid comfort. New York Times, p. C14.

14. EDITORIAL, LETTER TO THE EDITOR, REVIEW

MLA   "Facing Space, After the Cold War." Editorial. New
             York Times 1 May 1989: A16.

MLA   Childress, Glenda Teal. Letter. Newsweek 9 June
             1986: 10.

MLA   Linebaugh, Peter. "In the Flight Path of Perry
             Anderson." Rev. of In the Tracks of
             Historical Materialism, by Perry Anderson.
             History Workshop 21 (1986): 141–46.

APA   Facing space, after the cold war. (1989, May 1)
             [Editorial.] New York Times, p. A16.

APA   Childress, G. T. (1986, June 9). [Letter to the
             editor.] Newsweek, p. 10.

APA   Linebaugh, P. (1986). In the flight path of Perry
             Anderson [Review of In the tracks of historical
             materialism]. History Workshop, 21, pp. 141–
             146.

15. UNSIGNED ARTICLE FROM A DAILY NEWSPAPER

MLA   "Hospitals, Competing for Scarce Patients, Turn to
             Advertising." New York Times 20 Apr. 1986: 47.

Alphabetize in Works Cited by first word of title.

APA   Hospitals, competing for scarce patients, turn to
            advertising. (1986, April 20). <u>New York Times</u>,
            p. 47.

Alphabetize in References by first word of the title.

16. ARTICLE FROM A WEEKLY OR BIWEEKLY MAGAZINE OR NEWSPAPER

MLA   Toufexis, Anastasia. "Dining with Invisible
            Danger." <u>Time</u> 27 Mar. 1989: 28.

If a periodical is published every week or every two weeks, give
the complete date. First cite the day, then the month (abbreviated if necessary), and finally the year. Drop any introductory
A, An, or *The* from the title of a periodical.

APA   Toufexis, A. (1989, March 27). Dining with
            invisible danger. <u>Time</u>, p. 28.

17. ARTICLE IN A MONTHLY OR BIMONTHLY PERIODICAL

MLA   Roosevelt, Anna. "Lost Civilizations of the Lower
            Amazon." <u>Natural History</u> Feb. 1989: 74–83.

If a periodical is published monthly or every two months, give
the month(s) and year.

APA   Roosevelt, A. (1989, February). Lost civilizations
            of the lower Amazon. <u>Natural History</u>, pp. 74–
            83.

18. UNSIGNED ARTICLE FROM A WEEKLY OR MONTHLY PERIODICAL

MLA   "A Salute to Everyday Heroes." <u>Time</u> 10 July 1989:
            46+.

APA   A salute to everyday heroes. (1989, July 10).
            <u>Time</u>, pp. 46–51, 54–56, 58–60, 63–64, 66.

19. ARTICLE IN A JOURNAL WITH CONTINUOUS PAGINATION

MLA   Cochran, D. D., W. Daniel Hale, and Christine P.
Hissam. "Personal Space Requirements in
Indoor versus Outdoor Locations." <u>Journal of
Psychology</u> 117 (1984): 132–33.

If a journal pages its issues continuously through an annual volume, give only the volume number before the year. (*National Geographic* is such a journal. If the first issue of a volume ends on page 224, for example, the second issue starts on page 225.) Notice that all numbers, even the volume, are arabic numerals.

APA   Cochran, D. D., Hale, W. D., & Hissam, C. P.
(1984). Personal space requirements in indoor
versus outdoor locations. <u>Journal of
Psychology</u>, <u>117</u>, 132–133.

The volume number is underlined.

20. ARTICLE IN A JOURNAL THAT PAGES EACH ISSUE SEPARATELY

MLA   Hashimoto, Irvin. "Pain and Suffering: Apostrophes
and Academic Life." <u>Journal of Basic Writing</u>
7.2 (1988): 91–98.

Some journals page each issue of an annual volume separately. (Each issue begins with page 1.) To cite articles from such journals, give both the volume number and the issue number (7.2 says that 7 is the volume and 2 is the issue).

APA   Hashimoto, I. (1988). Pain and suffering:
Apostrophes and academic life. <u>Journal of Basic
Writing</u>. <u>7</u>(2), 91–98.

The volume number is underlined, and the issue number appears immediately after it, within parentheses.

21. INTERVIEW

MLA   Friedman, Randi.   Telephone interview.   30 June
                1991.

In APA style, a personal interview is considered personal cor-
respondence and is not included in the References list. Cite the
interview parenthetically in the text: Randi Friedman (personal
communication, June 30, 1989).

22. LECTURES, SPEECHES, AND ADDRESSES

MLA   Kennedy, John Fitzgerald.   Address.   Greater
                Houston Ministerial Association.   Houston,
                Sept. 12, 1960.

APA   Kennedy, J. F. (1960, September 12).   Address.
                Speech presented to the Greater Houston
                Ministerial Association, Houston.

23. FILMS AND VIDOETAPES

MLA   <u>Erendira</u>.   Writ. Gabriel Garcia Marquez.   Dir. Ruy
                Guerra.   With Irene Pappas.   Miramax, 1984.

APA   Marquez, G. G. (Writer), & Guerra, R. (Director).
                (1984).   <u>Erendira</u> [Film].   New York: Miramax.

24. RECORDINGS

MLA   Smetana, Bedřich.   <u>My Country</u>.   Cond. Karel Anserl.
                Czech Philharmonic Orch.   Vanguard, SV-9/10,
                1975.

MLA   Turner, Tina.   "Show Some Respect."   <u>Private
                Dancer</u>.   Capitol, ST-12330, 1983.

Begin the citation of a recording with either the composer, conductor, or performer, depending on whom or what you are em-

phasizing in your paper. Then give the information shown in the examples. If no date is available, use the abbreviation "n.d."

APA   Smetana, B. (Composer). (1975). <u>My country</u>.
Anserl (Conductor). Czech Philharmonic Orch.
(Recording No. Sv-9/10).

APA   Turner, T. (Performer). (1983). Show some respect.
On <u>Private dancer</u> [Album].

The word *On* is used to show where the selection came from.

25. Live Performance

MLA   <u>The Real Thing</u>. By Tom Stoppard. Dir. Mike
Nichols. With Jeremy Irons and Glenn Close.
Plymouth Theatre, New York. 3 June 1984.

Begin with the title or a particular individual (for example, writer, conductor, or director) depending on your emphasis.

APA   Stoppard, T. (Author), Nichols, M. (Director),
Irons, J. (Performer), & Close, G. (Performer).
(1984, June 3). <u>The Real Thing</u> [Live
performance]. New York: Plymouth Theatre.

26. Radio and Television Programs

MLA   <u>The Little Sister</u>. Writ. and dir. Jan Egleson.
With Tracy Pollan and John Savage. Prod.
Rebecca Eaton. American Playhouse. PBS.
WGBH, Boston. 7 Apr. 1986.

To cite radio or television programs, include all information shown in the example: the title of the program (underlined); the network; the local station and its city; and the date of the broadcast. For a series, also supply the title of the specific episode (in quotation marks) before the title of the program (underlined) and the title of the series (neither underlined nor in quotation marks) if it is different from the program title.

APA Egleson, J. (Writer and Director), Pollan, T.
(Performer), Savage, J. (Performer), & Eaton, R.
(Producer). (1986, April 7). <u>The little sister</u>
[Television program]. Boston: WGBH, PBS
American Playhouse.

27. COMPUTER SOFTWARE

MLA <u>Microsoft Word</u>. Vers. 5.0. Computer software.
Microsoft, 1989. MS–DOS 2.0 or higher or OS/2
1.0 512K, disk.

To cite computer software, give the writer of the program (if known), the title (underlined), a descriptive label, the distributor, and the year of publication. Add any other important information, such as the computer on which the program can be used, number of kilobytes or units of memory, operating system, and form of the program (cartridge, cassette, or disk).

APA <u>Microsoft word</u>. Vers. 5.0 [Computer software].
(1989). Microsoft. MS–DOS 2.0 or higher or
OS/2 1.0. 512K, disk.

41e Using content endnotes or footnotes in MLA style

When you want to add observations to your paper that do not fit into your text, use endnotes or footnotes. In the MLA system, the page is headed *Notes* (in the APA system, the page is headed *Footnotes*).

In MLA style, footnotes or endnotes serve two specific purposes. You can use them for commentary that does not fit into your paper but is still worth relating.

TEXT OF PAPER

Eudora Welty's literary biography, <u>One Writer's Beginnings</u>, shows us how both the inner world of self and the outer world of family and place form a writer's imagination.[1]

ENDNOTE WITH COMMENTARY

[1] Welty, who values her privacy, has resisted investigation of her life. However, at the age of 74, she chose to present her own autobiographical reflections in a series of lectures at Harvard University.

Also, you can use notes for extensive lists of bibliographic information supporting points you make in a paper. Otherwise, such information interrupts the flow of your paper.

TEXT OF PAPER

Barbara Randolph believes that enthusiasm is contagious (65).[2] Many psychologists have found that panic, fear, and rage spread more quickly in crowds than positive emotions do, however.

ENDNOTE WITH ADDITIONAL SOURCES

[2] Others agree with Randolph. See Thurman 21, 84, 155; Kelley 421–25; and Brookes 65–76.

41f Documenting sources with endnotes or footnotes in MLA style

You can put documentation information in notes either at the bottom of pages (footnotes) or on a separate page or pages

471

following the end of your paper (endnotes). The content is the same, whether you use footnotes or endnotes. Unless your instructor requires footnotes, use endnotes because they are easier to manage when you are typing a paper. For an example of a page of endnotes, see page 10 of Amy Brown's research paper in Chapter 42.

When a research paper refers to only one or two primary sources, some instructors permit students to use simplified documentation. A single note tells where quotations come from. When the full text of the primary source is not given in the paper's appendix, give full publication information:

¹ All quotations are from Alfred Lord Tennyson, "Break, Break, Break," <u>Literature: An Introduction to Reading and Writing</u>, 3rd ed., Edgar V. Roberts and Henry E. Jacobs. Prentice, 1992: p. 629.

Note form in MLA style for first reference

In a note system of documentation, the first time you refer to a source in your writing, the note gives complete bibliographic facts as well as the specific place you are referring to or quoting from in that source. Here are first-reference note forms for common sources.

BOOK WITH ONE AUTHOR—MLA NOTE FORM

¹ Joan Didion, <u>Salvador</u> (New York: Simon, 1983) 64.

BOOK WITH TWO OR THREE AUTHORS—MLA NOTE FORM

² Irving Wallace, David Wallechinsky, and Amy Wallace, <u>Significa</u> (New York: Dutton, 1983) 177.

WORK IN SEVERAL VOLUMES OR PARTS—MLA NOTE FORM

³ Robert Kelley, <u>The Shaping of the American Past</u>, vol. 2 (Englewood Cliffs, NJ: Prentice, 1975) 724–25.

WORK IN AN ANTHOLOGY OR A COLLECTION—MLA NOTE FORM

⁴ Wayne Tosh, "Computer Linguistics," <u>Linguistics Today</u>, ed. Archibald A. Hill (New York: Basic, 1969) 200.

ARTICLE IN A REFERENCE WORK—MLA NOTE FORM

⁵ "Fraudulence in the Arts," <u>The New Encyclopaedia</u>
<u>Britannica</u>, 1979 ed.

ARTICLE FROM A JOURNAL WITH CONTINUOUS PAGINATION—MLA NOTE FORM

⁶ William A. Madden, "<u>Wuthering Heights</u>: The Binding
Passion," <u>Nineteenth-Century Fiction</u> 27 (1972): 151.

ARTICLE FROM A JOURNAL THAT PAGES EACH ISSUE SEPARATELY—MLA NOTE FORM

⁷ Michael C. T. Brookes, "A Dean's Dilemmas," <u>Journal of</u>
<u>Basic Writing</u> 5.1 (1986): 65.

Note forms for second and subsequent references in MLA style

After the first note for a source, shorten all further references to the source. If you are citing only one work by the author, the author's last name and the page references are enough:

¹⁵ Kelley, 731.

If you are citing more than one work by the same author, also include a shortened form of the title.

¹⁶ Didion, <u>Salvador</u> 45.

List of sources when note is used in MLA style

When you use MLA note style, you have two options for listing your sources at the end of a paper. You can list all sources consulted, not only the sources referred to or quoted from. If you do this, call the list Bibliography. Alternatively, you can list only the sources referred to or quoted from. If you do this, call the list Works Cited. Whatever your choice, MLA style calls for the format for Works Cited (see 41c and 41d).

41g Using other styles to document sources

MLA style (41c-1) and APA style (41c-2) are not the only documentation styles. Many academic disciplines have manuals that explain the documentation style common to their professional journals. In each course, ask your instructor what documentation style is required. If the choice is yours, use the style of your major field so that you can practice it, or follow the style of the subject of your course. If you are writing in a field that does not have a style manual, refer to a journal in the field and imitate its documentation style.

BIOLOGY

Council of Biology Editors Style Manual Committee. *CBE Style Manual.* 5th ed. Bethesda: Council of Biology, 1983.

CHEMISTRY

American Chemical Society. *Handbook for Authors of Papers in American Chemical Society Publications.* Washington, DC: American Chemical Society, 1978.

MATHEMATICS

American Mathematical Society. *A Manual for Authors of Mathematical Papers.* 8th ed. Providence, RI: American Mathematical Society, 1984.

PHYSICS

American Institute of Physics. *Style Manual for Guidance in Preparation of Papers.* 3rd ed. New York: American Institute of Physics, 1978.

42 Case Study: A Student's Research Process

This chapter presents a case study of a student, Amy Brown, going through the processes of conducting research and writing a paper based on her findings. Section 42b shows Brown's final draft, along with annotations about the paper and Process Notes about Brown's decisions during her writing process.

Here is the assignment given to Amy Brown: Write a research paper on the general subject of "communication." The paper should run 1800 to 2000 words and should be based on a variety of sources. The final paper is due in five weeks. Interim deadlines for parts of the work will be announced. To complete this assignment, you need to engage in two interrelated processes: conducting research and writing a paper based on the research. Consult the *Simon & Schuster Concise Handbook,* especially Chapter 40.

42a Observing the research process

Amy Brown faced many challenges as she worked on her assignment. Narrowing the subject of *communication* to a more suitable topic proved to be the most difficult challenge. Brown decided to concentrate on *nonverbal communication* because the idea of unspoken messages among people interested her. She started her research by compiling a list of **headings and key words** (see 40f) that she found by looking up *nonverbal communication* in periodical indexes (see 40j) and the book catalog (see 40k) in her college library. She located many terms: *eye movements, gesture, sign language, body language, touch, expression, space perception, space and time,* and *territory.* Such a varied list confirmed what Brown had suspected: Nonverbal communication was too broad a subject for her paper. She thought about expressions on people's faces when they use public transportation, but she found that that topic was too narrow for the available resources in the library. At this point, Brown was tempted to switch to an entirely different aspect of communication, but she did not want to give up too soon. Brown wrote in her **research log** to keep track of her progress and to think on paper and discover ideas.

Deciding that more information would help her think of a suitable topic, Brown browsed through a psychology textbook and interviewed a psychology professor. One book that the professor recommended was especially interesting to Brown: *The Hidden Dimension,* by Edward T. Hall, which talks about personal space as a major factor in nonverbal communication. Personal space concerns the amount of physical distance people expect to maintain between themselves and other people during social interaction. The idea of space as a part of communication intrigued her. Brown was intrigued by the concept, so she decided to see what she could find in the library.

The key term *personal space* produced an important title: *Personal Space,* by Robert Sommer. Brown also looked under *body language,* a term she had seen in the titles of a few articles listed in the *Social Science Index.* She found *Body Language,* by Julius Fast. At the back of Fast's book is a bibliography of key references which includes Hall's book and Sommer's book. The listings helped Brown confirm that Hall and Sommer were **authoritative, reliable sources,** two among a number of criteria used to evaluate sources (see 40f).

476

Next, Brown was ready to formulate a **research question** (see 40a), which would further narrow her topic. Brown was most interested in Hall's discussion of differing standards for personal space in different cultures. After brainstorming some research questions, Brown settled on "How do standards for personal space differ among cultures?"

Now Brown was ready to think about her purpose (see 1b). While reading and taking notes to answer her research question, however, Brown realized that she could not explain basic cross-cultural concepts *and* argue a position within the time and length limits of the assignment. She settled on an informative purpose. For an audience (see 1c), she chose a **general reader**—rather than a specialized reader—because she wanted to assume that the audience would know little about the topic of personal space.

Brown's research process now shifted to finding additional sources and taking notes. Earlier Brown had used a search strategy (see 40g) to help her think of a suitable topic. Now she used the search strategy again, this time to take notes on the sources she had found before and to find additional sources that would permit her to give a full picture in her paper.

While taking notes, Brown realized that some of the articles she had found were not as useful as she had thought. She rejected a few sources that were duplications of what she already had. By now Brown was evolving a working bibliography. Using MLA documentation style (see 41-c and 41d) she made bibliography cards.

In organizing her paper, Brown looked through her notes and saw that she could place them into two piles: standards for personal space in North America and standards in other countries. She tried to outline the material and quickly realized that she had to start with a definition of personal space. Going back through her cards, she created a third pile for definitions.

Composing her thesis statement was next. Brown knew that her thesis statement would be the last sentence of her introductory paragraph. She drafted a preliminary thesis statement to use as she wrote the first draft of her paper. Later she revised the thesis statement (see 40n).

42b **Analyzing Amy Brown's research paper**

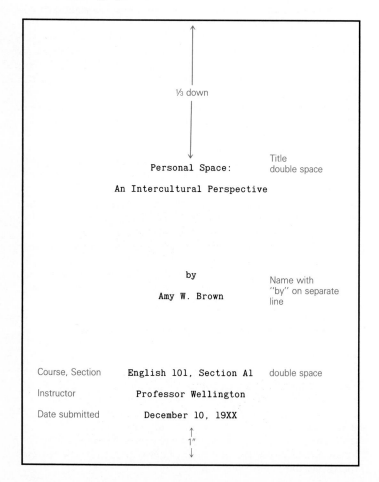

↑ ⅓ down ↓

Personal Space: Title
double space

An Intercultural Perspective

by   Name with
"by" on separate
Amy W. Brown   line

Course, Section   **English 101, Section A1**   double space

Instructor   **Professor Wellington**

Date submitted   **December 10, 19XX**

↑ 1" ↓

Cover page. If your instructor requires a cover page, use the format and types of information shown on the opposite page. Then on page 1 of your paper, repeat only the paper's title. A cover page is needed when an outline is included with the paper, as is the case with Amy Brown's paper. The outline appears on the next two pages.

First page. If your instructor does not require a cover page, follow the style shown below for heading your first page (which shows MLA format). If you do use a cover page, use the format on the first page of Amy Brown's paper on page 478.

HEADING FOR FIRST PAGE WITHOUT COVER PAGE

1

Amy W. Brown   Name

Professor Wellington   Instructor

English 101, Section A1   Course, Section

10 December 19XX   Date submitted
                                      double space

Personal Space:

An Intercultural Perspective
                                      quadruple
                                      space

    When she returned home after a year in South

America, Judith Martin, a North American writer,

realized that many people kept interpreting her

behavior as flirtatious. She was not flirting,

however. What she realized was that most South

Americans talk to each other face-to-face, and

they stand closer together than do North Ameri-

Brown i

Outline

<u>Thesis.statement</u>: Everyone has expectations concerning the use of personal space, but accepted distances for that space are determined by each person's culture.

  I. Observations about personal space began about thirty years ago.

    A. Most people are unaware that interpersonal distances exist.

    B. Personal space depends on invisible boundaries.

    C. Personal space moves with people as they interact.

 II. Research reveals North Americans' expectations for personal space.

    A. Hall identifies four zones for personal space.

    B. Subcultures help determine expectations for personal space.

    C. Gender influences people's use of personal space.

Brown ii

III. Expectations concerning personal space vary
   greatly from culture to culture.

   A. Conversational distances vary in different
      cultures.

      1. Western Europeans use fingertip-to-
         shoulder distance.

      2. Eastern Europeans use wrist-to-shoulder
         distance.

      3. Mediterraneans use elbow-to-shoulder
         distances.

      4. Arabs prefer close interpersonal
         distances.

      5. Japanese do not prefer close
         interpersonal distances.

   B. Amounts of touching vary in different
      cultures.

Outline. Brown's instructor required that a formal outline be submitted with the final draft of each student's research paper. To format her outline, Brown referred to sections 2n and 40o in this handbook. She wrote the outline as a **sentence outline,** not a topic outline (see 2n).

If your instructor does not want a cover page (see page 479) but does require an outline, ask whether the outline should be placed at the beginning or end of the paper.

A

1

B

Personal Space:

An Intercultural Perspective

C

1   When she returned home after a year in South America, Judith Martin, a North American writer, realized that many people kept interpreting her behavior as flirtatious. She was not flirting, however. What she realized was that most South Americans talk to each other face-to-face, and they stand closer together than do North Americans (9). Martin was confronted by the phenomenon known as personal space—the amount of physical distance people expect during social interaction. Everyone has expectations concerning the use of personal space, but accepted distances for that space are determined by each person's culture.

D

2   Observations about personal space began about thirty years ago. Anthropologist Edward T. Hall was a pioneer in the field. He became very interested in how interpersonal distances affected communication between people. In his aptly titled

E

General Note: Amy Brown uses MLA style for format and for documentation, which includes parenthetical references (see 41b-1) and Works Cited (see 41c and 41d).

A. **Page number.**   Because Brown used a cover page, she typed the number 1 in the upper right-hand corner, placed a half inch from the top edge. On continuation pages, she typed the page number preceded by her last name.

B. **Title.**   Brown's title prepares readers for her paper in two important ways. It gives the paper's major term (personal space) and the focus of the paper's discussion (more than one culture).   ❖ PROCESS NOTE: In an earlier draft, Brown's title was "Proxemics: An Intercultural Perspective on the Need for Space." She rejected it because "space" was too general and "proxemics" was too technical. She then tried "Being Close: An Intercultural Perspective." Brown liked the second half because it was an accurate description of her focus, but the first half had multiple meanings. ❖

C. **Introductory device.**   Brown uses an anecdote (see 5e). She felt it made the abstract concept of personal space concrete and familiar; it tied into the paper's title; it led into the thesis statement°; and it captured readers' interest.

D. **Thesis statement.**   The last sentence of Brown's introductory paragraph is her thesis statement, which presents the central idea of the paper. Emerging from the paper's title and opening anecdote, the thesis prepares readers for what to expect.   ❖ PROCESS NOTE: To see the evolution of Brown's thesis statement, see 40n. ❖

E. **Evaluation of source.**   Brown establishes Hall as an expert by identifying him as an anthropologist and as a pioneer on the subject of personal space.   ❖ PROCESS NOTE: To see how Brown was able to confirm that Hall was an authoritative, reliable source, see 42a. ❖

Brown 2

F

book <u>The Hidden Dimension</u>, Hall coined the word
"proxemics" to describe people's use of space as a
means of communication (1). As Hall's book title
indicates, most people are unaware that interpersonal distances exist and contribute to people's
reactions to one another (109).

3

G

    Personal space depends on invisible bound-
aries. Those boundaries move with people as they

H

interact. Personal space gets larger or smaller
depending on the circumstances of the social
interaction at any moment (Fisher, Bell, and Baum

I

149). Robert Sommer, an environmental psychologist, uses literary[1] and visual similes to

J

describe personal space:

K

> Like the porcupines in Schopenhauer's
> fable, people like to be close enough to
> obtain warmth and comradeship but far
> enough away to avoid pricking one
> another. Personal space . . . has been
> likened to a snail shell, a soap bubble,
> an aura, a "breathing room." (26)

F. **Parenthetical reference to author and book named in the text.** Brown uses two sources by Edward T. Hall (see "Works Cited" on Brown's page 10). She has to be sure to keep them separate. In this paragraph, therefore, she mentions Hall's name and the title of the work she is referring to, and her two parenthetical references include only the page numbers. The references are inserted before the periods that end the sentences. Brown uses quotation marks to set off the coined word "proxemics." (The other work by Hall is cited in paragraph 7.)

G. **Topic sentence.** Brown uses a topic sentence (see 5a) to start many of her paragraphs. ❖ PROCESS NOTE: Brown did not want to plagiarize. She thought carefully about what she could say in her paper without citing a source. Because she had read a great deal and had categorized her notes into logical units, she decided that her topic sentences—which she usually put at the beginning of her paragraphs—were her own and did not need citations. ❖

H. **Paraphrase of original source.** ❖ PROCESS NOTE: In an earlier draft, Brown quoted this material. In her final draft, she uses a paraphrase to avoid too many quotations. ❖

I. **Parenthetical reference to author not named in the text.** The source (author and page) is added in parentheses.

J. **Comment in an endnote.** An endnote number is placed a half line above, without a space between the word and the endnote number. See annotation DD for Brown's endnote.

K. **A long quotation.** A quotation of more than four typewritten lines is set off from the rest of the text. Brown introduces it with a colon because she has written a complete sentence. She indents the material 10 spaces and does not paragraph indent the first line. In the fourth line Brown uses a three-dot ellipsis to indicate the place where she omitted words. The page reference for the quotation is given in parentheses after the punctuation that ends the quotation. The words "breathing room" are in quotation marks because they appear that way in the original source.

Brown 3

4   Research provides information about the distances that North Americans prefer when interacting. The pioneering work was done by Hall. He observed the behavior of a group of middle-class adults in business and professions in the northeastern United States. He saw four zones of personal space; they are summarized and explained in Table 1 on the next page.   **L**

5   Researchers working with Hall's data found that accepted interpersonal distances in the United States also depend on other factors. For example, subcultures[2] help determine expectations   **M** concerning personal space. Fisher, Bell, and Baum report that groups of Hispanic-Americans generally interact more closely within their subculture than Anglo-Americans do within theirs. They further explain that in general all "subcultural groups   **N** tend to interact at closer distances with members of their own subculture than with nonmembers"   **O** (158).   **P**

6   Gender also influences people's use of   **Q** personal space. For example, sociologists Worchel

L. **Table placement.** In MLA style, a table must be placed as close as possible to where it is mentioned. If the table fits on one page, it should not be broken into two parts; in such cases, the table should start on the next page, as Brown has done here.

M. **Comment in an endnote.** Brown uses an end note to comment on her information.

N. **Quotation within sentence.** Brown fits a quotation into her prose, and she uses quotation marks to avoid plagiarism. ❖ PROCESS NOTE: Brown worked a quotation into paragraph 5 because she felt that the material comparing one subgroup with another might be sensitive. She wanted her readers to have particular confidence in her presentation of the information. This is Brown's second quotation her paper; the other one (paragraph 3) is a long quotation, which is displayed. This is a short run-in quotation, which Brown felt would demonstrate her skill at using both types of presentations for quotations. ❖

O. **Count of quotations** ❖ PROCESS NOTE: Brown used quotation in the following paragraphs: 3, 5, 7, and 9. She did not want to overuse quotations (see 39e), but she felt that all of these were justified because of their content. She also wanted to demonstrate her skillat using both run-in quotations (paragraphs 5 and 7) and displayed quotations (paragraphs 3 and 9). ❖

P. **Placement of parenthetical references.** Parenthetical references go immediately after a quotation or after a block of information from a source, as long as the material is not interrupted by the writer's own thinking.

Q. **Word choice.** Brown uses "gender," rather than "sex," here. ❖ PROCESS NOTE: In an early draft, Brown used "sex," not "gender." As she was reading journal articles, she saw that "gender" is used in discussions of comparisons between men and women. The psychology professor she had interviewed also used "gender," so she decided to use "gender" here. ❖

Brown 4

Table 1

Hall's "Distance Zones"[a]

	Intimate	Personal	Social	Public
Close	0 to 6"	1½' to 2½'	4' to 7'	12' to 25'
Far	6" to 1½'	2½' to 4'	7' to 12'	25' +

Source: Discussion in Hall, <u>Hidden</u> 110–20; also
    Henley 32–33; Fisher, Bell, and Baum 153.

[a] Selected illustrations of each zone are: <u>Close</u>
<u>Intimate</u>: lovers, children with parents; <u>Far</u>
<u>Intimate</u>: strangers in crowds; <u>Close Personal</u>:
husband and wife talking on the street; <u>Far</u>
<u>Personal</u>: friends talking on the street; <u>Close</u>
<u>Social</u>: boss and subordinate at a meeting; <u>Far</u>
<u>Social</u>: receptionist and people in a waiting room;
<u>Close Public</u>: teacher and students in a classroom;
<u>Far Public</u>: actors or public speakers with
audiences.

R. **Table.**   A table is an excellent way to summarize complex information that involves numbers and/or repeated categories. Brown uses the format described in the *MLA Handbook:* the table number and title at the left margin, a lettered—not numbered—footnote, and source information immediately below the data, before the footnote. In MLA style, footnotes in tables are signaled with lowercase letters, and endnotes or footnotes are signaled by numbers (see paragraphs 3 and 5). A table should be placed as close as possible to the paragraph in which it is first mentioned. If a table cannot fit in the space remaining on the page, it can be placed on the following page after the end of the first paragraph on that page. Some instructors permit students to put tables on a separate page at the end of the paper, before "Notes," if any, or before "Works Cited." ❧ PROCESS NOTE: In an early draft, Brown wrote sentences to present the information in this table. She did not think of using a table until she showed her early draft to a friend who said that the material was hard to follow and boring in prose form. She then tried to condense the material, and as she was writing she thought a table would be a concise, clear way to present numerical information. ❧

S. **Source identification.**   Because Brown uses two works by Hall, she includes a shortened title *(Hidden)* here so that readers will know which Hall work she is referring to. She uses semicolons to separate each item in a series of multiple references. The other Hall work is cited in paragraph 7.

T. **Choice of examples.**   ❧ PROCESS NOTE: In writing the footnote to the table, Brown had many choices of illustrations for each zone. She chose the ones that she thought her audience would find as useful as she did. ❧

Brown 5

and Cooper observe that North American males' most
negative reaction is reserved for anyone who
enters their personal space directly in front of
them. Females, on the other hand, feel most   **U**
negative about approaches from the side. Also,
females have smaller interpersonal distances than
do males, although pairs of the same sex communicate across larger spaces than do pairs of males   **V**
and females (535). The gender factor shifts,
however, in high density situations such as
crowded subways or elevators in the United States.
As Maines points out, when people have some choice
about where they stand or sit in crowded settings,
they gravitate to people of the same sex (100).

7   Expectations concerning personal space vary
greatly from culture to culture (Fast 29). Conversational distances vary between people from
different countries, according to Desmond Morris,   **W**
a British zoologist. He notes that when people
from Western Europe stand on the street and talk,
the space between them is the distance it would

U. **Paraphrase of an original source.** Brown uses a paraphrase here. ❖ PROCESS NOTE: The original source contains all the information here, but as Brown paraphrased she reordered its sequence slightly to fit the logic of her paper. She knew that reordering of sequence of material is permitted as long as the rearrangement does not distort the meaning of the original. Here is the original, from Worchel and Cooper, page 535 (the elipsis indicates intervening material): "One of the most consistent findings in the personal space literature is that females have smaller personal spaces thanmales. . . . Further, smaller personal-space zones are found between male-female pairs than between same-sex pairs. . . . Males responded most negatively to frontal invasions of their space, whereas females reacted most negatively to invasions from the side." ❖

V. **Multiple uses of sources.** ❖ PROCESS NOTE: Brown wondered whether she needed a parenthetical reference three times (after the second, third, and fourth sentences in paragraph 6). Her instructor explained that the parenthetical reference is needed only once as long as the information does not spill over to another paragraph and the material was not interrupted by information from another source or by a comment of the writer. ❖

W. **Summary of original source.** Brown uses a summary to condense the source. Here is the original, which uses British, not American, rules for quotation marks.

> Unfortunately, different countries have different ideas about exactly how close is close. It is easy enough to test your own 'space reaction': when you are talking to someone in the street or in any open space, reach out with your arm and see where the nearest point on his body comes. If you hail from western Europe, you will find that he is at roughly fingertip distance from you. In other words, as you reach out, your fingertips will just about make contact with his shoulder. If you come from Eastern Europe you will find you are standing at 'wrist distance'. If you come from the Mediterranean region you will find that you are much closer to your companion, at little more than 'elbow distance'.

Brown 6

take one person's fingertip to reach the other's
shoulder. People from Eastern Europe converse at a
wrist—to—shoulder distance. People from the
Mediterranean, however, prefer elbow—to—shoulder
distance (131). In an interview, Hall commented that   **X**
Arabs know the practicality of close conversational distances: "If you are interested in
something, your pupils dilate: if I say something
you don't like, they tend to contract" ("Silent
language" 47) Japanese generally do not prefer
close distances for conversations. Because the
island of Japan is quite small for its population
of about 120 million, public places are often very
crowded. To cope, the people remain formal and
aloof even when in very close proximity to one
another (Fast 38).

8   Permitted amounts of touching also illustrate
intercultural differences in standards for
personal space. Touching while conversing differs
in Germany, Italy, and the United States, reports
Robert Shuter, a communications specialist. His   **Y**
research shows that Germans and North Americans

X. **Quotation from an interview.**   Brown quotes what Hall said at an interview. She can be sure of the exact wording because the interview is reported in a respected magazine. ❖ PROCESS NOTE: While reading her sources, Brown was repeatedly impressed with the language of Edward T. Hall. She felt that her paraphrases and summaries could not possibly do justice to Hall, but she resisted the temptation to quote him extensively. She was aware that a student research paper, in one sense, is an exercise in which a student is expected to demonstrate the ability to paraphrase and summarize well. ❖

Y. **Transferring information from note to paper.**   In paragraph 8, Brown uses the summary from her note card.

> Shuter, p. 305
> Intercultural differences
>
> Summary:
> Germans and N. Americans behave alike in that males stand farther apart and touch less while talking than do male - female pairs. The opposite is true in Italy, where males interact more closely and touch more during conversations than do male-female pairs or female pairs. Thus, Italian males expect to use personal space as females do in Germany and the United States.

Brown 7

behave alike in that males stand farther apart and
touch less when talking than do male—female pairs
or female pairs. The opposite is true in Italy,
where males interact more closely and touch more
during conversations than do male—female pairs or
female pairs. Shuter concludes that Italian males   **Z**
expect to use personal space as females do in
Germany and the United States (305). In another
experiment, adults were asked to put dolls in
position for what was called "comfortable
interaction." People from Italy and Greece placed
the dolls closer together than did people from
Sweden, Scotland, or the United States. Also, in
doctors' waiting rooms, Australians were less
likely to start conversations with strangers than
were Indonesians (Worchel and Cooper 536).

9   People can easily be misunderstood if they
are insensitive to how people from another culture
use personal space. Clearly, what is considered
obnoxious in one culture might be considered
polite in another (Fisher, Bell, and Baum 167).

Z. **Word choice.**   ❖ PROCESS NOTE: In an early draft, Brown used the word "explains" in most places where she presented information from a source. When she revised, Brown wanted to vary her word choice. She looked at the chart in 39e to get ideas for different words. In her final draft Brown uses forms of these words: "explain" (paragraph 5), "report" (paragraphs 5 and 8); "observe" (paragraph 6); "points out" (paragraph 6); "note" (paragraph 7); "commented" (paragraph 7); and "conclude" (paragraph 8). ❖

Brown 8

As Hall says, virtually everything people are and do

> is associated with the experience of
> space. . . . Therefore, people from
> different cultures, when interpreting
> each other's behavior, often misin-
> terpret the relationship, the activity,
> or the emotions. This leads to
> alienation in encounters or distorted
> communications. (<u>Hidden</u> 171)

AA

As international travel and commerce increase, intercultural contact is becoming commonplace. Soon, perhaps, cultural variations in expectations for personal space will be as familiar to everyone as are cultural variations in food and dress. Until then, people need to make a special effort to learn one another's expectations concerning personal space. Once people are sensitive to such matters, they can stop them- selves from taking the wrong step—either away from or toward a person from another culture.

BB

10

AA. **Combined quotation from two paragraphs in original source.** Brown combines into one quotation material from two paragraphs in Hall. She uses a four-dot ellipsis to show that the quotation has one or more sentences between the quoted material. Here is the original source (Hall, *Hidden* 171):

This book emphasizes that virtually everything that man is and does is associated with the experience of space. Man's sense of space is a synthesis of many sensory inputs: visual, auditory, kinesthetic, olfactory, and thermal. Not only does each of these constitute a complex system—as, for example, the dozen different ways of experiencing depth visually—but each is molded and patterned by culture. Hence, there is no alternative to accepting the fact that people reared in different cultures live in different sensory worlds.

We learn from the study of culture that the patterning of perceptual worlds is a function not only of culture but of *relationship, activity,* and *emotion.* Therefore, people from different cultures, when interpreting each other's behavior, often misinterpret the relationship, the activity, or the emotions. This leads to alienation in encounters or distorted communications.

BB. **Concluding paragraph.** Brown concludes her paper with a call for action (see 5e). ❖ PROCESS NOTE: Brown rewrote her concluding paragraph many times. She wanted to use a call for action and to make the paragraph as concise and interesting as possible. Here is a very early draft of paragraph 10. ❖

> Contact between cultures is happening more fre-
> quently. After all, international travel and com-
> merce increase daily. It is urgent, therefore, that
> everyone knows that there are lots of variations among
> cultures in personal space. That means there are more
> differences than those in food and dress. Researchers'
> observations of the sort discussed in this paper help
> people understand more about the wide variety of expecta-
> tions concerning proper amounts of interpersonal
> closeness and distance.

CC

1″
Notes

½″
Brown 9

[1] Sociologists Worchel and Cooper reprint a rarely anthologized poem by the reknowned poet W. H. Auden, who explains his unique way of handling instrusions into his personal space (539):

DD

> Some thirty inches from my nose
> The frontier of my person goes
> And all the untilled air between
> Is private pagus or demense.
> Stranger, unless with bedroom eyes
> I beckon you to fraternize
> Beware of rudely crossing it
> I have no gun but I can spit.

EE

[2] Age also affects how people use personal space. Worchel and Cooper report that North American children seem unaware of boundaries for personal space until the age of four or five. As the children get older they become more aware of them. By puberty, children have completely adapted to their culture's standards for interpersonal distances (535–37).

CC.   **Endnotes.**   In MLA style, endnotes appear on a separate numbered page headed "Notes." Notes can offer a comment, present, or explain information that the paper itself cannot include. Each note starts with a number raised a half line and indented five spaces, paragraph style. It is followed by a single space before the text begins. Double spacing is used within and between all notes.

DD.   **Use of endnote.**   ✤ PROCESS NOTE Brown was impressed to find that W. H. Auden had written a poem about personal space. She wanted to include it in her paper because she felt that it would suit her audience well, given that the paper was for her Freshman English class. She decided that its best location would be in an endnote. ✤

EE.   **Use of endnote.**   ✤ PROCESS NOTE Brown wanted to include this information, but she realized it was not related to cultural differences. She decided it would be appropriate in an endnote. ✤

Brown 10

Works Cited

Fast, Julius. <u>Body Language</u>. New York: Evans,
    1970. **FF**

Fisher, Jeffrey D., Paul A. Bell, and Andrew Baum. **GG**
    <u>Environmental Psychology</u>. 2nd ed. New York:
    Holt, 1984.

Hall, Edward T. <u>The Hidden Dimension</u>. New York:
    Doubleday, 1966.

---. Interview. "Learning the Arabs' Silent **HH**
    Language." With Kenneth Friedman. **II**
    <u>Psychology Today</u> Aug. 1979: 44–54.

Henley, Nancy M. <u>Body Politics: Power, Sex, and</u>
    <u>Nonverbal Communication</u>. Englewood Cliffs:
    Prentice, 1977.

Maines, David R. "Tactile Relationship in the **JJ**
    Subway as Affected by Racial, Sexual, and
    Crowded Seating Situations." <u>Environmental</u>
    <u>Psychology and Nonverbal Behavior</u> 2 (1977):
    100–108.

Martin, Judith. "Here's Looking at You." <u>Newsday</u> **KK**
    27 Jan. 1981, sec. 2: 9+.

Morris, Desmond. <u>Manwatching: A Field Guide to</u>
    <u>Human Behavior</u>. New York: Abrams, 1977.

General Format.   A bibliography, called "Works Cited," is used in MLA documentation style (see 41c-1 and 41d). Entries are in alphabetical order by author's last name, with a five-space indention after the first line of each entry. Punctuation and spacing between words and lines are as shown. Double spacing is used within and between entries. Two spaces occur after each period in an entry.

FF.   **Entry for book by a single author.**   Inverted order for name (last name, first name).

GG.   **Entry for book by three authors.**   Inverted order (last name, first name) for name of first author, but regular order for others. *Second edition* abbreviated to *2nd ed.* Publisher abbreviated from *Holt, Rinehart and Winston* to *Holt.* (*Note:* In a work with three or fewer authors, all names are listed; in a work by four authors or more, the first author is named and then *et al.* is used.)

HH.   **Second work by same author.**   Three hyphens and a period stand for the repetition of the preceding author's name. (*Note:* In such instances, works by the same author are listed alphabetically by title, not chronologically according to date of publication.)

II.   **Entry for an interview published in a magazine.** Entry listed by person interviewed, not by the person doing the interviewing. The page numbers are not preceded by *pp.*

JJ.   **Entry for an article in a journal with continuous pagination.**   Article title in quotation marks. Journal title underlined. Then volume number, year (in parentheses), and page numbers without *pp.*

KK.   **Entry for article in a daily newspaper.**   Title of article in quotation marks. Name of newspaper underlined. Date of newspaper in this order: day, month (abbreviation permitted), year. Then newspaper section, columns, and page numbers without *pp.* The + symbol is used *only* for newspaper articles when material continues on another page.

Brown 11

Shutter, Robert. "A Field Study of Nonverbal
        Communication in Germany, Italy, and the
        United States." Communication Monographs 44
        (1977): 298–305.

Sommer, Robert. Personal Space: The Behavorial
        Bases of Design. Englewood Cliffs: Prentice,
        1969.

Worchel, Stephen, and Joel Cooper. Understanding
        Social Psychology. 3rd ed. Homewood, IL:
        Dorsey, 1990.

LL.

LL.   **Entry for book by two authors.**   Inverted order (last name, first name) for name of first author, but regular order for second name. Place of publication includes city *and* two-letter postal abbreviation for state because readers might not know that Homewood is in Illinois.

APPENDIX A: BUSINESS WRITING

Business writing requires of you what other kinds of writing call for: understanding your audience and your purpose. This chapter explains how to write business letters (see A1), job application letters (see A2), résumés (see A3), and memos (see A4). As you write for business, use the guidelines listed in the chart below.

GUIDELINES FOR BUSINESS WRITING

Consider your audience's needs and expectations.

Show that you understand the purpose for a business communication and the context in which it takes place.

Put essential information first.

Make your points clearly and directly.

Use conventional formats.

Writing and formatting a business letter

Business letters are written to give information, to build good will, or to establish a foundation for discussions or trans-

BUSINESS LETTER FORMAT

AlphaOmega Industries, Inc.
123456 Motor Parkway
Fresh Hills, CA 55555

December 28, 19xx

Ron R. London, Sales Director
Seasonal Products Corp.
5000 Seasonal Place
Wiscasset, ME 00012

Subject: Spring Promotional Effort

Dear Ron:

Since we talked last week, I have completed plans
for the Spring promotion of the products that we
market jointly. AlphaOmega and Seasonal Products
should begin a direct mailing of the enclosed
brochure on January 28th.

I have secured several mailing lists that contain
the names of people who have a positive economic
profile for our products. The profile and the
outline of the lists are attached.

Do you have additional approaches for the
promotion? I would liked to meet with you on
January 6 to discuss them, and to work out the
details of the project.

Please call me and let me know if a meeting next
week at your office accommodates your schedule.

Sincerely,

Alan Stone

Alan Stone, Director of Special Promotions

AS/kw

cc: Ken Lane, Vice President of Marketing

Enc.: Brochure; Mailing Lists;
      Customer Profile

actions. Experts in business and government agree that letters likely to get results are short, simple, direct, and human.

A standard format for a business letter is shown on the opposite page and for a business envelope is shown below. Also, to avoid sexist language in the salutation of the letter, use the guidelines on below.

```
AlphaOmega Industries, Inc.
123456 Motor Parkway
Fresh Hills, CA 55555


                    Ron R. London, Sales Director
                    Seasonal Products Corp.
                    5000 Seasonal Place
                    Wiscasset, ME 00012
```

GUIDELINES FOR WRITING A NONSEXIST SALUTATION

You may want to send a business letter when you do not have a specific person to whom to address your letter. Use the following steps to prepare a salutation.

1. Telephone the company to which you are sending the letter. State your reason for sending the letter, and ask for the name of the person who should receive it.

2. Use a first name only if you know the person. Otherwise, use *Mr.* or *Ms.* or an applicable title. Avoid sexist language.

3. If you cannot find out the name of the person who should read your letter, use a generic title.

   YES   Dear Personnel Officer

   No   Dear Sir [obviously sexist]

          Dear Sir or Madam [few women want to be addressed as "Madam"]

The best written letter means nothing if it does not reach its destination. For letters in the United States, do not forget the five digit zip code. When a nine-number code is available, use it. For letters to other countries, use as complete an address as you have available, including the postal code. If a printed envelope is not available, type your company's name and address in the upper left corner. In the center of envelope, type in block style the receiver's name and address.

 ## Writing and formatting a job application letter

GUIDELINES FOR JOB APPLICATION LETTERS	
YOUR ADDRESS	Type your address in block style as you would on an envelope. Use as your address (with a zip code) for a place where you can be reached **by letter.**
DATE	Put the date below your address. Make sure that you mail your letter on either the same day or the next day. A delayed mailing can imply lack of planning.
INSIDE ADDRESS	Direct your letter to a specific person. Telephone the company to find out the name of the person to whom you are writing. Be accurate; a misspelled name can offend the receiver. Also, a wrong address will likely result in a lost letter.

GUIDELINES FOR JOB APPLICATION LETTERS *(continued)*

SALUTATION	Be accurate; no one likes to see his or her name misspelled. To avoid sexist language, use the chart on page 506. In replying to an ad that gives only a post-office box number, omit the salutation and start your opening paragraph after skipping one line below the inside address.
INTRODUCTORY PARAGRAPH	State your purpose for writing and your source of information about the job.
BODY PARAGRAPH(S)	Interest the reader in the skills and talents you offer by mentioning whatever background and experience you have *that relate to the specific job.* Mention your enclosed résumé, but do *not* summarize it.
CLOSING PARAGRAPH	Suggest an interview, stating that you will call to make arrangements.
CLOSING	*Sincerely* is generally appropriate. Other choices include Sincerely yours, Very truly yours, and Respectfully yours.
NAME LINES	Type your full name below your signature. Leave about four lines for your signature.
NOTATION	If you are enclosing any material type *Enc.:* and briefly list the items.

JOB APPLICATION LETTER

422 Broward
University of Texas at Arlington
Arlington, Texas 75016
May 15, 19XX

Rae Clemens, Director of Human Resources
Taleno, Ward Marketing, Inc.
1471 Summit Boulevard
Houston, Texas 78211

Dear Ms. Clemens:

I am answering the advertisement for a marketing trainee
that Taleno, Ward placed in today's <u>Houston Chronicle</u>.

Marketing has been one of the emphases of my course work
here at the University of Texas, Arlington, as you will
see on my enclosed résumé. This past year, I gained
some practical experience as well, when I developed
marketing techniques that helped to turn my typing service
into a busy and profitable small business.

Successfully marketing the typing service (with flyers,
advertisements in college publications, and even a two-
for-one promotion) makes me a very enthusiastic novice.
I can think of no better way to become a professional
than working for Taleno, Ward.

I will be here at the Arlington campus through August 1.
You can reach me by phone at 555-1976. Unless I hear
from you before, I'll call on May 25 about setting up an
interview.

Sincerely,

Lee Franco

Lee Franco

Enc.: Résumé

A3   Writing and formatting a résumé

A **résumé** is an easy-to-read, factual document that presents your qualifications for employment. All résumés cover certain standard items: name, address, phone number; education; past experience; skills and talents; publications, awards, honors, membership in professional organizations; list of references or a statement that they are "available upon request."

A résumé gives you an opportunity to present a positive picture of yourself to a prospective employer. Employers understand that college students may have limited experience in the business world. Think of headings that allow you to emphasize your strengths. For example, if you have never done paid work, do not use *Business Experience.* You can use *Work Experience* if you have done volunteer or other unpaid work. If the experience you offer an employer is that you have run school or social events, you might use *Organizational Experience.* If your greatest strength is your academic record, put your educational attainments first.

You may choose to arrange your résumé in emphatic order with the most important information first and the least important last. Or you may choose to arrange information in chronological (time) order, a sequence that is good for showing a steady work history or solid progress in a particular field.

Lee Franco's résumé which was sent with the job application letter uses chronological order. It appears on page 509. If he had used emphatic order for the same information, he could have used these categories in this order: marketing experience, business experience, additional experience, education, extracurricular.

A4   Writing and formatting a memo

A memo can serve many purposes. It can call for action or provide a record of action taken or of a conversation. It can make a brief informal report. A sample memo is shown on page

CHRONOLOGICAL RÉSUMÉ

Lee Franco
422 Broward
University of Texas at Arlington
Arlington, Texas 75016

713–555–1976

CAREER QUALIFICATIONS

The experience I acquired marketing my typing service
provided me with a good practical background for a
position as a marketing trainee.

EDUCATION

University of Texas, Arlington
B.A. May 19XX, Psychology, Marketing

EXTRACURRICULAR
Marketing Club, Computer Graphics Society

BUSINESS EXPERIENCE

Type–Right Typing Service: Ran campus typing service
for two years. Duties included word processing
(Wordstar, Displaywrite, SuperCalc), proofreading,
billing and other financial record–keeping, and
customer contact. August 19XX to present.

Archer & Archer Advertising: Worked as general
assistant in the copy department under direct
supervision of John Allen, Director. Duties included
proofreading, filing, direct client contact. June
19XX to August 19XX.

Coordinated student–employment service at Hawthorne
High School, Baton Rouge, Louisiana. Duties included
contacting students to fill jobs with local
employers, arranging interviews, and writing follow–
up report on placements.

References available upon request.

Note that paragraphs are not indented in block style, so double spaces are used between paragraphs.

Use the **subject line** to define the memo's contents. In the **message,** give information in decreasing order of importance, and include only essential points. Be concise (see Chapter 20). When possible, set off listed items for ease of reference. If you expect action as a result of the memo, clearly state your expectations at the end of the memo.

MEMO FORMAT

Date	12 March 19XX
"To" Line	To: Len DeBeers
Sender	From: Ann Soukolov
Subject Line	Subject: Annual Meeting Publications Support

For the annual meeting of our stockholders on 3 April we need the active participation of the following people:

       —speech writer
       —graphic artist
       —graphics production specialist
       —one copy editor
       —typists and proofreaders

Message

We will use the office space on the second floor of the office building next to the auditorium. Word processing equipment should be in place by Monday. Six phones were installed today.

Art Smith, the meeting manager, will be here on Monday for a kick-off meeting at 10:00 a.m.

Please prepare a detailed list of critical items for that meeting.

Initials of writer/or typist	AS/ls
Distribution	Dist: A. Adams
	R. Traub
	T. Ziff-Smith

APPENDIX B: USING CORRECT MANUSCRIPT FORMAT

B1 Following standard practices when preparing the final copy of a paper

The appearance of a paper suggests to your instructor that you took the assignment seriously and that you value what you have written.

APPEARANCE

Paper: For typed papers, use 8½ × 11-inch white, standard typing paper. Do not use onionskin or erasable paper: onionskin is for copies only, and erasable paper smudges easily and resists handwritten corrections. Double space between lines. Type on only one side of each sheet of paper.

If your instructor accepts handwritten papers, use ruled 8½ × 11-inch standard white, lined paper. Do not use colored paper or paper torn from a spiral-bound notebook. Write on only one side of each sheet of paper. Some of your instructors might require that you write on every other line, to provide space for you to make neat corrections and for them to write comments. If you are unsure of your instructor's requirements, ask. Make your handwriting as clear as you can. Be consistent in your presentation; letters and spacing should be uniform.

Ink: Use a black typewriter ribbon, and keep the typewriter keys clean so that the letters will be clear, not blurred. For handwritten papers, use dark blue or black ink only. Do not use pencil.

Computer printouts: If your computer uses continuous feed paper, be sure to tear off the hole-punched edges and separate the pages.

FORMATS

First page: For a sample of a first page without a cover page see page 479. The format conforms to MLA style°. For sample of a cover page, along with a first page when a cover is used, see page 478 and 482.

Page from the body of a paper: For sample pages from the body of a paper, see 42b.

Works Cited page: See the sample Works Cited list in MLA style on pages 500 and 502.

Displaying quotations: When a prose quotation runs more than four typed lines or four handwritten lines, it is displayed. It starts on a new line, and all lines are indented ten spaces. The first line of a paragraph within a displayed quotation is indented an additional three spaces. See examples in 33a-1 and on pages 484, 496, and 498.

When you quote more than three lines of poetry, set the quotation off from your own words. Start a new line, indent ten spaces, and lay the quoted poetry out so that it looks like the printed version you are quoting from. If indenting ten spaces requires you to break lines of the poem, you can indent less than ten spaces. See the example on page 498.

Punctuation leading into a displayed quotation: When the words that lead into a displayed quotation are a complete sentence, end the sentence with a colon (for an example, see 33a-1). When the words are not a complete sentence and flow directly into the wording of the displayed quotations, use no punctuation (for an example, see page 496).

B2

Making careful handwritten corrections and insertions in typed papers

If your typewriter lacks special characters for accent marks, handwrite them. You can make a few handwritten corrections in a paper to hand in using the standard correction marks shown below. If you have more than three handwritten corrections on a page, retype the page.

Draw one line through words you want to take out.

> These ~~extra words~~ are deleted.

To insert words, make a caret (∧) where the missing words should be, and then write them in above the caret:

> A caret shows ∧ should be inserted.
> *where words*

To transpose letters, use a mark like this:

> squiggle

You can transpose words in a similar way:

> Transpose |in the|words| wrong order.

You can indicate the start of a new paragraph like this:

> Molly's actions primarily met her needs. ¶ Overall, Molly
> exemplifies the behavior of one type of typical toddler.

You can close up space between letters this way:

> Avoid in⌣correct spacing.

You can open space between letters this way:

> Leave one space between words in|a sentence.

You can drop a letter and close up the remaining letters this way:

> Some spellers have trouble with doubbΘle letters.   **515**

Usage Glossary

This **usage glossary** lists the customary manner of using particular words or phrases. "Customary manner," however, is not as firm in practice as the term implies. Standards for language use change. If you think a usage practice might have changed, consult a dictionary with a publication date later than this handbook's.

This usage glossary uses two terms frequently: *Informal* indicates that the word or phrase occurs commonly in speech but should be avoided in academic writing. *Nonstandard* indicates that the word or phrase should not be used in standard spoken English and in writing. As in the rest of this book, words marked with a degree symbol (°) are defined in this handbook's Glossary of Terms that appears after this Glossary.

a, an Use *a* before words beginning with consonant sounds: *a dog, a grade, a hole*. Also, use *a* before words beginning with vowels that sound like consonants: *a unit, a European*. Use *an* before words beginning with vowel sounds or a silent *h*: *an apple, an onion, an hour*: (7a)

accept, except To *accept* means "to agree to" or "to receive." To *except* (verb°) means "to exclude or leave out"; *except* (preposition°) means "leaving out." (26b)

> **Except** [preposition] for one or two details, the striking workers were ready to **accept** [verb] management's offer. The workers wanted the no-smoking rule **excepted** [verb] from the contract.

advice, advise *Advice* (noun°) means "recommendation"; to *advise* (verb°) means "to give a recommendation." (26b)

> I **advise** you to follow your doctor's **advice**.

affect, effect To *affect* means "to influence" or "to arouse the emotions"; to *effect* means "to bring about"; *effect* (noun°) means "result or conclusion." (26b)

> One **effect** [noun°] of the weather is that it **affects** [verb°] some people's moods. We **effected** [verb] some changes in our system for weather forecasting.

aggravate, irritate *Aggravate* is used colloquially to mean *irritate*. Each word has a precise meaning, however: to *aggravate* means "to intensify or make worse"; to *irritate* means "to annoy or make impatient."

ain't is a nonstandard contraction for *am not, is not,* and *are not.*

all ready, already *Already* means "before or by this time"; *all ready* means "completely prepared." (26b)

> The new players were **all ready**; the warmup had **already** begun.

all right is two words, never one (not *alright*). (26b)

all together, altogther *All together* means "in a group, in unison"; *altogether* means "entirely or thoroughly." (26b)

> The sopranos, altos, and tenors were supposed to sing **all together**, but their first attempt was not **altogether** successful.

allusion, illusion An *allusion* is a reference to something; an *illusion* is a false impression or idea. (26b)

a lot is informal for *a great deal* or *a great many*; avoid it in academic writing.

a.m., p.m. (or **A.M., P.M.**) are used only with numbers, not as substitutes for the words *morning, afternoon,* or *evening.* (37a)

among, between Use *among* for three or more people or things; use *between* for two people or things.

> The three students discussed the problem **among** themselves. They had to choose **between** staying in school and getting full-time jobs.

amount, number Use *amount* for concepts or things that are collective rather than separate (wealth, work, happiness); use *number* for anything that can be counted (coins, jobs, joys).

> A small **number** of people had to do a great **amount** of work.

an, and *An* is an article° (see *a, an*). Do not confuse it with *and,* which is a conjunction°. (7g)

anyplace is informal for *any place* or *anywhere.* Avoid it in academic writing.

apt, likely, liable *Apt* and *likely* are loosely interchangeable. Strictly, *apt* indicates a tendency or inclination; *likely* indicates a reasonable expectation. *Liable* means "having undesirable consequences."

> Although the roads are **apt** to be icy, you **likely** will arrive on time.
> You are **liable** to have an accident if you speed on icy roads.

as, like, as if
1. Use *like,* not *as,* in a comparison when resemblance but not equivalence is suggested.

> Mexico, **like** [not *as*] Argentina, is a Spanish-speaking country.

2. Use *as,* not *like,* in a comparison when equivalence is suggested.

> John served **as** [not *like*] debate moderator. [John = moderator]

3. *As* functions as a subordinating conjunction° or a preposition°, depending on the meaning of the sentence. *Like* functions only as a preposition. To start a clause°, use *as.*

> That hamburger tastes good, **as** [not *like*] a hamburger should. [subordinating conjunction]
> That hamburger tastes **like** chopped leather. [preposition]

4. Use *as if,* not *like,* with the subjunctive mood°. (9m)

> This hamburger tastes **as if** [not *like*] it was grilled for an hour.

awful, awfully *Awful* (adjective°) means "causing fear". Do not use it as a substitute for intensifiers such as *very* or *extremely. Awfully* (adverb°) is informal for *very* or *extremely* and should be avoided in academic writing.

a while, awhile A *while* is an article° and a noun° that functions as a subject° or object°. *Awhile* is an adverb°; it modifies verbs°. In a prepositional phrase°, the correct form is *a while: for* **a while,** *in* **a while.**

bad, badly *Bad* is an adjective° (*bad* feelings); use it after linking verbs° such as *feel* or *felt* (He *felt* **bad**). *Badly* is an adverb° and is nonstandard after linking verbs. For more information, see 4d.

> The farmers felt **bad** [not *badly*]. The **bad** drought had **badly** damaged the crops.

been, being *Been* is the past participle° of *to be; being* is the progressive form° of *to be.*

> *Alcohol abuse has* **been** [not *being*] on the rise recently. Lives are **being** [not *been*] ruined.

being as, being that are nonstandard for *because* or *since.*

beside, besides *Beside* means "next to or by the side of"; *besides* (when functioning as a preposition) means "other than or in addition to"; *besides* (when functioning as an adverb°) means "also or moreover."

> With keys in her hand, she stood **beside** the new car. No one **besides** her had a driver's license. **Besides,** she owned the car.

breath, breathe *Breath* is a noun°; *breathe* is a verb°.

bring, take Use *bring* for movement from a distant place to a near place; use *take* for any other movement.

but, however, yet Use *but, however,* and *yet* alone, not in combination with each other. (7g)

can, may *Can* indicates ability or capacity; *may* requests or grants permission. In the negative, however, *can* is acceptable in place of *may.*

can't hardly, can't scarcely are double negatives and are nonstandard; use *hardly* and *scarcely* only. For more information, see 4c.

censor, censure To *censor* means "to judge" or "to delete objectionable material"; to *censure* means "to condemn or officially reprimand."

choose, chose *Choose* is the simple form of *to choose; chose* is the past tense of *to choose.* (9d)

cloth, clothe *Cloth* (noun°) means "fabric"; to *clothe* (verb°) means "to dress" or "to cover with garments."

conscience, conscious *Conscience* (noun°) means "a sense of right or wrong"; *conscious* (adjective°) means "being aware or awake."

consensus of opinion is a redundant phrase. Use *consensus* only.

continual, continuous *Continual* is occurring repeatedly; *continuous* is going on without interruption in space or time.

> All essential spacecraft systems had to operate **continuously,** so the astronauts **continually** checked their instrument panels.

data is the plural of *datum,* a rarely used word. Informal usage treats *data* as singular, but use the plural in academic writing.

different from, different than *From* is the preferred preposition after *different,* although *than* is commonly used in speech.

> Football is **different from** [not *different than*] soccer.

disinterested, uninterested *Disinterested* means "impartial"; *uninterested* means "indifferent or not concerned with."

don't is a contraction for *do not,* not for *does not (doesn't).*

> She **doesn't** [not *don't*] like loud music.

emigrate from, immigrate to To *immigrate to* means "to enter a country to live there." To *emigrate from* means "to leave one country to live in another."

etc. is the abbreviation for the Latin *et cetera,* meaning *and the rest.* Do not use it in academic writing; acceptable substitutes are *and the like, and so on,* or *and so forth.*

everyday, every day *Everday* is an adjective°; it means "daily" and modifies nouns. *Every day* is an adjective-noun combination that functions as a subject° or object°. (26b)

> I missed the bus **every day** last week. Arriving at work late has become an **everyday** occurrence.

explicit, implicit *Explicit* means "directly stated or expressed"; *implicit* means "implied or suggested."

> The warning on cigarette packs is **explicit:** Smoking is dangerous to health. The **implicit** message is: "Don't smoke."

farther, further are used interchangeably, although many writers prefer to use *farther* for geographical distances and *further* for all other cases.

fewer, less Use *fewer* for anything that can be counted (*fewer dollars, fewer jobs, fewer joys*); use *less* for concepts or things thought of collectively, not separately (*less money, less work, less happiness*). (4c)

fine, find *Fine* can be a noun° (*The fine was $100*). *Fine* can be an adjective° (*She bought a fine electric drill*). *Find* is the simple form of the verb *to find* (*We find new evidence each day*).

former, latter When two ideas or things are referred to, *former* refers to the first of the two, and *latter* refers to the second of the two. When more than two ideas or things are referred to, do not use these words.

goes, says *Goes* is nonstandard for *says*.

good, well *Good* is an adjective° (*good idea*); it is nonstandard as an adverb; *well* is an adverb° (*run well*). (14d)

> The **good** writer spoke **well**.

have, of Use *have*, not *of*, after such verbs such as *could, might, must*.

hopefully is an adverb° that means "with hope," "in a hopeful manner," or "it is hoped that." It can modify a verb°, an adjective°, or another adverb. Some people use it as a sentence modifier° meaning "I hope," but this usage is not appropriate in academic writing. Always say in your sentence who is doing the hoping.

> **No** **Hopefully,** the plane will land safely.
> **Yes** They waited **hopefully** for the plane to land safely.
> **Yes** They **hoped** that the plane would land safely.

if, whether *If* is a subordinating conjunction°. *Whether* occurs in three situations: in an indirect question (*She asked whether I had heard from the hikers*); to express doubt (*She was not sure whether they would be safe in the storm*); and to express alternatives, with or without *or not,* (*I did not know whether* [or *whether or not*] *to search for them*).

imply, infer To *imply* means "to hint or suggest without stating outright"; to *infer* means "to draw a conclusion from what has been written or said."

irregardless is nonstandard for *regardless*.

is when, is where In giving definitions, *is* should not be followed by *when* or *where*.

its, it's *Its* is a personal pronoun in the possessive case *(The dog lost **its** bone)*. *It's* is a contraction of *it is* or *it has* (**It's** *a warm day)* (26b)

kind, sort are singular words and should therefore be paired with *this*, not *these*. *These* can be paired with *kinds* or *sorts*.

kind of (a), sort of (a) *Kind of* and *sort of* are nonstandard if used as adverbs° meaning "in a way" or "somewhat." Also, *a* with these phrases is nonstandard.

> The hikers were **somewhat** [not *kind of*] tired when they got home.

later, latter *Later* means "after some time" or "subsequently"; *latter* refers to the second or a pair of ideas or things. (26b)

> That restaurant opens **later** today. It serves lunch and dinner, the **latter** starting at 5 p.m.

lay, lie *Lay* is always followed by a direct object°. As a substitute for *lie*, *lay* is nonstandard. (9d)

> **Lay** the blanket on the beach so that you can **lie** [not *lay*] down

loose, lose, loss *Loose* means "not tight"; to *lose* means "to be unable to find"; *loss* means "that which cannot be found or retrieved."

lots, lots of, a lot of are informal for *many, much, a great deal*.

may be, maybe *May be* is a verb phrase°; *maybe* is an adverb°. (26b) *(Our team **may be** out of practice, but **maybe** we will win anyway)*

media is the plural of *medium* and therefore requires a plural verb.

mind, mine *Mind* is a noun° *(She had a good **mind**)*; *mine* is a personal pronoun° *(That key is **mine**)*.

myself, yourself, himself, herself are nonstandard when used as a subject° or an object in a prepositional phrase°.

> The dean and **I** [not *myself*] will explain the facts to the president. First, however, the class has to explain them to the dean and **me** [not *myself*].

OK, O.K., okay are acceptable, but avoid them in academic writing in favor of a word more specific to the meaning of the sentence.

percent, percentage *Percent* is used with specific numbers *(two percent, 95 percent). Percentage* is used with descriptive words or phrases (a *small percentage*), but do not use it as a synonym for *part, portion, number, amount,* or other words denoting quantity.

plus is acceptable as a preposition° meaning "in addition to." Do not use *plus*, (1) as a substitute for *and* between independent clauses° and (2) as a transitional word° such as *besides, moreover, in addition.*

pretty is informal for words such as *rather* and *very.* Avoid it in academic writing.

principal, principle *Principle* means "a basic truth or rule." *Principal* (noun°) means "chief person" or "main or original amount"; *principal* (adjective°) means "most important." (26b)

> The school **principal** paid interest on the **principal** of her bank loan.
> One of the **principal** values in the United States is the **principle** of free speech.

raise, rise *Raise* needs a direct object° *(Please **raise** your hand); rise* does not take a direct object *(The sun will **rise**).* Do not use these verbs interchangeably.

> The governor will **rise** [not *raise*] to speak after we **raise** [not *rise*] the flag.

really is informal for intensifiers such as *very* and *extremely.*

reason is because is redundant; drop *because.* (19a-2)

> The **reason is** [not *the reason is because*] we want to lower taxes.

respectful, respectfully; respective, respectively *Respectful* and *respectfully* relate to showing respect; *respective* and *respectively* refers to items that are in the given sequence.

The staff **respectfully** requested that the dean hear their complaints. He suggested that the typist and telephone operators go back to their desk and switchboards, **respectively.** They then returned to their **respective** jobs.

seen is nonstandard for *saw. Seen* is the past participle° of *to see.* (9d) (*They **saw** [not seen] the film. I **had seen** [not I seen] it last week.*)

set, sit *Set* is nonstandard as a substitute for *to sit. Set* means "to place" and is followed by a direct object°. *Sit* means "to be seated."

> After you carefully **set** [not *sit*] the rare Chinese vase on the table, please **sit** [not *set*] down.

should, would Use *should* to express obligation (*They **should** practice what they preach*) or condition (*If you **should** need advice, call me*). Use *would* to express a wish (*I wish my family **would** buy a VCR*) or habitual action (*I **would** tape all the football games*).

sometime, sometimes, some time *Sometime* means "at an unspecified future time"; *sometimes* means "now and then"; *some time* is a span of time. (26b)

supposed to, used to The final *d* is essential in both expressions. (9d)

sure is nonstandard when used as an adverb° meaning *surely* or *certainly. I **surely** [not sure] hope to go to college).*

than, then *Than* indicates comparison (*One is smaller **than** two). Then* relates to time (*He tripped and **then** fell*).

that, which Use *that* with restrictive (essential) clauses°; *which* can be used today for both restrictive and nonrestrictive (nonessential) clauses°, but most writers prefer to use it only with nonrestrictive (nonessential) clauses. (11g)

> We visited the house **that** Jack built. Jack built the house, **which** is on Beanstalk Street, for his large plant collection.

their, there, they're *Their* is possessive; *there* means "in that place" or serves as an expletive°; *they're* is a contraction of *they are.* (26b)

to, too, two *To* is a preposition° *(to the game); too* is an adverb° *(It was hot too); two* is the number *(two balls). (26b)*

toward, towards are both acceptable, although some writers prefer *toward.*

try and, sure and are nonstandard for *try to* and *sure to.*

> She wanted to **try to** [not *try and*] get a part-time job. Therefore, she had to be **sure to** [not *sure and*] prepare a résumé.

unique is an absolute word and therefore cannot be modified by intensifiers such as *very* or *most.*

> Her talent was **unique** [not *very unique* or *most unique*].

used to, supposed to See *supposed to, used to.*

wait on is informal when used instead of *wait for.* It is correct when used in the context of waiting on tables.

ways is colloquial for *way.*

> California is a long **way** [not *ways*] from New York.

where is nonstandard when used for *that.*

> I read in the newspaper **that** [not *where*] tuition will be increased.

who, whom Use *who* for the subjective case° *(The person **who** can type has an easier time in school).* Use *whom* for the objective case° *(I asked to **whom** my professor was speaking). (10e-2)*

who's, whose *Who's* is the contraction of *who is; whose* is possessive. (**Who's** going to run for mayor? Whose campaign is well organized?)

Xmas is an abbreviation for *Christmas;* avoid using it in academic writing.

GLOSSARY OF GRAMMATICAL AND SELECTED COMPOSITION TERMS

Throughout this handbook a degree symbol (°) signals that a term is defined in this glossary. Also, in this glossary terms that are themselves defined here are marked with a degree symbol. See the handbook section(s) given in parentheses after each definition for more information.

absolute phrase A phrase containing a subject° and a participle° and modifying an entire sentence: *Summer being over, we left the seashore.* (8e)

acronym A word made up of the first letters of other words and that acts as an abbreviation for those words: *NASA*. (37b)

active voice The form of a verb° in which the subject° performs the action named by the verb. This voice° emphasizes the doer of the action, in contrast to the passive voice°, which emphasizes the action. (9n, 9o)

adjective A word that describes or limits (modifies) a noun°, pronoun°, or word group functioning as a noun: *silly, three.* (7d, 14)

adjective clause A dependent clause° that usually begins with a relative pronoun° and that modifies nouns° or pronouns°. (8f)

adverb A word that describes or limits (modifies) verbs°, adjectives°, other adverbs, or whole sentences: *wearily, very.* (7e, 14)

adverb clause A dependent clause° that begins with a subordinating conjunction° and that modifies verbs°, adjectives°, adverbs°, or whole sentences. (8k)

agreement The match of number° and person° between a subject° and its verb° or a pronoun° and its antecedent°. (12, 13)

analogy An explanation of the unfamiliar in terms of the familiar comparing things not normally associated with each other. (5d, 25c)

analysis A thinking process, analysis divides something into its component parts to clarify the relationship between the whole and the parts. Sometimes called *division.* (5d)

antecedent The noun° or pronoun° to which a pronoun refers. (11, 13)

antonym A word opposite in meaning to another word. (24a)

APA style See *documentation style.*

appositive A word or group of words that renames a noun° or a noun group preceding it: *my favorite month,* **October.** (8d)

argumentative writing See *persuasive writing.*

articles The words *a, an,* and *the.* Also called *limiting adjectives, noun markers,* or *noun determiners.* (7a)

audience The readers to whom a piece of writing is directed. (1c)

auxiliary verb Also known as a *helping verb,* an auxiliary verb is a form of *be, do,* and others that with main verbs° make verb phrases°. (7c, 9b, 9c)

balanced sentence A sentence that uses parallelism° to enhance the message of similar or dissimilar ideas. (22c)

bibliography A list of sources used in a paper: in MLA style°, called Works Cited°; in APA style°, called References°. (41a, 41c)

brainstorming Listing all ideas that come to mind about a topic and about grouping them in patterns that emerge. (2g)

case The way a noun° or pronoun° changes form to show whether it is functioning as a subject°, an object°, or a possessive: *she, her, hers.* (10)

cause-and-effect analysis Examination of the relationship between outcomes (effects) and the rasons for them (causes). (5d)

chronological order Arrangement of ideas according to time sequence. (21-2, 5c)

classification A method of developing a paragraph° or a larger piece of writing in which separate categories that share some characteristics are grouped together. Classification is often used along with analysis°. (5d)

clause A group of words containing a subject° and a predicate°. A clause that delivers full meaning is called an *independent clause°* (or main clause). A clause that needs another sentence structure to deliver full meaning is called a *dependent clause°* (or subordinate clause). (8f)

cliché An overused, worn-out phrase that has lots its capacity to communicate effectively: *smooth as silk, ripe old age.* (25d)

climactic order An arrangement of ideas in a paragraph° or larger piece of writing from least important to most important. Climactic order is sometimes called *emphatic order.* (21-2, 5c)

climactic sentence See *periodic sentence.*

coherence The clear progression from one idea to another in content as well as grammatical structures and choice of words. (5c)

collective noun A noun° that names a group of people or things: *family, team.* (7a, 12h, 13e)

colloquial language Language characteristic of conversation and informal writing. (25a-3)

comma fault See *comma splice.*

comma splice The error that occurs when only a comma connects two independent clauses°. (6)

common noun A noun° that names general groups, places, people, or things: *dog, house.* (7a)

comparative The form of an adjective° or adverb° that reflects a different degree of intensity between two: *blue*, **bluer**; *easy*, **more easily**. See also *positive* and *superlative*. (4e)

comparison and contrast A discussion in which similarities (comparison) and/or differences (contrast) are presented. (5d)

complement A word or words in a sentence that renames or describes a subject° or object° in that sentence. (8d)

complex sentence A sentence containing one independent clause° and one or more dependent clauses°. (8g)

compound-complex sentence A sentence containing at least two independent clauses° and one or more dependent clauses°. (8g)

compound sentence A sentence containing two or more independent clauses° joined by a coordinating conjunction. (8g)

conjunction A word that is a coordinating conjunction°, correlative conjunction°, or subordinating conjunction°. (7g)

conjunctive adverb A kind of adverb° that creates logical connections between independent clauses°: *therefore, however*. (7c)

connotation The emotional associations suggested by a word that, along with its denotation°, make up its complete meaning. (246-1)

coordinate adjectives Two or more adjectives that equally modify a noun° or pronoun°. They are separated by a comma: **heavy, round** *paperweight*. (29e)

coordinating conjunction A conjunction that joins two or more grammatically equivalent structures: *and, or, for, nor, but, so,* and *yet*. (7g)

coordination The technique of using grammatically equivalent forms to communicate a sequence of ideas. (21a-21c)

correlative conjunction A pair of words that joins equivalent grammatical structures, including *both . . . and, not only . . . but also, either . . . or, neither . . . nor,* and *whether . . . or*. (7g)

cumulative sentence The most common kind of sentence, it begins with the subject° and verb° and then adds modifiers°. Also known as a *loose sentence*. (23c)

dangling modifier A modifier° that describes something implied but not stated: *Walking **down the street,** the Sears Tower came into view.* (18b)

deadwood Empty, unneeded words that increase the word count but do not add to the meaning. Also called *padding.* (20b)

declarative sentence A sentence that makes a statement: *I walked home.* (8a)

deduction The process of reasoning from general claims to a specific instance. (6e-2)

demonstrative pronoun A pronoun° that points out the antecedent°: For example, *this, that,* and *those.* (7b)

denotation The dictionary definition of a word. (24b-1)

dependent clause A clause° that cannot stand alone as an independent grammatical unit, usually preceded by a reltive pronoun° or subordinating conjunction°. (8e)

descriptive adjective An adjective° that describes the condition or properties of the noun° it modifies and has comparative° and superlative° forms: *round, rounder, roundest.* (7d)

descriptive adverb An adverb° that has comparative° and superlative° forms: *happily, **more happily, most happily.*** (7c)

diction Word choice. (24a, 24b)

direct discourse Words that repeat speech or conversation exactly, requiring the use of quotation marks. (17d, 29h, 33e)

direct object A word or group of words functioning as a noun that receives the action of a verb°. (8c, 9e)

direct quotation The exact words spoken or written by someone other than the writer of the paper; in your writing, such words must be enclosed in quotation marks. (29h, 33e, 39e)

division See *analysis.*

documentation Acknowledging the sources that you used in your writing, by giving full and accurate information about the source's author and the work's title, date of publication, and related facts. (39b, 40f, Chapter 41)

documentation style Any of various systems for providing information in your writing about the sources that you paraphrase, summarize, or quote. Two of the most widely used styles are those of the Modern Language Association (MLA) and the American Psychological Association (APA). (39b, 40f, Chapter 41)

double negative Two negative modifiers°, the second of which repeats the message of the first. (14c)

drafting A part of the writing process during which writers compose ideas in sentences and paragraphs. (2a, 3b)

edited American English Also called *standard English,* the language that conforms to established rules of grammar, sentence structure, punctuation, and spelling. (25a-2)

editing A part of the writing process° during which writers check the correctness of their grammar, spelling, punctuation, and mechanics°. (2a, 3d)

elliptical construction A sentence structure that deliberately omits words that have already appeared in the sentence and can be inferred from the context. (8f, 19b)

end punctuation A term that includes the period, the question mark, and the exclamation point. (28)

etymology The study of a word's origins and historical development, including its changes in form and meaning. (24a)

euphemism Language that attempts to hide harsh reality with more pleasant-sounding words. (25e-3)

exclamatory sentence A sentence that expresses strong emotion by making an exclamation: *That's ridiculous!* (18a)

expletive The function of *there* and *it* when they combine with a form of the verb *to be* to postpone the subject of the sentence: *It is Mars that we want to reach.* (12f)

expository writing See *informative writing.*

extended definition A definition that includes, in addition to the denotation° of a word or phrase, its connotations° as well as concrete details to clarify abstract terms. (5d)

faulty predication An error that occurs when a subject° and its predicate° do not make sense together. (9a)

finite verb A verb° form that shows tense°, mood°, voice°, person°, and number° to express an action, occurrence, or state of being. (9b)

freewriting Writing nonstop to generate ideas by free association of thoughts. "Focused freewriting" builds on a sentence or two taken from an earlier piece of freewriting. (2f)

fused sentence The error of independent clauses° together without a semicolon or a comma and a coordinate conjunction° between them. Also called a *run-on* or *run-together sentence*. (16)

future tense The verb tense that expresses an action yet to be taken or a condition not yet experienced: *they will talk.* (9e, 9f)

gender Concerning languages, the labeling of nouns° and pronouns° as masculine, feminine, or neutral. (25b)

gerund A verbal°, the present participle° functioning as a noun°: ***Walking*** *is good exercise.* (7c)

helping verb See *auxiliary verb.*

homonyms Words spelling differently that sound alike: *to, too, two.* (26b)

illogical predication See *faulty predication.*

imperative mood The mood° that expresses commands and direct requests: *Go.* It uses the simple form° of the verb. (9l)

imperative sentence A sentence that gives a command: *Go home now.* (8a)

indefinite pronoun A pronoun° that refers to nonspecific persons or things but that takes on meaning in context: *any, few.* (7b, 2g)

independent clause A clause° that can stand alone as an independent grammatical unit. (8f)

indicative mood The mood° of verbs° for statements about real things or highly likely ones and for questions about fact: *The rain stopped.* (9l)

G-17

indirect discourse Discourse that reports speech or conversation and is not enclosed in quotation marks because it does not give the speaker's exact words. (17d, 29h, 33e)

indirect object A noun° or pronoun° or group of words functioning as a noun that tells *to whom* or *for whom* the action expressed by a transitive verb° was done. (8c)

indirect question A sentence that is a qustion but ends with a period: *I wonder whether you are going. (28b)*

induction The process of arriving at general principles from particular facts or instances. (6e-1)

inferential meaning A part of the reading process that calls for the reader to read "between the lines" and thereby understand what is implied but unstated. (6c-2)

infinitive A verbal° made of the simple form° of a verb and usually, but not always, *to.* It functions as a noun°, adjective°, or adverb°. (7c, 9b)

infinitive phrase An infinitive° and its modifiers°. It functions as a noun°, adjective°, or adverb°. (8e)

informal language Word choice that creates a tone° appropriate for casual writing or speaking. (25a-1)

informative writing Also known as *expository writing,* informative writing gives information and, when necessary, explains it. In contrast to persuasive writing°, informative writing focuses on the subject being discussed rather than the reader's reaction to the information. (1b-1)

intensive pronoun A *-self* form of a pronoun°, which intensifies the antecedent. (7b, 10i)

interjection A word (or words) conveying surprise or another strong emotion. (7h)

interrogative pronoun A pronoun° that asks a question, such as *whose* or *what.* (7b)

interrogative sentence A sentence that asks a question: *Did you see that hat?* (8a)

intransitive verb A verb that does not take a direct object° and is not a linking verb°. (9p)

invention techniques Ways in which writers gather ideas for writing. (2d-2k)

irony Suggesting the opposite of the usual sense of the words. (25c)

irregular verb A verb that forms the past tense and past participle° in some way other than by adding *-ed* or *-d: see, saw, seen.* (9d)

jargon Specialized vocabulary of a particular field or group that a general reader might not understand or that is used to be pretentious. (25e-2)

limiting adjective An adjective° that limits the noun° it modifies. (7e, 7d)

limiting sentence A sentence that sometimes follows a topic sentence to narrow the focus of the paragraph. (5b-1)

linking verb A main verb° that connects a subject° with a subject complement°. Linking verbs indicate a state of being, relate to the senses, or indicate a condition. (7c, 12i)

logical fallacies Flaws in reasoning that lead to illogical statements. (6f)

loose sentence See *cumulative sentence.*

main clause See *independent clause.*

main verb A verb that expresses action, occurrence, or state of being. It shows mood°, tense°, voice°, number°, and person°. (7c, 9b)

mapping Generating ideas in a visual layout. Also called *webbing* or *clustering.* (2i)

mechanics Conventions regarding the use of capital letters, italics, abbreviations, and numbers. (35, 36, 37, 38)

levels of formality Levels of language. *Highly formal* language is used for certain ceremonial and other occasions when stylistic flourishes are appropriate. A *medium level of formality* is neither too scholarly nor too casual. This level is acceptable for academic writing. See also *informal language.* (25a-1)

metaphor A comparison between otherwise dissimilar things. (25c)

misplaced modifier A modifier° that is incorrectly positioned in a sentence and thus distorts meaning. (18a)

mixed construction A sentence that starts with one grammatical form and then suddenly switches to another, thus garbling the meaning of the sentence. (19a-1)

mixed metaphors An incongruously combined image. (25c)

MLA style See *documentation style.*

modal auxiliary verbs The auxiliary verbs° *can, could, may, might, should, would, must,* and *ought.* (9c)

modifier A word or group of words that describes or limits. The most common modifiers are adjectives° and adverbs°. (8d)

mood The ability of verbs° to convey the attitude expressed toward the action: indicative°, imperative°, and subjunctive°. (9l)

nonfinite verb A participle° or infinitive° functioning as a noun° or modifier°. Also known as a *verbal*°. (7c, 9b)

nonrestrictive element A word, phrase°, or dependent clause° that provides information not essential to understanding the element it modifies. A nonrestrictive element, sometimes called a *nonessential element,* is usually set off by commas. (29f)

nonsexist language See *sexist language.*

nonstandard Generally taken to mean language not written in edited American English°. (opening section Usage Glossary)

noun The name of a person, place, thing, or idea. (7a)

noun clause A dependent clause° that functions as a subject°, object°, or complement°. (8f)

noun phrase A noun° and its modifiers° functioning as a subject°, object°, or complement°. (8e)

number Relates to how many subjects act or experience an action, one (singular) or more than one (plural). (9a, 12a)

object A noun° or pronoun° or group of words functioning as a noun or pronoun that receives the action of a verb° (direct object°), tells to whom or for whom something is done (indirect object°), or completes the meaning of a preposition° (object of a preposition°). (8c)°

object complement A noun° or adjective° that immediately follows a direct object° and either describes or renames it. (8c)

objective case The case° of the pronoun° functioning as direct object. (10)

padding See *deadwood.*

paragraph A group of sentences that work together to develop a unit of thought. Most paragraphs in academic writing are topical paragraphs°; they state a main idea and offer specific, logical support of that idea. (5)

paragraph development Specific, logical support for a main idea or generalization. (5)

parallelism The use of equivalent grammatical forms or matching sentence structures to express equivalent ideas. (22)

paraphrase A restatement of someone else's ideas in language and sentence structure diffeerent from those of the source. (39c)

parenthetical documentation Information enabling a reader to identify the source of ideas or of direct quotations°. This information is placed in parentheses immediately after the quotation or information. (41b)

participial phrase A phrase that functions as an adjective° contains a present participle° or past participle° (8e)

passive construction See *passive voice.*

passive voice The form of a verb° in which the subject° is acted upon. This voice° emphasizes the action, in contrast to the *active voice°*, which emphasizes the doer of the action. (9n, 9o)

past participle The third principal part° of the verb°. In regular verbs°, it adds *-d* or *-ed* to the simple form° and is identical to the past tense°. In irregular verbs°, it often differs from the simple form and the past tense. (7c, 9b, 9c)

past tense The verb tense that expresses an action or occurrence or state of being completed in the past. The second principal part of the verb°. The past tense of regular verbs° add *-ed* or *-d* to the simple form°: *watched.* The past tense of irregular verbs° changes in various ways. (9b, 9c)

perfect tenses The three tenses—the present perfect°, the past perfect°, and the future perfect°—that show complex time relationships in the present, past, and future. (9i)

periodic sentence A sentence that begins with modifiers° and ends with the independent clause°, thus saving the main idea—and the emphasis—for the end of the sentence. Also called *climactic sentence.* (23c)

person Who or what acts or experiences an action. First person is the one speaking *(I, we);* second person is the one being spoken to *(you, you);* and third person is the person or thing spoken about *(he, she, it; they).* (12a)

personal pronoun A pronoun° that refers to people or things, such as *I, you, them, hers,* and *it.* (7b, 10)

persuasive writing Persuasive writing seeks to convince the reader about a matter of opinion. (1b-2)

phrase A group of related words that does not contain a subject° and predicate°. It cannot stand alone as an independent grammatical unit. (8c)

plagiarism Plagiarism occurs when a writer presents another person's words or ideas without giving credit to that person. Writers must use documentation° to give proper credit to their sources. Plagiarism is a serious offense, like stealing, and can lead to course failure or expulsion. (39a)

planning An early part of the writing process°, during which writers gather ideas. Also called *prewriting°.* (2a-2k)

plural See *number.*

possessive case The case° of a noun° or pronoun° that shows ownership or possession. (10)

predicate The part of the sentence that contains the verb° and tells what the subject° is doing or experiencing, or what is being done to the subject. (8b)

prefix One or more syllables added in front of a word° to modify its meaning. (26d)

preposition A word that shows a relationship between a noun° or pronoun° and other words in the sentence. (7f)

prepositional phrase A preposition° and its object° along with any modifiers°. (7f, 8c)

present participle The *-ing* form of verb°. It is used with an auxiliary verb° to create a verb phrase° that expresses an action, occurrence, or a state of being: *I am **running.*** As a verbal°, it functions as an adjective° *(**running** water)* or a noun° (***Running** pleases me*). (9b)

present tense The verb tense that expresses what is happening, what is true at the moment, and what is consistently true. It uses the simple form° *(**talk**)*. In the third person singular, it uses the *-s* form *(she **talks**)*. (9b, 9g, 9h)

prewriting A term for all activities in the writing process before drafting°. See *planning* and *shaping.* (2d-2k)

primary source An original work of an author—novels, poems, short stories, autobiographies, diaries—and firsthand reports of observations and of research. (40a)

progressive verb forms Verb forms in all tenses° that use the present participle° and forms of *to be.* These forms show that an action is ongoing. (9j)

pronoun A word that takes the place of a noun°. (7b)

pronoun–antecedent agreement The match in expressing number°, person°, and gender° required between a pronoun° and its antecedent°. (13)

pronoun case The way a pronoun changes in form to reflect its use as the agent of action (subject case°), the thing being acted

G-23

upon (objective case°), or the thing showing ownership (possessive case°). (10)

pronoun reference The relationship between a pronoun° and its antecedent°. (11)

proofreading The final step in the writing process°, proofreading calls for the writer to read the final copy of a piece of writing to find and correct typing errors or handwriting illegibility. (2a, 3e)

proper adjective An adjective° formed from a proper noun°: *Victorian, American.* (7d, 35d)

proper noun A noun° that names a specific person, place, or thing: *St. Louis, Toni Morrison, Corvette.* (7a, 35d)

purpose The goal of a piece of writing: to express oneself, to provide information, to persuade, or to create a literary work. (1b)

quotation Words another person has spoken or written. Direct quotation° repeats the words of the source exactly and encloses them in quotation marks. Indirect quotation° reports what the source said, without the requirement for using quotation marks unless some of the source's words are repeated as well. Quotation requires documentation° of the source in order to avoid *plagiarism.* (29h, 39e)

References In the APA style° of documentation, the list of sources cited in a research paper. (41c-2)

regular verb A verb° that forms its past tense° and past participle° by adding *-ed* or *-d* to the simple form°. Most English verbs are regular. (9d)

relative clause See *adjective clause.* (8f)

relative pronoun As a subordinating word, such as a pronoun° that introduces noun clauses° and adjective clauses° such as *who, which, that, what,* and *whomever.* (7b, 8f)

restrictive appositive An appositive° renaming a noun° or pronoun° by giving information that is essential to distinguish it from other things in its class: *the college instructor **Pat Murphy**.* (8d)

restrictive clause A dependent clause° that limits a noun° or pronoun° by giving information necessary to distinguish it from others in its class. In contrast to a nonrestrictive clause°, this kind of dependent clause is not set off with commas. (29f)

restrictive element A word, phrase°, or dependent clause° that provides information essential to the understanding of the element it modifies. In contrast to a nonrestrictive element, a restrictive element is never set off with commas. (29f)

revision A part of the writing process° in which writers evaluate their rough drafts and, on the basis of their decisions, rewrite by adding, cutting, replacing, moving, and often totally recasting material. (2a, 3c, 4)

rhetoric The area of discourse that focuses on arrangement of ideas and choice of words as a reflection of the writer's purpose° and sense of audience°. (1)

run-on (run-together) sentence See *fused sentence.*

secondary source A source that talks about someone else's original work. It explains events, analyzes information, and draws conclusions. (40a)

sentence fragment A portion of a sentence that is punctuated as though it were a complete sentence. (15)

sexist language Language that unfairly assigns roles or characteristics to people on the basis of sex. In contrast, *nonsexist language* avoids stereotyping according to sex. (25b)

shaping An early part of the writing process° during which writers consider ways to organize their material. (2l)

simile A comparison, using *like, as,* or *as if,* between otherwise dissimilar things. (25c)

simple form The form of a verb° that expresses action, occurrence, or state of being that is taking place in the present. It is also called the *dictionary form* or *base form.* (9b)

simple sentence A single independent clause° with no dependent clauses°. (8g)

simple tenses The present°, past°, and future tenses.° (9h)

singular See *number.*

slang Coined words or new or extended meanings for established words, appropriate only for informal communications. (25a-3)

source A book, article, document, other work, or person providing information. (40f)

spatial order A description of objects according to their physical relationship to one another. (21-2)

standard English See *edited American English*.

subject The word or group of words in a sentence that acts, is acted upon, or is described by the verb°. A *simple subject* includes only the noun° or pronoun°. A *complete subject* includes the noun or pronoun and all its modifiers°. A *compound subject* includes two or more nouns or pronouns and their modifiers. (8b)

subject complement A noun° or adjective° after a linking verb° that describes or renames the subject° of the sentence. (8d, 9e)

subject–verb agreement The match required of a subject° and verb° in expressing number° and person°. (12)

subjective case The pronoun° case° functioning as subject°. (10)

subjunctive mood The verb mood° that expresses wishes, recommendations, indirect requests, and speculations: *I wish I were going.* (9m)

subordinate clause See *dependent clause*.

subordinating conjunction A conjunction that introduces an adverbial clause°, showing its relationship to the independent clause°. (7g, 8f)

subordination The technique of using grammatical structures to reflect the relative importance of ideas. (21d-21g)

suffix A syllable or syllables added to a word to modify its meaning. (26e)

summary A condensed version of the essentials of ideas expressed in a longer version. (39d)

superlative The form of the adjective° or adverb° when three or more things are being compared: *green, greener, **greenest***; *quickly, more quickly, **most quickly**.* (14e)

syllogism The structure of an argument reflecting a reasoning process that uses deduc . . .°. (6e-2)

synonym A word that is close in meaning to another word. (24a)

synthesis A component of critical thinking that involves making connections among ideas. (5a)

tense The time at which the action of the verb° occurs—in the past, present, or future. (9g)

tense sequence The use of verbs° to reflect the logical time relationships in sentences that have more than one verb. (9g)

thesis statement A statement of the central theme of an academic essay that makes clear the essay's main idea, the writer's purpose, and the focus of the topic. (2m, 3c-2)

tone The writer's attitude towards his or her material and reader, especially as reflected in the writer's choice of words. (1d, 25a)

topic The subject of a piece of writing. (2c)

topic sentence The sentence in a paragraph° that contains the main idea of the paragraph. (5b-2)

transition The logical connection of one idea to another in a piece of writing. Transition can be achieved by use of various techniques of coherence°. (5c)

transitional expressions Words and phrases that signal connections among ideas and create coherence. (5c-1)

transitive verb A verb° that takes a direct object. (9f)

unity The clear and logical relationship between the main idea of a paragraph° and the supporting evidence for that main idea. (5b)

usage The customary manner of using particular words or phrases. (20a; opening section Usage Glossary)

valid A term applied to an argument based on deduction° when the conclusion logically follows from the premises°. (6e-2)

verb The part of the predicate° in a sentence that acts or describes a state of being. Verbs change form to show time (tense°), attitude (mood°), and role of the subject (voice°). (7c, 9)

verb phrase A verb° and its modifiers°. A verb phrase functions as a verb in the sentence. (8c)

verbal Verbals include infinitives°, present participles°, past participles°, and gerunds°. (7c)

verbal phrase A group of words that contains a verbal°—an infinitive°, participle°, or gerund°—and its modifiers°. (8e)

voice An attribute of a verb° showing whether the subject° acts (active voice°) or is acted upon (passive voice°). (9n, 9o)

webbing See *mapping*.

Works Cited In the MLA style° of documentation, the list of sources cited in a research paper. (41c-1)

writing process Stages of writing that include planning°, shaping°, drafting°, revising°, editing°, and proofreading°. The stages do not always proceed in a linear progression: that is, the writing process is recursive. (2, 3, 4)

CREDITS

We gratefully acknowledge permission to reprint from the following sources

THE NEW YORK TIMES
Excerpt from "Personal Computers" by Erik Sanberg Diment in *The New York Times*, June 1o, 1985. Copyright © 1985 by The New York Times Company. Reprinted by permission.
Excerpt from "The Sandpipers Politics" by Rick Horowitz in *The New York Times*, December 4, 1980. Copyright © 1980 by The New York Times Company. Reprinted by permission.

THE NEW YORKER "Democracy" from *The Wild Flag* by E. B. White (Houghton Mifflin). Copyright © 1943, 1971 E. B. White. This originally appeared in "Notes and Comments" from *The Talk of the Town* by E. B. White in *The New Yorker*, July 3, 1943. Reprinted by permission of The New Yorker.

RANDOM HOUSE, INC., "Prologue: The Birth of Architecture" from W. H. Auden. *Collected Poems*, edited by Edward Mendelson. Copyright © 1965 by W. H. Auden. Reprinted by permission of Random House, Inc. and Faber & Faber.

SIMON & SCHUSTER, INC., The Entry for *celebrate* is from *Webster's New World Dictionary*. Third College Edition. © 1988 Simon & Schuster, Inc. Reprinted by permission of the publisher.

TIME MAGAZINE. Excerpt from "Oops! How's That Again?" by Roger Rosenblatt from *Time*. The Weekly Newsmagazine. 1981 Copyright © 1981 by Time, Inc. and reprinted with their permission.

H. W. WILSON COMPANY. Entry on "Communication, nonverbal" is excerpted from *Readers' Guide to Periodical Literature*. March 1979–February 1980. Copyright © 1980 The H. W. Wilson Company and reprinted with their permission.

INDEX

A degree symbol (°) after an index entry signals that the term is defined in the Glossary of Grammatical and Selected Composition Terms. Some of the most commonly used words in the Usage Glossary are shown here in bold face. Section numbers are in boldface type and page numbers in regular type. Thus, the listing **8a**: 121 refers you to section 8a, which is on page 121.

Index

INDEX

Index

Prepositions°, **7f**: 117–18, **10b**: 158. *See also*
  Prepositional phrases
Present participles°, **7c**: 114, **9b**: 134, **9k**:
  147, **15a**: 207
Present tense°, **9k**: 144, 145, 146
Pressure, writing under. *See* Tests, essay
Pretentious language°, **25e-1**: 306–7
Prewriting°, **2d**: 20
Primary sources°, **40g**: 426. *See also* Sources
Process, writing. *See* Writing Process
Process, paragraph° development by, **5d**: 76–
  77
Progressive forms° of verbs, **9j**: 143–44
Pronoun-antecedent agreement°, **13**: 187–96
  with *and*, **13b**: 188
  with collective-noun antecedents, **13e**:
    191–92
  with indefinite-person antecedents, **13d**:
    189–91
  with closest antecedent, **13c**: 188–89
  patterns for, **13a**: 187, **13c**: 189
  understanding, **13a**: 187–8
Pronoun case°. *See* Case
Pronoun reference°, **11**: 167–73
  to definite antecedent°, **11d**: 169–70
  overuse of *it*, **11e**: 171
  placing pronouns° close to antecedents°,
    11c: 168–69
  to single antecedent°, **11b**: 167–68
  with who, which, and *that,* **11g**: 172–73
  understanding, **11a**: 167
  you for direct address, **11f**: 171
Pronouns°, **7b**: 111–13
  See also Indefinite pronouns°; Pronoun-
    antecedent agreement°; Relative
    pronouns°
  agreement with antecedent, **13**: 187–96
  adjective clauses° starting with, **8f**: 128
  case°, **10**: 155–66
  and comma splices° and fused sentences°,
    16a: 221
  intensive°, **7b**: 112, **10i**: 165–66
  interrogative°, **7b**: 112, **10e**: 160
  paragraph coherence° with, **5c-2**: 71–72
  personal, **7b**: 112, **10a**: 155, 156, **32b**: 364
  reflexive°, **7b**: 112, **10i**: 165–66
  sexist use of, **13c-2**: 190
  types of, **7b**: 112
Pronunciation, dictionary information about,
  24a: 293
Proofreading°, **2a**: 13, 14, **3e**: 49
  using computer for, **3f-3**: 51
  of final draft, **4c**: 58–62
  for incomplete sentences, **19b-3**: 251
  for spelling errors, **26**: 309–10
Proper adjectives°, **7d**: 115, **35d**: 386–89
Proper nouns°, **7a**: 111, **35d**: 386–89
Publication information in citations, **41c-1**:
  455–456, **41c-2**: 456–57
Punctuation. *See also names of punctuation
  marks*
  for commands, **9l**: 149, **28a**: 324, **28c**: 326
  in formal outline, **2n**: 36
Purpose(s)°
  for reading, **6b-1**: 90

in thesis statements°, **2m**: 29, 30
for writing, **1b**: 4–7, **2b**: 16

Question marks, **28b**: 325
  with parenthetical words, **34b-3**: 378–79
  with quotation marks, **33e-3**: 373–74
Questions
  capitalization of, **28b**: 325
  direct, **28b**: 325
  indirect, **28a**: 324
  journalist's, **2h**: 23–24
Quotation marks, **33**: 368–74, **39c**: 410
  for direct discourse°, **33a-3**: 370–71
  to enclose direct quotations, **33a**: 368–71
  misuse of, **33d**: 372–73
  other punctuation with, **33e**: 373–74
  single, **33a-2**: 369–70
  for special purposes, words, **33c**: 371–72
  for titles, **33b**: 371, **33d**: 373
Quotations°, **39c**: 413–17, **42b**: 485, 487,
  493, 497
  with brackets, **34c**: 379–80
  capitalization in, **35c**: 385–86
  displayed, **33a**: 368
  in manuscripts, **App. B**: 514
  omissions in, ellipsis for, **34d**: 380–81
  parenthetical references° to, **41b-1**: 448,
    41b-2: 452
  of poetry, **33a-3**: 370, **34e-1**: 381, **35a**: 385
  verbs° useful for, **39e**: 416

Radio programs, citation styles for, **41d**:
  469–70
***raise, rise,* U GL**: G–9
Readers. *See also* Audience°
  general, **1c-1**: 8–9, **42a**: 477
  informing, **1b-1**: 4–5
  instructor as, **1c**: 2
  persuading, **1b-2**: 5–7
  specialists as, **1c**: 3
  tone°'s effect on, **1d**: 10–11
Readers' Guide to Periodical Literature, **40j-
  1**: 432
Reading, **6**: 89–98
  critical, **6a**: 89, **6c**: 93–98
  for evaluating, **6c**: 93, **6c-3**: 95–98
  for ideas, **2j**: 25
  to make inferences, **6c**: 93, **6c-2**: 94
  to learn, **6b-2**: 90–92
  for literal meaning, **6c**: 93, **6c-1**: 93–94
  predictions during, **6b**: 89–90
  process, **6b**: 89–92
  purposes for, **6b-1**: 90
  SQ3R system of, **6b-2**: 90–92
  and writing, **1**: 3
Reason(s)
  paragraph° development using, **5b-2**: 68
Reasoning
  deductive, **6e-3**: 99, **6e-2**: 100–103
  faulty, **6c-3**: 95, **6d**: 98–99, **6e**: 99–103
  inductive, **6e**: 99, **6e-1**: 99–100
Recordings, citation styles for, **41d**: 468–69
Red herring fallacy, **6f**: 105
Redundancy, avoiding, **20c**: 262–65

I-9

CHARTS IN TINTED BOXES